HUMAN RESOURCE ISSUES OF THE EUROPEAN UNION

Mike Leat

FINANCIAL TIMES
MANAGEMENT

LONDON · HONG KONG · JOHANNESBURG
MELBOURNE · SINGAPORE · WASHINGTON DC

FINANCIAL TIMES MANAGEMENT
128 Long Acre, London WC2E 9AN
Tel: +44 (0)171 447 2000
Fax: +44 (0)171 240 5771
Website: www.ftmanagement.com

A Division of
Financial Times Professional Limited

First published in Great Britain in 1998

ISBN 0 273 62508 X

British Library Cataloguing in Publication Data
A CIP catalogue record for this book can be obtained from the British Library

1 3 5 7 9 10 8 6 4 2

Typeset by M Rules
Printed and bound in Great Britain by
Clays Ltd, St Ives plc

*The Publishers' policy is to use paper manufactured
from sustainable forests.*

CONTENTS

Part One
THE EUROPEAN UNION: CONTEXTS AND CONSTRAINTS

PREFACE

This book grew out of the absence of an adequate single source for those of us who both teach and study the European Union from the direction of Human Resource Studies and the Social Dimension. There are books that deal with the Economic dimensions of the Union and others that examine issues and developments from a particular legal perspective but none that seem to approach the activities of the Union from the viewpoint of its interest and implications for and impact upon the human resource and its employment. I have also tried in this one work to provide adequate contextual material to facilitate an understanding of the activities of the Union in this field and this material includes an examination of the influences of: National Culture, Demographic and Labour Market Developments and Trends, the Nature of Work and changes to it and the increasing internationalisation of business and the activities of the Multinational Corporation. The other major contextual area dealt with is the development, institutions and processes of the Union.

To some extent the major themes of the book are self selecting in that I have concentrated upon those areas of human resource studies in which the Union has been active, there are therefore chapters in Part Three of the book that examine: Labour Mobility and the notion of free movement, Vocational Education and Training, Health and Safety at Work, Equality between the sexes and the matter of Racial Discrimination, Employee Participation and lastly Unemployment.

I have tried to adopt a standard approach to each of these major themes. Each chapter has, as far as possible, been structured to provide readers with an understanding of the appropriate theoretical background and the major debates surrounding the particular issues, the initiatives that have been taken by the Union and its predecessors, and lastly an attempt has been made to appraise the initiatives in terms of achieving the objectives specified or implied. Treatment of the initiatives taken are generally structured chronologically.

The continually evolving and dynamic nature of the subject matter inevitably posed me with the problem of keeping the material as up to date as possible and also deciding upon the point beyond which further material would not be included. This dilemma was in some respects aided by the decision to revise the Treaties in the summer of 1997 via the Inter-Governmental Conference at Amsterdam, to have gone to press without incorporating these proposed changes would have run the risk of the book becoming out of date even more rapidly than will happen naturally. The decision was therefore taken to incorporate the Amsterdam summit and to take September of 1997 as the effective cut off point for the inclusion of new material, the only exception to this being a brief mention of the outcome of the so-called jobs summit in November of that year.

The decision to try and incorporate the Amsterdam Summit conclusions posed additional problems as far as the extent to which this material should be fully integrated into this book given that the agreements arrived at would remain provisional amendments to the Treaty until ratified by all member state governments. In the end the decision was taken to deal with the matter via the inclusion of a separate chapter dealing with this and the issue of monetary union and appropriate cross referencing throughout the rest of the book. Perhaps inevitably the project grew as time passed, as did the task of keeping the whole up to date and coherent. I've allowed myself the luxury of some overall conclusive and personal reflections and concerns at the end of the book.

I am extremely grateful to all the staff at Financial Times Management that have worked on the manuscript and its layout, correcting my spelling and grammar as they did so, and in particular Penelope Woolf, Glenda Bourne and Michelle Graham, who have been extremely helpful and forbearing.

I also want to thank my colleagues at Plymouth University Business School – Beryl Badger, Eugene Sadler-Smith, Liz Pearson and Nick Wiseman for their constructive comments on an early draft of some of the chapters in Part Three of the text.

I would like to dedicate this book to my children, Alex and Jacob and to my mother.

Mike Leat
January 1998

TABLE OF CASES

TABLE OF DIRECTIVES AND OTHER INSTRUMENTS

Regulations

Other instruments

GLOSSARY OF ABBREVIATIONS
AND ACRONYMS

ACAS	Advisory, Conciliation and Arbitration Service
ADAPT	Initiative to help employees adapt to industrial change and remain in employment
A-Gs	Advocates-General
CAP	Common Agricultural Policy
CAP	French vocational training certificate
CDS	Le Comité des Sages
CEDEFOP	European Centre for the Development of Vocational Training
CEEP	European Centre of Public Enterprises
CFSP	Common Foreign and Security Policy
CGT	Confédération Générale du Travail
COMETT	Community Programme in Education and Training for Technology
COREPER	Comité des Réprésentants Permanents (Committee of Permanent Representatives)
CSF	Community Support Frameworks
CVS	The Chinese Value Survey
DGB	Deutscher Gewerkschaftsbund
EAGGF	European Agricultural Guidance and Guarantee Fund
EC	European Community
ECHR	European Court of Human Rights
ECJ	European Court of Justice
EcoSoc	Economic and Social Committee
ECSC	European Coal and Steel Community
EEA	European Economic Area
EEC	European Economic Community
EFILWC	European Foundation for the Improvement of Living and Working Conditions
EFTA	European Free Trade Association
EIB	European Investment Bank
EIC	European Industry Committees
EIF	European Investment Fund
EIRR	European Industrial Relations Review
EMU	European Monetary Union
EP	European Parliament
ERDF	European Regional Development Fund
ERM	Exchange Rate Mechanism
ESF	European Social Fund
ETUI	European Trade Union Institute
ETUC	European Trade Union Confederation
EU	European Union
EURES	European Employment Services
EWC	European Works Council
FDI	Foreign Direct Investment
FORCE	Programme to promote occupational training, succeeded by LEONARDO

GDP	Gross Domestic Product
GNP	Gross National Product
GNVQ	General National Vocational Qualification
HASAW	Health and Safety at Work Act
HASTE	European Health and Safety Database
HRM	Human Resource Management
JIT	Just-in-time
IGC	Intergovernmental Conference
ILO	International Labour Organisation
IPD	Institute of Personnel and Development
IPPR	Institutes for Public Policy Research
IRR	Industrial Relations Research Unit, Warwick
ITBs	Industrial Training Boards
LEONARDO	Action Programme concerned with vocational training, dates from 1995
LTU	Long-term unemployed/unemployment
MEPs	Members of the European Parliament
MNC	Multinational Corporation
MNEs	Multinational enterprises
NAFTA	North American Free Trade Agreement
NCVQ	National Council for Vocational Qualifications
NOW	New Opportunities for Women
NVQ	National Vocational Qualification
OECD	Organisation for Economic Cooperation and Development
PEPPER	Promotion of Employee Participation in Profits and Enterprise Results
PETRA	Action Programme for the Vocational Training of Young People and their Preparation for Adult and Working Life
QC	Quality Circle
QMV	Qualified Majority Voting
RSI	Repetitive Strain Injury
SAC	Social Affairs Council
SAFE	Safety Actions for Europe
SAP	Social Action Programme
SEA	Single European Act
SEDOC	Système européan de diffusion des offres et demandés d'emploi en compensation
SLIM	Simpler Legislation for the Single Market
SMEs	Small and medium-sized enterprises
SMIC	Salaire Minimum Interprofessional de Croissance (French minimum wage)
SOCRATES	A programme of educational cooperation
SPASP	Social Protocol Agreement on Social Policy
SPEC	Support Programme for Employment Creation
TECs	Training and Enterprise Councils
TEN	Trans European Network
TEU	Treaty on European Union
TGWU	The Transport and General Workers' Union
TNC	Transnational Corporation
TQM	Total Quality Management
UEFA	Union of European Football Associations
UNCTAD	United Nations Conference on Trade and Development
UNICE	Union of Industrial and Employers Confederations of Europe
URTU	The United Road Transport Union
WHO	World Health Organisation

Part One

THE EUROPEAN UNION: CONTEXTS AND CONSTRAINTS

In this first Part of the book, we examine the key contexts influencing the operations of the Union at the end of the twentieth century. We consider the individual national cultures and ideologies of the member states that make up the Union and their influence at both national and Union level. The changing nature of the world of work and the implications it has for employment throughout the Union are covered, as are the increasing internationalisation of business and the significance of the growth in the power of the multinational organisation.

Part One ends with a thorough examination of the data available on the major demographic and labour market trends that affect the European Union.

1

NATIONAL CULTURES AND IDEOLOGY IN THE EUROPEAN UNION

LEARNING OBJECTIVES

When you have read this chapter, you should be able to understand and explain:

- the various definitions of 'culture';
- the models used to analyse different national cultures;
- the ways in which the member states of the European Union can be grouped together according to particular features of national culture;
- the forms of organisation which are most appropriate in particular cultures;
- the different ideological and regulatory frameworks of the member states of the Union.

INTRODUCTION

Over the last 20 years, it has become increasingly clear that an understanding of the diversities of national cultures is crucial, when conducting business on an international basis. This has been particularly important in the context of:

- the globalisation of markets and business activity;
- the development of the multinational organisation and the requirement to manage cultural diversity;
- the increasing propensity for companies to engage in international joint ventures and alliances; and
- the development of international defence and trade agreements and arrangements such as those which stimulated the initial formation of the European Economic Community (EEC) and which have facilitated the further development and integration of the member states of the European Union (EU) into a single market and towards monetary union.

An understanding and appreciation of cultural diversity and the implications of a lack of congruence or an incompatability between cultures have enormous potential benefits for managers seeking to do business with companies and governments from a different culture, and, of course, for an understanding of the difficulties and direction of policy formulation and the achievement of consensus within the EU.

As will become apparent in this and subsequent chapters, culture can influence national approaches to issues such as:

- the desirability and relevance of seeking to achieve equality between the sexes;
- the legitimate role of government and the relative benefits of centralised decision making;
- attitudes towards regulation of business and the labour market;
- approaches regarding an effective and peaceful interaction with peoples from other countries;
- the merit of facilitating collective organisation and representation compared with encouraging individualism; and
- perspectives relating to the working environment, risk and safety.

SO WHAT IS CULTURE?

Many have sought to define 'culture' and those definitions most useful in the current context tend to agree that it is a phenomenon that has some point of contact with values and attitudes and, in turn, with the behaviour that they generate.

Hodgetts and Luthans (1994) argue that culture is:

> acquired knowledge that people use to interpret experience and to generate social behaviour. This knowledge forms values, creates attitudes and influences behaviour.

They further suggest that culture can be characterised using the following terms.

- *Learned*. Culture is acquired by us all as we grow and as we experience; it is acquired through the process of socialisation.
- *Shared*. Culture is a group phenomenon and the group varies. For example, it may be members of a nation, an organisation or a sex.
- *Transgenerational*. It is passed down from one generation to the next.
- *Patterned and structured*.
- Adaptive. It changes over time and in response to many stimulae.

There is little doubt that, over the last two decades, the Dutch researcher, Geert Hofstede, has made the greatest contribution to the debate and understanding of the concept of national culture. He defines culture as:

> the collective programming of the mind which distinguishes the members of one group or category of people from another. (Hofstede, 1991, pp. 4–5)

He adopts a computing analogy and explains that culture is like the software of the mind and encompasses patterns of thinking, feeling and acting. Culture is reflected in the particular assumptions, perceptions, thought patterns, norms and values of the group or category.

Hofstede (1991) also argues that culture as a group phenomenon can be distinguished from individual personality and from the notion of human nature. The former he characterises as being the set of mental programmes unique to the individual, whereas the latter is perceived as what all human beings – 'from the Russian professor to the Australian aborigine' – have in common and is inherited.

In explaining the determination of the group or category, Hofstede (1991, p. 10) suggests that culture can be perceived as occurring at a number of different levels or in layers. In addition to the national level, culture might also occur at the level of the sex or gender, region, religion, ethnic group, generation, social class or within a particular organisation. The implication of this is that within countries it is likely that there are also many sub-cultures based, for example, upon religion or ethnic origin or gender.

Culture is likely to be manifested in many ways but Hofstede, like many other writers, tends to see *values* as the core or central manifestations which are indicative of the culture. This is why much of the research undertaken to ascertain and compare the cultures in different countries and categories has sought to establish the values held by the members of the group. Other manifestations of a group's culture will include *symbols*, *heroes* and *rituals*, with the symbols being the most superficial and the values the deepest.

In many respects it is the shared values that provide the cement that binds the group together. However, it would be unwise to imagine that all members of such a group will necessarily share all the values with the same degree of intensity. There are bound to be differences in strength of feeling and commitment, but the central or core values, perceptions of reality and attitudes must be sufficiently shared to render the group distinctive.

Outsiders commonly stereotype group members; they perceive all the members as one on any particular dimension. For example, all women might be perceived by men as soft and caring, whereas all men might be perceived by women as ruthless, ambitious and uncaring; the young might stereotype the old as miserable and lacking in adventure and initiative, whereas the old might perceive the young as irresponsible and unwilling to work hard. Stereotypes, as we discuss in a later chapter, are at the root of much discrimination between the genders and between racial, ethnic and religious groupings and it is often the culture of the discriminating group that has to be addressed and changed if the discrimination is to be prevented.

MODELS OF NATIONAL CULTURE

Hofstede is by no means the only person to devise a model or framework which can be used to distinguish and compare national cultures and, while we do concentrate upon his work in this chapter, it is both useful and relevant to mention at least a couple of the others.

Culture according to Hall and Hall

Hall and Hall (1990) seek to distinguish cultures on the basis of whether communication between members of the group is explicit – that is, the majority of the meaning and therefore the understanding is derived from the written or spoken word (*low context*) –

compared to communication and understanding which relies to a great extent upon the assumption that much of the information necessary to the communication and understanding is already in the recipient or is in the physical context (*high context*). The implications are that in high context cultures considerable reliance will be placed on body language and gesture, informal and subtle face-to-face communication. This informality and lack of precision may well extend into the development of effective informal networks and into attitudes towards the need for clear and written rules and procedures. High context peoples also tend to have a more flexible approach to matters such as timekeeping and punctuality, are happy to undertake several tasks at any one time and are more likely to mix business and pleasure.

In low context cultures, on the other hand, not only will much greater reliance be placed upon unambiguous and explicit messages but it is also likely that greater emphasis and importance will be attached to time management, punctuality and both the setting and meeting of deadlines. Ambiguity will be avoided and low context peoples will think it reasonable that people seek to mitigate lack of understanding and ambiguity by formalising and specifying rules and procedures. They will be much more likely to try and separate their work and social lives and are likely to be task- as opposed to person-oriented.

Within the European Union (EU), high context countries include the UK and the southern member states and on the high-context side of the middle, France. The low context countries include Germany and the Scandinavian member states with Belgium, Holland and Denmark just on the low-context side of the middle.

Culture according to Trompenaars

Trompenaars (1993) undertook a study of values among a large sample from over 20 countries and focused upon a number of aspects of culture, including:

- how different cultures award status to each other;
- attitudes towards time and towards nature and the environment;
- attitudes towards individuals and groups and the way in which people deal with each other.

The EU countries covered by this research were Austria, Belgium, France, Germany, Italy, the Netherlands, Spain, Sweden and the UK. He sought to differentiate and compare national cultures according to the following dimensions.

1 *Universalism* v *Particularism*. *Universalism* is the belief that ideas and practices can be applied anywhere without modification, whereas *particularism* is the belief that the application of ideas and practices needs to take circumstances into account and to be tailored and modified in the light of those circumstances. Trompenaars found that in Germany, Sweden and the UK, there was high universalism. None of the EU member states were in the high particularism category.

2 *Individualism* v *Collectivism*. Here *individualism* refers to people regarding themselves as individuals whereas *collectivism* refers to the extent to which people regard themselves as members of a group – not quite the same definitions as those applied by Hofstede, but the concepts are similar. Of the EU member states covered, the UK exhibited the greatest degree of individualism, followed by Sweden and Spain. France was closest to the collectivist pole.

3 *Neutral* v *Affective*. *Neutral* in this context refers to keeping emotions in check: people try not to show their emotions or feelings. An *affective* culture, on the other hand, would be one in which people give vent to their emotions and express their feelings readily. The UK is an example of a neutral culture, whereas the Netherlands exhibits relatively high scores on the affective pole. The majority of the EU member states covered by the research are towards the middle of this index.

4 *Specific* v *Diffuse*. This is perhaps the most difficult to understand of the dimensions and refers to the ratio or proportion of public and private space. A *specific* culture is one in which individuals have large public space which they readily allow others to enter and a small private space which is jealously guarded and restricted to close friends. A *diffuse* culture is one in which the size of both public and private spaces are similar and entry into the public space is guarded because it easily facilitates entry into the other private space. In the former (specific) case, people will be quite open and extrovert in their public space or role – at work, for example – because they know that entry into their private space can be protected and restricted; work and non-work lives and relationships can be separated. Countries that score highly on the specific dimension include the UK and Austria; Spain and Sweden are closer to the diffuse end of the spectrum.

5 *Achievement* v *Ascription*. Here we are concerned with the basis upon which status is afforded individuals. This could be based on *achievement* – for example on how well they do their jobs – or on *ascription* – the position occupied, age, gender or social connections. The former would be characteristic of an achievement culture, whereas the latter would exemplify an ascription orientation. The EU member states covered were variously found to be more towards the achievement end of the spectrum with the UK, Sweden and Germany being those exhibiting the greatest orientation towards an achievement culture.

The research by Trompenaars is considerably more recent than that of Hofstede and while this means that it may more accurately reflect current situations, there have as yet been few, if any, independent attempts by others to verify the results.

Culture according to Hofstede

This brings us to the point where it is necessary to examine in some detail the work of Hofstede who, as noted earlier, has undoubtedly made the major contribution to the development of knowledge and understanding of this area of study. According to his article in 1994, Hofstede's five-dimension culture framework was developed as the result of three different research projects – the most famous and largest having been undertaken in the late 1970s and centring on the employees of IBM in 64 different countries. The other research projects were based on students from 10 and 23 different countries respectively.

Initially his researches led him to the identification and exposition of four cultural dimensions.

- Power distance
- Uncertainty avoidance
- Individualism *v* Collectivism
- Masculinity *v* Femininity.

The fifth was developed somewhat later (in the mid-1980s) as the result of concerns that the original framework might itself have been the product of Western cultural bias and might therefore not adequately enable the analysis and comparison of countries with a Chinese cultural base. Originally called *Confucian dynamism*, illustrating the Confucian roots of such cultures, the fifth dimension has subsequently been described by Hofstede as an orientation to, or concern with, either the long or short term, which can be applied to countries without such a Confucian base. (A very brief summary of relevant elements of the Confucian philosophy is given in Hollinshead and Leat (1995, pp. 60–1) and a more detailed exposition is given in Hofstede (1991, p. 165).)

Hofstede examines the impact of each of the first four dimensions for the family and at the school and workplace; it should be borne in mind that socialisation begins in the family and is continued in the school. The scores of all the EU countries covered in the research are incorporated into Table 1.1.

Table 1.1 Scores of EU member states on Hofstede's four original indices

	Power distance	Uncertainty avoidance	Individualism	Masculinity
Austria	11	70	55	79
Belgium	65	94	75	54
Denmark	18	23	74	16
Finland	33	59	63	26
France	68	86	71	43
Germany (FR)	35	65	67	66
Greece	60	112	35	57
Ireland	28	35	70	68
Italy	50	75	76	70
Netherlands	38	53	80	14
Portugal	63	104	27	31
Spain	57	86	51	42
Sweden	31	29	71	5
United Kingdom	35	35	89	66

Source: Adapted from Hofstede, G. (1980) *Culture's Consequences*. Sage, p. 315.

Power distance

Power distance is the extent to which the less powerful members both expect and accept that power within the society is distributed equally or unequally. A *high power distance* (score) indicates that the population are likely to expect and accept inequality in this power distribution. The implications of a high score on this dimension are that subordinates both expect and accept hierarchically organised societies and workplaces and, as Hofstede suggests, the ideal boss or manager is one who fits the stereotype of a benevolent autocrat, often also referred to in terms of paternalism. Consistent with this is centralised decision making. Both teachers and parents are treated as superiors to children and pupils and with obedience and respect. The hierarchy within society is reflected in both status and reward differentials, so that the expectation would be that the inequality in society would be reflected in quite wide differentials in income and wealth. Generally *low power distance* cultures would be expected to exhibit characteristics at the other end of the spectrum so that inequalities would be minimised, salary and income differentials would be narrow rather than wide, decision making would be decentralised, and the ideal boss would be a resourceful democrat.

As can be seen in Table 1.1, Austria, Denmark, Ireland, Sweden, Finland, Germany, the UK and the Netherlands all have relatively low scores on this dimension, whereas France, Belgium, Greece, Portugal and Spain all have scores on the high side.

Uncertainty avoidance

The uncertainty avoidance dimension is concerned with attitudes towards uncertainty and unfamiliar risk. Again societies may exhibit high or low scores on this dimension and a high score indicates that people seek to avoid uncertainty and ambiguity. Hofstede suggests that ultimately this dimension is concerned with people's desire or search for the truth. Those with a *strong desire to avoid uncertainty* will be uncomfortable with unstructured situations; they will look for order and safety, strict laws and rules, precision and clarity. *Low uncertainty avoidance* societies will be comfortable with informality and risk; they will tend to be tolerant of both people and things that are new and that they don't understand. There will be less emphasis upon security and less anxiety and stress.

On this dimension, the scores were on the low side for Denmark, the UK, Ireland and Sweden; however, some of the other member states scored very highly – in particular, Greece, Portugal, Belgium, France and Spain – with Italy, Austria and Germany not too far behind and above the mean score of all the countries covered in the research (*see* Table 1.1).

Individualism v Collectivism

Hofstede (1994, p. 151) refers to the third of his original four dimensions of culture as 'the degree to which people are integrated into groups', or, conversely, the extent to which people are expected to look after themselves and their own family. In *collectivist societies*, group loyalty is expected; in *individualist societies*, loyalty is to self and consciousness is of the 'I' as opposed to the 'We' variety. It is self-interest and self-actualisation that matters and motivates. In individualist societies the task prevails over relationships with others and the nature of the employment relationship is essentially calculative, as opposed to normative or moral.

There is some evidence of an association between high scores on the individualism index and national wealth. Most of the member states appear to be at the individualist end of this spectrum and only Greece and Portugal can be said to be clearly at the collectivist end (*see* Table 1.1).

Masculinity v Femininity

The last of the original four dimensions refers to the distribution of roles between the sexes. In *masculine societies*, competition, assertiveness, achievement and decisiveness are appreciated and stressed. The emphasis is upon success, money and things. In *feminine societies*, the stress is upon relationships, conciliation and compromise, the quality of life and caring for others.

Considerable differences are evident among the member states on this dimension with some countries exhibiting very feminine traits and values, Sweden being the furthest towards the feminine end, closely followed by the Netherlands, Denmark and Finland, with Portugal, France and Spain also on the feminine side of the mean. On the other hand, Austria, Germany, the UK, Ireland and Italy all exhibit scores putting them firmly into the masculine camp.

Interestingly, the IBM surveys found that womens' values varied less between societies than did mens' and this dimension encompasses both 'male and female values'. The IBM findings demonstrate that the values exhibited by men vary from the very masculine to the feminine and in feminine countries both the sexes tend to share feminine values, whereas in masculine countries the values of the women are not as male as those of the men. It may be that there is likely to be a clearer and greater division between gender roles in masculine societies than in those demonstrating a low score on the masculinity index.

Confucian dynamism – long-term orientation

As has been indicated, Confucian dynamism – Hofstede's fifth dimension – was established in a study of students from 23 countries and was the product of a questionnaire designed by Chinese scholars (the Chinese Value Survey (CVS)). It was an attempt to overcome the potential Western bias in the original IBM surveys and analysis (Hofstede, 1994). Hofstede has argued (1991) that there are profound differences between the ways in which the East and West think, and he acknowledges the importance of the Confucian roots of Chinese societies and cultures. He argues that one of the IBM survey dimensions – the uncertainty avoidance dimension – is absent from the CVS results. He suggests that the uncertainty avoidance dimension is associated with people's search for truth, whereas the fifth dimension is actually concerned with virtue, regardless of truth. This reflects the differing emphases placed in the respective traditions (East and West). In the East, what matters is meditation, ritual, what you do and how you attain virtue, whereas, in the West, the emphasis is more upon what you believe, the truth, and this is derived from the three common religions of Judaism, Christianity and Islam.

Hofstede also argues, however, that the values that indicate both long- and short-term orientations are found in non-Chinese cultures and therefore this fifth dimension should not be considered a dimension only relevant to Eastern societies.

According to Hofstede (1991, pp. 165–6), the values associated with a long-term orientation include:

- thrift
- perseverence
- the ordering of relationships by status and observing this order and
- having a sense of shame.

The values associated with a short-term orientation, on the other hand, include:

- a respect for tradition
- saving face
- personal steadiness and stability
- fulfilling social obligations and
- reciprocating favors and gifts.

The terms long- and short-term orientation have led to some confusion since it is arguable that they would be more appropriately labelled for Western readers and scholars as, on the one hand, values demonstrating a concern for the future (long term) and those demonstrating a concern for the past and the present (short term). Hofstede (1991, p. 166) uses this alternative as a means of explaining the terms:

> . . . the values on the one pole are more oriented towards the future (especially perseverence and thrift); they are more dynamic. The values on the opposite pole are more oriented towards the past and the present; they are more static.

What really drew attention to this fifth dimension, however, was the assertion that there was a correlation between the values on the long-term, future, pole and economic growth – at least for the period 1965 to 1987.

The survey that produced the 'new' dimension took in students from only a few EU member states: Sweden, the Netherlands, Germany and the UK. Of these the Netherlands scored highest on the long-term orientation pole but was only tenth out of the 23 and the UK was the lowest of the four in eighteenth place.

COUNTRY CLUSTERS

Inevitably, there is a temptation to compare countries on the various cultural dimensions and to assess whether there are groups or clusters of 'like' countries. We have already begun this process by referring to the scores of member states as we have briefly described each of the Trompenaars and Hofstede dimensions. Others have gone further and probably the most cited are the efforts of Ronen and Shenkar (1985) who examined previous efforts to cluster countries and concluded that it was possible to differentiate eight groups or clusters and four individual countries that didn't appear sufficiently culturally similar to warrant their inclusion in any cluster with others.

From the viewpoint of this work Ronen and Shenkar (1985) identified the following clusters:

- *a Germanic cluster* – containing Germany, Austria and Switzerland;
- *an Anglo cluster* – containing the UK and Ireland, as well as the USA and a number of the territories formerly part of the British Empire;
- *a Latin European cluster* – containing France and Belgium, as well as Italy, Spain and Portugal;
- *a Nordic cluster* – containing Finland, Sweden and Denmark, as well as Norway.

Leeds, Kirkbride and Durcan (1994) review the work of Ronen (1986), Peabody (1985), Trompenaars (1988), Mole (1990), Hall (1976) and Hofstede and come to the conclusion that there may be a case for a sixfold clustering of countries within Europe. In addition to the four clusters described above, they hive Belgium and France off into a separate cluster of their own which they name the *Northern* (quasi) *Latin cluster* and they locate Greece with Turkey in a *Near Eastern cluster*. Otherwise their clusters are the same as those identified by Ronen and Shenkar (1985). In seeking to explain the common characteristics between countries they acknowledge the relevance of many factors and influences including common experiences as the result of colonisation, common religions,

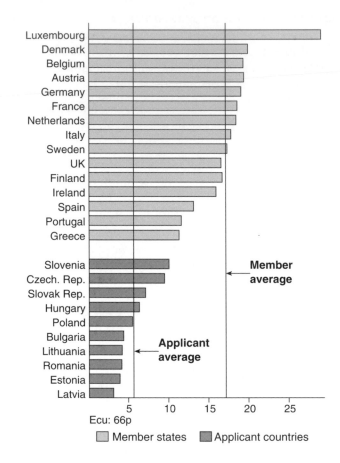

**Fig. 1.1 Relative GDP per capita of current and aspirant
EU member states ('000 ecus) (1995)**

Source: Eurostat, *The Guardian*, 17 July 1997.

climate and language and also point out that these influences may have their origin in the distant past.

Ronen and Shenkar also raise the issue of a relationship between wealth, in terms of Gross Domestic Product (GDP) per head of population, and values and suggest that, if there is a relationship, as wealth converges, so will culture. One of the implications of this view is that as the currently (relatively) underdeveloped economies of the Union become wealthier, and if there is a convergence between the wealth of the various member states, they will become more alike culturally – that is, there will be a cultural convergence.

The relative GDP per head of population within current and aspirant EU member states is shown in Fig. 1.1.

It is open to debate whether such a convergence would lead to the dominance of a particular current combination of cultural values (for example, those exhibited by Germany and Austria as two of the wealthier countries within the Union) or to the development of new hybrids of the cultural value clusters already identified by Ronen and Shenkar.

This debate raises a number of interesting questions.

1 *To what extent do national cultures themselves constitute a source of competitive advantage?* Are there particular dimensions and combinations of values and attitudes that facilitate or encourage the process of wealth generation and growth?

   Hofstede perceives a relationship between the long-term orientation values in Confucian-based, work-related value systems and economic growth and, if this is the case, we may in the future witness the emergence in European economies of an increasing acceptance of and emphasis upon such values, both in order to facilitate and then to reinforce further growth and development.

2 *Are values and cultures static or dynamic?* The suggested relationship between wealth and cultural values is indicative of the view that cultures are dynamic – they change over time – in this case, as wealth changes.

3 *Is it possible for national cultural characteristics to be engineered and manipulated?* For example, is it possible to adapt a culture to more readily achieve the objective of economic growth?

4 *What other influences may be at work on the values and attitudes that comprise cultures?* The following factors are all considered to play a role in forming the cultures within which we live:

   ● the creation of global communication and information systems that make developments, events, attitudes and values in other parts of the world more accessible to all and facilitate efforts at world-wide persuasion;

   ● the multinational organisation and its desire for a truly international or geocentric approach to the conduct of its activities, products and the management of its resources;

   ● the use being made of the threat of international competition in global markets to promote the values associated with economic liberalism, individualism and a diminished role for the state and social protection.

CULTURE AND FORMS OF ORGANISATION

Much of the interest in national cultures and cultural differences in recent times has been accompanied and reinforced by two emerging concerns:

● the relatively rapid and substantial development of international business activity and the problems posed to multinational business management of doing business across national and cultural boundaries and managing cultural diversity among their employees; and

● the relevance in other countries of the traditional and dominant American 'theories' about organisational structuring, management and organisational behaviour, since these are based in and reflect 'American culture'.

To some extent we address the second of these concerns in this section on culture and organisational form; the former is tangentially addressed in Chapter 2 on internationalism and the multinational. (For more detailed discussions of such issues, *see*: Adler (1997), Joynt and Warner (1996), Tayeb (1996), Hoecklin (1995), or Schneider and Barsoux (1997).)

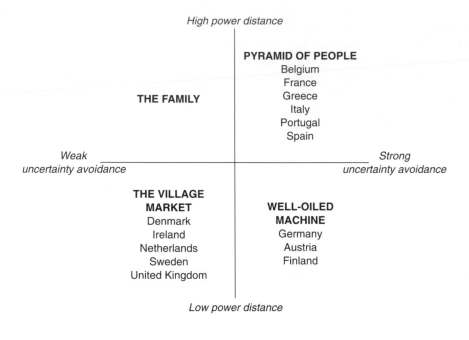

Fig. 1.2 EU member states in the context of Hofstede's typology of organisational forms

Source: adapted from information in Hofstede (1991) Chapter 6.

In his 1991 work, Hofstede produced a matrix of the scores on both the power distance and uncertainty avoidance dimensions which he suggests provides an indication of the kind of organisation that is ideal in each of the four categories produced by the mapping. In essence, the results are the four combinations of high and low scores on both of the dimensions. He characterised each of the organisational forms and produced the classification shown in Fig. 1.2.

- *Large power distance and low or weak uncertainty avoidance.* This combination indicates an organisational form that he calls *the family*. This combination tends to be found in the Far East and some parts of Africa, but not in Europe and is typified by an organisation in which there is a strong central source of authority, the corresponding inequality being accepted and expected but without the need for order and structure that one would expect in societies demonstrating a lack of comfort with the unknown. The family form of organisation combines the elements of central and benevolent authority without the security afforded by highly structured arrangements and activities. The boss is like a father to an extended family.

- *Large power distance with strong uncertainty avoidance.* The organisational form implicit to this combination is called the *pyramid of people*. Here we have the combination of inequality, centralisation of decision making and paternalist authority and hierarchy with a desire for order, security, rules and regulations and a fear of the unfamiliar risk. This is the most common of the four possible combinations and a number of the EU members fall into this category, including Belgium, France, Greece, Italy, Portugal and Spain.

- *Small power distance and weak uncertainty avoidance.* This combination implies an organisational form that is called the *village market.* The lack of acceptance of inequality in power distribution mitigates against any form of hierarchy and centralisation of decision making with decentralisation and democracy being preferred. Allied to this is a level of comfort with uncertainty that implies an acceptance of difference, tolerance, and the absence of order, rules and regulations. Society tends towards decision making of an *ad hoc* nature. Countries within the Union falling into this group include the UK, Denmark, Ireland, the Netherlands and Sweden.

- *Small power distance combined with strong uncertainty avoidance.* Again there is poor acceptance of inequality in the distribution of power so that one might expect the implicit organisation to be relatively flat and with decentralised decision making and an emphasis upon democracy. However, this is combined with a desire for order, security, rules, procedures and structure. It is for this reason that the name given to this form of organisation is *the well-oiled machine.* EU member states falling into this group include Germany, Austria and Finland.

Trompenaars (1993) also devised a fourfold typology illustrating the potential impact or implications of national culture for preferred or ideal organisational forms and cultures (*see* Fig. 1.3). This typology or framework is based upon two main dimensions of organisation – the tendency towards either egalitarianism or hierarchy (which is also sometimes perceived as the degree of centralisation) and the relative emphasis given to either the person or the task (which is also sometimes translated into the difference between formal and informal relationships).

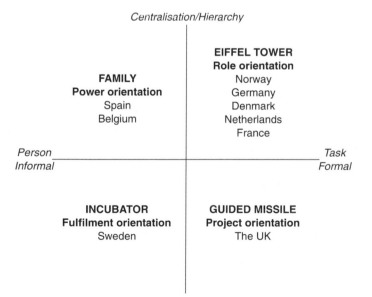

Fig. 1.3 Tentative location of some EU member states in the context of Trompenaars'
typologies of national and organisational cultures
Source: adapted from Trompenaars (1993).

He divided organisations and organisational cultures into four categories or types.

- *The family*. This depicts organisations in which there is a strong orientation towards hierarchical relationships and structures combined with a person and power orientation. The result is an organisation in which there is a leader who is regarded as a caring parent who knows what is best for the members of the group. Paternalism is combined with internal group cohesion that may well act as a barrier to outsiders.

- *The Eiffel Tower*. This is a combination of a task orientation with a preference for highly structured and well defined roles and relationships. Everyone knows what their role is and everything is coordinated from the top. Relationships tend to be job specific and confined to the work environment and people are perceived as both transferable and replaceable. Status is associated with and derived from the job or role. There is a reliance upon rules and procedures and change tends to be difficult.

- *The guided missile*. This is where the orientation is towards a project-based structure but with an emphasis upon egalitarianism between the members of the group and a reliance upon intrinsic motivations. This is a form that is consistent with the formation of project and other teams that do whatever it takes to get the job done. A number of European organisations demonstrate both the Eiffel Tower and guided missile forms; the two in combination are frequently referred to as *a matrix structure*. Change and flexibility should be easy in such forms.

- *The incubator*. This form exhibits little or no formal structure and has a person orientation which sees the group members emphasising self-fulfilment and self-expression. There is a considerable emphasis upon equality. The organisation itself is secondary to the fulfilment of the individuals within it; it is an incubator for the fulfilment and development of those who work there. There is an empathy with creativity and change is easy.

There is a tendency to think of the above implicitly ideal forms of organisation as applying predominantly in the workplace, but they also have implications for the ordering of society and perhaps for the role of government.

In this book, our interest is particularly related to the problems and challenges that cultural differences may pose for the development of the EU as a group of independent member states. The potential impact and influence of cultural diversity within the Union are described in the following section on ideology and political approach, since these are both influenced by many of the same features and processes that mould the values and attitudes that have been accepted as cultural indicators.

POLITICAL AND REGULATORY FRAMEWORKS AND IDEOLOGY

The political and regulatory approaches and frameworks within the Union are the products of belief and perception. Governments, political parties and the many other interest groups each have sets of beliefs and perceptions which will partially determine their objectives, the kind of society that they perceive as desirable and therefore the economic, social and industrial policies pursued.

Hollinshead and Leat (1995) suggest a threefold typology of ideological perspectives on the employment relationship which distinguishes between the *liberal individualist*, *liberal collectivist* or voluntarist, and the *corporatist* perspectives. Adnett (1996) refers to four social policy regimes: the *traditional rudimentary model*, *liberal individualism*, *conservative corporatism* and the *social democratic model*.

Gold noted in 1993 the wide variations in social philosophies, traditions and legal practices of the different member states and suggested that a broad distinction could be detected between the *social protection aims* of the Commission and the *deregulatory approach* of the UK government of that time. The social protectionist perspective encompasses the Socialist, Social Democrat and Christian Democrat philosophies, all of which, though to varying degrees and with differing priorities, accept the principle of intervention and the need for government to regulate the labour market, insist upon minimum employee rights and promote social justice.

The tensions between the social protection approach of the Commission, and indeed many of the member states, and the deregulation and reliance upon market forces promoted by the Conservative UK governments of 1979–97 are evident in a number of the policy debates that surround issues such as job creation and unemployment, employee participation and vocational education and training – issues to which we shall return later in this book.

Adnett (1996) also distinguishes three labour market policy regimes – *laissez-faire*, *supportive* and *active* – each of which tends to be related to or derived from a particular perspective and which, he also suggests, is likely to be identified with a particular legal framework.

Within the Union, the legal frameworks are often categorised using a threefold distinction: the Roman-German, the Anglo-Irish and the Nordic systems (Due *et al*, 1991).

- *The Roman-German system*. Here the state plays a crucial role and a core of fundamental rights and freedoms are guaranteed by the Constitution. It is common in such systems for there to be quite extensive legal regulation of terms and conditions of employment, of the rights of employees to be represented and of the mechanisms of that representation. Germany, France, the Netherlands, Belgium and Italy are quoted as being in this category/tradition.

- *The Anglo-Irish system*. Here the role of the state is more limited and there is a much less extensive set of legislatively created and supported basic rights and protections. Governments in these countries have traditionally left more to the parties themselves and stepped in to regulate and defend only when necessary to defend either the national interest and/or the interests of certain vulnerable minorities, such as children. In this context, Hall (1994) refers to these systems as *voluntarist*.

- *The Nordic system*. The difference between this system and those in the Anglo-Irish group is in the degree of emphasis and reliance placed on and in the collective agreement. It is suggested that in these countries more emphasis is placed upon the national or sectoral level basic agreement. The state has intervened to regulate only at the request of the parties. Denmark, Sweden and Finland share this tradition.

There are similarities between this classification system by Due *et al* and that of Ronen and Shenkar (1985) which clusters countries together in terms of culture (*see* p. 11). The ideological perspectives described in this chapter are summarised below, using the typology adopted by Hollinshead and Leat (1995). As noted earlier, these various perspectives are affected by many of the same influences and processes as are the values and attitudes that have been accepted by the various researchers and analysts as cultural indicators.

Liberal individualism

This perception, frame of reference, set of beliefs, values and attitudes are often also referred to as *market liberalism* or *market individualism*. The central assumptions or beliefs are that individuals are rational, free and able to look after themselves in an exchange situation. There also tends to be an assumption that the market is the most effective and efficient means of allocating resources to different uses and that, within the market, there is a rough equality of bargaining power between buyers and sellers. In this context, collective organisation for the purpose of defending and promoting a collective interest is both unnecessary and disruptive of the market mechanism's efficiency, and of course there is either no or only a very small role for the state as regulator. The state should intervene only in order to preserve the freedom and efficiency of the market mechanism and, where unavoidable, to protect the national interest or the interests of those who are obviously unable to look after their own interests and/or have little or no market power. Where such protective intervention is necessary, the support provided is of the minimum variety since to do more distorts the market and destroys the incentive for people to look after themselves.

This perception is one that supports a *laissez-faire* and a *deregulatory* approach to labour markets and to social, economic and industrial policy. It is an approach that is consistent with a non-interventionist stance on the part of government. In fact it could be argued that this set of beliefs and assumptions in a pure form denies the validity of government at all; as a result it has not been a particularly popular perspective among political parties. However, it is an approach that has underpinned many of the positions adopted by UK governments of a Conservative persuasion between 1979 and 1997 and supports the call that has echoed around the Union in the 1990s for a deregulated and flexible labour market.

If we relate this perspective to the traditions of legal regulation within the Union it comes closest to that categorised by Due *et al* (1991) as the Anglo-Irish. It is also the perspective that underpins Grahl and Teague's (1991) competitive flexibility trajectory (*see* final chapter).

Liberal collectivism

The essence of the distinction between this perspective and the former is a recognition that individuals are not necessarily able to look after their own interests in the market effectively and that it is extremely unlikely that individual sellers of labour will have a rough equality of bargaining power with individual buyers. It is a perspective that acknowledges the likelihood that liberal individualism will result in the acquisition of market power by the buyers of labour to the point at which they are able to exploit labour. This recognition that free markets seem likely to result in inequality has led to the acknowledgement that it may be both necessary and justifiable that employees combine together in collectives in order to represent their interests effectively in the labour market and to use this collective strength to resolve conflicts between buyer and seller, through forms of collective as opposed to individual bargaining.

In the context of this perspective there is a greater role for government in ensuring that a satisfactory legal framework exists to regulate the interaction of the parties and to protect those unable to protect themselves. However, it is a perspective that still encompasses a minimalist approach to this intervention and a preference for the parties to voluntarily resolve their differences and to do so through a modified form of market exchange. The recognition of the weakness of individuals and their inability to pursue their own interests effectively is likely also to encourage government to insist that the legal system provides employees with minimum rights and protections and that, where necessary, a social safety net is available to those least able to look after themselves. It may be that this willingness to achieve adequate social protection extends into measures designed to achieve a degree of redistribution from rich to poor.

This perspective seems to be consistent with both the model that Adnett refers to as the *conservative corporatist model* and a *limited social protection regime*. It implies a supportive labour market policy regime. The system of legal regulation that is most consistent with this perspective is the one that Due *et al* (1991) call the Nordic model, in which government intervenes to ensure minimum rights and protections but still leaves the parties to conclude their own resolution of the conflicts between them. This perspective is consistent with an industrial relations system that emphasises collective bargaining as the means through which these conflicts are voluntarily resolved.

Corporatism

This perspective goes further in recognising the imperfections, weaknesses and failures of the market, and the inadequacies and inequities of resource allocation and income and wealth distribution that are the product of decisions arrived at through relatively unregulated bargaining between competing forces.

It is a perspective that acknowledges that the market is an inadequate mechanism through which to order society and that social equity and order will not be achieved through the free or almost free operation of market forces, which arguably promote inequity and disorder. Similarly, reliance upon market forces results in unpredictability of outcome. Social equity and order and the predictability of economic outcomes are objectives that are the proper concern of government and, where possible, these should be achieved through mechanisms that emphasise consensus rather than competition. Where necessary, these objectives should be invested with priority over the interests of individuals and collectives in the marketplace.

According to this, the interests of order and equity can be best pursued at a central level and through mechanisms that involve and integrate the interests of the various parties; the decentralised decision making associated with the operation of market forces is one of the sources of market weakness. In effect government mediates between the interests of labour and capital and may invoke the national interest as justification.

In practice, therefore, this is a perspective that implies and relies upon tripartite decision making and this often takes the form of tripartite bargaining, hence the term *bargained corporatism*. This tripartism may also extend from decision making into administration. It is in this context that the term 'social partners' has emerged to describe organised labour and capital.

For many, corporatism has provided the ideal solution to the central problem of modern capitalism – that is, the maintenance of order where market relations are no longer supreme, where both capital and labour are organised and where it is no longer tenable to maintain a separation between economy and polity.

This is a perspective that one would expect to encourage governments in the pursuit of active labour market policy regimes and is consistent with the legal regulation traditions of the Roman-German model. Commonly this perspective has been associated with a Keynesian approach to the determination of economic objectives and policy.

Radical /Marxist perspective

While not a perspective that has yet formed the basis of government within the Union, the radical perspective is nevertheless a perspective that has informed the attitudes and activities of a number of the labour movements within the Union, in particular in France and Italy. The essence of the perspective is that capitalism has as its objective the accumulation of capital and this is achieved through the employment and exploitation of the labour resource. Labour is paid less than the value of its product and the surplus accumulates to capital. In such a system where market forces operate to the advantage of one of the parties, labour is right to distrust initiatives by either capital or government to involve their representatives in the decision-making process, whether it be collective bargaining, consultation or corporatist tripartism, since the motives of the other parties will be dominated by concerns for the maintenance of order and the status quo. The interests of labour in this context are only likely to be improved through radical change and the other parties are not interested in securing such change since it would appear to be against their self-interest. In the absence of the willing participation of labour in voluntary mechanisms directed at the maintenance of capitalism and order, it may be that governments are prompted into the pursuit of a more interventionist and regulatory role than would otherwise be their inclination.

References

Adler, N.J. (1997) *International Dimensions of Organisational Behaviour* (3rd edn). South Western.

Adnett, N. (1996) *European Labour Markets: analysis and policy.* Longman.

Due, J., Madsen, J.S. and Jensen, C.S. (1991) 'The Social Dimension: Convergence or Diversification of Industrial Relations in the Single European Market', *Industrial Relations Journal,* 22(2), Summer, 85–102.

Gold, M. (1993) *The Social Dimension – Employment Policy in the European Community.* Macmillan.

Grahl, J. and Teague, P. (1991) 'Industrial Relations Trajectories and European Human Resource Management', in Brewster, C. and Tyson, S. (eds) *International Comparisons in Human Resource Management.* Pitman Publishing, pp. 67–91.

Hall, E.T. (1976) *Beyond Culture.* Doubleday.

Hall, E.T. and Hall, M.R. (1990) *Understanding Cultural Differences.* Intercultural Press.

Hall, M. (1994) 'Industrial Relations and the Social Dimension', in Hyman, R. and Ferner, A. (eds) *New Frontiers in European Industrial Relations.* Blackwell.

Hodgetts, R.M. and Luthans, F. (1994) *International Management* (2nd edn). McGraw-Hill.

Hodgetts, R.M. and Luthans, F. (1997) *International Management* (3rd edn). McGraw-Hill.

Hoecklin, L. (1995) *Managing Cultural Differences: Strategies for Competitive Advantage.* Economist Intelligence Unit and Addison Wesley.

Hofstede, G. (1980) *Culture's Consequences: International Differences in Work-related Values.* Sage.

Hofstede, G. (1991) *Cultures and Organisations: Software of the Mind.* McGraw-Hill.

Hofstede, G. (1994) 'The business of international business is culture', *International Business Review*, 3(1), 1–14. Reprinted in Jackson, T. (1995) *Cross Cultural Management*. Butterworth–Heinemann.

Hofstede, G. and Bond, M. (1988) 'The Confucius Connection: From Cultural Roots to Economic Growth', *Organisational Dynamics*, 16(4), 4–21.

Hollinshead, G. and Leat, M. (1995) *Human Resource Management : An International and Comparative Perspective on the Employment Relationship*. Pitman Publishing.

Jackson, T. (1995) *Cross Cultural Management*. Butterworth–Heinemann.

Joynt, P. and Warner M. (1996) *Managing Across Cultures*. Thomson.

Kirkbride, P. (ed) (1994) *Human Resource Management in Europe*. Routledge.

Leeds, C., Kirkbride, P. and Durcan, J. (1994) 'The Cultural Context of Europe: a tentative mapping', in Kirkbride, P. (ed) *Human Resource Management in Europe*. Routledge.

Mole, J. (1990) *Mind your Manners: Managing Culture Clash in the Single European Market*. Industrial Society.

Peabody, D. (1985) *National Character*. Cambridge University Press.

Ronen, S. (1986) *Comparative and Multi-national Management*. Wiley.

Ronen, S. and Shenkar, O. (1985) 'Clustering Countries on Attitudinal Dimensions: A Review and Synthesis', *Academy of Management Journal*, Sept, 435–54.

Schneider, S.C. and Barsoux, J.-L. (1997) *Managing Across Cultures*. Prentice-Hall.

Tayeb Monir, H. (1996) *The Management of a Multicultural Workforce*. Wiley.

Trompenaars, F. (1988) *The Organisation of Meaning and the Meaning of Organisation* (modified printed version of Doctorate dissertation). University of Pennsylvania.

Trompenaars, F. (1993) *Riding the Waves of Culture – Understanding Cultural Diversity In Business*. Economist Books.

Additional reading

Briscoe, D.R. (1995) *International Human Resource Management*. Prentice-Hall.

Ghauri Pervez, N. and Prasad, S.B. (1995) *International Management: A Reader*. Dryden Press.

Hickson, D. J. and Pugh, D.S. (1995) *Management Worldwide*. Penguin.

Institute of Personnel and Development (1994) *The Culture Factor. Corporate and International Perspectives*.

Randlesome, C. (1993) *Business Cultures in Europe* (2nd edn). Butterworth–Heinemann.

Torrington, D. (1994) *International Human Resource Management*. Prentice-Hall.

2

THE NATURE AND ORGANISATION OF WORK

LEARNING OBJECTIVES

When you have read this chapter, you should be able to understand and explain:

- the principles and characteristics of Fordist and post-Fordist production strategies and systems;
- models of the flexible firm and their implications;
- perceptions of the relationships between the notions of involvement, commitment, satisfaction, quality and performance;
- a number of common mechanisms for reorganising work and the evidence and arguments for and against them;
- the significance of the desire for high levels of employment for the reorganisation of work.

INTRODUCTION

One of the dominant themes in recent literature relating to human resource management (HRM) has been a concern with the development and introduction of new forms of work and work organisation which facilitate flexibility, improved quality and which encompass and accommodate the new technologies. Guest's (1987) model or theory of HRM identifies *quality*, *flexibility* and *commitment* as desirable outcomes, as do many of the Anglo-American models of HRM that have emerged in the last 15 years.

The implementation of these developments in work design and working practices has often been contingent upon a number of interrelated factors, including:

- the degree and nature of the legislative regulation of work practices and organisation;
- the extent of managerial autonomy; and
- the power, influence and interest of the trade unions.

Beyond health and safety at work, the EU has had relatively little involvement in these issues until recently, but this is changing as various internal interests press the argument that enhanced flexibility and the new forms of work organisation are integral to the achievement of enhanced competitiveness and employment.

The scale and nature of unemployment in the 1990s have encouraged EU institutions to become more concerned with issues of structural and functional, as well as temporal and numerical flexibility (*see* 'The flexible firm' later in this chapter). Recent documents and agreements have emphasised the importance of flexibility to the pursuit of high employment; this is apparent in the Commission report on *Employment in Europe in 1996* (*see* Chapters 4 and 15) and in the *Title on Employment*, agreed at the IGC in Amsterdam in 1997 (*see* Chapter 9).

Further impetus has been given to the debate on the desirability of new flexible forms of work organisation by the publication of a Commission Green (Consultative) Paper in April 1997, entitled *Partnership for a New Organisation of Work*. The Green Paper adopts a relatively specific focus with respect to the concept of work organisation:

> work organisation is taken to mean the way in which the production of goods and services is organised at the workplace. The focus is upon a new organisation of work . . . this concept implies, in particular, the replacement of hierarchical and rigid structures by more innovative and flexible structures based on high skill, high trust and increased involvement of employees.

The introduction to this consultative document makes clear both the objectives and assumptions of the policy makers.

> This . . . is about the scope for improving employment and competitiveness through a better organisation of work at the workplace . . . while much has been written about the need for flexibility of the labour market and its regulation, much less has been said about the need for flexibility and security in the organisation of work at the workplace . . . An improved organisation of work can make a valuable contribution, firstly to the competitiveness of European firms, and secondly to the improvement of the quality of working life and the employability of the workforce.

As one might expect, employers and managers often tend to take the view that they should have autonomy over issues of this kind, though the strength of this view will depend to some extent upon the culture and political traditions of the country concerned.

It is clear that there are interests within the Union that seek stronger rights for employees and their collective organisations so that employees have at the least the right to information and consultation on these matters. Indeed, the Green Paper referred to above does highlight the advantages of an approach to change which is based on partnership and the involvement of all the actors including employees and their representatives.

Stimulus to change has in many instances come from the influence of multinational enterprises; foreign firms importing different attitudes and practices as they invest in host countries have played an especially important role. The most obvious and well reported examples of this are the changes in work and job design, working practices and attitudes that Japanese firms have arguably introduced into Europe in the 1980s and 1990s, some of which we examine in more detail later in this chapter.

There is scant evidence available regarding the incidence and impact of these changes within the EU and it seems that some developments have been popular in some member states and not others, but nevertheless it is possible to form some judgements.

The changes discussed in this chapter relate also to other themes in this book. There may be important health and safety considerations to the new forms of work and the need to reform work organisation may have implications for both competitiveness and employment. As we shall see, many of the initiatives that have been taken also impinge on issues related to employee participation and involvement; changes to production technologies and working practices are also likely to have vocational education and training implications.

This chapter begins with a brief introduction to the form of production system and work organisation that supposedly dominated American and European economies for much of the twentieth century. This is the system characterised by mass production and often referred to as *Fordism*. In describing this system, we must identify the underlying principles which owe much to the work of F.W. Taylor (1911) and which are frequently referred to collectively as *Taylorism* and *scientific management*.

THE DEVELOPMENT OF WORK ORGANISATION

It is often suggested that, prior to the intervention of Taylor, work was typified by the craftsman exercising his skills in the conception and planning of a job, as well as in its execution. This no doubt presents a somewhat idealised view; however, it is useful for the purposes of contrasting pre- and post-Taylorist scenarios.

Taylorism and scientific management

Taylor's great contribution was his attempt to apply the principles of scientific analysis to work and its organisation. He placed great emphasis upon measurement and time and conceived the idea that there was a 'one best way' of organising work – one way that would yield greater efficiencies in terms of time and costs than any other. He assumed that the nature of human motivation was essentially instrumental; workers could and would be motivated by the prospect of earning more.

Armed with these beliefs, Taylor began the process of measurement and experimentation that led to the development of the means whereby the labour process could be designed and so organised to facilitate the mass production of standardised products. This was achieved through the design and fragmentation of work into a large number of small tasks, each of which required very little skill and was performed by units of labour on a repetitive basis. Each of the tasks was to be as simple as possible, and the belief was that, with experience, labour would become more and more proficient at the individual constituents of the process and efficiency would improve almost without end.

Responsibility for the design, planning, organising and control of the process of production was to be divorced from the labour engaged in the production process and performed by others. This contributed in large measure to the development of the specialised functions that we today associate with management, and formed a basis for the development of a managerial élite or cadre.

Where possible, the machine – the technology – was to control the pace of production, and as labour became more and more proficient, the speed of the machine could be increased and the rate of production enhanced. As long as pay was linked to performance or output, labour would accept these conditions since they would be content as long as they earned more.

According to Taylor, labour would also become cheaper if jobs were broken down into a number of smaller tasks which could be performed repetitively since largely unskilled units could be used that required relatively little training to perform the simplified tasks.

The effectiveness of these principles was enhanced further by the technological developments that facilitated the emergence of the conveyer belt and assembly line. It was when all these came together that capital really had the opportunity to engage in mass production.

Fordism and mass production

One of the major disciples and champions of these techniques and principles was Henry Ford, the automobile manufacturer, and it is because of this that such production systems have often been referred to as *Fordist*.

The development of large-scale manufacture that was facilitated by the work of Taylor must be seen as part of the process of industrialisation and urbanisation that has characterised developing economies in the twentieth century. Large-scale manufacture required a large labour force and in the early days that labour had to live close to the place of work given the absence of quick and cheap transport.

Mass production of standardised products also required mass markets for standardised products and the labour employed in the factories that developed became a part of these markets, as their own living standards improved. Furthermore, in this way both full employment and economic growth were stimulated.

Criticisms of Fordist systems

As these systems matured, problems and disadvantages did become apparent.

1 Alienated workforce

Fordist systems tended to result in bored and alienated labour forces which posed both motivational and control problems. Employees seemingly learned how to manipulate the socio-technical systems to relieve the pressures of alienation, boredom and task control. The most apparent evidence of this is often in levels of absenteeism and other mechanisms of temporary withdrawal from the work situation, as well as in the development of means by which employees are able to exert some unofficial controls over the pace of work and the technology.

Taylor assumed that since people could and would be motivated by monetary returns for effort expended, control would be easily achieved through the manipulation of the link between pay and performance in terms of output or, more mechanistically, through management's control over the pace of the machine. As these systems became established, however, it became apparent that this was by no means always possible. As we shall see later (*see* p. 33), this has led to a number of experiments in job design that have been driven by alternative views on motivation – by softer approaches by managements concerned to ally employee satisfaction with productive efficiency, competitiveness and profitability.

2 Massive investment resulting in inflexibility

These systems require massive investment in plant and technology to facilitate the production of large numbers of standard items relatively cheaply. Once installed, this plant and equipment are relatively fixed and inflexible. These production systems are rarely amenable to change and, of course, labour also tends to be relatively inflexible in terms of what it can do – the tasks and functions that it can perform. The massive fixed overheads also pose problems if competition emerges from parts of the world where labour and other materials may be cheaper.

3 Specialised labour and technology resulting in inflexibility

The advantages of Fordist systems, when confronted with mass markets for standardised products, become disadvantages the moment the product needs to be changed or customised. Both technology and labour tend to be highly specialised. In this context, it is important not to confuse specialisation with skill: the application of Taylorist principles resulted in a specialised labour force, not a skilled one.

Arguably, the greatest threat to the viability of these systems occurs if and when customers change their requirements. For example, they may decide that they want something a little different from the man next door – the emergence of variated demand and a desire for customisation. As living standards improve, it seems that many people tend to become more discriminating and less prepared to have the same as everyone else. They not only want something different; they want something better.

4 Reduction in quality and control

The degree of specialisation and the separation of tasks and functions that are central to this system mean that unskilled and semi-skilled labour engaged in the production process is not required, or able, to exercise control over quality. Furthermore, the technology often doesn't lend itself to inspection prior to the end of the process. As a result, this control function is either not performed or is performed at the end of the production process by expensive specialist quality inspection and control functions. The disaffection of the labour force probably also contributes to a decline in the quality of the product. In addition, it seems that as the size of the operation increases and problems of control and quality emerge, there is a tendency for the overhead element that is attributable to the employment of specialist management and administration to become a greater burden upon production costs.

5 Large concentrations of labour

Mass production generates large concentrations of labour in one place, resulting in pressure for the standardisation of terms and conditions of employment. These production systems created the circumstances in which trade unions could flourish due to the disaffection and alienation of the labour employed. This disaffection could be harnessed to exert pressure upon the traditional technical and managerial control mechanisms and to demand their replacement by mechanisms of control that are jointly agreed and in some circumstances jointly exercised. Logistically, trade unions have tended to flourish in circumstances of this kind which might be characterised as the ideal circumstances for recruiting members.

In recent years there have been some outspoken critics of Fordist production systems, the principles underpinning them and their consequences for the labour resource.

Chief among these is probably Braverman (1974). He alleges that Fordist production systems have caused a general de-skilling of the labour force, a degradation and cheapening of the labour resource and that such systems have been influential in facilitating the exploitation of labour and its input into the labour process. According to the radical perspective (*see* Chapter 1), these twentieth-century, mass-production strategies and processes have facilitated capital's control over both the labour process and the price of labour.

The Braverman critique of Fordist production systems and their implications for the labour resource has itself been subject to criticism. This had related in particular to the view that it is both over-simplistic and inaccurate to suggest that the dominant concern of management is the exploitation of labour and the creation of surplus value through processes that are concerned to de-skill among other things.

The application of Fordism in Europe

Although the Fordist design has been the dominant model of the twentieth century, both in America and in Europe, it is not the case that the model has demonstrated the same level of appeal to employers or the same degree of acceptability across all the national borders within the EU. In Chapter 1 a number of cultural differences were observed between the countries within the Union and these same cultural patterns are likely to have influenced the acceptability and appeal of the Fordist regime. If you look back to the cultural dimensions identified and measured by Hofstede (*see* Chapter 1) it isn't too difficult to envisage ways in which, for example, attitudes regarding the acceptance of power distance, individualism or collectivism and the characteristics associated with masculinity and femininity might all be influential in determining the attraction and acceptability of the Fordist stereotype.

In Europe the stereotype was modified in practice and cultural influences can be detected in this modification both directly and indirectly. Lane (1989), in contrasting the nature and degree of penetration of the principles of scientific management, suggests that in most countries there are certain conditions, traditions and institutions that might create a favourable climate for the implementation of a Fordist production strategy and others that might mitigate against it.

She suggests that the First World War placed considerable emphasis upon the development of facilities for mass production, thereby creating favourable conditions for the introduction of scientific principles in both France and Britain. In France, the educational system and traditions also favoured acceptance of the stereotype. However, there is also a strong radical tradition within the labour movement in France, as well as a traditional dominance of the small family-owned firm producing for relatively small markets and competing on the grounds of price. Each of these might be perceived as factors that would mitigate against the easy acceptance and smooth introduction of the stereotype system.

Lane suggests that in Britain, despite the need to engage successfully in mass production that can be associated with both the World Wars, the militant and craft traditions of the labour force, the preference for individual as opposed to collective solutions and the absence of a technical élite would act as mitigating influences. She also suggests that, on an intellectual level, Germany was the country in which one might have expected the greatest level of acceptance and this can indeed be detected in the redevelopment of German industry since the end of the Second World War.

Post-Fordism

The appropriateness of Fordism has been thrown into doubt in Europe and America in recent years by the increasing demand by customers for customised products and for products that place a higher priority on issues of quality. Allied to this has been competition on both price and quality from manufacturers and plants located in lower cost and developing economies. It is argued that the combined effect has encouraged employers to search for production systems that are more flexible, in which fixed costs are less signifi-cant, in which a greater emphasis is placed upon quality and in which quality can more easily and cheaply be achieved.

Many of the amended and new work practices that have been introduced in recent years should properly be seen as management responses to these changed market and competi-tive circumstances and requirements, although other associated motives, such as concerns about employee satisfaction and commitment and the quality of work life, should not be ignored.

Flexibility in this context needs to include both technology and labour, and in the latter case the flexibility requirement may apply to both the quantity and capacity of the labour input. The demand for labour in the new post-Fordist production systems has been influ-enced by the technological innovations that have enabled the development of robotics and vastly improved systems for controlling activity at a distance. The demand for large quan-tities of relatively unskilled labour – characteristic of Fordist systems – has been replaced by a demand for labour that is multi-skilled and flexible, that does not need external super-vision and that is both familiar and comfortable with the new technologies.

The requirements that these post-Fordist systems – sometimes referred to as *flexible spe-cialisation* – make of the labour resource can be seen in many of the 'softer' HRM models which refer to the desirability of quality, flexibility, commitment and cost effectiveness (*see* Guest (1987), Singh (1992), Beer *et al* (1984)).

The term 'flexible specialisation' seems to have been coined by Piore and Sabel (1984) and refers to a model of production that stresses:

- functional flexibility;
- higher levels of responsibility and autonomy on the part of the workforce;
- a degree of overlap between skills and specialisms; and
- a degree of judgement and skill on the part of labour, more commonly associated with the craft worker – particularly interesting in the context of Taylorism and the criticisms by Braverman.

This model places considerable and specific demands upon the labour force and Lane (1989), in assessing the degree of fit between this form of production and the circumstances in individual EU member states, suggests that circumstances in Germany and Italy might fit best with the new model, whereas the UK and France might well find its introduction and effective operation more difficult.

So far we have confined our discussion of Fordism and post-Fordism to matters of pro-duction, the organisation of work and working practices. It is important to also mention, however, that the terms have often been used to describe broader social and socio-eco-nomic systems. Fordism has been used to identify a socio-economic system combining mass production with full employment and mass consumption; often Keynesian demand man-agement policies, social democracy and the welfare state are perceived as natural bedfellows with the 'Fordist' production system. It is in this context that Crouch (1995) comments that:

> Within Europe the countries that developed Fordist use of semi-skilled production line workers most intensely were France, Italy and in a different way the Soviet Union.

He suggests that Scandinavia and post-war Britain were the main exemplars of the social democrat welfare state, but that their economies were less Fordist. Crouch points out that, as in the case of Fordism, various meanings have also been attached to post-Fordism. He comments that use of the term 'post-Fordism' indicates that we tend to be more certain of where we are coming from than of where we are going to.

THE FLEXIBLE FIRM

By the early 1980s, the developments outlined above, allied to changes in the political and regulatory environments, had encouraged a new approach to the organisation of work and the demand for labour. This was summed up in the model of the flexible firm, devised by Atkinson (1984) (*see* Fig. 2.1). This model became to some extent a blueprint, in Western economies, for the successful firm of the 1980s and 1990s; at the same time it represents for many the ideal model for a post-Fordist regime. It constitutes a form of organisation that satisfies the requirements of the employer and the market, is consistent with HRM, but would appear to do little to satisfy the requirements of labour.

The model in Fig. 2.1 indicates the important distinctions between the external and internal labour markets, core and peripheral workers and the different dimensions of

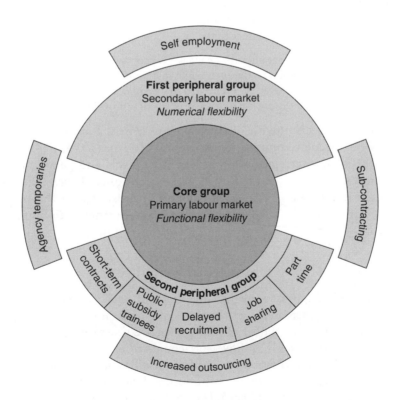

Fig. 2.1 The flexible firm
Source: Atkinson, J. (1984) 'Manpower strategies for flexible organisations',
Personnel Management, Aug.

flexibility, both functional and numerical. In this context, *functional* means a flexibility of task and/or skill, the ability to do different things and to vary the actual deployment of labour. The core group needs to be functionally flexible; *numerical* flexibility is primarily derived from the selective use of labour in the secondary labour markets. Other dimensions of flexibility include *temporal* (involving times and hours of work) and *locational* and demand for each of these may also be a product of these same influences.

1 The members of the *core group* benefit from security of employment and demand for the skills that they possess; the organisation might even be prepared to invest in the training and development of this group.

2 In *the secondary internal labour market*, labour may be given the status of an employee but this labour is likely to be less skilled and more vulnerable than that in the core group.

3 In the *external market*, there is no security but there may be both high levels of skill and good pay. The providers of many professional services fall into this category along with the 'losers' – the part-time, temporary and relatively unskilled who are likely to be used as any other resource and effectively discarded when no longer required. It is extremely unlikely that the labour in this group will be developed by the employer and of course many of them will not have the means to finance their own development.

The Commission (1997d) acknowledges the dangers of change and flexibility to the security of employees. They assert that achieving a balance between flexibility and security is a key issue. In particular they assert that:

> Workers need to be assured that after the changes . . . they will still have a job and that this job will last for a reasonable period of time . . . while there are considerable benefits for firms and workers engaged in core activities, care is needed to ensure that all workers, irrespective of their contractual status, share in the potential benefits of the new work organisation.

In the context of the EU, the use of atypical employment contracts to achieve numerical flexibility has become common. Sparrow and Hiltrop (1994, p. 495) suggest that in Europe there is an interrelationship between the levels and persistence of employment protection – whether achieved by legislation or collective agreements – and the pursuit of functional flexibility. The greater the persistence of the protection, the greater the benefit from the achievement of functional rather than numerical or temporal flexibility.

Obstacles to flexibility

It is important at this point to highlight some of the obstacles in the path of this flexibility trend. For example, there may be boundaries or demarcations between jobs and skills and allied to these may be a number of other restrictive practices operated by employees. Often managements have tacitly approved or acquiesced in these practices. These barriers can be particularly difficult to overcome, if different skills and grades jealously guard their position in what effectively constitutes an informal hierarchy or pecking order. This is made worse if each job has a different rate of pay associated with it, and if those in one grade, skill or job are members of one trade union while those in adjoining ones are in others. Inevitably, therefore, the strength of managerial autonomy, the political approach of government and the nature of the regulatory environment are all factors likely to impinge upon the rate and effectiveness of change. In many European countries, job categories have been legally defined and defended, particularly in areas such as the civil service and the professions.

Criticisms of the flexible firm model

Concerns have already been voiced about the value to and impact of the flexible firm upon labour. Members of the core group may well benefit, but outside the core, life may be very unpredictable, characterised by uncertainty and high levels of anxiety and stress.

Marchington and Wilkinson (1996, p. 30) identify a number of reservations and concerns about the flexible firm model.

1 The flexible firm model has the tendency to fuse together description, prediction and prescription into what becomes a self-fulfilling prophecy (Pollert, 1988). Writings on the subject tend to veer between *describing* flexible practices in the workplace, *predicting* that the model is the ideal design for the future and *prescribing* that, if organisations want to be successful in the future, this is the model that they should take as the blueprint. Furthermore, in the UK the model was 'talked up' because it was consistent with government ideology concerning the efficiency of the market and the need for markets to be deregulated and for organisations to be lean (Legge, 1995).

2 Flexibility, particularly functional flexibility, is not as common or extensive as the proponents of the model and deregulation would have us believe. Again in the particular context of the UK, surveys by ACAS (1988) and by Beatson (1995) indicate that the introduction of flexibility in terms of working practices was not as extensive as reported and Beatson concludes that 'full blown flexibility is a rarity'. There are often gaps between the rhetoric and the reality.

3 There are reasons to doubt the benefits claimed for flexibility and there may well be costs that are not realised or acknowledged. Studies have cast doubts on the productivity, attendance rates, levels of commitment, quality of work and loyalty of employees employed on a flexible basis. Core workers may well be disaffected by witnessing events around them, particularly when they see friends and colleagues losing their jobs through rationalisation and redundancy. It is suggested that in such circumstances core worker commitment and feelings of security may well be damaged and that the nature of their attachment to the organisation may revert from commitment to compliance.

Sparrow and Hiltrop (1994, p. 496) assert that across Europe there have clearly been moves towards the flexible organisation, but also point out that there are doubts about the extent to which it will continue to advance. These doubts arise due to:

● the differential limitations to temporal and numerical flexibility;

● criticisms of the logic that flexibility is automatically associated with increased competitiveness; and

● acknowledgement that it may not be easy to sustain differential HRM policies for different sectors of the labour force – that is, the core and the periphery.

ALTERNATIVE STRATEGIC MODELS

In addition to those who cast doubt upon the extensiveness of the introduction of the flexible firm model, Crouch (1995) and others suggested that there are a range of post-Fordist scenarios and possibilities for development. Regini (1995) found that a range of competitive and production strategies were being adopted by managements in Europe. By no means all of these were consistent with the models of post-Fordist production that emphasise competition on the basis of quality, product differentiation and customisation, flexible specialisation and adaptability of response.

In all, Regini identified five ideal types of strategy, each of which can be seen to embody a different pattern of human resource utilisation, only some of which are similar to that depicted in the flexible firm model.

1 *Diversified quality production.* This involves competition on both quality and product diversification, thereby avoiding competition on price with low-wage economies. Often this takes the form of a high level of customisation of the product and requires the kind of labour resource that is a mix of high and broad-based skills – that is, adaptive, willing and able to learn new tasks rapidly and capable itself of contributing to innovation and product development.

2 *Flexible mass production.* The strategy is to mass produce a number of different goods, thereby competing in a number of different markets and to do so on price, if necessary. Production can be extensively automated and the organisation tends to require a mix of labour – low and unskilled at the production end and highly skilled middle-management, marketing, sales and technical staff.

3 *Flexible specialisation.* Here the term is not being used wholly consistently with the Piore and Sabel model referred to earlier (*see* p. 28). The emphasis of this particular strategy, as identified by Regini, is upon the organisation's ability to adapt to changes in demand. This strategy may be more common among small firms and the requirements of labour include both functional and numerical flexibility, allied to broadly based social and interactive skills.

4 *Neo-Fordist.* Even in the developed economies of Europe in the late twentieth century and in an era supposedly post-Fordist, there are in fact still in existence many firms that operate in a largely traditional Fordist fashion, relying upon Taylorist techniques of organising production and work practices with the traditional emphasis upon the fragmentation of the work and the de-skilling of the labour input. Such systems require labour that is unskilled; labour is not required to be functionally flexible.

5 *Traditional small firm.* These organisations seek to compete on price, but not through obtaining the economies that may come from scale and mass production; they can compete only by keeping down their costs, including their labour costs. Many survive only because they operate in product markets that make few demands upon the skills of the labour resource, thereby enabling the employment of cheap unskilled labour.

Each of these competitive and production strategies impose its own demand features upon the labour market in terms of types, levels and mixes of skill and only some require labour that is functionally flexible.

The Price Waterhouse Cranfield data (Brewster, Hegewisch and Mayne, 1994) supports the view that there has been a general widening of jobs and job definitions even though at varying rates from one country to another and between managerial and manual work. The authors assert that their evidence in this area is less supportive of there being clear cut and common trends across all countries. However, they do indicate that this widening of jobs has been occurring at a more rapid rate among manual jobs than among managerial categories, where in many countries the trend has apparently been in the opposite direction with jobs becoming more specific and specialised. The overall conclusion was that the survey data (1992) already indicated considerable task flexibility within European organisations, which continued to grow. (Numerical and temporal flexibility and trends within the Union are dealt with in Chapter 4.)

The Commission Green Paper, *Partnership for a New Organisation of Work*, adopts a somewhat different notion of the flexible firm. The authors suggest that the notion of flexibility in this context refers to and encompasses processes, structures and an environment of continuous change:

> a more fundamental change in the organisation of work is emerging, a shift from fixed (Fordist) systems of production to a flexible, open-ended process of organisational development, a process that offers new opportunities for learning, innovation, improvement and thereby increased productivity . . . This new concept of a process of continuous change is sometimes described as the flexible firm . . .

JOB DESIGN

The search for employee flexibility, satisfaction and commitment

In most instances, changes to working practices and the way in which work is organised and jobs designed have been introduced and motivated by the desire to compete more effectively. In capitalist economies, ultimately the driving force behind change is likely to be profit.

We must not forget, as the work of Regini (1995) clearly argues, that the nature of change and response to market pressures has by no means always been to try and achieve HR outcomes, such as functional flexibility, commitment and quality. It is also important to remember that flexibility has often been perceived by managements almost exclusively in terms of reducing labour costs by cutting down both the quantity and quality of labour input. Technological innovation and development have often assisted this process.

Nevertheless, although the motivation for change is likely to be related to issues of competitiveness and profit, it is the case that many organisations have pursued change in job design and working practices with the aim of enhancing the intrinsic satisfactions that employees derive from their experience at work, assuming both that they have such needs and that satisfied employees will contribute more to the organisation. Some of these schemes have been directed at adding variety and scope for achievement, while others have been more concerned to enhance employee involvement or participation in the task-related, decision-making process.

This view – that the new form of the organisation of work has potential for greater employee involvement and enhanced employee satisfaction – seems to underly the assertions and exhortations made in the Commission Green Paper (1997).

The surveys of work-related values referred to in Chapter 1 are potential sources of information in this regard.

1 *Hofstede*. Hofstede (1991) found a correlation between scores on two of his cultural dimensions – uncertainty avoidance and masculinity – and scores obtained by McClelland's (1987) survey for 'achievement motivation'. The implication of this is that in countries with low scores for uncertainty avoidance and high scores for masculinity (for example, UK and Ireland), there will be high achievement motivation, implying that job designs that provide employees with the opportunity to 'achieve' will effectively motivate. Countries exhibiting high scores for uncertainty avoidance and low scores for masculinity – for example, Spain, Portugal, Greece, France, the Netherlands and Finland – would not expect such returns from designing jobs so as to provide employees with the opportunity to achieve as individuals.

2 *Trompenaars*. Trompenaars' achievement–ascription dimension is also of some potential relevance to this issue, though it refers to the basis of awarding status within society rather than to individual motivation.

3 *Guest*. There is certainly evidence from the UK that employees do seek these rewards from work. Guest's (1995) study supports this contention. One of the categories supported by more than 70 per cent of those questioned as being essential or very important was:

> the type of work which they are doing, the opportunity to use their initiative and abilities whilst at work, in effect to be stretched in terms of problem solving and creativity.

4 *O'Brien*. There are some wider surveys of employee attitudes and feelings about work. O'Brien (1992) has summarised the results of a number of surveys in various countries that seek to identify the degree of employee commitment to work by asking the employees whether they would continue in work if they were to win the lottery or experience similar financial good fortune. The results indicated that British workers had the lowest levels of commitment in this context, though it must be added that over two-thirds of those asked indicated that they would continue to work in such circumstances. However, the reasons given for responses seem to reflect the deriving of social and esteem satisfactions, as well as work being important as a means of structuring time.

The question is whether designing work so as to give employees the opportunity to gain these intrinsic satisfactions then results in higher levels of *commitment*, despite the fact that many such schemes, and particularly those associated with Japanisation (*see* the next section), have been referred to as *high commitment management*. Commitment is a concept that is difficult to measure, and attitudinal commitment more so than behavioural commitment. There may be a relationship between them – that is, measuring behaviour may give an indication of attitudinal commitment – but this is by no means certain. In any event, the belief that it is realistic to envisage employees sharing the values and objectives of their employing organisation depends in part upon personal perspectives and in part upon the employees' needs.

Certainly the Commission Green Paper (1997d) envisages employees and employers having common interests and emphasises the benefits to be derived from a perceived relationship between cooperation, participation, commitment, trust and performance:

> Industrial relations will require, in a new organisation of work, to be built upon a basis of cooperation and common interest . . . Therefore, new forms of industrial relations have to be developed, including, for example, greater participation by employees, since efficient production requires enhanced levels of both trust and commitment in firms.

Forms of job design

The most common ways in which management has sought to add variety and provide scope for employee achievement through job design are:

- job rotation;
- job enlargement;
- job enrichment; and
- the creation of autonomous (or semi-autonomous) teams.

Job rotation

The essence of this re-design is the simple rotation of employees around jobs of a similar skill level so as to alleviate boredom. This requires flexibility from the members of the labour force as they undertake a number of jobs rather than just one. Assembly-line production systems may lend themselves to this kind of re-design, but it can also be applied in other circumstances. The danger is that, although variety has been introduced, employees are simply rotated around a number of jobs that are equally boring and potentially alienating.

Job enlargement

This involves adding tasks of a similar skill level and nature to the existing job, so that the job is enlarged in a horizontal dimension. The level of responsibility remains the same. This widening of the job can relieve the repetitiveness of a highly fragmented and specialised process and thereby arguably yield benefits for the employee in terms of interest and freedom from boredom. However, the counter view is that the situation may be made worse. With one repetitive and boring task, employees may become so proficient that they can effectively switch off and obtain relief; with two or more such tasks, the increased level of concentration required may prevent this relief giving escape and thereby breed resentment and even more dissatisfaction.

Job enrichment

In this case, the enlarging of the job is vertical rather than horizontal, so that responsibility is added to the job – for example, a production operator may be given the added responsibility for inspecting quality, ordering materials or maintaining schedules on the machinery or possibly even responsibility of a supervisory nature. Enrichment of this kind often occurs when management is seeking to delayer or reduce the number of different skill and responsibility levels within the organisation.

Autonomous work groups

In this case, both the principles of enlargement and enrichment are themselves extended and applied at a group level. A group of employees become collectively responsible for a wider range of tasks – often a complete job, such as building a complete car rather than just a part – and also for the kind of responsibilities that were previously performed by supervisors, such as the scheduling of the work and the pace at which the work is performed. For example, a group may be set a production target of 10 complete cars a week. They are then left to achieve the target as they see fit, allocating the work between themselves, ordering the necessary materials, scheduling the necessary maintenance and self inspecting for quality.

Autonomous, or semi-autonomous work groups (as is mostly the case in practice) are in many ways the design with the greatest potential for increasing employee satisfaction. They provide not only opportunities for individual achievement, but also opportunities for employees to satisfy any social and interaction needs that they may have. There is also scope for the team or group members to be more involved in decision making that is more decentralised. Sweden is usually acknowledged as the country in which modern attempts at the design of effective autonomous teams originated. Companies such as Saab and Volvo are perceived to have been at the forefront of these developments.

In each of the above cases, a measure of functional flexibility is achieved even if this is not the major motivation or prime objective.

In a sense these schemes have been dealt with in an order reflecting an increasing degree of re-design of traditional systems and work practices. It would be unwise to overestimate the frequency with which these more profound experiments have been tried.

The more profound the re-design, the greater the impact upon management; changes of this kind are likely to have implications for management style and both the degree of control that management remains able to exert and the mechanisms through which they seek to do so. Furthermore, integral to many of these initiatives is an enhancement of employee autonomy.

Many of these re-design techniques can be described as the antithesis of Taylorism and the principles of scientific management. In many instances, fragmented jobs are to some extent being recomposed by these mechanisms and in some instances tasks such as planning and controlling are being re-merged with execution.

'JAPANISATION': QUALITY, INVOLVEMENT AND COMMITMENT

Many organisations have sought to copy others who appear to have been more successful in confronting the challenges of the global economy and changing product markets. Within the EU, this has often involved studying the methods of Japanese organisations in which the emphasis upon quality and employee involvement and commitment are seen as sources of competitive advantage. As a result, we have seen organisations experimenting with methods, such as:

- quality circles (QCs) and other forms of problem-solving groups;
- cell/team working;
- total quality management (TQM) processes;
- Kaizan or continuous improvement processes; and
- just-in-time (JIT) and lean production policies and systems.

The significant increase in the outward foreign direct investment (FDI) of Japanese organisations since the mid-1980s, much of which has been into the EU, has almost certainly had a significant impact on the publicising and popularising of these practices and techniques.

The quality circle

The quality circle (QC) is probably the most famous technique associated with 'Japanisation' and became popular in the UK and some other parts of Europe in the 1970s and 1980s. Sparrow and Hiltrop (1994) suggest that by 1980 63 per cent of industrial workplaces were running quality circles. These comprise relatively small numbers of employees (6 to 10), meeting voluntarily on a regular basis to identify, examine and resolve quality or other operational problems concerned with their own work and immediate environment. Their remit may primarily be to deal with quality problems, but they are commonly also expected to devise ways of reducing costs and means for improving the design of work. Generally, they are centred around a particular part of the production process.

These groups rarely have the authority to implement their own recommendations and, as the problems are resolved, there is a danger that there may be a loss of momentum. The formation and successful operation of such groups are not quite as easy as they may at first sight seem; experience has tended to reinforce the view that these groups need to be both guided and led. It is quite common for the participants to also need training and some access to resources. As with many of the other mechanisms referred to here, it is important that management is seen to take note and implement at least some of the recommendations of such groups. The effective continuation of problem-solving groups, whether quality circles or others, tends to depend upon evidence that their work is valued.

The popularity of quality circles has waned in recent years, perhaps in part because organisations have introduced one or more of the more comprehensive approaches dealt with later in this chapter. The Price Waterhouse Cranfield data (Brewster and Hegewisch, 1994, pp. 164–5) indicates that quality circles were operating in approximately 30 per cent of indigenous companies in Europe (with the use in multinationals at a higher average of approximately 45 per cent). They were least popular in the Scandinavian countries and were more popular in large companies, as compared with small companies, and in the private sector rather than the public sector. Goetschy and Rozenblatt (1992) asserted that quality circles had become more widespread in France than in any other European country and they thought this was at least partially a response to the very limited role played by the trade unions in French workplaces.

The success of these quality circles has been the subject of debate over the years. They certainly were introduced into hundreds of companies and some success was claimed in terms of factors such as quality improvements, increased job satisfaction and employee involvement. Much of the criticism has focussed on ambiguity about the true purpose of such schemes. Some commentators (for example, Batstone and Gourley, 1986, pp. 117–29) believed that the true purpose of these experiments was not so much to secure improvements in quality and employee involvement and thereby employee satisfaction, but rather to provide a means whereby management could bypass the traditional collective mechanisms of industrial relations and develop a more individual relationship with its employees. From this perspective, the demise of the QC movement in the mid- and late 1980s was due to change in the industrial relations environment and climate. By then, management felt more able to confront a very much weakened trade union movement, without having to camouflage its true intentions.

Another explanation for the relative lack of success and longevity of quality circles was that their voluntary nature gave the impression that a concern for quality improvement was voluntary and therefore not crucial to the success of the organisation. More recently, the need to convince employees that quality is integral to competitive advantage has encouraged the development of more comprehensive approaches.

Total quality management

Total quality management (TQM) encompasses a number of the techniques typically associated with Japanese organisation and, in this context, it is important to bear in mind the general warning that systems effective in one culture may well not transfer very easily into others . . . The essence of the TQM approach is a comprehensive and continuous search for improvement – the production of goods and services with 'zero defects', that involves most employees and knows few boundaries in terms of organisational activity.

In many respects it is an approach that seeks to generate a culture of quality throughout the organisation.

1 *The driver for this attention to TQM should be the customer.* This should include internal as well as external customers. The internal customers are the employees involved in the next stage of the process.

2 *The focus of improvements in quality should be the employees doing the job.* A fear of failure should be replaced with a search for failure. If people are blamed for failure, they are unlikely to take risks. They are unlikely to search for faults and put them right; they are more likely to try and hide them (Marchington and Wilkinson, 1996, pp. 353–4).

3 *The formation of cells, or teams, and the devolution of some additional responsibilities to these semi-autonomous teams are commonly part of this overall approach.* This may also involve the formation of quality circles and other problem-solving groups. Concerned with issues of wider impact than can be coped with by a QC, these other groups may be cross-functional.

The customer-driven nature of such initiatives and the implications for employees are illustrated in the Guiding Principles governing a programme initiated within Ford in the UK and quoted in Storey (1992, p. 57):

- Quality comes first.
- Customers are the focus of everything we do.
- Continuous improvement is essential to our success.
- Employee involvement is our way of life.
- Dealers and suppliers are our partners.
- Integrity is never compromised.

TQM programmes are likely, therefore, to include an emphasis upon employee involvement as the means through which the search for continuous improvement is to be achieved.

Just-in-time

The essence of the just-in-time (JIT) approach is to eliminate waste and this may seem to have little to do with either flexibility or quality. However, there are interdependent relationships between these concepts and systems – sometimes referred to as *'lean production'*.

The basic theory of JIT is that, at all stages of the production of a good or the provision of a service, consideration should be given to minimising the time between the product or a raw material being needed and its acquisition. As a result, systems should be designed which mean that:

- the final product is produced just before it is required in the marketplace;
- sub-assemblies are produced just before final assembly; and
- bought components are acquired just before they are needed.

This enables the company to respond more quickly to market demand and it confirms demand as the driver of the production process. This contrasts with traditional Fordist systems in which vast quantities of standardised products are made and may be stockpiled until they are sold.

In JIT systems the production time is reduced to a minimum; the various contributions to the final product are performed and acquired at the last reasonable moment and the likelihood is that the system will be geared towards and capable of satisfying the demand for relatively small batches of differentiated goods and services.

It is a system, therefore, which places an emphasis upon both quality and flexibility. The materials, labour and sub-assembly processes have to be of the right quality and a premium is placed upon this by the shortness of the timescale. If materials are only acquired just before they are needed, they have to be of the desired quality or else the system fails. If the object is to respond to market demand and undertake relatively short production runs, given that the demand in the market is for customised or variated products, then both the labour and machinery must be flexible. Quality, ideally TQM, and flexibility are crucial to the effective operation of these schemes and they are very vulnerable to failure or shortcomings in either.

From an employee relations perspective, these systems give labour and the suppliers of other materials a pivotal role with the capacity to directly influence the ability of the company to satisfy demand in the marketplace, since the system operates without stocks at both ends of the process.

These same constraints place similar pressures upon the efficiency and effectiveness of the entire system and arguably act as the impetus for the application of continuous improvement. The effective operation of this type of production system also places an emphasis upon trust, since the relationship between management and employees is one of high dependency.

Some of these 'innovations' involve a much more comprehensive and coherent degree of and approach to change than others. TQM and JIT imply change throughout the organisation, whereas many of the other initiatives can more easily be introduced on a piecemeal basis.

As with some of the more fragmented initiatives in the arena of job design (for example, job enrichment programmes and autonomous teams), it would appear that employees must be given autonomy in decision making with respect to many production issues, if these comprehensive zero defect systems are to work effectively.

CONCLUSIONS

There are at least three different sets of views and conclusions about the incidence and impact of these latter comprehensive culture-changing approaches to the challenge of competitiveness in the global market:

1 *The avid proponents*. The members of this group tend to greet these schemes with such a degree of messianic zeal that one tends to wonder about the veracity of their claim (for example, Wickens (1987) and Jones (1990) on Nissan at Sunderland). While perhaps not messianic, the authors of the Commission Green Paper (1997) are certainly avid proponents.

2 *The relative neutrals*. These include many academic researchers (for example, Hill (1991), Wilkinson *et al* (1992), Storey (1992) and Oliver and Wilkinson (1992).

3 *The radical perspectives*. These are perhaps likely to be suspicious and sceptical of the initiatives (for example, Turnbull (1988) and Garrahan and Stewart (1992)).

The claims of the proponents have already been aired in outlining the various initiatives. We are more interested at this stage in trying to ascertain the extent to which it seems that these claims are being realised, what other effects the schemes may have and indeed whether any of these other effects or implications may be consistent with or counter-productive to the claims made for these programmes.

Legge (1995) summarises the conclusions of the neutrals in respect of the UK as:

- evidence of much enthusiasm among managers;

- variable success in implementation; and

- the suspicion that in all but a few companies the magnitude of the cultural change and the time over which the enthusiasm and commitment needs to be maintained combine to hamper effective implementation. The notorious short termism of British business may not be suited to these kinds of change programmes – in the words of Legge, 'a lack of stamina associated with endemic short-termism'.

The more sceptical third group view these initiatives as having both very different objectives and effects to those claimed by the proponents. They view functional flexibility – as acquired through methods such as job enlargement, enrichment, team working, multi-skilling – as the means through which the pressure upon labour is intensified and labour is further exploited. Parker and Slaughter (1988) coined the term 'management by stress' to depict the outcome. The emphasis upon quality and team working are perceived as mechanisms through which a culture of blame is introduced (rather than eradicated, as the theory proclaims). This, allied to the influence of peer pressure, combine to produce a situation in which there is more effective control of the labour resource through peer surveillance. The impact is very far from the production of an involved, satisfied and committed workforce; it is much more a case of management through compliance.

So we have very different interpretations of the impact of these changes upon the nature of work and the employment relationship.

- On the one hand, compliance is being replaced by commitment, conflict by cooperation, dissatisfaction and alienation by satisfaction and management control by employee involvement, autonomy and discretion.

● On the other hand, the view is that these changes are motivated by the desire for increased productivity, competitiveness and profit and that they result in the intensification of labour use and exploitation, an increase in management control through means that are often insidiously based on peer surveillance, as well as the never ending search for faults and the apportionment of blame. Through the continuous search for improvement these systems place unacceptable levels of stress and anxiety upon the labour resource. What is presented as employee involvement and participation is in fact no more than a sham designed to give employees the opportunity to acquiesce to pre-ordained management decisions.

Geary (1995) in his review of the evidence in the UK and assessment of the impact of these new work structures upon employees' working lives presents a fairly depressing picture of the extent to which these working lives have in any real sense been improved. He concludes that the dominant impacts have included:

● increased stress and effort levels;

● little significant upskilling with task specialisation and gendered divisions of work remaining pretty much as they were;

● little increase in employees' control of the work process and its organisation, with managements remaining opposed to extending employees' autonomy and to any other moves that might impair its ability to define the content of acceptable work behaviour;

● more assertive managements that have been successful in gaining greater control over the labour process;

● little or no lasting impact upon employees' commitment to the organisation and its objectives and no significant improvements in the extent to which employees trust their managements; and

● no change in the fundamentally conflictual nature of the employment relationship.

Sparrow and Hiltrop (1994) discuss the proposition that future success is likely to be linked to the successful development of 'learning organisations' – organisations in which innovatory practices are sought out and communicated quickly to employees and suppliers. This is a view shared by the authors of the Commission Green Paper (1997d) who suggest that the document is an invitation to:

> the social partners and public authorities to seek to build a partnership for the development of a new framework . . . such a partnership could make a significant contribution to achieving the objective of a productive, learning and participative organisation of work.

Sparrow and Hiltrop (1994) contrast the Japanese 'lean' approach with the more human-centred German–Scandinavian approach as alternatives for achieving this objective. This may also serve to remind us that cultural and ideological differences are likely to influence the successful introduction and implementation of changes to the nature of work and the way in which work is organised and people motivated.

References

ACAS (1988) *Labour Flexibility in Britain*. Occasional Paper No 41. HMSO.

Atkinson, J. (1984) 'Manpower Strategies for the Flexible Organisation', *Personnel Management*, Aug, 28–31.

Batstone, E. and Gourley, S. (1986) *Unions, Unemployment and Innovation*. Blackwell.

Beatson, M. (1995) *Labour market flexibility*. Employment Dept. Research Series No. 48.

Beer, M., Spector, B., Lawrence, P.R., Quinn, M.D. and Walton, R. (1984) *Managing Human Assets*. Free Press.

Braverman, H. (1974) *Labour and Monopoly Capital*. Monthly Review Press.

Brewster, C., Hegewisch, A. and Mayne, L. (1994) 'Flexible Working Practices: the controversy and the evidence, in Brewster, C. and Hegewisch, A. (eds) *Policy and Practice in European HRM*. Routledge, pp. 168–93.

Brewster, C., Hegewisch, A., Mayne, L. and Tregaskis, O. (1994) 'Employee Communication and Participation', in Brewster, C. and Hegewisch, A. (eds) *Policy and Practice in European HRM*. Routledge, pp. 154–67.

Crouch, C. (1995) 'Exit or Voice: Two Paradigms for European Industrial Relations After the Keynesian Welfare State', *European Journal of Industrial Relations*, 1(1), 63–81.

European Commission (1997d) *Partnership for a New Organisation of Work*. Green (Consultative) Paper COM(97), 128.

Garrahan, P. and Stewart, P. (1992) *The Nissan Enigma: Flexibility at Work in a Local Economy*. Mansell.

Geary, J.F. (1995) 'Work Practices: The Structure of Work', in Edwards, P. (ed) *Industrial Relations: Theory and Practice in Britain*. Blackwell.

Goetschy, J. and Rozenblatt, R. (1992) 'France: the Industrial Relations System at a Turning Point', in Ferner, A. and Hyman, R. (eds) *Industrial Relations in The New Europe*. Blackwell, pp. 404–44.

Guest, D. (1987) 'Human Resource Management and Industrial Relations', *Journal of Management Studies*, 24(5), 503–21.

Guest, D. (1995) Employment in Britain Survey – Why do People Work? Presentation to IPD Conference. Harrogate.

Hill, S. (1991) 'How Do you Manage a Flexible Firm: the Total Quality Model', *Work, Employment and Society*, 5(3), 397–415.

Hofstede, G. (1991) *Cultures and Organisations: Software of the Mind*. McGraw-Hill.

Hollinshead, G. and Leat, M. (1995) *Human Resource Management: An International and Comparative Perspective on the Employment Relationship*. Pitman Publishing.

Jones, A.K.V. (1990) 'Quality management the Nissan way', in Dale, B. and Plunkett, J. (eds) *Managing Quality*. Philip Allan, pp. 44–51.

Legge, K. (1995) *Human Resource Management: Rhetorics and Realities*. Macmillan.

Marchington, M. and Wilkinson, A. (1996) *Core Personnel and Development*. IPD.

Marchington, M., Wilkinson, A., Ackers, P. and Goodman, J. (1992) *Recent Developments in Employee Involvement*, Employment Department Research Series No. 1. HMSO.

McClelland, D.C. (1987) *Human Motivation*. Cambridge University Press.

Mowday, R.T., Steers, R.M. and Porter, L.W. (1982) *Employee–Organisation Linkages: The Psychology of Commitment, Absenteeism and Turnover*. Academic Press.

O'Brien, G. (1992) 'Changing meanings of work', in Hartley, J. and Stephenson, G. (eds) *Employment Relations*. Blackwell, pp. 44–66.

Oliver, N. and Wilkinson, B. (1992) *The Japanisation of British Industry: New Developments in the 1990s*. Blackwell.

Parker, M. and Slaughter, J. (1988) *Choosing Sides: Unions and the Team Concept*. Labour Notes.

Piore, M.J. and Sabel, C. (1984) *The Second Industrial Divide*. Basic Books.

Pollert, A. (1988) 'The Flexible Firm: Fixation or Fact', *Work, Employment and Society*, 2(3), 281–306.

Regini, M. (1995) 'Firms and Institutions: The Demand for Skills and their Social Production in Europe', *European Journal of Industrial Relations*, 1(2), 191–202.

Singh, R. (1992) 'Human Resource Management: a sceptical look', in Towers, B. (ed) *The Handbook of Human Resource Management*. Blackwell, pp. 127–43.

Sparrow, P. and Hiltrop, J. (1994) *European Human Resource Management In Transition*. Prentice-Hall.

Storey, J. (1992) *Developments in the management of human resources*. Blackwell.

Taylor, F.W. (1911) *Principles of Scientific Management*. Harper and Row.

Turnbull, P. (1988) The limits to Japanisation – just-in-time, labour relations and the UK automative industry, *New Technology, Work and Employment* 3(1), 7–20.

Wickens, P. (1987) *The Road to Nissan*. Macmillan.

Wilkinson, A., Marchington, M., Ackers, P. and Goodman, J. (1992) 'Total Quality Management and Employee Involvement', *Human Resource Management Journal*, 2(4), 1–20.

3

THE INTERNATIONALISATION OF BUSINESS AND THE MULTINATIONAL ENTERPRISE

LEARNING OBJECTIVES

When you have read this chapter, you should be able to understand and explain:

- the development of multinational enterprises;
- the different forms of multinational enterprise;
- the emergence and characteristics of the Euro-company;
- managerial problems associated with cultural diversity;
- the meaning and significance of the term 'community-scale undertaking';
- the employment and employee relations implications of the expansion in the activities of multinational enterprises within the EU.

INTRODUCTION

In recent decades we have witnessed the increasing internationalisation of business and the emergence of many multinational enterprises (MNEs). We have seen:

- substantial increases in the volume of international trade;
- the development of more global product markets;
- the growth of international free trade areas (for example, the North American Free Trade Agreement(NAFTA)) and other forms of multinational trading alliance;
- increases in the volume of cross-national investment and ownership; and
- growth in the number of joint ventures and alliances.

Hodgetts and Luthans (1994) assert that all nations are becoming financially more interdependent with industrialised economies investing in those that are developing and the developing economies investing in those that are already more advanced. This *globalisation* or *internationalisation* of business has been significantly enabled by the development and use of new technologies, particularly in the arena of information transfer and communications.

FOREIGN DIRECT INVESTMENT

In the EU, the UK has had a special place both as the source of outward foreign direct investment (FDI) and as a home for inward foreign investment. Traditionally, UK companies have invested more overseas than any other country except the USA, although in the period 1989 to 1994 Japanese outward investment increased substantially and accounted for 13 per cent of the world total of outward FDI, compared to the USA share of 19 per cent, France at 12 per cent, the UK at 11 per cent and Germany at 10 per cent. These figures also demonstrate the extent to which the source of outward FDI is concentrated.

As a recipient of foreign direct investment, the UK has by far the largest stock of the world total when compared with any other EU country. In 1994, the total stock in the UK stood at US $214 billion, whereas those for France and for Germany were US $142 billion and US $132 billion respectively (*source: United Nations World Investment Report 1995*).

The Organisation for Economic Cooperation and Development (OECD) asserts that in recent years the UK has been the single greatest recipient of foreign direct investment into the EU (*see* Exhibit 3.1). The figures for 1996 show that the UK's share of inward FDI into the EU was in the region of 40 per cent and this amounted to US $32.8 billion – more than double the inflow into France which was the next most popular destination. These figures positioned the UK as the second most popular destination in the world behind the USA; for the period 1991 to 1995 the UK total was US $81 billion which put it in third place behind the USA and China over the same period. UK outflows for the year 1996 were US $43.7 billion putting it in second place behind the USA and confirming that the UK is a net investor abroad (*source: OECD Financial Market Trends, 1997*).

Exhibit 3.1

Britain doubles share of EU inward investment   FT

By Guy de Jonquières

Britain received about 40 per cent of the inward direct investment reported by European Union members in 1996 – almost twice its share a year earlier – and attracted bigger inflows than any industrialised country except the US.

UK inflows, which rose from $22.8bn in 1995 to $32.8bn (£19.4bn) were more than double those into France, the next most popular European country, according to the Organisation for Economic Co-operation and Development.

France received inflows of $14.4bn last year, up from $13.4bn. But inward investment into most other EU members fell. Germany reported net disinvestment by foreign inflows of $12bn in 1995.

The OECD said inward direct investment in Britain totalled $81bn between 1991 and 1995, making it the world's third-largest host country after the US and China. France was in fourth place, with inflows of $63.5bn.

The OECD data contrast with recent United Nations figures, suggesting France overtook Britain in the first half of the 1990s to become the largest recipient of inward investment in Europe.

The Labour party used the UN statistics this year to attack the Conservative government's claim that maintaining the UK's opt-out from the European social chapter was essential to attract inward investment.

The OCED said much of the recent inward investment in Britain took the form of mergers and acquisitions, rather than greenfield investment.

Britain was also the world's second-largest source of outward foreign direct investment after the US last year, when its outflows reached a record $43.7bn, up from $42.7bn in 1995.

The total inflows and outflows reported by the OECD's 29 member countries fell slightly last year to $198.3bn and $259.2bn respectively.

The declines were chiefly due to sharply lower outward investment by companies in Germany, the US and Sweden, and big falls in inflows into Australia, Canada, Germany, the Netherlands and Sweden.

Nonetheless, the US remained by far the world's biggest outward investor, with outflows of $88.3bn, and attracted $84bn in inward investment, about $24bn more than in 1995.

Financial Market Trends, June 1997.
OECD, 2 rue André Pascal, 75775
Paris Cedex 16. Tel: 331-45 24 82 00.
Fax: 49 10 42 76.
E-mail: Compte.PUBSINQ@oecd.org.

Source: Financial Times, 14 July 1997.

There has been some debate within the EU as to the relative positions of the UK and France as recipients of FDI. While the OECD seems to confirm the UK as the major recipient of FDI, other sources have argued that for at least part of the time in the 1990s the situation was reversed with France being on the receiving end of more FDI than the UK. For example, Barrell and Pain (1997) refer to IMF data which suggests that in the period 1991 to 1995 the yearly average FDI inflows were US $17.2 billion for the UK, compared with an average of US $19 billion in France.

Debate about these matters has been fuelled by the debate about the relative merits of regulated and unregulated labour markets, relative wage costs and the costs and benefits of social protection. Those figures showing that the UK has been the major recipient have been used to justify the emerging UK model, whereas figures showing that other EU member states have been able to attract inward FDI at the same rates as the UK have been used to support the more traditional, regulated European model. Barrell and Pain argue that the fact that the UK is a net outward investor within Europe and elsewhere casts doubt upon the supposed attractiveness of low labour costs and deregulated labour markets. That doubt is confirmed by the fact that France is such a close competitor for inward FDI. They suggest that investment and location decisions within the EU are influenced by factors such as:

- corporate tax burdens;
- the skills and training of the labour force;
- the quality of the infrastructure;
- language and cultural factors; and
- the cost of labour.

The more high-tech the operation, the less important are labour costs in the investment and location decision.

A survey by KPMG Corporate Finance (reported in *The Guardian* of July 1997) suggests that in the first half of 1997 Germany was the EU member state that attracted the highest amount of foreign corporate investment into the EU – US $14.7 billion, whereas the UK figure was US $11.6 billion. At the same time, the UK retained its position as the EU's biggest foreign investor with US $13.5 billion being invested abroad in the same period. (Switzerland was the only European country that invested more abroad in this same six month period.)

THE RISE OF THE MULTINATIONAL

The growth in the number of companies that now not only buy and sell across national borders, but also own or control production or service facilities in one or more countries other than the home country, is one of the most apparent indications of this internationalisation. It is this dimension of ownership and/or control which sets multinational enterprises (MNEs) apart from other organisations that simply trade or liaise internationally, and which provides us with a simplified definition of the multinational company. It is also this element of ownership or control which tends to bring with it the challenge of managing human resources in different national contexts and poses for the organisation's management the problems associated with international human resource management.

Griffiths and Wall (1996) refer to United Nations figures which suggested that there were in excess of 35 000 multinational enterprises in the world and that the top 200 control approximately one-third of global production. They point out that some multinationals have annual turnovers that exceed the GDP of the majority of countries; their estimate was that only 14 countries had a GDP that exceeded the annual turnover of companies such as General Motors, Ford, and Exxon. Hodgetts and Luthans (1994) list the 25 largest multinational corporations by sales in 1994 and these three companies were fifth, seventh and eighth respectively – the top four and the sixth corporations all being Japanese in origin: Mitsubishi, Mitsui, Itochu, Sumitomo and Marubeni respectively. All of these corporations had sales running in excess of US $101 000 million. The largest European corporation in these terms was Royal Dutch/ Shell which was tenth in the list with sales figures of nearly US $95 000 million.

Griffiths and Wall state that, of the top 500 companies operating in the UK, some 313 were foreign owned, with the USA and Japan being the two most common locations of ownership, and that multinationals account for some 30 per cent of UK GDP.

Ultimately companies become multinationals in order to generate more profit. However, there are other common and specific reasons why companies decide to become multinational and several different approaches to achieving that goal.

A company may go multinational for one of the following reasons:

- to protect themselves from the risks associated with the business cycle in the country of origin – a kind of hedge against events in any one country;
- to protect themselves from the risks associated with allowing another company to produce 'their' product under licence and thereby acquire access to their technological expertise;
- to take advantage of developing markets in other parts of the world;
- to avoid tariff and other barriers that may be erected to international trade, by locating or investing in a particular country and thereby gaining access to that market as if it were the company's country of origin;
- to take advantage of production cost (including labour) differentials and less strict legislative or regulatory regimes.

Exhibit 3.2 illustrates some of the reasons for becoming multinational, some of the different strategies employed and is also indicative of some of the forms of multinational organisation.

In the context of the EU, the last two reasons may be of particular significance since the decision in 1985 to create the single market and to provide for the free movement of capital, labour, goods and services across the internal national borders. The avoidance of tariff barriers has been a dominant motive for companies originating from and owned outside the EU to invest within one or more of the member states. As noted above, there are differences of view about the significance to investment and location decisions of differences in production costs and regulatory regimes within the EU. This applies to both determining the member state destination of foreign direct investment (FDI) from outside the Union and to the investment decisions of companies that originate from one of the member states and expand in to others.

Exhibit 3.2

Flashes of opportunity amid the gloom

FT

By Tony Jackson

Europe's industrial performance varies across sectors, as illustrated below. The picture is not one of unrelieved gloom. There are plenty of opportunities as well as problems.

Cars: The EU is the world's largest car market and the world's largest car producer. However, close to 30 per cent of European production is foreign-owned, with the figure likely to rise to about a third as new Japanese plants reach full production in the next few years. The European industry is also more parochial than its US or Japanese rivals, though it is striving to catch up. BMW and Mercedes are building their first plants in the US. In China, European carmakers have established an early lead.

Europe is still at an early stage of a huge phase of rationalisation and restructuring. There are six true volume car makers left: Volkswagen, Fiat, Renault and Peugeot Citroen, plus Ford and General Motors of the US. Almost all the smaller players have been absorbed. Though Volvo's merger with Renault has fallen through, Rover is about to become part of BMW. Among the big players, at least one further merger looks likely within the next few years.

The industry is likely to emerge from this phase more competitive than before. It also has the geographical advantage of a potentially enormous market on its doorstep, in the form of eastern Europe and the former Soviet Union.

Drugs: The pharmaceutical industry is a European success story. The EU is the world's biggest producer of prescription drugs, and many of the world's best-selling drugs have been invented and developed in Europe over the years. Between 1987 and 1991, EU production grew by 36 per cent in real terms, compared with 16 per cent for the US. This is also an industry in which Japan has yet to make its mark.

The chief threat to Europe lies in the rise of biotechnology, which may supplant much of the traditional chemistry-based drug industry. The US has a substantial lead here, based largely on its entrepreneurial tradition and huge pool of venture capital.

Electronics/telecommunications: The picture is mixed. In telecommunications, Europe has a number of internationally successful equipment suppliers, such as Siemens, Alcatel, Ericsson and Nokia. It has also struck lucky in mobile phones, where the European GSM standard is now becoming a global standard outside the US. This puts US suppliers at a significant disadvantage in an important growth market.

In electronics, however, Europe is sandwiched between Japan's dominance in consumer electronics and America's overwhelming strength in high-tech hardware and software. Unlike the US, Europe has chosen to confront Japan in consumer electronics, the result being heavy losses for companies such as Thomson and Philips. Across the high-tech field of computer hardware, software, semiconductors and micro-processors, Europe as a whole is weak and risks getting weaker.

Aerospace/defence: Perhaps the EU's biggest industrial success in recent years has been the establishment of the Airbus consortium as the world's only real rival to Boeing in civil aircraft manufacture. The financial cost has been heavy, though, and Airbus's eventual success as an independent entity cannot be taken for granted.

In the defence industry, European contractors traditionally enjoyed preferential treatment from their own governments, while the US government was reluctant to allow sophisticated weaponry into foreign hands. With the collapse of the Soviet Union, the picture has changed dramatically. Since 1989, US defence exports have risen from $6bn a year to $15bn, while Europe's have halved to around $5bn. It is not clear that this process is over. On the other hand, the European industry also lags the US badly in terms of rationalisation. As in cars, this should make for greater efficiency, provided it is undertaken in time.

Chemicals: The EU is still by a narrow margin the world's biggest producer of basic chemicals, just ahead of the US and well ahead of Japan. The threat comes in petrochemicals, more than half the sector.

Though Europe invented many of the basic plastics, it has some fundamental handicaps. The US and Middle East have cheaper natural gas as raw material. The Far East is the main growth market, and Far Eastern producers are raising capacity accordingly. Several of Europe's leading producers see the long-term outlook as bleak.

Labour price falls offshore

FT

Fila, the fast-growing sportswear and shoe maker based in the north Italian textile town of Biella, has found one way of coping with a fundamental problem of European manufacturing. It is trying not to have any.

The company started business in 1926 as a family-owned knitwear manufacturer. After widespread changes over the past two decades, Fila's production is now carried out by about 50 independent low-cost subcontractors around the world. Roughly 85 per cent of output came from the Far East last year, with just under 10 per cent of its goods made in Italy.

Fila has switched to Asian production as part of 'globalisation of sales, sourcing and creativity', according to Mr Enrico Frachey, the company's 59-year-old managing director. This has also involved an intense attack on the booming US market, which accounted for 63 per cent of sales last year.

Sitting in his office in front of a large wall map of China – 'more and more important for our future' – Mr Frachey says: 'We are a kind of textbook. The only chance for US and European companies to survive in this field is to do what we did.'

Mr Frachey worked for Fila during the 1970s, presiding over its diversification into sportswear, helped by promotional deals with stars like Bjorn Borg, the Swedish tennis champion. He left in early 1980. After rejoining in 1987, he pushed Fila's US expansion and built up subcontracting.

Fila's basketball shoes, tennis gear and ski outfits compete for retain supremacy around the world with leading brands such as Reebok, Nike and Adidas. Now 70 per cent owned by the holding company Gemina, Fila closed its last production line in Biella in 1983. The old factory floor has been refurbished into a lavish auditorium for displaying its latest outfits to the sportswear trade.

Staff in Italy, which totalled 2,500 in the 1950s and 1,800 in the 1960s, has now declined to 270, with a further 670 employed abroad – mainly in quality control, design, distribution and marketing. Turnover has rocketed 10-fold since the late 1980s.

Overall sales increased last year to L741bn ($441m) from L515bn in 1992. Fila hopes to achieve turnover of L1,000bn by 1995.

Of its show production, roughly 40 per cent is made in Indonesia, and 30 per cent in China. In sportswear, the two countries each account for 20 to 25 per cent.

CASE STUDY: FILA

A north Italian clothing and footwear company has closed its factory and shifted production to Asia: 'The only chance of survival.'

Davi Marsh reports

Mr Frachey says making up a track suit in an Indonesian or Chinese garment factory costs L5,000, against L35,000 to L40,000 in Italy. Even South Korea is now a relatively high-cost site, with production about 40 per cent more expensive than in China.

Saving manufacturing costs releases funds for the company's huge budget for promotion and marketing – last year L60bn or 8 per cent of sales.

With 70 per cent of its costs and revenues in dollars, Fila has become progressively less Italian. Reflecting US dominance in leisure wear, even Italian design is now becoming less important. 'Fila is losing the Italian look. there is more feeling for American brands,' says Mr Frachey.

He does not exclude the possibility that, one day, the company may sever its Italian ties altogether. 'The European market is a small project. We are beyond this. Our market is the world.'

Gains via R&D, market share and cost-cuts   FT

Three leading European manufacturers employ very different strategies against their international competitors

ROCHE

By Tony Jackson

The Swiss pharmaceutical giant Roche is an example of European industry at its most effective. Last year, the steady rise in its share price made it the most highly valued drug company in the world, overhauling Merck of the US.

Roche's success is based on the performance of European workers at home and European managers abroad. Swiss-based researchers have discovered a wealth of commercially valuable drugs. Roche has also proved shrewd in acquiring assets overseas, notably Californian biotechnology company Genentech.

The achievement owes much to the immense and, no doubt, excessive profitability of the international drug industry, which governments around the world are now seeking to control. The results for Roche have been extraordinary.

Its spending on R&D has been heavy even by the standards of its industry: in 1992, for instance, its pharmaceuticals research bill came to SFr1.6bn ($1.1bn), or 24 per cent of its pharmaceutical turnover.

It was also able to plonk down $2bn in 1990 for 60 per cent of Genentech, a company which had only $500m in sales and very little profit. Despite all that, Roche has cash and securities currently estimated at SFr20bn ($13.5bn).

In the field of conventional drugs, it is worth recalling that Roche's success represents a fairly recent comeback. It had a previous glory phase in the 1960s, based largely on the tranquilliser Valium.

As Valium went off patent, Roche spent heavily on the search for replacement drugs. For a while, it seemed the money was being wasted. The real strength of the resulting research pipeline has become apparent only recently.

Roche has also built a formidable position in hospital drugs, claiming to sell more drugs to US hospitals than any other company in the world.

At the same time, the purchase of Genentech was a particularly bold strategic move, since biotechnology is a field in which the US has a clear lead over Europe. Roche has thus hedged its bets against a possible shortfall in European technology.

MICHELIN

By John Ridding

Michelin of France, the world's biggest tyre maker, made it the hard way. In 1960 it was the 10th biggest, by 1970 it was number six and by the end of the 1980s it was number one. Michelin's approach had a Japanese ring: aggressive international expansion and concentration on market share.

Greenfield investments, followed by the acquisition of Uniroyal Goodrich in 1990, have resulted in a 20 per cent share of the world market and a clear lead over Goodyear of the US and Bridgestone of Japan. At the same time, Michelin has invested heavily in quality and in R&D, being the first company to develop and market the radial tyre.

Michelin's rise has been far from smooth. The Uniroyal acquisition was completed as the US market collapsed. Last year, the European market did likewise. For several years, the group suffered large losses. But

▶

Exhibit 3.2 continued

most industry observers believe the worst is over.

Michelin's ability to pursue its aggressive and sometimes risky strategy partly reflects its ownership. As a family-controlled group in the continental European mould, it can afford to be less concerned with quarterly earnings and more with dominance in markets and technologies. The benefits are evident in the initially costly but ultimately lucrative development of radial tyres and in the strengths of geographical diversity.

But now a different message is emanating from Michelin's headquarters at Clermont-Ferrand. With its market position established and little remaining scope for growth through acquisitions or new capacity, the company is shifting emphasis towards increased efficiency and higher margins.

This is to be achieved partly through new, higher value-added products, such as the green tyre, which reduces fuel consumption.

The company has also embarked on job cuts which have seen staff numbers fall from 140,000 at the end of 1991 to 125,000. Further reductions are expected from the introduction of its C3m automated and flexible production process.

PHILIPS

By Tony Jackson

Philips, the Dutch electronics group, is a classic case of a once-great European company caught between the Japanese hammer and the American anvil. On the one hand, its battles with Japan in consumer electronics have led to huge losses. On the other, it has been obliged to abandon high-tech areas to computers and semiconductors.

Philips's basic problem can be illustrated by comparison with one of its chief competitors, the Japanese electronics company Matsushita. A decade ago, Matsushita's sales in dollar terms were smaller than Philips's. They are now twice as large. The growth of the Japanese company in the 1980s owed much to the strength of its domestic market, from which Philips was largely excluded by a combination of protectionism and the peculiarities of the Japanese retail system.

But the Japanese advantage, whether fair or foul, was a fact of life. Philips' determination to tackle the competition head-on has been impressive, but also smacks of arrogance and inflexibility. Despite the company's recent enormous losses, the struggle continues. In the field of consumer audio, Philips is confronting Sony's mini-compact disc with its new digital compact cassette. It has also just opened a factory in Holland to make flat screen panels, a vitally important technology in which even the Americans have conceded Japan a virtual monopoly.

Philips could be past the worst. Its cost-cutting and rationalisation in the past couple of years have been on a scale to suggest that even the notorious Philips bureaucracy has become genuinely alarmed. And the Japanese electronics industry is facing problems which may prove structural rather than cyclical.

Certainly, the investment community is inclined to optimism. In the past year, Philips's shares have outperformed the Dutch market by two thirds.

However, the company has seen false dawns before. For the pessimists, it may be more relevant to reflect that the shares have halved relative to the Dutch market in the past decade.

Source: *Financial Times*, 25 February 1994.

FORMS OF MULTINATIONAL ORGANISATION

In this work we use the term multinational enterprise (MNE) as the generic for organisations that own or control production or service facilities in one or more countries other than the home country. It is relevant to point out, however, that there are a number of different and potentially confusing terms and definitions used in the literature and it is appropriate to identify some of these.

Arguably the most influential of the typologies that have been devised to further distinguish multinationals is that of Bartlett and Ghoshal (1989) who devised a fourfold typology of the forms of organisation used to manage international businesses.

- *The multinational*. In many respects this form is a collection of decentralised and independent national units, each having a tendency towards a domestic orientation serving local markets and retaining knowledge locally – almost like a decentralised federation.

- *The global.* These are centralised organisations which operate on a global basis consistent with notions of global markets, with overseas operations implementing centrally determined policies and strategies. Knowledge is developed and retained at headquarters; these organisations exhibit a high degree of internal integration.

- *The international.* This is a more mixed stereotype with some things being determined and retained centrally and others decentralised. It is likely in this form that knowledge developed at the centre is transferred to the overseas units and resources are shifted around within the whole. This is a form of organisation that may respond quite easily to global markets becoming more diverse with much less emphasis upon the world-wide production and consumption of standardised products. These firms are more flexible than either of those above.

- *The transnational.* In this case we are describing a mentality as well as an organisational form. This is the culmination of flexibility and diversity in structure and systems. Here the objective is to be globally competitive through multinational flexibility and a world-wide learning capability; there is an interdependence not present in the international organisation described above. These are almost stateless organisations with a world-wide ownership base. National boundaries and regulatory systems tend to be irrelevant and headquarters can be anywhere in the world.

Bartlett and Ghoshal (1989) argued that the transnational form was the one that would provide the base or template for success in the future – effectively, a stateless organisation with activities and systems in various parts of the world, the location of which is determined by considerations of least cost. This is the form of international organisation that many perceive as providing the greatest threat to the traditions and regulatory and protective systems typical of social/welfare capitalism in Europe.

In many respects this typology can be viewed as stages in the development of the MNE. Some authors no longer seek to distinguish between the various forms of MNE identified by Bartlett and Ghoshal and are satisfied to distinguish between *transnational* and *uninational* corporations (Ietto-Gillies, 1997).

The multinational enterprise may operate multinationally in either a *horizontally* or *vertically integrated* fashion. Horizontal integration refers to the situation in which basically the same production or service functions are carried out in each of the countries in which the company is located (for example, retail operations such as Toys 'R' Us and Marks and Spencers), whereas vertically integrated multinationals are those that undertake different stages of the same production process in different countries (for example, a car manufacturer that makes engines and gearboxes in its plant in one country, chassis and bodykits in another and carries out final assembly in another.

In an examination of the approaches to the organisation of production and production strategies, Schulten (1996) cites UNCTAD (1994) and identifies three different types:

- *the stand-alone strategy*, whereby the subsidiaries in foreign countries operate as mini replicas of the parent organisation and the whole value-added process is organised in the host country with few functional links to the parent;

- *the simple integration strategy*, whereby the subsidiaries in the host countries supply the parent with components – a simple division of labour between the parties;

- *the complex integration strategy*, developed since the 1970s and supported by modern communications technology, which may see, for example, production within the MNE integrated and organised in one way with other functions integrated and organised in another. Schulten quotes the example of the MNE in which:

. . . some functions may be integrated globally, e.g. finance, others regionally, e.g. production, while again others may remain entirely local, e.g. training . . .

The first two of these strategies correspond quite closely to the traditional distinction between horizontal and vertical integration, while the third is more a hybrid that represents in some respects a more genuine and comprehensive European approach to the problems of integration.

In terms of the Bartlett and Ghoshal (1989) typology, the first of Schulten's categories seems to correspond reasonably closely to their multinational form and the second to the global form of organisation. Schulten's third form of production strategy is more complex and more integrated and would appear to have more in common with the international or transnational forms or stages of development identified by Bartlett and Ghoshal, but on a European as opposed to a global scale.

Many MNEs acquire this status through merger with or the acquisition of a going concern, although the establishment from scratch of a new production or service facility in the other country is often the only alternative available; the term 'green field investment' is sometimes used to distinguish this latter approach. UNCTAD (1994) asserts that in the second half of the 1980s some 70 per cent of FDI into developed countries was via the mechanism of cross-border acquisition.

THE EURO-COMPANY

Once the decision to create the single European market was taken, the latter part of the 1980s and the early 1990s became a period characterised by a considerable restructuring of European capital and expansion of cross-border amalgamations and mergers.

Nicolaides and Thomsen (1991) summed up these developments succinctly:

Cross border mergers and amalgamations within Europe and relentless investment by Japanese, American and other non-EU firms in the EU are reshaping the European economy.

This capital restructuring was accompanied in some instances by corporate restructuring and rationalisation, reflected in the development and strengthening of management structures at a European level. Marginson and Sisson (1994) refer to companies that have repositioned themselves in this way on a Europe-wide footing as *Euro-companies* and while they acknowledge that these may be relatively few in number, they suggest that they are of considerable influence in economic and employment terms.

However, the decision to go ahead with the single market and these subsequent developments have also awakened many of the concerns and pressures that have been behind the increased emphasis given in the 1990s to the achievement of a social dimension within the EU – the subject matter of this book.

Marginson and Sisson's (1994) Euro-company fits more closely with the third of the integration strategies within Europe identified by Schulten (*see* p. 51). They suggest that while it may be a characteristic of such MNEs that strategic decision making and integration become centralised at the level of the company or division, they also point out the converse trend towards the decentralisation and devolution of operational responsibility and financial accountability to individual business units and cost and profit centres within the larger transnational or Euro-company.

Marginson and Sisson (1996) argue that there are trends in most companies involving simultaneous increasing decentralisation to individual business units and increasing centralisation to the European level and they suggest an inverse relationship between the two. The greater the degree of devolution to individual business units located within national systems, the greater is the tendency towards centralisation and coordination of strategy at the Euro-company level.

MANAGING DIVERSITY IN THE MULTINATIONAL ENTERPRISE

Some of the problems facing MNEs are related to managing effectively in different cultures and managing cultural diversity. Multinationals have a number of choices when they address these matters and these are illustrated effectively by the work of Perlmutter (1969) in which he distinguishes four possible approaches.

- *The ethnocentric approach.* The culture of the home country is allowed to determine the organisational culture and no account is taken of local cultures and characteristics. Home-country nationals are likely to be used to staff and manage foreign operations. This will facilitate communications between the HQ and the foreign operation and many American and UK multinationals have adopted this approach in the past.

- *The polycentric approach.* The MNE seeks to take account of the host country culture and is likely to try and staff and manage from the host country. This can cause communication problems between the centre and the foreign operations.

- *The regiocentric approach.* The company seeks to organise and manage on a regional basis and will seek to appoint or develop staff from within the region to manage and staff operations in that region. The company may try to develop and inculcate a hybrid regional culture within the organisation. The cultures of regions – for example, Europe or Africa – are by no means as homogeneous as this approach might imply.

- *The geocentric approach.* This is very much like the regiocentric approach, but on a global scale. For example, operations may be staffed and managed by the best people available, irrespective of their country or region of origin.

In the context of the Perlmutter typology, the complex integration strategy of Schulten and the international and transnational forms of multinational organisation identified by Bartlett and Ghoshal might all be perceived as indicative of and consistent with a regiocentric or geocentric approach to the organisation of the companies' activities.

Within Europe, the Price Waterhouse Cranfield studies have established that MNE attitudes and approaches to the management of human resources and employee relations have so far been primarily polycentric, implying that they work with and within the relevant national regulatory systems and traditions. These findings have contributed to the reinforcement of the *societal effect theory* (Maurice *et al*, 1980) which argues that the activities and organisational practices of MNEs are significantly influenced by specific national cultures and sets of social institutions to the extent that it tends towards a reproduction of national patterns.

THE COMMUNITY-SCALE UNDERTAKING

Within the EU, a new concept in business organisation has been created in recent years – the 'community-scale undertaking'. This is the term used in the European Works Council (EWC) Directive to depict those multinationals that employ more than 1000 employees with at least 150 in each of two member states. These companies need not have their headquarters within the EU and national origin and/or ownership are not factors relevant to whether an undertaking is of community-wide scale.

Estimates vary as to the number of companies in the EU that fit into this category, but there seems to be a measure of agreement among commentators that there are in excess of 1100 of them. Rivest (1996) cites the European Trade Union Institute (ETUI) (1995) estimate that there were 1144 companies employing approximately 15 million employees that would be covered by the Directive, and that the largest number are based in the UK, with more than 300 qualifying companies estimated as having their home or their European base/headquarters in the UK. Original estimates suggested that 106 UK-owned companies would be covered by the Directive in respect of their non-UK EU activities and that in all just over 400 of the companies covered by the Directive were owned in countries not directly subject to the Directive, of which nearly 200 were from the USA and 32 were from Japan.

MULTINATIONALS, EMPLOYMENT AND EMPLOYEE RELATIONS

As noted earlier, multinationals are important from both an economic and employment perspective and, within the EU, in recent years we have witnessed considerable competition between member-state national and regional governments to be on the receiving end of direct inward foreign investment as one dimension of multinational activity. This competition has been heightened by the relatively high rates of unemployment within the EU generally and within certain countries and regions in particular.

The impact of multinationals for employment

The belief is that attracting such inward investment by a multinational has the potential for beneficial effects upon levels of employment.

Generally, the net impact of multinational activity upon employment depends upon the combined effect of three factors:

- *Direct job creation*. This depends upon both the size and the capital–labour mix in the production process; highly capital-intensive investment will have relatively poor returns in terms of direct job creation.

- *Indirect job creation*. This depends upon links with local suppliers and the extent to which the company imports components and other factors of production.

- *The Trojan horse or displacement effect of the investment*. If the investment merely means that other local producers are forced out of the market, then overall the effect upon employment may not be what it first seems.

It is important that we also bear in mind that FDI that takes the form of merger or acquisition of a going concern may have no beneficial impact upon employment at all and indeed it may in the long term lead to employment decline, as activities and structures are rationalised and reorganised on a Euro- or transnational basis. Furthermore, potential complication to these calculations and issues within the EU is that investment in one country may have beneficial net effects upon employment in that country at the expense of employment in one of the other member states.

The European Works Council (EWC) Directive (discussed in more detail in Chapter 14) is one of the first successful attempts by the EU (in the sense that the measure was actually adopted, as opposed to being proposed but not adopted – the fate of several proposals before it) to regulate the employee relations activities and regimes within MNEs.

The adoption of this measure should be viewed at least partially as a symptom of the awareness among the officials and representatives of national governments and other interest groups within the EU that the single market has provided the MNE with an even greater ability to go **regime shopping** – that is, to pick and choose between regimes in individual member states, to locate activities where production costs may be low, to close plants in one country and move them to other countries where conditions may be more favourable. In so doing, multinationals pose national governments and their peoples with substantial employment implications. This diversion of investment towards those national regimes which favour lower production costs or enhanced labour flexibility is often referred to as 'Social Dumping' (*see* Chapter 6).

Two of the most famous, or infamous examples of this are the decision by Hoover in 1993 to close one of its plants in France and relocate the activity to a plant in Scotland and the decision of Renault in 1997 to close a plant in Belgium – one of their most efficient plants – at the same time as the company was negotiating with local government and officials from the EU to obtain grant aid to open a new plant in Spain. The latter decision was greeted with a storm of protest in Belgium and industrial action by Belgian workers which was supported by workers from other Renault plants in France – but ultimately, to no avail.

It should be borne in mind that both governments and employees can be pressured into forms of concession and pattern bargaining by the knowledge that the MNE can act in this way. There are many examples of governments being persuaded to provide financial and other assistance to MNEs, rather than lose a potential job-creating or protecting investment – a recent case being the British government offering grant aid in response to the threat by Ford to relocate the production of Jaguar cars.

Internally, the MNE is in a position to encourage competition for work between groups and divisions and between locations and groups of employees within the company. This can be used to exert a downward pressure on terms and conditions of employment and hence costs, as employees compete against each other for the available work. The decision by Hoover to switch resources to Scotland was explicitly linked to agreement to certain concessions on the part of the Scottish employees.

The impact of multinationals on employee relations

There has been considerable debate regarding the likelihood of the formation of Euro-companies acting as a stimulus for the convergence of employee relations and human resource systems within the EU. The use of internal competition is one way in which this might occur on a piecemeal basis over time.

However, Schulten (1996) highlights another way in which this may be encouraged. Companies that are concerned to enhance flexibility or quality will examine the entire organisation for instances of best practice and will then seek to implement these on a company-wide basis. He also suggests that the European Works Council (EWC), which is depicted as a form of micro-corporatism at Euro-company level, may actually be of great benefit to management as a mechanism through which best practice can be ascertained and the message spread to other units and locations. The EWC may be used as the conduit by which management seeks to achieve convergence and a form of transnational human resource management.

There is little evidence, however, to suggest that companies will forgo regime shopping and the social dumping approach referred to above, simply because the EWC provides a mechanism for the transfer of best practice. Indeed it is possibly more likely that MNEs will seek to utilise both approaches as means by which they can enhance efficiency, productivity, competitive advantage and profit.

The effect of social dumping outside the EU

In this section we have concentrated upon activities and restructuring within and internal to the Union, but it is important also to remember that many of the multinationals active in the Union have also expanded into labour markets in other parts of the world. The social dumping phenomena applies equally to the ability of the MNE to relocate investment from plants within the Union to plants in other countries and areas of the world in which even greater cost savings may be available. As a result, in the 1990s there have been numerous instances of European MNEs closing production and other facilities in relatively high-cost Europe and relocating in lower cost and developing economies. Much of this diversion of investment has been into the former Soviet Bloc countries of Eastern and Central Europe – many of which are aspirant members of the EU – and into Asia, Africa and other low-cost and 'friendly' regulatory regimes.

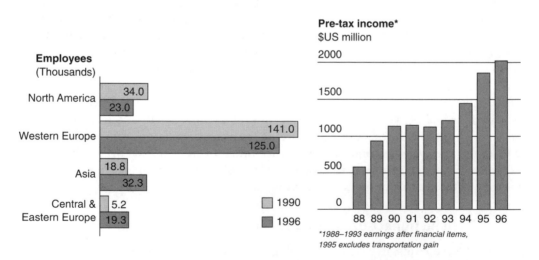

Fig. 3.1 The financial performance (1988–96) and employment record (1990 and 1996) of the ABB Group

Source: ABB, *The Guardian*, 27 Sept 1997.

Developments of this nature can pose significant employment problems for the EU and the labour force within it. In June 1997, the Asea Brown Boveri (ABB) group – itself a product of a Swedish–Swiss cross-national merger (*see* Kennedy (1992)) – decided to cut its European workforce by some 57 000 at the same time as it expanded its operations in Asia. Figure 3.1 shows how the company had shifted its employment pattern in the 1990s prior to the decision.

Decisions of this nature inevitably fuel the debate about the need to somehow limit the autonomy of the MNE to locate and relocate at will. If limiting their autonomy is inconsistent with the spirit of the single market and the freedom of mobility of capital upon which the single market is built, then this issue fuels the debate on the desirability of a social dimension, as opposed to the argument for deregulation and flexibility. This is seen by many as the only means by which the EU can hope to retain such employment-creating investment within the Union. This is a debate to which we return at various points in this book.

References

Barrell, R. and Pain, N. (1997) 'EU: an attractive investment', *New Economy*, 4(1).

Bartlett, C.A. and Ghoshal, S. (1989) *Managing Across Borders: The Transnational Solution*. Harvard Business School Press.

Brewster, C. and Hegewisch, A. (eds) (1994) 'Policy and Practice in European HRM'. *The Price Waterhouse Cranfield Survey*. Routledge.

European Trade Union Institute (ETUI) (1995) *Les comités d'entreprises européens: inventaire des entreprises concernées*.

Griffiths, A. and Wall, S. (1996) *Applied Economics*. Longman.

Hodgetts, R.M. and Luthans, F. (1997) *International Management* (2nd edn). McGraw-Hill.

Ietto-Gillies, G. (1997) 'Working with the big guys: hostility to transnationals must be replaced by co-operation', *New Economy*, 4(1).

Kennedy, C. (1992) 'ABB: model merger for the new Europe', *Long Range Planning*, 25(5), 10–17.

Marginson, P. and Sisson, K. (1994) 'The Structure of Transnational Capital in Europe: the Emerging Euro-company and its Implications for Industrial Relations', in Hyman, R. and Ferner, A. (eds) *New Frontiers in European Industrial Relations*. Blackwell.

Marginson, P. and Sisson, K. (1996) 'Multi-national Companies and the Future of Collective Bargaining: A Review of the Research Issues', *European Journal of Industrial Relations*, 2(2), 173–97.

Maurice, M., Silvestre, J.-J. and Sellier, F. (1980) 'Societal Differences in Organising Manufacturing Units: A Comparison of France, West Germany and Great Britain', *Organisational Studies*, 1, 59–86.

Nicolaides, P. and Thomsen, S. (1991) 'The Impact of 1992 on Direct Investment in Europe', *European Business Journal*, 3(2), 8–16.

OECD (1997) *Financial Market Trends*. June.

Perlmutter, H. (1969) 'The Tortuous Evolution of the Multi-national Corporation', *Columbus Journal of World Business*, 4(1), 9–18. Reprinted in Ghauri Pervez, N. and Prasad, S.B. (eds) (1995) *International Management: a Reader*. Dryden.

Rivest, C. (1996) 'Voluntary European Works Councils', *European Journal of Industrial Relations*, 2(2), 235–53.

Schulten, T. (1996) 'European Works Councils: Prospects of a New System of European Industrial Relations', *European Journal of Industrial Relations*, 2(3), 303–24.

United Nations (1995) *World Investment Report 1995*.

United Nations Conference on Trade and Development (UNCTAD) (1994) *World Investment Report 1994: Transnational Corporations, Employment and the Workplace*. United Nations.

4

DEMOGRAPHIC AND LABOUR MARKET DEVELOPMENTS

LEARNING OBJECTIVES

When you have read this chapter, you should be able to understand and explain:

- the implications of an ageing population for social protection expenditure;
- trends in the sectoral and occupational structure of the labour force;
- trends towards more flexible employment;
- developments in the participation and employment rates of men and women;
- the significance of people staying on in education longer and the relationship between level of education and employment;
- the distinction between active and passive labour market policies.

INTRODUCTION

It is possible to identify a number of trends of a demographic nature and in the structure and constituents of the labour force. To some extent, the trends in the make-up of the labour force can be seen as responses to changes in technology and the nature of work, the structure of industry and the demands placed upon employers and industry within the Union by global competitive developments. It has become commonplace to argue that the increase in global competition is at the root of moves by employers and governments within the Union to deregulate labour markets and the employment relationship, to reduce labour costs, social protection and associated costs and that it is also responsible for the imperatives for more flexible forms of production, work organisation and use of labour. As noted in Chapter 2, this requirement for a more flexible labour resource may be for flexibility in terms of times and hours of work (temporal), numbers of employees (numerical), function and/or location. In this section we are concerned with flexibility of a temporal and numerical nature and not of working practice, function or location.

MAIN DEMOGRAPHIC AND LABOUR MARKET TRENDS

Before proceeding to a presentation and discussion of these developments, it is perhaps useful to briefly outline the main trends that affect the social dimension of the Union.

1 Demographic trends

The two main demographic trends are the declining birth rates and mortality rates which in combination project to a significant ageing of both the population and workforce of the Union as we move into the early decades of the twenty-first century. This has significant implications for the level and costs of social protection, health and welfare services, the quantitative adequacy of the labour force and the demand for immigration, future levels of employment/unemployment, attitudes towards the employment of the elderly, retirement ages, and education and training strategies.

2 Labour market trends

The main labour force and labour market trends appear to be:

- an increasing participation of women in the labour force and as a share of the labour force;
- the continuing shift from the agriculture sector through the manufacturing sector to the services sector, with those economies that are most developed being those also furthest down this road;
- increased flexibility in terms of the use and prevalence of so-called atypical contracts – part-time, temporary and fixed-term;
- increased flexibility in the hours worked, the use of shift work and weekend working;
- increased levels of unemployment, particularly among women, the young and the over 55s;
- a greater proportion of long-term unemployment;
- a tendency towards a shift of emphasis in the direction of public expenditure upon supply-side and active labour market policies and initiatives;
- a decline in the demand for unskilled labour outside the service industries;
- an increasing propensity for men and women to remain longer in education and training and an increase over time in the general levels of educational attainment.

AN AGEING POPULATION

The two main explanations or driving forces behind the ageing population are that people are living longer and birth rates are falling throughout the Union. Projections indicate that this will lead to changes in age distribution both within the population as a whole and within the labour force. The Commission (1996b) has produced a report entitled *The Demographic Situation in the European Union 1995* in which these developments are both identified and discussed.

The population of the Union in 1995 was 372 million and it is anticipated that population growth will remain slow (or that it will fall) excluding the effects of future enlargement. This will mean that the EU's share of the world population will almost

Table 4.1 EU spending on social protection, 1980 and 1994

	% of GDP	Old-age pensions as % of total benefits		Employment as % of total benefits	
	1994	1994	1980	1994	1980
Belgium	27.0	44.2	41.5	11.0	11.6
Denmark	33.7	36.6	35.7	16.8	12.9
Germany[1]	30.8	41.2	42.6	9.2	4.5
Greece	16.0	66.8	66.1	2.7	2.7
Spain	23.6	42.6	41.0	18.1	15.7
France	30.5	43.7	43.9	8.1	5.1
Ireland	21.1	27.5	31.4	17.2	8.8
Italy	25.3	64.0	55.1	2.5	2.3
Luxembourg	24.9	46.0	47.5	2.3	0.9
Netherlands	32.3	36.8	31.0	10.4	6.1
Portugal	19.5	40.1	39.4	5.8	2.8
UK	28.1	41.3[2]	42.8	7.3[2]	9.6
E12	**28.6**	**44.2**	**43.3**	**9.2**	**6.4**
Austria	30.2	44.5		5.3	
Finland	34.8	32.3	15.2		

[1]All 1994 figures include new German Länder [2]1993
No data for Sweden

Source: Eurostat in *Europ News*, 2, 1997.

certainly contract in the early decades of the twenty-first century. In 1993, the population of the EU comprised 6.7 per cent of the world population and the projection is that this proportion will fall to 4.7 per cent by 2025 (European Commission, 1996b, p. 8).

The report shows that the proportions of the EU population in the under-20 and over-60 categories seem set to experience reversals. In recent decades the proportion under 20 has outweighed those over 60, but they are expected to equate around 2004, after which the proportion over 60 will grow consistently and the proportion under 20 will continue to decline, though at a slower rate. It is anticipated that between 1995 and 2025 the numbers above the age of 60 will increase by 37 million to the point where they constitute almost 30 per cent of the total EU population, and the numbers in the 'adults of working age' category will decline by some 13.25 million. Those under the age of 20 will decline by some 9.5 million over the same period to just under 21 per cent of the total. The potential impact of these developments on employment policies and the costs of social protection and health care is significant.

Table 4.1 shows the proportions of national and EU GDP taken up by spending on social protection in 1994 – with an EU average of 28.6 per cent. Of this total, approximately 44 per cent was taken up by the provision of old-age pensions (representing close to 12 per cent of GDP) with a further 9.2 per cent of total social protection expenditure relating to employment/unemployment-related benefits. The data also demonstrates that the proportion of GDP spent on social protection has increased since the beginning of the 1980s, reflecting the higher incidence of early retirement, unemployment and the slow down in the rate of growth in GDP.

As already noted, above the two main driving forces behind this demographic ageing of the total population and the population of working-age adults are the falls in fertility and mortality. The Commission report makes the point that the decline in the number of children born per woman seems to have begun in most countries in the Union around 1965. While there are four identifiable groups according to the pattern of decline, by 1994 the range varied between just under 2 children per woman in some of the Scandinavian member states to between 1.25 and 1.5 children per woman in the southern countries, Portugal, Spain, Italy and Greece.

The combined effect is the creation of an age pyramid which is steadily narrowing at the base. Life expectancy has increased in all the countries in the Union, but the greatest rates of improvement have been in those countries where, initially, the life expectancy was the shortest. Inevitably, this has resulted in a narrowing of the range of life expectancy within the Union. In all member states women have a life expectancy which exceeds that for males; the 1993 averages throughout the Union work out at approximately 72 for men and almost 80 for women, compared with 67.5 and 73 respectively in 1960.

Addressing the problem

It would seem reasonable to conclude that, if these issues remain unaddressed, fewer and fewer people will be working and these people through their efforts will be required to support an increasing population that is not working. In such a situation there is potential for conflict and social unrest between the two sections of the population, with those of working age resenting the costs of supporting the older members of the population.

There are a number of ways of addressing the problem.

1 *Immigration*. If the effects of these demographic developments were to be balanced out through immigration, this would require a massive increase in the rate of immigration into the Union, from the current rate of just over one million in the early 1990s (a rate which was not expected to continue) to somewhere approaching seven million per year by 2025.

2 *An increase in the activity rates of those of working age*. There is considerable scope for such increases to be achieved, in particular among the female population where activity rates are generally lower than those of men.

3 *Increased activity rates in the age groups above 60 and below 20*. In the latter case, the scope for increased activity rates will be influenced by the proportion of the population remaining in full-time education. The scope for securing increased levels of activity among the over-60s may be dependent upon amending retirement and pension ages as well as changing attitudes towards both the provision of training and the employment of the elderly. The European Commission report points out that an ageing population should not be confused with a decrepit one; the former does not imply the latter.

There are considerable national variations in current activity rates and this imposes a need for these issues to be addressed at national level.

4 *The achievement of significant improvements in the productivity and the output per unit of labour of those who are working.*

TRENDS IN SECTORAL AND OCCUPATIONAL EMPLOYMENT

Employment sector changes

The dominant trends in the sectoral distribution of employment are described by the European Commission (1996c, p. 101):

> the most pronounced aspect of this is the long-term shift of employment initially away from agriculture to industry and then from industry to services, reflecting the changing pattern both of demand and of specialisation in production, and trade, as economic development takes place. This is coupled with a simultaneous tendency for the nature of the jobs to alter, for the manual content to diminish and for other skills to become more important, requiring a more educated workforce.

These trends are demonstrated in Table 4.2 which shows employment by sector as a proportion of the total in each of the years 1975 and 1995.

The scale and rate of change varies from one member state to another. As is implied by the European Commission in the above quotation, the member states are at different stages in the process of economic development. In the EU as a whole, the proportions of total employment in each of three main sectors in 1995 were 5.3 per cent in agriculture, 30.2 per cent in industry and the remainder, 64.5 per cent, in services.

Table 4.2 Employment by sector as a percentage of total, 1975 and 1995

	Sector					
	Agriculture		Industry		Services	
	1975	1995	1975	1995	1975	1995
Belgium	3.8	2.7	39.6	28.2	56.5	69.1
Denmark	9.8	4.4	31.5	27.1	58.7	68.5
Germany*	6.8	3.2	45.4	36.0	47.8	60.8
Greece	33.2	20.4	29.2	23.2	37.5	56.4
Spain	22.1	9.3	38.3	30.2	39.7	60.5
France	10.3	4.9	38.6	27.0	51.1	68.1
Ireland	22.4	12.0	31.8	27.8	45.8	60.2
Italy	15.8	7.5	38.5	32.1	45.7	60.4
Luxembourg	6.8	3.7	43.6	25.6	49.6	70.6
Netherlands	5.7	3.7	34.9	22.6	59.4	73.7
Austria	12.5	7.3	40.9	32.1	46.5	60.6
Portugal	33.9	11.5	33.8	32.2	32.3	56.4
Finland	14.9	7.7	36.1	27.6	49.0	64.6
Sweden	6.4	3.3	36.5	25.8	57.1	71.0
United Kingdom	2.8	2.1	40.4	27.4	56.8	70.5
E15*	11.1	5.3	39.5	30.2	49.4	64.5

* Figure for 1995 includes new Länder.

Source: adapted and derived from European Commission (1996) *Employment in Europe 1996*.

- The member states with the highest and lowest percentages in *agriculture* are Greece at 20.4 per cent and the UK at 2.1 per cent respectively; in general, the proportions employed in this sector are greater in the southern member states.

- The Netherlands at 73.7 per cent has the greatest proportion in the *services* sector, closely followed by both Sweden at 71 per cent and the UK at 70.5 per cent.

- Germany at 36 per cent has the highest proportion in *industry* and the only other member states with over 30 per cent in this sector are Italy, Spain, Austria and Portugal.

The Commission examines these changes in the structure of industry and the associated trends in the distribution of jobs and employment in considerably more detail than is appropriate or possible in this text, but these changes are both informative of and important to an understanding of the employment context within the union and are summarised here.

Comparisons with USA and Japan

In comparing the EU with both Japan and the USA, the Commission points out that, in terms of the sectoral location of net jobs growth, the three economies exhibited very similar characteristics over the period 1980 to 1993.

1 In the EU, jobs in the services sector increased by just over 18 million and this amounted to a percentage increase over the period of 25 per cent – compared with figures of 22 million and 33 per cent in the USA, and 28 per cent in Japan.

2 The kinds of service activities in which the expansion occurred were also very similar and included personal and communal services, such as health care, social services and education (the leading growth area) and banking, insurance, and business services and distribution, hotels and catering.

3 Only in Japan were there increases over the period in the number of jobs in manufacturing; in both the EU and the USA the number of jobs in manufacturing declined over the period.

4 The EU also suffered significant job losses in both other areas of industry, such as construction, and in the agriculture sector. In both the other economies, there were gains in construction and while the agricultural sector in Japan experienced a sizeable contraction of jobs, in the USA the decline was very much smaller.

5 In the EU, the decline in the number of jobs in the industrial and agricultural sectors combined was approximately 13 million over the 13-year period, compared with a decline of 2 million in the USA and an increase in Japan of just over half a million.

These figures lead the Commission to conclude that:

in quantitative terms, therefore, the poor overall performance of the European economies in expanding employment relative to the USA and Japan owes much more to the scale of job losses in the primary and secondary sectors than to the low rate of net gains in services.

Identifying areas of low, medium and high growth

The Commission identifies the low, medium and high growth sectors within the EU as:

- *Low growth/Declining*   – agriculture
      – manufacturing
      – mining
      – electricity, gas and water

- *Medium growth*   – construction
      – wholesale, retail and repairs
      – transport and communications
      – banking and insurance
      – public administration

- *High growth*   – hotels and catering
      – education
      – personal and business services
      – health, social and recreational services

The above are EU-wide conclusions and it is important to note that within these there are likely to be hidden both member state variations and even variations within the various sectors. For example, within the manufacturing sector there are sub-sectors that have exhibited growth over the decade 1986 to 1995 – including instrument engineering, rubber and plastics and paper and printing.

If we look solely at the developments in 1995, we find that the main areas of growth were in the service sector; however, this growth was not uniform across all services and the main growth occurred in business, health and personal services while there were declines in public administration, banking and insurance and transport and communications. It was also the case that in this particular year there was a significant increase in the number of jobs in construction, particularly in the new eastern Länder in Germany, and jobs in manufacturing grew in Denmark, France and Ireland.

Adnett (1996, p. 7) gives another important warning that much of the increase in the numbers and proportions employed in the service sector are comprised of part-time workers. If the total numbers of hours worked in the various sectors were to be compared, the distribution in favour of the service sector in some of the member states would not be anywhere near so dramatic.

The Commission also concludes that there is evidence of convergence between the member states in the respective shares of the total employed in each of the sectors – that is, that the distribution of employment between the three sectors in all of the member states is becoming more alike over time. This convergence in the broad pattern of economic activity, the Commission suggests, is linked to the development and growing prosperity of the less advanced economies. This reinforces the earlier suggestion that there is a relationship between the sectoral distribution of the workforce and the stage reached in the process of economic development.

Changes in occupation

In general the changes in the structure of industry and the sectoral labour force have been accompanied by changes in the occupational distribution of jobs within the Union. In the main the occupations that have experienced growth over recent years have been those with relatively high skill and responsibility content, including those classified as managers, professional and technical. In the three years leading up to 1995 there were also fairly widespread increases in the employment of sales and service workers.

Decline has been the norm for jobs such as clerks, craft and trade workers, agricultural workers and for those with so-called elementary skills. The European Commission report (1996c) states that this was also what happened in 1995.

Information on the occupational distribution of the workforce within the EU is not so plentiful as for the sectoral distribution. Nevertheless, it seems that in the early 1990s the proportions in the various occupational groupings were approximately:

Legislators and managers	8%
Professionals	11%
Technicians	12%
Elementary occupations	10%
Agriculture and fishermen	3%
Plant and machine operators	9%
Craft workers	15%
Clerical	13%
Service workers	12%

Given that there is a degree of segmentation within the labour markets in the EU, with particular occupations undertaken and dominated by the members of one sex, it is quite likely that occupational change will have differential impacts upon the opportunities for and employment of men and women (*see* Chapter 11).

All of this information about the sectoral and occupational distribution of the EU labour force forms an essential part of the context within which advisers and policy makers within the EU analyse and address the issues of unemployment, the equality of opportunities for men and women, the demand for skills, vocational education and training and levels of educational attainment, all of which are examined in some detail in later chapters.

FLEXIBLE EMPLOYMENT

Since the early 1980s it has become almost the accepted wisdom that the emergence and development of global markets, greater international competition, changes in the patterns of consumer demand and new technologies have all contributed to the new imperative that industries in the EU need to be able to react quickly and, where possible, reduce labour costs. Producers and suppliers of services have been confronted by a much less comfortable and certain environment and this, combined with pressures upon speed of response and costs, has encouraged employers to devise means by which they can become more able to vary their labour input more easily.

Having discussed functional flexibility in some detail in Chapter 2, we shall focus in this chapter on employers' attempts at achieving greater flexibility in both numbers of employees and the time and hours they work.

We are concerned here with evidence of the extent to which labour markets within the

Union have begun to demonstrate the presence of such greater flexibility. In particular, it is important to ascertain the extent to which the incidence of part-time, temporary and fixed-term working has increased and also whether there is proof of greater flexibility in the hours worked and a greater incidence of shift and weekend working.

The term 'atypical' is used in the EU to refer to these 'flexible' forms of employment contract or working pattern and Brewster (1995, p. 316) suggests that in recent years the major motivation for employers to make greater use of these forms of flexible working has been the focus upon organisational cost-effectiveness:

> People employed are the major operating cost for most organisations, so a focus on more efficient ways of working has led to a challenge to 'typical' employment contracts.

It is important to note at this point that many of the practices associated with the new labour flexibility desired by employers were and still are effectively outlawed in many of the member states, whether by legislatively backed regulatory regimes or by collective agreement. As a result, the introduction and use of such flexibilities have often required legislative change, deregulation and/or the agreement of the trades unions. Employers have been confronted by varying levels of willingness to participate in the necessary deregulation on the part of member state governments and trade union movements.

In many instances – both at the level of the nation state and the individual employing organisation – employers have only gained the additional flexibility against the backdrop of high unemployment and, as we discuss in Chapter 15, further deregulation of labour markets is at the heart of many of the proposals to create jobs and reduce unemployment levels. In essence, greater flexibility is perceived as an aid to employment creation and generation in a number of main ways.

- Enhancing the competitiveness of business facilitates economic growth and this feeds through into employment growth.
- Reductions in the numbers of hours worked and, in particular, the expansion of part-time work create opportunities for others also to work, facilitating the sharing out of the work among a greater number of people.
- In countries where employers have in the past been dissuaded from employing people by restrictions upon their freedom to hire and fire or by limitations upon working hours, working at night or the weekends, deregulation acts as an incentive for employers to employ more people.

Naturally, employees and their organisations perceive these developments as something of a double-edged sword: they are often asked to trade less employment and social protection (which is what deregulation all too often means) for work. We must certainly not imagine that increases in numerical and temporal flexibility are always the product of employees' wishes.

Part-time working

Throughout the Union there has been a considerable, though inevitably varied, increase in those employed on a part-time basis as a proportion of the total employed (*see* Table 4.3). In 1985, the EU-wide total was 12.5 per cent of all those employed and by 1995 this had increased to 16.0 per cent.

Table 4.3 Men and women employed part-time as percentage of each category's total employment, 1985 and 1995

	Total		Men		Women	
	1985	*1995*	*1985*	*1995*	*1985*	*1995*
Belgium	8.6	13.6	1.8	2.8	21.1	29.8
Denmark	24.3	21.6	8.4	10.4	43.9	35.5
Germany[1]	12.8	16.3	2.0	3.6	29.6	33.8
Greece	5.3	4.8	2.8	2.8	10.0	8.4
Spain	5.8[2]	7.5	2.4[2]	2.7	13.9[2]	16.6
France	10.9	15.6	3.2	5.1	21.8	28.9
Ireland	6.5	12.1	2.4	5.5	15.5	23.0
Italy	5.3	6.4	3.0	2.9	10.1	12.7
Luxembourg	7.2	8.0	2.6	1.0	16.3	20.7
Netherlands	22.7	37.4	7.7	16.8	51.6	67.2
Austria	6.7	13.9	1.4	4.0	14.9	26.9
Portugal	6.0[3]	7.5	3.4[3]	4.2	10.0[3]	11.6
Finland	7.8	11.8	4.3	8.1	11.6	15.7
Sweden	25.7[2]	25.8	6.9[2]	10.3	46.0[2]	43.0
United Kingdom	21.2	24.1	4.4	7.7	44.8	44.3
E15	**12.5**	**16.0**	**3.4**	**5.2**	**27.3**	**31.3**

[1] 1995 figures include new Länder.
[2] 1987 figures
[3] 1986 figures
Source: adapted and derived from European Commission (1996) *Employment in Europe 1996*.

Women are more likely to be employed in a part-time capacity than are men. The figures for the two sexes are: men, 3.4 per cent in 1985, 5.2 per cent in 1995; women, 27.3 per cent in 1985 and 31.3 per cent in 1995. In each case the percentage is of the total of the sex in employment.

The EU has tried to regulate the employment of part-time workers with a view to providing them with employment rights and social protections on a pro-rata basis with those employed full-time. For many years this objective was prevented by the opposition of the UK government who, with other interests, took the view that the provision of such rights and protections would harm industry's competitiveness by limiting the ability of employers to use labour flexibly. It was also argued that such regulation would also harm the interests of those that wanted to work part-time since it was felt that, if employers had to grant the same rights, benefits and protections to part-time workers as they did to full-time workers this would render the employment of part-time labour less attractive. In 1997, however, the Social Partners did reach agreement on proposals for a Directive through the Protocol procedures (*see* Chapter 11).

Much of the protection that has been afforded at an EU level has been the product of the Courts making use of the sex equality/discrimination directives and articles in the Treaty to grant rights to part-time workers, on the grounds that the substantial majority of them are female, and to prevent part-time workers being discriminated against in comparison with full-time workers. In the main, as Gregory and O' Reilly (1996, p. 227) point out, these decisions have been the product of individuals and trade unions pursuing claims and cases:

Improvements in the employment status of part-timers since the 1980s have largely resulted from individual cases of sexual discrimination.

National variations range between the Netherlands where the total percentage working part-time in 1995 was 37.4 per cent with the figure for men 16.8 per cent and for women 67.2 per cent and Greece which in 1995 had the lowest proportion employed on a part-time basis at 4.8 per cent (men 2.8 per cent and women 8.4 per cent). The Scandinavian countries and the UK also have relatively large proportions of those in employment working part-time. Gregory and O' Reilly (1996) group the EU member states according to the extent to which they use part-time work and they locate the Netherlands, Denmark and Britain as high-use countries, Germany, France and Belgium as moderate users and Ireland, Italy, Spain, Luxembourg, Greece and Portugal as low users.

The Commission report (1996c) makes the point that the majority of the jobs created in the recession years of the early 1990s were part-time, and that this was as true of jobs for men as of jobs for women. Between 1991 and 1994 the numbers of men and women in full-time jobs fell and the numbers in part-time jobs increased. In 1995 the same pattern of change was evident with the majority of the new jobs created being part-time. The Commission estimates that some 71 per cent of the jobs for men created in 1995 were part-time and this compares with a figure of 85 per cent for women.

The Commission (1996c) takes the view that this expansion in the numbers and of part-time jobs and their proportion to full-time jobs would not be a cause for concern if it were the product of employee choice and/or accompanied by people doing second jobs. It appears, however, that in the main this is not the case. The 1995 Labour Force Survey suggests that only a very small proportion of those in employment (3.5 per cent) have more than one job and of those working part-time, some 38 per cent of men and 18 per cent of women would have preferred to work full-time if they could have found a full-time job.

One of the traditional features of part-time working has been that, where men were engaged in such work, it tended to be the case that they were either approaching retirement age or were young and combining part-time work with study, whereas women working part-time tended not to vary significantly with age range. Evidence that patterns of part-time working are changing is provided by the fact that between 1991 and 1995 there was a significant increase in the proportion of men working part-time in the prime working age category – the 25 to 49 age group (from 2 per cent to 3 per cent) and it is estimated that men in this age range accounted for approximately 60 per cent of the total increase in men working part-time.

Temporary work and fixed-term contracts

As with part-time working, there has been a considerable increase in the 1990s in the proportions and numbers of those in employment who are not employed on 'normal' contracts – that is, contracts which do not specify the duration of the job and are in that sense therefore permanent. The shift towards temporary working was common to all the member states except Greece. The Commission (1996c) asserts that in 1995 the expansion of temporary working among men was responsible for all of the increase in the number of men in employment across the Union as a whole and that by contrast there was a net decline in permanent jobs.

Throughout the Union, in 1995 the proportion of those in employment who were employed on fixed-term contracts was 11.5 per cent and the corresponding figures for men and women were 10.7 per cent and 12.5 per cent respectively.

Temporary work is of particular importance to those in the age group below 25, of whom in 1995 approximately a third were employed on such contracts. Among the under-25s over half of those gaining employment after unemployment, education or training moved into work on contracts of this type in 1995. This was higher than in preceding years and considerably higher than the figures for the whole age group that were in employment. The Commission (1996c, p. 57) also concludes that:

> . . . in very few cases was there the formal prospect of a temporary contract becoming a permanent one after an initial period of time.

The proportions in the prime working age group (25 to 49) that are employed on such contracts are relatively small (8 per cent for men and 10 per cent for women). However, in recent years the main growth of such temporary working has occurred in this age range. The Commission (1996c, p. 56) suggests that of all those previously unemployed or inactive who obtained employment in 1995 about half (49.5 per cent men and 51.5 per cent women) moved into employment on the basis of a contract of this type. They further assert that, in the under-25 age group, in the majority of such cases (over 80 per cent) this was because it was the only kind of work that people could find and not because they wanted to work on such a basis or because the job involved a probationary or training period. Importantly, the evidence cautions against an assumption that the vast majority of these jobs are either low-skilled or that they are filled by people with low educational attainment levels.

Hours of work

The European Commission report (1996c) examines changes in working hours in some detail (more so than we can in this text) and the findings and conclusions are summarised below.

Number of hours worked

The report highlights the need to identify the causes of the changes in average hours worked and distinguishes three main potential contributors:

- *The process of development.* This tends to involve shifts in employment between sectors, from agriculture through manufacturing and other industrial into services, and it is common that the normal hours worked in these sectors differ with fewer hours being worked in the service sector.

- *Changes in the composition of the labour force.* As more women enter the labour force and as the incidence of part-time work increases, the average number of hours worked per person in employment will decline.

- *Changes in the actual number of hours that constitute the normal working week for a full-time employee in a particular sector.*

These are distinguished as the *sectoral*, *compositional* and *residual* sources of change respectively.

The Commission's investigations conclude that, if allowance is made for the impact of the first two of these contributors, there has been very little decline in the length of a normal working week for a full-time employee over the period 1983 to 1995 – probably no more than 10 minutes a week over the full period. Indeed, in the period 1990 to 1995 the evidence suggests that there was actually an average increase of about five minutes a week. The Commission's figures confirm this and the respective contributions of the three main causes. It is the compositional changes due to the increase in part-time working that account for the majority of the gross changes identified.

According to the Commission report (1996c):

> This suggests that there is no general trend towards a decline in the typical length of the working week or, if there is, it has been disguised over the early 1990s by the effect of the recession on working time.

Times of work

In addition to the number of hours worked, we are also interested in the times at which work is carried out. The advantages to employers of extending the working day to incorporate working in the evening and at night and/or to extend work into the weekend are fairly straightforward. This enables more use to be made of capital and, where appropriate, it enables the business to better meet the needs of consumers who may want to purchase goods and services at these times. It may also be the case that employees are beneficiaries in that working at such times may better enable parents or others with caring responsibilities to discharge these responsibilities and work.

Generally, the number of people working at night and at the weekend has increased in recent years in most parts of the Union. There are also people who remain reluctant to do so, however, and, as far as Sunday working is concerned, there are significant religious interest groups and objections to be overcome in some member states and, of course, in people's minds.

- *Night-time working.* Women are much less likely to work at night. The sectors in which such working is most prevalent are communications and transport and public administration, which includes the police and the armed forces. In 1995, 5.5 per cent of the total employed usually work at night with a further 9 per cent sometimes working at night; the figures for men were 7 per cent and 12 per cent and for women 3.5 per cent and 5 per cent respectively.

- *Saturday working.* Some 23 per cent of the employees in the Union usually work on Saturday, 22 per cent of men and 24 per cent of women. Saturday working is still relatively uncommon in the industrial sector but in the services sector, as one would probably expect, it is much more common with over 40 per cent of those in the distribution and hotels and restaurants sectors usually working on a Saturday.

- *Sunday working.* Sunday working is less prevalent than working on Saturday and in all some 9 per cent of the total of employees usually work on a Sunday. Working on Sunday is most common in the same sectors as is Saturday working.

In all the UK appears to be the member state with the most flexible working arrangements, particularly for men, if one puts together these three elements of working at night and on Saturday and Sunday. The Commission concludes that there is evidence of a move towards more variable hours of work in most member states in recent years.

ACTIVITY RATES FOR MEN AND WOMEN

One of the most distinctive developments within the labour force in Europe in recent decades has been the increase in the proportion of women working and the increased share they now possess of the employment available within the Union. In 1995, the overall employment rate in the Union was 60 per cent, less than the figure of 63 per cent in 1991 (the recent peak) and less than the 1975 figure of 64 per cent. Women accounted for approximately 41 per cent of all those in employment and yet in 1995 they constituted 62 per cent of the increase in the number employed. Women have made up pretty well the whole increase in the growth of the workforce that has occurred over the last two decades.

By 1995, the activity rate of women throughout the Union was 57.3 per cent compared with figures of 78.3 per cent for men and 67.7 per cent combined. These compare with the figures for 1975 of 45.6 per cent, 88.6 per cent and 66.7 per cent respectively (*see* Table 4.4).

Even these relatively bald figures indicate the decline in the activity of men and the increase in the activity of women. In the 1990s the decline in the activity rate of men of working age has been attributed to two specific developments: an increase in the proportions in the younger age groups staying on in education and initial training and an increase in the number of early retirements.

Table 4.4 shows considerable member state variations, both in terms of the overall activity rates of women and the direction of change in recent years. Female activity rates have been traditionally very high in the Scandinavian countries of Sweden and Denmark. This is still the case but in both instances there has been a decline in the last few years. At the

Table 4.4 Activity rates in the EU as a percentage of 15 to 64 year olds, 1975 and 1995

	Total		Men		Women	
	1975	1995	1975	1995	1975	1995
Belgium	60.9	62.8	83.2	73.1	38.7	52.4
Denmark	76.5	81.3	89.6	87.9	63.4	74.6
Germany[1]	67.5	69.5	87.4	78.4	49.1	60.4
Greece	58.4	62.0	85.6	80.0	33.8	45.3
Spain	60.6	60.2	93.6	75.1	30.0	45.6
France	71.7	68.3	89.9	75.6	54.0	61.2
Ireland	64.0	63.3	90.6	78.7	36.1	47.9
Italy	57.8	58.1	83.6	73.5	33.2	43.0
Luxembourg	67.6	78.9	94.2	99.8	39.9	57.8
Netherlands	63.7	69.1	91.8	79.3	35.3	58.5
Austria	67.8	73.6	86.1	82.7	50.8	64.5
Portugal	69.5	70.5	88.2	80.3	52.0	61.4
Finland	73.6	74.6	80.2	77.3	67.3	71.8
Sweden	80.1	79.4	89.3	80.8	70.8	78.0
United Kingdom	73.1	76.6	92.1	85.7	54.0	67.5
E15	**66.7**	**67.7**	**88.6**	**78.3**	**45.6**	**57.3**

[1]1995 figures include new Länder.
Source: adapted and derived from European Commission (1996) *Employment in Europe 1996*.

other extreme, female activity rates have been on the low side in the southern states and Ireland and in recent years some of these states have experienced the fastest rises. Italy, Ireland, Spain and Greece all still had female activity rates of less than 50 per cent in 1995.

It is important to point out at this stage that there appears to be some correlation between the proportion of the employed population in the service sector and female activity rates. In 1995 throughout the Union almost 80 per cent of female employment was in the services sector, compared with 54 per cent of male employment. Generally, the larger the size of the service sector, the more equal are the activity rates between men and women. As yet there are no member states in which female activity rates exceed those for men but in most member states there has been notable convergence in the last two decades and in Sweden the gap between them is the smallest – 81 per cent for men and 78 per cent for women.

ACTIVITY RATES BY DIFFERENT AGE GROUPS

We have already noted that the decline in the activity rates of men within the Union in recent years is attributed to two dominant influences:

1 the tendency for more of those in the young age groups (under 25) to stay on in education and/or training for longer; and

2 among the older groups, an increase in the rate of early and premature retirement.

These trends are examined further in the Commission's (1996c) report and, while these trends are confirmed, it is also pointed out that the 25 to 49 age group also shows a decline in activity rate. This contrasts with activity rates among women in the over-25 groups which continued to increase during the same time period. Figure 4.1 identifies the extent to which the overall impact upon the size of the labour force is due to both participation and demographic influences. The Figure demonstrates that in the 1990s the size of the labour force within the EU has increased and that this increase is predominantly the product of positive demographic influence among both sexes centered to some extent by negative participation trends among the men. Female participation rates increased in all age groups other than the under-25 group, whereas rates of men have been declining in all age groups above 25. The largest rate of annual decline is in the under-25 group, followed by the over-50s, which is in turn followed by the 25 to 49 age group.

The report concludes that there is evidence that the trend towards more early retirements continued in 1994 to 1995, despite the renewed growth of employment, and there is also evidence of an increase in the incidence of men in the 25 to 29 group in education or training. Nevertheless, the evidence also demonstrates decline in male participation in the labour force of the Union throughout the range of ages in the 25 to 49 category; it is not a phenomenon that is restricted to the 25 to 29 group or to any single five-year band.

In looking for the explanation of the decline in male activity in this prime working age group (25 to 49) the report notes that in 1995, according to the inactive themselves, they included sizeable numbers that were classified as being permanently disabled as well as some that were employed but not actually working at the time of the survey – for example, because they were temporarily laid off. In 1995 the figures were approximately 25 per cent in education/training, 20 per cent disabled, 20 per cent laid off, etc. and 8 per cent retired.

It is important to point out that there are considerable differences across the member states in the proportions in the disabled and retired groups and this may well reflect

(a) 1990–94

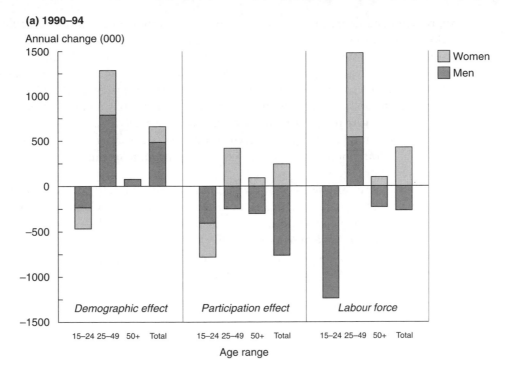

(b) 1994–95

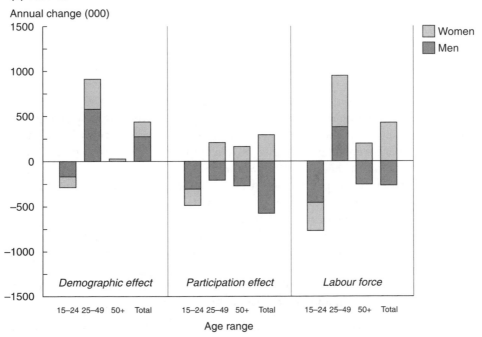

Fig. 4.1 **Changes in the labour force in the EU: (a) 1990–94, (b) 1994–95**

Source: European Commission (1996) *Employment in Europe 1996*. European Commission.

different approaches and definitions within member states as to what constitutes disablement and also the extent to which either or both may be used as alternatives to redundancy and unemployment and supported by state benefits. In the UK, the Netherlands and Luxembourg, relatively large proportions of those inactive in these age groups gave disability as the reason, whereas in other countries the proportions stating disability as the reason were very small – Italy, Spain and Portugal, for example. In Italy a much larger proportion stated that they were temporarily not working and it is likely that this is related to the Italian government funding temporary lay-off schemes as an alternative to redundancy. (For further information on the schemes operating in some of the member states, *see* Hollinshead and Leat (1995).)

The trend towards more early retirement may in part be the result of deliberate policies to facilitate employment for younger people in the context of relatively high unemployment within the Union in the early nineties. As noted earlier, demographic developments projected over the next 20 to 30 years imply not only that such policies need to be reversed but that it may be necessary to encourage employment in even older age groups in order to compensate for the declining birth and mortality rates and to minimise the cost burden of an ageing population.

The trends apparent in the Union encourage the Commission (1996c, p. 46) to comment that:

> . . . perhaps the most disturbing feature of changes in participation in recent years is the common tendency across the Union for a growing proportion of men in the 25 to 49 age group to withdraw from the labour force. Coupled with the growth of part-time working among men in this age group, often contrary to their preference . . .

As for activity rates for women by age, it is clear from the evidence presented in the Commission report that the decline in activity of females below the age of 25 has continued into 1995 (*see* Fig. 4.1). This is most likely to also be the product of the trend towards a greater proportion staying on in education and training and for longer. Above the age of 25, however, the trend in the 1990s has been increasing activity both in the groups of prime working age, between 25 and 49, and among the over-50s. Activity rates vary from one member state to another and, if we examine the nature of change in the 1990s, it is apparent that while in the majority of countries overall female activity rates have been increasing, there are some member states in which the 1990s have not been a period of continuous expansion in the activity of women. This applies particularly in Denmark, Sweden, Finland and Ireland and to a lesser extent in Germany. The countries showing the greatest decline are those in Scandinavia which had, and still have, the highest rates of activity and the explanation for this decline is presumed to be recession-related. Post-reunification Germany has had its own peculiar problems of recession and declining female activity rates in the East, where prior to reunification female activity was very high (*see* Hollinshead and Leat (1995, p. 42)).

Rubery and Fagan (1994) illustrate and discuss the different lifetime working patterns of females within the Union and identify three different types or models:

- a pattern in which there is a left-hand peak somewhere in the 20s followed thereafter by steadily declining activity rates as each age group is reached;

- a so-called 'M'-shaped pattern with a left-hand peak followed by decline through the late 20s and early 30s, but which is then followed by increasing rates as women return to the labour market having given birth and brought up their children;

(a) Left-handed peak: southern countries, Ireland, Belgium, Luxembourg

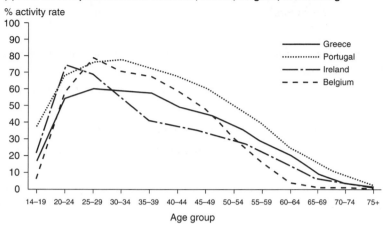

(b) M-shaped curve: Germany (ex-FRG), the Netherlands, UK

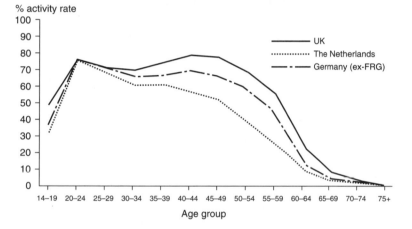

(c) Plateau curve: Denmark and France

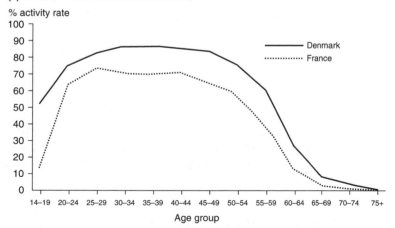

Note: Spain, Italy, Luxembourg not shown on Figure (a) but similar to the four countries shown for illustration.

Fig. 4.2 Patterns of women's activity rates by age group (1990)

Source: Eurostat 1992, Labour Force Survey Results (1990) in *Official Publications of the European Communities*

- a pattern often described as a plateau pattern where the initial left-hand peak in the early 20s is not followed by substantial decline in activity rates until women reach the age of 50 and over.

Figure 4.2 depicts these different patterns and indicates which of the member states fit into each category. The trends in female activity in the 1990s impact upon these patterns and over time and if continued one would expect a certain degree of convergence between the three models with:

- the initial peak moving to the right as those under 25 remain in education and training;
- a gradual elimination of the dip that is associated with childbirth in the 'M' shape pattern; and
- perhaps more immediately, a flattening upwards of the decline in the left-hand peak pattern among the older age groups as participation among these groups rises.

EMPLOYMENT AND UNEMPLOYMENT

As has been noted earlier, there has been and continues to be considerable concern within the Union at what appears to be relatively poor performance in securing employment growth. In comparison with both the USA and Japan, the Union has tended to exhibit relatively low rates of employment creation for given levels of growth in GDP. It must be remembered that growth in GDP results from a combination of increases in employment and net output per person employed. Decreases in the number employed can accompany growth in GDP if the increases in net output per person are great enough; in both Germany and Italy this has happened in the period from 1993 to 1995.

It has also been noted already that there are reasons to believe that the Union's relatively poor performance in net employment terms compared with the USA and Japan is not so much due to a considerably worse rate of job creation in the service sector, but that Europe has lost far more jobs in the agricultural and manufacturing sectors than have the other two. Nevertheless, the Commission estimates that job creation performance in the service sector in the USA was about one third better than in the EU over the period 1980 to 1993. This may be attributable to the following factors:

- *greater wage flexibility*, including a wider dispersion of wages at the lower end of the wage scale and a lower rate of wage increase in the USA compared with the Union;
- *the greater propensity for services to be supplied through the private sector in the USA*, compared with the Union where public sector provision is more entrenched;
- *the relatively low rate of coverage and benefit of the unemployment benefit insurance schemes in the USA*, which, it is suggested, may provide more of an incentive for people to take work at relatively low rates of wages and facilitates the creation of low productivity jobs.

Overall in the Union the employment rate in 1995 was just over 60 per cent; this was some 5 per cent less than in 1973 and substantially less than the 1995 rates in both the USA and Japan which were 73 and 74 per cent respectively (*see* Fig. 4.3). Again it is important to bear in mind that these employment rates take no account of the volume of hours worked by each person employed; if this is taken into account and the figures are

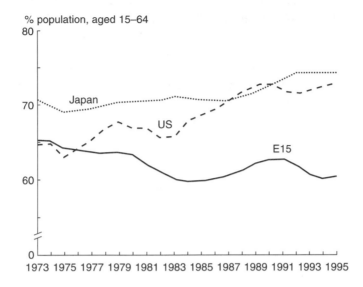

Fig. 4.3 Employment rates for Japan, USA and E15, 1973 to 1995
Source: European Commission (1996) *Employment in Europe 1996*.

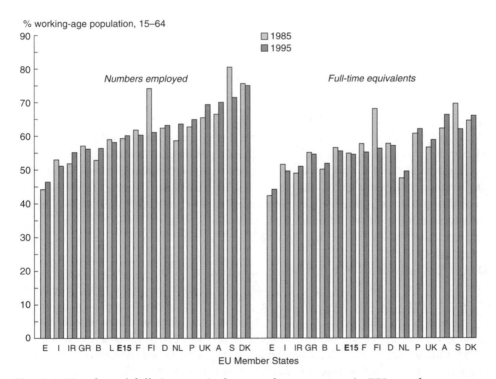

Fig. 4.4 Simple and full-time equivalent employment rates in EU member states, 1985 and 1995
Source: European Commission (1996) *Employment in Europe 1996*.
Note: E: Spain, I: Italy, IR: Ireland, GR: Greece, B: Belgium, L: Luxembourg, E15: EU total, F: France, FI: Finland, D: Germany, NL: the Netherlands, P: Portugal, UK: United Kingdom, A: Austria, S: Sweden, DK: Denmark.

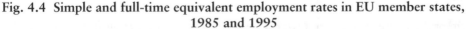

recalculated as full-time equivalents a different picture emerges which gives an EU-wide employment rate closer to 55 per cent. Such a calculation also throws a different light on the apparent employment rates in some of the member states – for example, in the Netherlands which has the highest rate of part-time employment in the Union. The adjusted employment rate in 1995 works out at approximately 50 per cent compared to the unadjusted rate of 64 per cent (*see* Fig. 4.4).

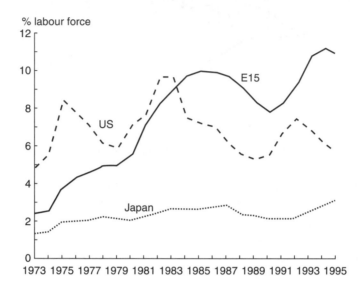

Fig. 4.5 Unemployment rates for Japan, USA and E15, 1973 to 1995
Source: European Commission (1996) *Employment in Europe 1996*.

Unemployment in the Union has been at historically high levels over the period 1993 to 1995. Figure 4.5 illustrates this, as well as the differences of both level and trend between the unemployment rates in the Union and those in both the USA and Japan. A peak rate of unemployment of 11.3 per cent was reached in April 1994 and even in July 1996 the overall rates remained high at 10.9 per cent. There are considerable differences of both level and trend among the member states (*see* Fig. 4.6). Arguably the rates of unemployment within the Union would have been, and would continue to be even higher, had the Union not also been experiencing a decline in activity rates among the young of both sexes and men of all ages.

Despite the increase in the employment of women in recent years there is still within the Union a gap between the unemployment rates for women and men with the female rate being higher than the rate for men. As Fig. 4.7 shows, this is the case for the populations both below age 25 and above. In 1995 the only three member states in which the gross unemployment rate for men exceeded the unemployment rate for women were Sweden, the UK and Finland (see Table 4.5). The member state with the highest rate of unemployment was Spain where the gross rate was 22.9 per cent and the rate for women was 30.5 per cent.

Two of the features of unemployment within the Union that have attracted considerable interest in recent years are those of unemployment among the young and the phenomenon of long-term unemployment.

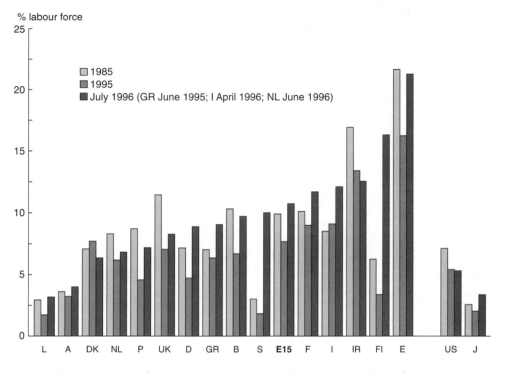

Fig. 4.6 Unemployment rates in EU member states, USA and Japan, 1985, 1990 and July 1996

Source: European Commission (1996) *Employment in Europe 1996*.

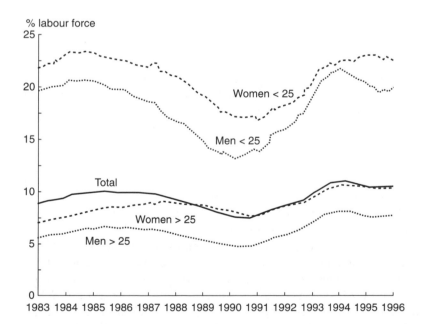

Fig. 4.7 Unemployment rates by sex and age in the EU, 1983 to July 1996

Source: European Commission (1996) *Employment in Europe 1996*.

Table 4.5 Unemployment as a percentage of labour force in EU member states, 1975, 1985 and 1995

	Total			Male			Female		
	1975	1985	1995	1975	1985	1995	1975	1985	1995
Belgium	3.8	10.3	9.9	2.4	6.5	7.8	5.7	16.7	12.9
Denmark	3.9	7.1	7.1	3.7	5.8	5.8	4.0	8.6	8.7
Germany[1]	5.5	7.2	8.2	3.2	6.2	7.1	3.9	8.7	9.8
Greece	1.5[2]	7.0	9.1	1.1[2]	5.0	6.2	2.5[2]	10.6	13.8
Spain	4.4	21.7	22.9	4.9	20.2	18.2	4.6	25.1	30.5
France	3.9	10.1	11.5	2.7	8.3	9.5	5.8	12.5	13.8
Ireland	7.3	16.9	12.4	6.7	16.1	12.2	8.2	18.5	12.6
Italy	4.8	8.5	11.9	3.2	5.8	9.2	8.7	13.5	16.4
Luxembourg	1.1	2.9	2.9	0.3	2.2	2.1	0.5	4.4	4.4
Netherlands	4.3	8.3	7.3	3.8	7.0	6.0	3.5	10.8	9.1
Austria	1.7	3.6	3.8	1.3	3.5	3.0	2.2	3.5	5.0
Portugal	4.4	8.7	7.3	4.1	6.6	6.5	5.0	11.7	8.2
Finland	2.6	6.3	17.2	2.7	6.5	17.6	2.6	6.1	16.7
Sweden	1.8	3.0	9.2	1.5	3.1	10.1	2.2	2.9	8.2
United Kingdom	3.2	11.5	8.8	3.8	11.8	10.1	1.8	11.0	7.0
E15[1]	3.7	9.9	10.7	3.3	8.8	9.4	4.4	11.7	12.5

[1]Figures for 1995 include new Länder.
[2]1977 data.
Source: adapted and derived from European Commission (1996) *Employment in Europe 1996*.

Youth unemployment

Table 4.6 shows that between 1985 and 1995 total rates of youth unemployment – that is, among those aged 15 to 24 – in the Union as a whole varied between 16.4 and 22 per cent and that in 1995 it was 21.5 per cent. There are significant variations between the member states; Spain exhibits the highest unemployment rates among this group with the rate in 1995 being 42.4 per cent – lower than in 1994 and a number of the years before that.

If we examine the evidence on youth unemployment further, we see that of this age group in 1994 not only are more than a fifth of those active in the labour force unemployed, but almost 45 per cent of them had experienced at least one period of unemployment in the previous five years (European Commission, 1996c, p. 89) and that in some countries the evidence indicated that over 60 per cent had experienced at least one period of unemployment – Spain, Italy, Greece and France. Overall, of the population in this age category, it is usual that less than half are 'active', the rest being engaged in education and training of one kind or another.

Among the older age groups within the Union there tends to be an inverse relationship between educational attainment level and the likelihood of being unemployed – the better your educational attainment, the less likely you are to be unemployed. For the groups under the age of 25, however, there is not so clear a relationship. While there is the expected relationship between those with low and medium levels of attainment, when those with university-level attainments are considered, the likelihood of experiencing unemployment does not decline below the levels associated with middle-level attainment.

Table 4.6 Youth unemployment as a percentage of the
labour force (15–24 years), 1985 and 1995

	Total	
	1985	*1995*
Belgium	23.0	24.4
Denmark	11.2	10.2
Germany[1]	10.3	8.8
Greece	21.9	27.9
Spain	47.8	42.4
France	25.4	27.0
Ireland	24.2	21.8
Italy	29.4	33.2
Luxembourg	6.7	7.1
Netherlands	13.1	12.5
Austria	N.A.	5.6
Portugal	20.0	16.6
Finland	9.7	29.9
Sweden	7.1	19.4
United Kingdom	18.5	15.9
E15	**21.9**	**21.5**

[1]1995 figure includes new Länder.
Source: adapted and derived from European Commission (1996) *Employment in Europe 1996*.

The Commission (1996c, p. 91) does caution against placing too much credence upon this latter observation, however, since it feels that the data may not be as reliable as that for the other groups. The Commission does, nevertheless, comment that:

> Finding a job, therefore, seems to pose almost as many problems for graduates in many Union countries as for those with lower educational qualifications.

It suggests that the problems of finding employment may be shifting towards those in their twenties rather than being predominantly an issue for those in their teens.

Long-term unemployment

Long-term unemployment is classified as that which extends beyond one year in duration and, if we look at the Union overall in 1995, 50 per cent of those unemployed had indeed been so for more than a year. Between 1986 and 1995 this proportion varies between 56 and 41 per cent. In 1995 some 60 per cent of the long-term unemployed had been out of work for more than two years.

There is a general tendency for long-term unemployment to be a greater problem for those who are over 50 years old and unemployed. There are also some sectoral connections in that people who have previously worked in sectors that were and/or continue to be in decline generally exhibit a greater propensity to long-term unemployment than those who have worked in expanding sectors.

Labour costs and unemployment

It is frequently argued that high labour costs cause unemployment in that they contribute to uncompetitiveness. There tend to be rival camps arguing, on the one hand, for the need to reduce labour costs in order to gain competitiveness and through that increased employment and, on the other, that high labour costs will not generate unemployment if the labour costs are accompanied by high productivity (*see* Chapter 15). The conclusion of the Commission (1996c) is that:

> Over the Union as a whole, there is a negative correlation between average hourly labour costs in industry and unemployment rates. The higher the rate of unemployment, the lower the labour costs tend to be and vice versa . . . high increases in labour costs do not necessarily have an adverse effect on unemployment if they are related to high rates of productivity growth.

EDUCATION AND THE LABOUR FORCE

There is evidence that an increasing proportion of the population under 30 are staying longer in the education and training systems within the Union and that this is true for both men and women and across all the member states. The Commission (1996c, p. 67) notes that this may in part be a reaction to the lower numbers of jobs available in recent years but points out that nevertheless:

> . . . there has been a significant and continuous increase in the average educational attainment level of the workforce

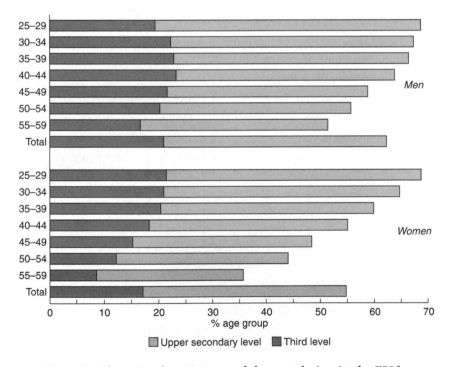

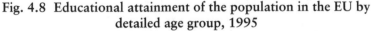

Fig. 4.8 Educational attainment of the population in the EU by detailed age group, 1995

Source: European Commission (1996) *Employment in Europe 1996*.

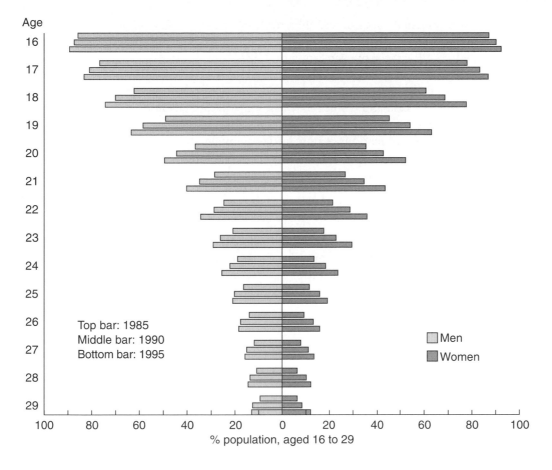

Age

Top bar: 1985
Middle bar: 1990
Bottom bar: 1995

☐ Men
▨ Women

100 80 60 40 20 0 20 40 60 80 100

% population, aged 16 to 29

Fig. 4.9 Participation of men and women, aged 16 to 29, in education and training in the EU, 1988, 1990 and 1995

Source: European Commission (1996) *Employment in Europe 1996*.

and that this should be reflected in rapidly rising skill levels and a greater capacity to adapt to technological developments and changes in working practices in the future. (This is discussed in greater detail in Chapter 13.)

There is a generally positive relationship between educational attainment levels and the ability to find and remain in employment. Figure 4.8 shows the greater propensity for both the male and female population to remain in education or training and attain higher qualifications in recent years, as is evidenced by the levels of educational attainment being consistently greater the younger the age group. The figure also suggests the convergence noted elsewhere between men and women in recent years; among the younger age groups there is little difference between the sexes. Indeed in the 25 to 29 age group a greater proportion of women have attained third level (graduate level) qualifications than men.

The participation of men and women below the age of 30 in education and training between 1985 and 1995 is shown in Fig. 4.9. This again clearly indicates a convergence between the proportions of men and women participating in education and training in recent years. It is at around the age of 24 that the participation rate of men (in education and training) starts to exceed that for women to any significant degree. There are member state variations as usual and, interestingly, the proportion of 16 to 18 year olds in education or training in 1995 was lowest in the UK at just 67 per cent; this compares with a Union-wide figure for the same age group of 85 per cent.

We have already noted that there are still differences between the activity rates of men and women in all the various age groups and that while there has been a convergence between the rates for men and women in recent years the activity and employment rates for women are still below those of men.

Comparison of the education attainment levels by age and sex with the appropriate employment, activity and unemployment rates encourages the Commission to draw the following tentative conclusions:

- For women a good level of education seems to be even more important in finding a job than for men.
- Many women with low educational attainment do not enter the labour market at all.
- Women tend to be more qualified than men for the jobs they do.
- The less well educated men and women are more likely to be unemployed and the relationship between level of educational attainment and propensity to be unemployed is more marked for women.
- Long-term unemployment is also more likely the lower the level of educational attainment.

LABOUR MARKET POLICIES

One of the trends that is arguably common to all member states in recent years is the shift of member state government policy away from *passive* policies – geared towards the protection of those out of work and involving interventions and arrangements that make unemployment more bearable – towards those more *active* policies and interventions that have as their objectives:

- the provision of additional employment opportunities;
- the protection of existing employment; and
- making it easier for those out of work to find another job.

Initiatives to attain these objectives might be concerned with creating jobs – either directly or through some form of employer subsidy or business start-up scheme – providing additional training opportunities and improving the public job search and matching arrangements.

Passive policies and interventions are likely to include schemes and arrangements such as:

- improved unemployment benefits/social security payments;
- redundancy schemes and pay; and
- early retirements not linked to health.

It has been noted earlier that male activity rates have been declining at all age ranges and the popularity of schemes of this nature does go some way towards providing an explanation of this trend among the over-40s.

There are some difficulties in correctly categorising particular schemes since objectives and effect may not coincide – for example, training schemes that are predominantly concerned to provide income support rather than to provide meaningful training in the context of job opportunities and demand for labour.

According to the Commission report (1996b, p. 128) in 1995 the Union spent in all some 180 billion ECU on labour market policies, of which approximately one third was on active as opposed to passive initiatives. This total spend is equivalent to approximately 3.5 per cent of Union-wide GDP, so that the proportion of Union GDP spent on active measures was little more than 1 per cent. Figure 4.10 shows the proportions of GDP spent on labour market policies in each of the member states and this demonstrates quite clearly that there are considerable variations in the amount spent, as well as the distribution of it between active and passive measures. The three Nordic states – Sweden, Denmark and Finland – top the list with each spending in excess of 5.5 per cent of GDP on labour market measures, whereas Greece and Luxembourg each spend less than 1 per cent of GDP. In the latter case, this probably was related to the fact that Luxembourg had the lowest rate of unemployment, but this was not so for Greece. The distribution of expenditure between active and passive policies varies considerably between the member states with Sweden leading the way spending approximately 54 per cent of the total on active measures, compared to Austria and Spain at the other extreme spending only 20 per cent of the total on active measures. Sweden has a tradition of emphasising active labour market initiatives (*see* Hollinshead and Leat (1995, pp. 53–4)).

From an examination of the distribution of labour market expenditure throughout the Union, it is clear that the single greatest object of the expenditure is the maintenance of the

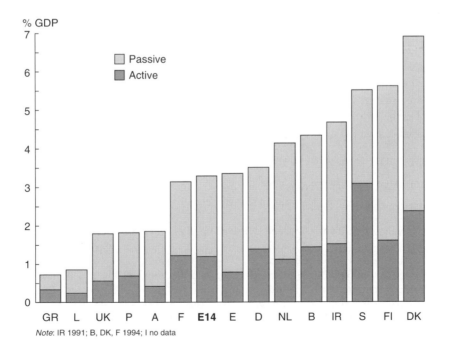

Fig. 4.10 Labour market expenditure in EU member states, 1995

Source: European Commission (1996) *Employment in Europe 1996*.

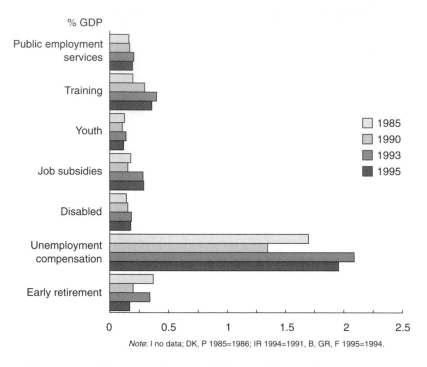

Fig. 4.11 Public expenditure on labour market policies in the EU, 1985, 1990, 1993 and 1995

Source: European Commission (1996) *Employment in Europe 1996*.

unemployed and their dependants and that this has not changed in recent years (*see* Fig. 4.11). It is also the case that there tends to be a relationship between the distribution of labour market expenditure and the rate of unemployment with the proportionate spend on passive measures (including unemployment benefits) rising as the rate of unemployment increases. Furthermore, as unemployment rises so there is a tendency for the proportion of GDP spent on active measures per person unemployed to decline.

References

Adnett, N. (1996) *European Labour Markets: analysis and policy*. Longman.

Brewster, C. (1995) 'HRM: The European Dimension', in Storey, J. (ed) *Human Resource Management: A Critical Text*. Routledge, pp. 309–31.

European Commission (1996b) *The Demographic Situation in the European Union 1995*. European Commission.

European Communities Publication Office (1997) *Eur-Op News*, 2.

Gregory, A. and O' Reilly, J. (1996) 'Checking Out and Cashing Up: The prospects and paradoxes of regulating part-time work in Europe', in Crompton, R., Gallie, D. and Purcell, K. (eds) *Changing Forms Of Employment: Organisations, Skills and Gender*. Routledge.

Hollinshead, G. and Leat, M. (1995) *Human Resource Management: An International and Comparative Perspective on the Employment Relationship*. Pitman Publishing.

Labour Force Survey Results (1990) In *Official Publications of the European Union*.

Labour Force Survey (1995) In *EC Report* (1996) p. 54.

Rubery, J. and Fagan, C. (1994) 'Does Feminisation Mean a Flexible Labour Force?' in Hyman, R. and Ferner, A. (eds) *New Frontiers in European Industrial Relations*. Blackwell.

Part Two

THE EUROPEAN UNION: ITS ORGANISATION, INSTITUTIONS AND PROCEDURES

Having explained some of the more important contexts and background to the operations of the European Union in the late 1990s, it is now time to examine the Union itself: its membership, its institutions, its procedures and decision making processes. Particular attention is given to the social dimension of the Union's activities.

This Part concludes with an analysis of the Intergovernmental Conference which ended in Amsterdam in June 1997 and a consideration of monetary union and its implications for individual member states.

5

MEMBERSHIP AND ENLARGEMENT

LEARNING OBJECTIVES

When you have read this chapter, you should be able to understand and explain:

- the legislative basis of the European Union and the terminology used;
- the history of the development of the European Union;
- the current membership;
- the issue of enlargement of the Union, the countries concerned and the criteria to be applied;
- the implications of enlargement and the problems it may create.

INTRODUCTION

The European Union is currently made up of 15 member states, with a number of countries aspiring to join the Union over the coming years. This chapter describes the legislative basis of the Union and its development since it was created in the 1950s. The issue of enlargement is discussed in some detail as it has major implications for the future of the Union.

THE LEGISLATIVE FRAMEWORK AND TERMINOLOGY

The term 'European Union' (EU) is derived from the *Maastricht Treaty on European Union* (TEU) which was initially agreed by the Heads of Government in December 1991, signed on 1 February 1992, and came into force on 1 November 1993. It was the Maastricht Treaty that created the European Union.

This Treaty on European Union also renamed the European Economic Community (EEC) Treaty – which was the founding Treaty of Rome 1957, as amended by the Single European Act (SEA) 1986 – as the European Community (EC) Treaty and it is this EC Treaty that provides the legislative base for European-level initiatives in the area of social and employment matters.

It was the Maastricht TEU that introduced provisions regarding the achievement of economic and monetary union into the EC Treaty. The EC is part of the EU as is made clear in the preface to the EC Treaty which now states that:

> the EU is a term describing all of the EC, European Coal and Steel Community (ECSC), Euratom [these are technically three distinct communities], the Common Foreign and Security Policy(CFSP) and home affairs co-operation.

Technically, the Union is to be comprised of and based upon three 'pillars' with the three communities above comprising one of the pillars, and the CFSP and home affairs (including justice) comprising the other two.

The Union is made up of 15 member states that have agreed to act together in a number of areas and the creation of a single market and cooperation in economic, monetary and social issues are provided for and covered by the EC Treaty.

There is considerable scope for confusion regarding terminology. In this book, the term EU is used to encompass the others (both EEC and EC) and to indicate the level at which action may be taken or matters discussed. In order to avoid confusion, this term EU is also used retrospectively to encompass relevant policies, initiatives and actions prior to the Maastricht summit and the Treaty on EU, even though they preceded the creation of the EU.

Where reference is made to a particular treaty, title or article, these will be reproduced accurately. The EU is almost certainly the term that will be used in the future; it is indicative of both wider and deeper integration, political as well as economic, and it seems sensible to use it now as the generic.

CURRENT AND ASPIRANT MEMBERS

Since January 1995, the Union has comprised 15 member states. These include the six founder members (1957):

- Germany
- France
- Italy
- Netherlands
- Belgium
- Luxembourg

three countries who joined in 1973:

- United Kingdom
- Denmark
- Ireland

three countries who joined during the 1980s:

- Greece (1981)
- Spain (1986)
- Portugal (1986)

and the three countries who joined in January 1995:

● Austria

● Sweden, and

● Finland.

There are a number of other countries queuing up to join the Union, although there is no prospect of additional members being admitted until after the year 2000 and probably not many before the year 2005. In all, there are around 12 countries in East and Southern Europe that have applied to join the Union – for example, Poland, the Czech Republic, Hungary, Slovenia, Slovakia, Romania, the three Baltic states (Estonia, Latvia and Lithuania), Bulgaria and Cyprus. In addition, Turkey has been keen to join, although its potential membership poses problems of a particular nature given its history of conflict with Greece and the partition of Cyprus.

A number of these aspirant countries have signed agreements giving them a form of associate or partnership status, although there are different degrees of association involved and not all of the aspiring members are at the same stage of development and proximity to full member status.

THE CRITERIA FOR ENLARGEMENT

The criteria against which applicants for membership would be judged were established at the Copenhagen Summit in 1993 and comprise a mix of economic, social and industrial, and political standards. On the political front, the criteria relate to institutional stability with a view to guaranteeing the principles of liberty, democracy, the rule of law and respect for human rights, fundamental freedoms and minorities. The other criteria relate to commitment to monetary and political union, a market economy and the ability to handle the competition and market forces.

Full membership requires the adoption of the '*acquis communitaire*' – the body of laws, rights and obligations already adopted by the EU – and these encompass both the creation of the single market and the convergence criteria agreed as the basis for a future monetary union.

As Sassoon (1996) puts it, adopting the 'acquis' principle as the basis for enlargement means that aspirants 'must accept all that has been achieved so far, lock, stock and barrel'. He criticises this approach as being both unnecessary and unrealistic given the complexity of the acquis and the current positions of the aspirants. He argues that the principle has in any event already been diluted in the following ways.

● The temporary derogations and transitional arrangements agreed with recent entrants mean that the acquis is no longer a pre-entry condition.

● There are already precedents for existing members not accepting the acquis fully – for example, being the partial opt-outs of the social dimension and the timescale for monetary union acquired by the UK at Maastricht and, more recently, the refusal of the UK and Ireland to accept the Schengen Convention (*see* Chapter 10).

He argues that the acquis already has the status of a statement of intent. His criticisms are part of a more extensive debate regarding the need for a Charter of core or fundamental rights, duties and obligations, acceptance of which would form both the basis of membership and the basis upon which the EU might become a 'citizens' Europe' – that is, a Europe consistent with the principles and traditions of social democracy – as opposed to the intergovernmental arrangement that it has become, dominated by business and those only interested in the creation of a single market.

The Madrid Summit at the end of 1995 agreed that negotiations with the countries of Eastern and Central Europe should begin six months after the completion of the Intergovernmental Conference (IGC) – in effect, early in 1998.

By the middle of 1996, the idea had been floated that some form of partial membership (distinct from the various associate and partnership agreements already signed with individual countries) might be devised which provided for membership of the foreign and home affairs 'pillars' of the Union. Membership of the third 'pillar' would be delayed due to the fact that this is the one that comprises social, agricultural and industrial policies.

The individual aspirant countries have much work to do in order to meet the requirements of the Union on many of the economic, social and industrial criteria. The Union will have to reform both the regional aid budgets (the structural funds) and the Common Agricultural Policy (CAP) before allowing other countries to join; otherwise, there is the danger of massive and unrealistic subsidies being payable to farmers and others in the new member countries, combined with a loss of support for existing beneficiaries.

The European Parliament's Budget Committee produced a report in December 1996 in which these points were stressed. The report also highlighted the fact that there had been no reliable and accurate assessments of the costs to the Union of allowing further enlargement. It was argued that aspirant countries should be expected to meet the obligations of full membership upon entry. The report urged the aspirants to pursue the necessary policies and, in particular, to reform their command-derived economies down the road of privatisation and the encouragement of private enterprise. The report rejected notions of enlargement *en bloc* and argued that each aspirant be treated on its own merits.

Nevertheless, enlargement is perceived as desirable by many in the Union for reasons similar to those that prompted the creation of the original communities, paramount among which is the belief that membership of such communities or such a Union is an extremely important hedge against the likelihood and dangers of war within the continent of Europe. The German and French have been in the vanguard of the movement within the Union promoting economic, monetary and political integration and the conflict-ridden history of relations between these two countries is an important motivating influence in their championing of these developments.

It was envisaged by some that the Intergovernmental Conference (IGC) – commenced in 1996 and completed at the Amsterdam Summit meeting of the Heads of Government in June 1997 – would lead both to agreement on the reform of institutions and processes necessary to enable a larger Union to work efficiently, and to agreement on which applicant states would be the first to join. However, the IGC did not achieve these objectives, although there were some relevant agreements on the maximum size of the European Parliament (*see* Chapter 7), the make-up of the Commission (*see* Chapter 7) and on simplifying the Co-Decision Procedure (*see* Chapter 8).

It seems likely that enlargement will take place in phases, given the different stages of development and proximity to meeting the convergence criteria for monetary union and other criteria for membership, including those relating to democracy and human rights.

AGENDA 2000

The likelihood of a phased enlargement was confirmed by the European Commission immediately after the IGC in its communication, *Agenda 2000*, which was published in July 1997 (European Commission 1997a). In this communication, the Commission indicated the countries that were closest to meeting the requirements for membership of the Union and also commented upon the progress that had been made by those countries that were unlikely to be in the first wave. The Commission concluded that, while none of the aspirant countries yet met the criteria for membership, there were six countries that were at the stage where negotiations could be commenced – Poland, Hungary, the Czech Republic, Estonia, Slovenia and Cyprus.

The intention was expressed at the IGC in June 1997 that the *Agenda 2000* document was to form the basis for discussions at the meeting of the heads of state in Luxembourg in December 1997 and that this meeting would take the decisions necessary to enable negotiations on accession to start early in 1998.

The Commission also took the opportunity in this communication to identify the need for far-reaching reforms of the Common Agricultural Policy (CAP) and the regional aid budgets (structural funds) as being essential prior to enlargement. It argued that the failure to reform the institutions and processes at the Amsterdam IGC meant that another would be needed prior to any enlargement of the Union.

Perhaps inevitably, the Commission's assessment in *Agenda 2000* of the progress of aspirant countries provoked some dissent from both within and outside the Union.

- Turkey was particularly unhappy at criticism of its performance on human rights, democratic deficiencies and the achievement of economic stability; the Turkish government was also critical of the Commission proposals to open negotiations with Cyprus.

- Slovakia was singled out as having satisfied the economic criteria but not those relating to democracy, human rights and political stability.

- Bulgaria, Romania, Latvia and Lithuania were considered to pass the tests of democracy and human rights but were advised that they have much to do in terms of economic and legal reform.

Other difficulties began to emerge from the beneficiary member states and powerful farm lobbies in France and Germany who were concerned at the impact on their financial positions if the CAP and structural funds were reformed. A minority of the member states – particularly Italy, Denmark and Sweden – expressed the initial view that it would be better to open negotiations on accession with all aspirants at the same time.

Exhibit 5.1 (on p. 94) illustrates some of the problems the EU faces as it considers enlargement.

Exhibit 5.1

EU brace for enlargement war

FT

Brussels blueprint will make the flak fly. **Lionel Barber** reports from the front

The phony war over the European Union's plans to admit new members from the former communist countries of central and eastern Europe is about to end.

On Wednesday the European Commission will unveil its blueprint for managing the historic process of enlargement under the code name Agenda 2000.

The Commission blueprint offers comprehensive assessments of each of the 10 applicant countries which want to join the 15-member EU. But it also offers a foretaste of problems which lie ahead.

As the authors note, enlargement involves increasing the EU's total population by more than a third, from 370m to almost 500m people, but only increasing the total gross domestic product of the union by around 5 per cent. Thus enlargement seems certain to pit rich versus poor countries, small versus large, north versus south.

The commission hopes that, although EU governments will have the last word on the terms of enlargement, Agenda 2000 will be pivotal in shaping the final agreement. The blueprint, which runs into more than 1,000 pages, falls into five broad categories:

■ Short-listing new members. After a bruising internal debate, the commission decided last week to clearly identify which of the 10 applicant countries are ready to open accession negotiations next year.

The five favoured candidates are Estonia, the Czech Republic, Hungary, Poland and Slovenia, plus Cyprus; but Brussels would like Bulgaria, Romania, Latvia, Lithuania, and Slovakia to have their applications reviewed each year along with special financial aid to help them qualify for membership.

■ Strengthening institutions. The commission is calling for a new EU intergovernmental conference to agree on a substantial increase in majority voting and a weakening of the rules on unanimity to avoid paralysis in decision-making in a union of 20-plus countries.

'Any delay can only compromise an effective enlargement of the union,' the document warns. The commission is insisting on a new IGC even if the first wave of new members is restricted to three.

Enlargement seems certain to pit rich versus poor countries, small versus large, north versus south

---

■ Common agricultural policy. Agenda 2000 proposes reinforcing the 1992 McSharry reforms which have led to a movement towards world market prices and direct income payments to farmers. The Commission proposes sharp cuts in intervention to support prices in the beef, cereal and dairy sectors. However the commission package would involve CAP spending increasing by up to Ecu4bn (£2.7bn) a year.

■ Regional aid. Agenda 2000 proposes a radical reform of the 'structural fund' budget, designed to help poor areas within countries. Mrs Monika Wulf-Mathies, the commissioner responsible, would like to shrink the population of the EU eligible for special assistance from around 50 per cent to between 35 and 40 per cent. The Commission also intends to cut programmes

funnelling aid to poorer regions, and target unemployment.

The central reform will fall in the category called Objective One which channels money to areas with a GDP of less than 75 per cent of the Union average. Most applicant countries will need at least 15 years to reach this level.

The Commission makes clear it would like more efficient use of the 'cohesion funds', the special assistance agreed in 1992 for the poorest EU countries: Ireland, Greece, Spain and Portugal. Ireland has rapidly improved its GDP per capita, so it is likely to find its share of the cohesion funds tapering away.

■ Future financing. Agenda 2000 says the first wave of new members can be accommodated without increasing the present 1.27 per cent of GNP ceiling due to take effect in 1999 but more fundamental reform would be required if the EU were to go above that.

When the phony war ends the battle lines will be seen to run across the entire union. Germany, though nominally in favour of eastward enlargement, opposes increases in EU funding and is hostage to powerful farming interests in Bavaria. Britain also supports enlargement for political reasons but is opposed to increasing the EU budget.

Spain, Italy, Greece and Portugal are determined to keep their share of EU regional aid while smaller countries, such as Belgium and Luxembourg, are worried expanding membership without deepening political integration would undermine their rights.

France has accepted that enlargement is historically inevitable, but will defend its farmers against radical CAP reform.

Source: Financial Times, 14 July 1997.

References

European Commission (1997a) *Agenda 2000*.
European Parliament Budget Committee (1996) *Report on Financing of Enlargement of EU*. 11/96
Sassoon, D. (1996) *Social Democracy at the Heart of Europe*. IPPR.

6

THE SOCIAL DIMENSION

LEARNING OBJECTIVES

When you have read this chapter, you should be able to understand and explain:

- the concept of the social dimension – its scope and aims – and the reasons for its development;
- the significance of the absence of a legal basis for the social dimension and other issues affecting EU activities in this area;
- the creation of the European Social Fund, its history, its level of funding and its current operations;
- the practice described as social dumping and its implications for the Union;
- the major Treaties and Agreements relating to the social dimension and their impact on member states;
- the issues raised by the growing acceptance of the principle of subsidiarity.

INTRODUCTION

It was recognised in the early years of the European Community that the desired economic integration would inevitably result in benefits for some and costs for others. A social dimension to the Union's activities was seen as a way of balancing out the effects on individual member states and regions, so that no single area was harmed by the integration. The social programme has had its critics, however. We consider here the development of the social dimension and the main issues affecting its successful implementation.

DEFINING THE SOCIAL DIMENSION

The use and meaning of the term 'social' in this context encompasses employment and related issues, as well as matters of social protection and benefits. The term's scope is apparent from an examination of the rights encompassed within the *Social Charter* or the *Agreement on Social Policy* appended to the Treaty agreed at Maastricht (*see* later in this chapter). The social dimension is not something that exists on its own or outside the Union and commonly the term is used to refer to the social dimension of the EU or some element of it, such as the single market.

In the same way as the single market concept implies a process of economic integration, so the notion of a social dimension encompasses a series of steps in a process of integration in specific areas, such as:

- welfare systems, including charges and benefits;
- labour market regulation, encompassing both individual and collective elements; and
- processes leading to an international redistribution of wealth and living standards.

Completion of the process would result in a single model or system and arguably this should be the objective and the long-term outcome of the social dimension (Paque, 1997).

THE DEVELOPMENT OF THE SOCIAL DIMENSION

The development of the social dimension within the Union has been the subject of much debate and disagreement over the years with different perspectives regarding the need for and desirability of action and regulation at the level of the Union. Generally, social issues and the 'need' for action and regulation have been addressed in the context of the implications of economic integration. They have been given greater significance by the decision to create a single market (with effect from January 1993) and, as we shall see later, the Single European Act (SEA) of 1986 made some important amendments to the founding treaties in order to facilitate action in some of the relevant social policy areas.

It was recognised at the outset that the market and economic integration process would inevitably create some dislocation of industry and employment and a need for restructuring. There would be losers as well as winners. In the main the debate has been between those who considered that intervention was necessary in order to cushion these effects and promote restructuring and a more efficient use of labour, and those who took the view that while integration might have these effects the solution was to leave the market to cope and that to intervene would simply prevent the adjustment mechanisms of the market working effectively. If there were circumstances justifying intervention, they should be limited to those in which the intervention itself contributed to the process of market integration. As Hall (1994) explains, the Commission and most of the member states have viewed the social dimension as:

> an important vehicle for securing the support of the European labour movement for the single market project and for enhancing the 'social acceptability' of the consequent economic restructuring . . . the human face of the EC.

This is a debate that has not been resolved within the Union and in the mid-1990s essentially the same debate informed the deliberations within the Union on solutions to the problems of unemployment and international competitiveness – with the Commission and the European labour movements, on the one hand, arguing the case for the protection of those in employment and the regulation of the labour market to ensure social justice and the UK government (prior to the defeat of the Conservatives in May 1997) and the employers, on the other hand, arguing the case that economic performance in Europe, including job creation, is actually being undermined by excessive intervention and regulation leading to labour market inflexibility.

These different perspectives can also be seen to inform and underpin the different traditions in the member states: the former being consistent with notions of corporatist integration and social or welfare capitalism and the latter being consistent with the notions of economic liberalism and liberal individualism (*see* Chapter 1).

Even at the creation of the Community back in the 1950s, these differences of view can be seen to have contributed to the fudging of the issue of social policy and as Hall (1994) states:

> To date, the evolution of the EC's [Community's] social policy role has been uneven and limited. The Treaty of Rome did not establish a clear Community competence in this sphere.

HARMONISATION OF SOCIAL POLICY

This fudging and lack of a clear Treaty basis for action on social policy are reflected in Article 117 of the Treaty of Rome in which the member states agree on the need to

> promote improved working conditions and an improved standard of living for workers, so as to make possible their harmonisation while the improvement is being maintained . . . such a development will ensue not only from the functioning of the common market, which will favour the harmonisation of social systems, but also from the procedures provided for in this Treaty and from the approximation of provisions laid down by law . . .

This one Article contains references to a number of the issues that have occupied the member states and institutions over the years:

1 *The need to promote improvements.* This involves the concept of *upward harmonisation*. Harmonisation in EU terms refers not to the process of equalisation, but to closer alignment; the two most popular uses of the term are 'upward harmonisation' – the process of raising standards and levels up to the level of the best – and 'partial harmonisation' – the process of seeking to more closely align only some of the standards, usually those considered to be key.

2 *The role of the market in this process.* Harmonisation is seen as one of the outcomes of market integration.

3 *Treaty procedures and legislative regulation.*

However, in Article 118, while the Commission is given the role of promoting close cooperation between member states in the social field, the mechanisms through which this objective is to be achieved are described as:

> by making studies, delivering opinions and arranging consultations.

There are no provisions within these two Articles which unambiguously give the Commission, as the initiator of EU legislation, a basis which can be used to set up any form of legislative or otherwise enforceable interventions and regulations in the area of social policy.

In the early years the absence of such a base doesn't appear to have posed major problems, partly because there were specific Treaty articles covering matters such as:

- equal pay between the sexes;
- the free movement of labour; and

- assistance with the relocation and retraining of individuals harmed by the integration process as it caused dislocation and restructuring.

The last two areas were both considered essential to the process and objective of integration since failure to take measures to facilitate in this regard might have produced, on the one hand, imperfections in the market allocating process and, on the other, opposition to and negative impressions of integration.

Articles 48 and 49 covered the free movement of labour and Article 123 provided the basis for the creation of the *European Social Fund (ESF)* which has been the main mechanism for achieving improved employment opportunities and enhancing geographic and occupational mobility (*see* later in this chapter). The principle of equal pay for equal work was covered by Article 119, which we deal with at some length in Chapter 11.

The absence of specific Treaty bases enabling the Commission and the member states to intervene legislatively, where necessary, on issues of employee rights and the development of a social policy came to the fore for the first time in the mid-1970s and a solution was obtained through the uncertain means of using Article 100. This Article provides for the unanimous adoption of directives for the approximation of provisions in the member states as they directly affect the establishment or functioning of the common market.

This provides only dubious grounds for the enactment of directives granting employee rights because of the tenuous logic that has been used to justify the few directives adopted using this device. These include directives concerning collective redundancies (75/129, extended by 92/56) and the transfer of undertakings (77/187) and the procedures to be followed by employers. The argument used was that the failure to require the approximation of such procedures would distort competition and give employers in one member state a competitive advantage over those in another where the national requirements were more onerous, thereby affecting the functioning of the common market. The dangers of this argument and use of Article 100 were such that, apart from a burst of activity in the mid-1970s, the parties have been reluctant to use this Article as the base for the harmonisation or approximation of employee rights.

The Single European Act addressed some of these concerns but not the major one of the absence of a clear and definite base for the adoption of measures leading to the harmonisation of employment rights and industrial relations systems. The Act contained new Articles 100a and 118a and these provided for the adoption by majority voting using the *Co-operation Procedure* (*see* Chapter 8) of measures for the approximation of provisions in member states having as their objective the establishment and functioning of the internal market. However, Article 100a specifically excluded its use in respect of provisions relating to the rights and interests of employees (this was at the instigation of the UK government). Article 118a is specifically concerned with the working environment, in particular the health and safety of workers, and the objective of achieving harmonisation at a high level but with certain safeguards for small and medium-sized undertakings.

As a result the requirement of unanimity was relaxed for most measures and interventions concerned with achieving economic integration and specifically geared to the creation and effectiveness of the single market, but with the specific exception of employee rights and interests to which the requirement of unanimity continued to apply.

However, where the measures were concerned with the health and safety of workers, qualified majority voting was to apply. As we have seen with a number of proposals introduced since, the vagueness of the line that separates health and safety from other employee rights and interests has led to a number of arguable proposals and eventual adoptions.

The most famous or infamous being the directive adopted under this provision that sought to regulate working hours (*see* Chapter 12). The then UK government objected to the argument that this was a health and safety issue and appealed to the European Court of Justice (ECJ) who in November 1996 ruled that the directive was properly adopted under these provisions. The directive on maternity pay and leave (*see* also Chapter 12) was also, but less contentiously, adopted under these new qualified majority procedures.

There are still those that argue that a radical interpretation of the terms 'establishment and functioning of the internal market' would enable action across a much wider range of social policy areas and that the exclusion of employee rights and interests need not be as limiting as most of the parties have accepted.

THE EUROPEAN SOCIAL FUND

Created in 1960, the main objectives of the European Social Fund (ESF) were to assist through the provision of funds with the retraining of redundant workers and, where necessary and appropriate, with their resettlement into areas of the Community where there were alternative work opportunities. The early creation of this fund indicates that the architects of the Community were aware that the formation and operation of the Community would mean that, in terms of economic growth and prosperity, some industries and regions and hence groups of employees would gain and others would lose. Closer economic integration would inevitably lead to structural change.

The ESF was envisaged as an instrument that would cushion the impact for the losers and enhance their re-employability, and, in addition, would dilute the effect of unemployment upon incomes by providing payments directed at the maintenance of incomes for workers whose employment was temporarily suspended or where there was a need for short-time working.

The development of the ESF

As the Community developed, so did the ESF and by the mid-1970s the Fund's activities were primarily directed at:

- providing retraining for those groups suffering unemployment and dislocation as a result of technological change or Community policies in particular industries – for example, textiles, clothing and agriculture; and

- helping certain disadvantaged regions or members of certain social groups – for example, the disabled, migrant workers, women and the young unemployed.

The Fund has always been a means of providing additional funds and support for policies initiated and implemented at a national level. Usually the *matching funds principle* applied – in other words, the financial support and contribution from the Fund could not exceed 50 per cent of the required total funding, and funds from the ESF had to be matched by equal funding from public sources within the country concerned. The term 'additionality' is commonly used to depict this founding principle.

In 1983, there were further reforms and a re-prioritising of ESF objectives. A new emphasis was given to the problems of the young unemployed and, as Casey (1993) points out, in the following five years programmes to counter and mitigate youth unemployment accounted for over 75 per cent of the assistance provided. The other disadvantaged groups referred to above were not completely ignored, but the level of assistance was inevitably scaled down. Schemes for women returners, the disabled, long-term unemployed and migrants still qualified for assistance but were not the ESF's main priority in this period. Small and medium-sized enterprises could also qualify for support for re-training programmes directed at facilitating the introduction of new technologies or management techniques.

Subsequent to the decision in 1986 to create the single market, it was realised that there might be an even greater dislocation and negative impact upon employment in certain regions and for certain groups of workers. Consequently, in 1988, there was further and substantial reform of the ESF's objectives and a substantial increase in the funds available to assist projects. The opportunity was also taken to introduce a greater degree of coordination between the ESF and other structural funds with which there were close or overlapping responsibilities and areas of interest. The other structural funds were:

- the *European Regional Development Fund* (ERDF) which had an indirect job-creating role through its support of infrastructural projects; and

- the *European Agricultural Guidance and Guarantee Fund* (EAGGF) which, not surprisingly, had a specific responsibility for adjustment projects in agricultural areas.

The reforms of 1988 resulted in a revised list of objectives for the ESF and other funds and a *modus operandi* as to which fund was to have prime responsibility for which objective. The five objectives were to be:

1 *The promotion of growth and adjustment of the regions considered to be lagging.* The criterion adopted for determining which regions might qualify was to be a per capita income average of less than 75 per cent of the Community average. The ESF could provide funding for training and re-training, but primary responsibility for this objective was to be the ERDF, which provided funding of a capital nature for infrastructure and equipment.

2 *Support for regions affected by industrial decline.* Again the prime responsibility was with the ERDF, but the ESF shared some of the responsibility. The intention was that the funds would encourage new activities and also enhance the productivity of existing industries. There were 60 qualifying regions in eight different countries. The region had to be one in which industry had declined and where both general unemployment and industrial unemployment were above the Community average.

3 *Combating long-term unemployment (LTU).* This was the prime responsibility of the ESF. Funding could be for the provision of training to improve qualifications, financial incentives to employers to encourage them to recruit from the ranks of the LTU. There was also a specific provision that funding could be provided for schemes to aid the training of women who had been out of the labour market for some time – sometimes referred to as women returners.

4 *The employment of young people by the provision of vocational training for school leavers.* A particular emphasis was given to training in new technologies and to the attainment of qualifications and also to the promotion of self-employment. Again the ESF was to have particular responsibility for this objective.

5 *The reform of the Common Agricultural Policy (CAP) and coping with the fallout from that reform.* In the main, the aid was intended to alleviate low incomes, under-employment and unemployment. This objective was of relatively minor importance in comparison with the others and was the responsibility of both the EAGGF and ERDF.

It is clear from the above list that the ESF was intended by these reforms to be particularly interested in and responsible for funding schemes to combat unemployment, with a particular role in helping the young and long-term unemployed.

In addition to the changed objectives, revised administrative procedures were also introduced in an attempt to improve the degree of coherence between Community and national policies and within nations between central government and the parties involved on the ground. This last group was no longer able to make direct application to the Commission; applications had to be submitted by national governments, who had to draw up coordinated programmes demonstrating the partnerships involved and the linkages between the applications supported and national economic and social policies and programmes. The Commission now had to describe the measures being supported and how they fitted into the network of national and Community policies in a Community Support Framework (CSF).

The level of funding

The amounts allocated to these funds constitute a relatively small amount of the total EU budget. Wise and Gibb (1993, pp. 139–40) point out that in 1989 funds allocated by the ESF (3.23 billion ECU) amounted to only 7.2 per cent of the total EU budget and this compared with an allocation to the CAP of approximately 67 per cent of the total. They further comment that it is hard to escape the conclusion that the ESF was an essentially cosmetic policy, designed to give the impression that the Union was tackling the problems while in fact:

> little of substance was in fact being achieved to counter growing mass unemployment.

The reforms of 1988 were accompanied by an increase in funding for the structural funds over the five-year period to 1993 with the total over the period increasing to approximately 60 billion ECU. However, the proportionate spend on combating long-term and youth unemployment was only to equal about 20 per cent of the total; the largest proportion, approximately 60 per cent, was allocated to expenditure on promoting growth in regions that were considered to be lagging.

One of the debates surrounding expenditure on interventions of this kind is that to some extent they run counter to the specified objectives associated with the single market – that labour, as well as other resources, goods and services, should be mobile between different uses and regions, thereby facilitating the achievement of the efficiencies that are argued to be the product of the operation of the market. Interventions of the kind financed by the structural funds have as specified objectives the correcting of regional and other labour market imbalances – for example, by encouraging and financing training and job creation initiatives for groups and in areas that would otherwise experience greater unemployment. Once again economic and social and political agendas exist that do not always coincide.

Current ESF operations

In July 1993, further reforms to the funds were introduced to cover the period from 1994 to 1999. Some additional areas were identified as lagging regions – in particular, several of the new Länder formed as a product of the reunification of Germany – which qualified them to receive funding, as appropriate, within Objective 1. The 1988 Objectives 3 and 4 were merged into a new Objective 3 which was also to facilitate the integration of those threatened with exclusion from the labour market. The new Objective 4 was to facilitate adaptation to industrial change, including changing production systems. The new Objective 3 was primarily concerned with assisting the unemployed, whereas the new Objective 4 was concerned with providing assistance to those in employment but whose employment may be threatened by change.

In addition, the ESF also supports a range of specific employment creation initiatives:

- *HORIZON.* The initiatives within this programme are concerned primarily to provide help for the disabled disadvantaged in their search for work using the new technologies.

- *NOW.* (New Opportunities for Women) These initiatives promote opportunities for women, in particular through the promotion of the attainment of qualifications, changing company cultures so as to create greater opportunities for women in management, and encouraging women to establish their own businesses.

- *ILEs.* These initiatives encourage women to employ other women, particularly those in groups that are most susceptible to exclusion – for example, migrants and breadwinner mothers.

- *ERGO.* This initiative encourages the pooling and exchange of information on successful programmes to help the long-term unemployed.

- *SPEC.* These are support programmes for employment creation and are concerned with providing technical and financial support to some of the more innovatory employment creation projects.

- *Transnational schemes.* The intention is to support schemes assisting the young and the long-term unemployed that are cooperatively managed across at least two member states.

In June 1994 a new initiative – ADAPT – was introduced, consistent with the new Objective 4, the aim of which was to help employees adapt to change and by so doing remain in employment. The programme has four objectives, all of which are concerned with assisting adaptation to industrial change:

1 to help both workers and companies to adapt to industrial change by anticipating trends;

2 to enhance competitiveness through the more effective use of resources in introducing new technology and production systems;

3 to improve the flexibility and mobility of the workforce; and

4 to anticipate and encourage the creation of new jobs and activities, with particular emphasis upon the small and medium-sized enterprise sector.

The ESF represents a long standing recognition that certain regions, industries and groups of people would be relatively disadvantaged by European integration. The objectives of this and other structural funds have been to try and mitigate the impact of these developments and to do so through the partial financing of schemes that enable those in disadvantaged groups to better compete in the marketplace for work. This may involve the provision of training and retraining opportunities or financial incentives for job creation and the employment of the unemployed.

Estimates of the success and adequacy of these initiatives vary; it is clear, however, that the funding allocation to these schemes and Union-wide expenditure on active labour market policies of this kind represent relatively small percentages of the Union budget and Union GDP respectively (See earlier figures 4.10 and 4.11). This raises doubts about the degree of seriousness and commitment invested by the governments of the member states in the initiatives.

The Commission is clearly aware that further reform of these funds is necessary. The Commissioner with responsibility for these areas, Padraig Flynn, argued in 1997 that there should be a simplified overall structure and that the seven current activities should be reduced down to two main activities:

1 dealing with assistance to the poorer regions and areas with problems of industrial adaptation and rural development; and

2 dealing with human resource development in the Union as a whole.

He also suggested that the guiding principle of additionality or matching funds should be dropped (*Eur-op News 2*, 1997).

SOCIAL DUMPING

After the adoption of the Single European Act, the Commission, the labour movements and some member state governments became increasingly concerned at the dangers of *social dumping* – that is, the tendency for large national or multinational companies to locate, and in some instances relocate, their production facilities in those parts of the Union where the social costs of production and/or the degree of regulation of the labour market are lowest. It is this fear that has been responsible for much of the impetus behind efforts to ensure the development of a social dimension to the single market. The fear was particularly acute in those countries with the most developed labour standards and standards of social protection and correspondingly the highest social costs.

Putting it bluntly, the fear was that employers, faced with competition from companies operating in regimes with lower social costs and the threat of losing market share, would go 'regime shopping' and would use the variation in labour costs and degree of flexibility within the labour market to guide their location decisions and/or to beat down the social costs and standards in those countries in which they were most developed. This latter tactic might involve putting pressure on both governments and workers; employees in turn might engage in concession bargaining as an alternative to unemployment.

An example of this process can be seen in Exhibit 6.1 which reports survey evidence indicating an upward trend in German companies relocating production abroad, mostly into Central and Eastern Europe, and citing high labour costs as the reason.

In a single market, where barriers to the mobility of labour are removed, there might also be pressures upon social standards and protections from the process of labour mobility between low-wage regimes and high-wage regimes, the explanation being that factors of production that are mobile will gravitate towards those uses in which returns are greatest. The

Exhibit 6.1

Germans flee high labour costs

FT

Companies' shift of production abroad shows no signs of abating

By Ralph Atkins in Bonn

The exodus of German companies relocating production abroad shows no sign of abating in the next three years as the disadvantages of remaining at home – particularly high labour costs – continue to bite, according to a survey published today.

DIHT, the umbrella body for the country's chambers of industry and commerce, found 28 per cent of west German industrial companies plan to shift production abroad in the next three years. That compared with the 25 per cent that said they relocated production abroad in the past three years.

The results come amid signs of a significant setback in federal government attempts to cut Germany's labour costs. Research released yesterday by WSI, the Düsseldorf-based economics and social science institute, showed that unions representing 2m employees had struck deals in the past week which

kept sick pay at 100 per cent of wages.

Sick pay has been preserved despite legal changes this year which permitted a cut to 80 per cent of wages. The move was significant because unions regarded 100 per cent sick pay as one of the movement's biggest post-war gains. But a landmark deal last week in the Lower Saxony electrical and metal industry preserving the 100 per cent figure – albeit partially compensated with other savings – is rapidly becoming a yardstick for agreements across Germany.

Meanwhile, domestic Lufthansa airline flights are threatened with warning strike action tomorrow after the breakdown of pay talks. The DAG union is proposing two-hour stoppages by flight crews and some ground staff which could affect a number of airports.

The DIHT survey, based on more than 6,000 responses, found labour costs cited by 62 per cent of industrial companies as the

main reason for locating abroad. The next most important reason, cited by 21 per cent, was tax and other charges. Middle and east European states remained the most popular alternative location.

DIHT said the results demonstrated Germany's labour cost problem had not been under-estimated. 'Where production is relocated, the higher productivity and better training of German workers are not covering wage costs and increasingly high additional wage costs.'

Figures earlier this year from the Bundesbank showed investments abroad by German companies nearly doubled in 1995 to a record DM50bn (£19.5bn). The DIHT survey suggests the trend will remain upwards, with 38 per cent of west German industrial companies expected to increase foreign investment in 1997 against 17 per cent expecting a fall.

Source: *Financial Times*, 11 December 1996.

high standards of social protection and high wages would attract labour from the poorer regions and this influx of labour, as an increase in labour supply, would itself facilitate the competing down of wages and social standards. The market mechanism would eventually lead to adjustment and a new equilibrium somewhere between the two opening positions.

Of course, other factors influence location decisions and critics have alleged that too much attention has been paid to the dangers of social dumping (*see* also Chapter 3).

THE SOCIAL CHARTER

It was concern about social dumping, allied to the influence of the then President of the Commission, Jacques Delors, that provided whatever additional incentive was needed for the Commission to propose the adoption by the Council of the statement of minimum social rights that was contained in the document known as the *Social Charter*. By the time the Charter was presented to the Council in Strasbourg in December 1989, the Commission had also developed a *Social Action Programme* (SAP) containing 47 proposals for Union-level action to give effect to many of the minimum rights contained within the Charter.

The rights incorporated in the Charter fall into 12 main sections:

1 *Freedom of movement*. This includes the removal of obstacles arising from the non-recognition of diplomas and equivalent occupational qualifications.

2 *Employment and remuneration.* This involves the rights to fair and equitable wages thereby enabling a decent standard of living.

3 *Improvement of living and working conditions.* Specific reference is made to working hours, weekly rest periods and annual leave, temporary, fixed-term and part-time contracts. It is clearly the intention that there should be an upward approximation.

4 *Social protection.* In this context, social protection should be the employee's particular situation.

5 *Freedom of association and collective bargaining.* Both workers and employers should have the right to form and join, or not, associations for the defence of their economic and social interests. The associations should have the right to negotiate and conclude collective agreements and the right to take collective action, including strike action. Conciliation, arbitration and mediation should be encouraged and in all cases these rights should be subject to and exercised in accordance with existing national conditions and practice. This section also refers to improvement in the dialogue between the Social Partners at European level.

6 *Vocational training.* All workers should have the right of access to such training and retraining throughout their working life with particular reference made to the acquisition of new skills in the light of technological developments.

7 *Equal treatment for men and women.* This should be assured and equal opportunities should be developed. Particular mention is made of equality of access to employment, remuneration, working conditions, social protection, education, vocational training and career development. Measures to facilitate both men and women reconciling their work and family lives/obligations are also included.

8 *Information, consultation and participation of workers.* This section takes into account the practices in each member state and makes particular reference to organisations with establishments or companies in two or more member states. In particular these rights should apply in cases where:

- technological change has major implications for the workforce in terms of working conditions and/or work organisation;
- where restructuring or mergers has an impact upon the employment of workers; and
- in cases of collective redundancy procedures.

9 *Health, protection and safety at the workplace.* This section refers to satisfactory health and safety conditions in the working environment and harmonisation while improvements are maintained. Specific mention is also made of training, information, consultation and the balanced participation of workers as regards both the risks involved and the measures taken to eliminate or reduce them.

10 *Protection of children and adolescents.* Children and adolescents should receive equitable remuneration, be protected from working below a certain age and particular arrangements should be made to ensure that their development, vocational training and access to employment needs are met. There should also be limits on the duration of such work and their working at night. They should also be entitled to initial vocational training upon leaving full-time education.

11 *Elderly persons.* The elderly, upon retirement, should have an entitlement to a decent standard of living.

12 *Disabled persons.* Disabled persons should be entitled to measures aimed at improving their social and professional integration and, in particular, to vocational training, ergonomics, accessibility and mobility.

The document was acceptable to 11 of the 12 member states, the odd one out being the UK, but because the document could only be adopted via unanimity the UK had an effective veto. The Charter therefore remained only as a statement of intent on the part of all member states other than the UK. (*See* also the discussion in the next section on the Social Protocol and the Agreement on Social Policy, agreed at Maastricht in 1991, and Chapter 9 in which the agreement, made at the IGC in June 1997, to bring the Social Charter into the Treaty is discussed.)

As noted earlier, a Social Action Programme (SAP) was devised that was designed to give effect to some of the specified Charter rights, but not all of them. Some of the proposals involved legislative intervention in order to put particular rights in place throughout the Union, but many others were either not addressed at all in the action programme or the proposals were of a non-legislative and binding nature.

An explanation of the full contents of the SAP is beyond the scope of this chapter, but it is important to note that there were no proposals in this programme for the legislative imposition of rights for workers in the areas of freedom of association, collective bargaining, information, consultation and participation and the entitlement to an equitable wage.

Considerable care was taken in both the Charter and the SAP to not impose rights in a manner that was inconsistent with the traditions, practices and laws of the various member states. This conformed with what has become one of the guiding principles of the Union – the principle of *subsidiarity* (*see* later in this chapter). Some of the actions and interventions consequent upon and involved with the SAP are examined in more detail in the following two sections of this chapter.

MAASTRICHT AND THE SOCIAL PROTOCOL AGREEMENT (SPASP)

The Social Charter's position as a statement of intent was not the end of the episode, however, since the contents of the Charter formed the basis of the draft *Social Chapter* of the Treaty on European Union agreed at Maastricht in December 1991. Again it was the UK government that refused to accept the proposals and it was at its insistence that the draft Chapter was removed from the Treaty – the condition of the UK government's agreement to the remaining contents which included the criteria and timetable for monetary union.

The intention of the parties in drafting the Social Chapter was to significantly amend the original Treaty Articles 117 to 122 on social provisions, and in so doing to redress some of the omissions from the Treaty that had hampered the ability of the Union to take action in certain areas – for example, regarding equality and employee participation (*see* Chapters 11 and 14), both areas in which the Union had found it difficult to take action due to the absence in the Treaty of specific authority to do so, whether by qualified majority voting (QMV) or unanimity.

The reactions of the other parties to the UK refusal was to devise the *Social Protocol* and the *Agreement on Social Policy* that, with the agreement of the UK, were annexed to the Treaty. This gave all the other member states the authority to proceed (without the UK) down the road of implementing the rights referred to in the Charter and to use the Union institutions to do so. This is what became known as 'the UK's opt out of the Social Chapter' – technically incorrectly, since the Social Chapter was actually removed from the Treaty and had no status other than that its contents became the subject matter of a separate agreement on social policy between the other member states.

There are, however, different views as to the precise legal status of the contents of the Social Policy Agreement between the member states, excluding the UK. Some suggest that it does not form part of the Treaty, while others cite Article 239 of the Treaty to support their argument that since this Article states that Protocols form an integral part of the Treaty and the Agreement on Social Policy forms part of the Protocol, the Agreement contents must be part of the Treaty (Lasok and Lasok, 1994, p. 706). To some extent the significance of this latter view has been superseded by the agreement of the Labour government, elected in the UK in May 1997, to allow the contents of the Protocol Agreement on Social Policy to be brought back into the Treaty – one of the outcomes of the IGC of June 1997. We must bear in mind, however, that this agreement is yet to be ratified by the member states and that this may take some time.

The Protocol Agreement, as it is commonly known, specifies clearly in Article 1 what the objectives of the agreement are:

> The Community and the member states shall have as their objectives the promotion of employment, improved living and working conditions, proper social protection, dialogue between management and labour, the development of human resources with a view to lasting high employment and the combating of exclusion. To this end . . . shall implement measures which take account of the diverse forms of national practices, in particular in the field of contractual relations, and the need to maintain the competitiveness of the Community economy.

Some would undoubtedly argue that this statement of objectives includes the elements of the major dilemma confronting the Union in the 1990s – how to achieve what to many appear to be the conflicting objectives of:

● competitiveness in the global economy;
● the maintenance of employment;
● improved living and working conditions; and
● the maintainance of social protection.

The pre-1997 UK government and employers associations certainly saw these as unattainable together and argued that, if necessary, priority must be given to competitiveness and employment over social protection and social justice. The debate over and after the publication at the end of 1993 of the Commission's (1993b) *White Paper on Growth, Competitiveness and Employment* demonstrated this divergence of perspective perhaps more clearly than any other (*see* Chapter 15).

The SPASP sets out clearly the areas to which it applies and indicates which adoption procedure is to be used in respect of each. The outcome of this is that qualified majority voting is to apply to:

● improving the working environment in order to protect worker's health and safety;
● working conditions;
● the information and consultation of workers;

- equality between the sexes; and
- the integration of those excluded from the labour market.

These are extensions to the range of areas to which QMV was to apply. Unanimity is still required before measures can be adopted in respect of:

- social security and social protection of workers;
- employee protection in circumstances of termination of their employment contract;
- the representation and collective defence of both employers and workers interests to include the issue of codetermination;
- conditions of employment for third-country nationals resident in the Union.

It is also quite clearly stated that the provisions of the Agreement are not intended to apply to pay, the right of association, the right to strike or the right to impose a lock out. There are no means by which the member states signatory to the Agreement can via the Agreement take action to implement rights related to these areas. Such matters remain subject to the unanimous agreement of all members of the Union and arguably there is still no clear treaty base that gives the Union the ability to act in these areas.

In addition, the Agreement sets out a new procedure whereby the Social Partners at European level can more fully participate in the legislative process (*see* Chapter 8 for more detail). The means are also created for the Social Partners through agreement to establish contractual relations and to implement by agreement at the level of the member state (at their request and with the approval of the member-state government) Directives otherwise adopted within the terms and provisions of this Agreement. These are specific additional mechanisms involving the Social Partners which are set in the context of a more general task imposed upon the Commission by Article 3 of the Agreement to promote the consultation of management and labour at European level.

This agreement was implemented along with the other 'Maastricht' Treaty provisions in 1993. (*See* Chapter 8 for information on the early operation of these new procedures.)

THE IGC REVIEW

The various Treaties and associated developments were to be reviewed in 1996–7 at the Intergovernmental Conference. There was considerable pressure for the revised Treaty to finally provide the Commission and the other interests with a firm Treaty base for the creation, development and implementation of a social dimension. There was specific pressure to extend the scope of the Co-operation Procedure and qualified majority voting (QMV), beyond that already incorporated within the SPASP, in the area of social policy.

However, the IGC did not agree to any significant extension of QMV, other than that provided for within the SPASP, despite the extra pressures for reform implied by the prospects of enlargement of the Union (*see* Chapter 5).

The UK governments formed by the Conservative party between 1979 and 1997 were clearly opposed to any such extension of QMV which they thought would lead to a further dilution of national sovereignty and provide the means for even further regulation of the labour market – regulation which they perceived as a barrier to international competitiveness and thereby employment.

Detailed discussion of the outcome of the IGC and the Treaty revisions agreed in draft is contained in Chapter 9.

THE PRINCIPLE OF SUBSIDIARITY

The Maastricht Treaty confirmed the increasing importance of the *principle of subsidiarity* as a constraint upon action and interventions at the level of the Union. For some time before the Council meeting to agree the Treaty, the UK government had been at the forefront of the argument on this subject with its view essentially being that the Commission in particular was seeking to act inappropriately at the level of the Union, and when action was unnecessary, and was thereby diminishing national sovereignty and flexibility. As a consequence of this discussion, the EC Treaty as amended at Maastricht clearly specifies in Article 3b:

> In areas which do not fall within its exclusive competence, the Community shall take action, in accordance with the principle of subsidiarity, only if and in so far as the objectives of the proposed action cannot be achieved by the member states and can therefore, by reason of the scale or effects of the proposed action, be better achieved by the Community . . . Any action by the Community shall not go beyond what is necessary to achieve the objectives of this Treaty [sometimes referred to separately as the *principle of 'proportionality'*].

This Article is the nearest thing to a definition of the principle of subsidiarity as has yet been produced by the Union. Its implications are clear:

1 The Commission and the Union should seek to act only when it is clear that the objectives cannot be achieved at the level of each of the member states.

2 Furthermore, they should only act when it is clear that objectives can be better achieved through action at the centre.

It can be argued that primary responsibility for action to achieve Union objectives has been returned to the nation state by this Article but there no doubt remains considerable scope for differing interpretations, both of the meaning and intentions of the Article and its relevance in individual instances. For example, by whom and how are words like 'better' to be interpreted?

Further subsequent attempts were made to clarify the issue. There was an agreement at the European Council meeting in December 1992 on the overall approach to the application of the principle of subsidiarity and this was followed by an interinstitutional agreement on implementation procedures in October 1993.

These developments are significant in that they do indicate:

● a shift of intent away from the production of Union-wide and convergent systems through Union-level interventions and upward harmonisation; and

● a greater willingness to try and achieve common objectives while retaining national and diverse traditions and practices.

This has implications for debates about unity and convergence as well as federalism, and the feasibility and desirability of interfering with national-level systems and procedures, particularly where these procedures are integral to the traditional distribution of power within the national system. In many respects the debate about subsidiarity goes right to the heart of the debate about the future nature of the Union. Recent events bring into question whether an approach that seeks a Union-wide social policy to be achieved through interventions consistent with the principle of subsidiarity is a realistic possibility.

The meaning and application of the principle of subsidiarity have been further developed in the Amsterdam Treaty draft. The IGC at Amsterdam agreed a new Protocol on the subject and the introduction to this Protocol clearly specifies the purpose:

> . . . to establish the conditions for the application of the principles of subsidiarity and proportionality enshrined in Article 3b of the Treaty . . . with a view to defining more precisely the criteria for applying them and to ensure their strict observance and consistent implementation by all institutions . . . wishing to ensure that decisions are taken as closely as possible to the citizens of the Union.

In the main the conditions to be complied with consist of:

- a requirement that the Union states how proposals for Union legislation satisfy both the principles of subsidiarity and proportionality and the reasons for concluding that a Union objective can be better achieved by the Union must be substantiated by qualitative and, where possible, quantitative indicators (para. 3);

- a requirement that both aspects of the subsidiarity principle are met (*see* above) and a number of guidelines are given as to what should be taken into account in such an examination – for example, whether the issue concerned has transnational aspects and whether action by the Union would produce benefits by reason of its scale or effect compared with action at the level of the member state;

- the guideline that action at Union level should be as simple as possible and should leave maximum scope for national decision making, wherever feasible, leaving member states a choice between alternative methods for achieving the objective specified;

- a requirement that the Council and the Parliament should consider their consistency with Article 3b and in both the Co-operation and Co-Decision Procedures (*see* Chapter 7), where a Council position is adopted and put to the Parliament, that the issue of consistency with Article 3b is addressed by the Council.

References

Casey, B. (1993) 'Employment promotion', in Gold, M. (ed) *The Social Dimension – Employment Policy in the European Community*. Macmillan.

Council of the European Union (1997) *Intergovernmental Conference Draft Treaty*. Office for Official Publications of the European Communities.

European Commission (1993b) *White Paper on Growth, Competitiveness, Employment*. European Commission.

European Commission (1994c) *White Paper on Social Policy*. European Commission.

European Communities Publication Office (1997) *Eur-Op News*, 2.

Hall, M. (1994) 'Industrial Relations and the Social Dimension', in Hyman, R. and Ferner, A. (eds) *New Frontiers in European Industrial Relations*. Blackwell.

Lasok, D. and Lasok, K.P.E. (1994) *Law and Institutions of the European Union* (6th edn). Butterworth.

Paque, K.-H. (1997) 'Does Europe's Common Market Need a Social Dimension? Some academic thoughts on a popular theme', in Addison, J.T. and Siebert, W.S. (eds) *Labour Markets in Europe: Issues of Harmonisation and Regulation*. Dryden.

Wise, M. and Gibb. R. (1992) *A Single Market to a Social Europe*. Longman.

7

INSTITUTIONS OF THE EUROPEAN UNION

LEARNING OBJECTIVES

When you have read this chapter, you should be able to understand and explain:

- the four main Union institutions, their structure and areas of operation;
- the main Union institutions concerned with the implementation of social policy;
- the role of the European Investment Bank.

INTRODUCTION

There are four main Union institutions:

- the European Commission (EC);
- the Council of the European Union (often also known as the Council of Ministers);
- the European Parliament (EP); and
- the Court of Justice of the European Communities (ECJ).

This is not the place for extensive analysis of these various institutions, but an understanding of the institutions' various and respective roles is important. Special note should be taken of the fact that the *Council of Europe* is a completely separate organisation that has absolutely no connection with the European Union other than that some nation states are members of both. This chapter also refers to some of the other relevant Union institutions:

- the European Foundation for the Improvement of Living and Working Conditions (EFILWC);
- the Economic and Social Committee (EcoSoc); and
- the European Investment Bank.

European trade union and employers organisations, the Social Partners, are also discussed.

THE EUROPEAN COMMISSION

The European Commission provides the secretariat for the Union and, perhaps more importantly, has the Right of Initiative with respect to proposals for union-level policy and legislative interventions, although there are plenty of opportunities for interest groups to lobby the Commission and the Commissioners. In many ways it is the institution that sets the agenda for the Union.

At the head of the organisation are the President of the Commission and the Commissioners (currently 20). The President of the Commission is appointed unanimously by the member-state governments and individual member states therefore have the power of veto over the appointment. The Amsterdam IGC draft states that it is the intention that the President of the Commission's appointment be subject to the assent of the European Parliament.

The President and the Commissioners formally constitute the Commission and it is they who collectively agree policy and other proposals and initiatives before they are presented for the purposes of consultation and discussion.

The Commissioners are nominated by individual member-state governments; they are appointed for a five-year term and their appointment is subject to the approval of the European Parliament. The big five member states – Germany, France, Italy, the UK and Spain – all have the right to nominate two Commissioners each and the other ten each nominate one. While Commissioners, they are supposed to work for and represent the Commission and the Union as a whole and not the member states from which they come.

The work of the Commission is split into various areas of subject matter, or policy areas, and administrative sections. The subject matter or policy areas are each allocated to a Directorate General (D-G) and each of these is headed up by one of the Commissioners. Currently, there are 23 D-Gs and some Commissioners therefore look after more than one policy area. For example, the D-G that deals with the subject matter of employment and other areas of social policy is D-G V(five) and is given the title 'Employment, Industrial Relations and Social Affairs'.

Future enlargement of the Union is likely to necessitate revision of the numbers and distribution of Commissioners; if, as seems possible, the decision is to reduce the number of Commissioners, this may mean that some member states will not always have one of their own nationals as a Commissioner. There was hope that this may have been achieved at the Amsterdam IGC but it was not. Some of the smaller countries were particularly concerned not to lose their right to appoint a Commissioner. The issue therefore remains unresolved.

The IGC summit did produce a draft Protocol indicating awareness of the issues and this Protocol states in Article 1 that:

> at the date of entry into force of the first enlargement of the Union, the Commission shall comprise one national of each of the member states, provided that by that date the weighting of the votes in the Council has been modified, . . . in a manner acceptable to all member states, taking into account all relevant elements, notably compensating those . . . which give up the possibility of nominating a second member of the Commission.

This leaves many issues and questions unanswered but it does seem that at least the first five member states to join as part of the enlargement process may be guaranteed a Commissioner. It is unclear, however, whether the intention is that this would also apply to later entrants; the suspicion is that it would not. It is clear that the parties are contemplating the need to reform and to reduce the number of member states that have a right to nominate two Commissioners. It also seems that some kind of trade-off is envisaged whereby those losing the right to nominate two Commissioners might in return have a real-location of votes within the Council.

The Commission has already indicated in its *Agenda 2000* communication that in its view another IGC will be required prior to enlargement in order to address and resolve some of these matters.

In addition to initiating policy, the Commission is also responsible for managing policy and for seeking to ensure that policy and other legislative decisions are actually implemented and complied with in all the member states. It has an enforcement role and this role sometimes brings the Commission into conflict with individual member states. There have been numerous occasions upon which the Commission has taken action against a member state for non-compliance. In some areas it is given the right to decide issues of compliance (competition policy being one such area) and a Commission decision has legal effect in such circumstances upon the parties to the dispute. As implied above, this will often include one or other of the member-state governments.

THE COUNCIL OF THE EUROPEAN UNION

Sometimes known as the Council of Ministers, this body has the decision-making role in respect of EU policy, the role of the various institutions and legislation. There are various consultation and other checks and balances built into the decision-making processes (*see* later in this chapter) but at the end of the day the Council decides as it wishes, subject that is to its ability to actually come to an adequately supported decision. The Council must reach some decisions unanimously or else it cannot act.

Actual membership of the Council varies according to the subject matter under discussion. The object is to have present for decision-making purposes the appropriate government minister from each member state. For example, when the Council meets as the Social Affairs Council each member state is represented by the member of government with responsibility at home for the subjects to be discussed. Normal Council meetings tend to occur on a regular monthly basis. The Council, therefore, is not a directly elected body and the members are not accountable to any particular constituency of electors; they are accountable to their own member-state governments of which they are a member.

The Council is an intergovernmental institution. Despite pressures from many quarters, it is extremely unlikely in the foreseeable future that change of any substantive nature will be accepted by the Council that diminishes the right of the various member-state governments collectively to make the decisions on policy, the nature and role of the institutions and legislation.

As is noted in the following section on the European Parliament and in Chapter 9 on the Intergovernmental Conference, there are pressures for the Parliament to have a more influential role and for the EU to be perceived as a more democratic Union. However, there seems to be little chance of significant inroads being made into the policy- and law-making roles of the Council, despite the extension of the co-decision making powers of the European Parliament agreed at Amsterdam. The most likely reason for this is that not enough of the member-state governments, worried as some are by issues of sovereignty and with a perception of the Union as a community of nation states, will be prepared to give additional influence to a body that they cannot control and that is directly elected.

When issues can be decided by a qualified majority (QMV), each member state is afforded a number of votes linked indirectly to population, so that the unified Germany, Italy, France and the UK all have the same and largest number of votes – ten each. This distribution and the very loose nature of the relationship between population size and votes have become an issue of some concern in the light of the intention to enlarge the Union, reduce the size of the Commission and expand the use of QMV.

Understandably, Germany with a population in excess of 80 million and ten votes in the Council has a case for arguing that it should be assigned more votes when the smallest member state in terms of population – Luxembourg with its population of 450,000 – has two votes. At the moment it looks as if reform will wait until enlargement is closer to a reality.

Twice a year the Heads of Government meet as the *European Council* and it is to this body that issues of a general and significant nature go for decision including proposals for revision of the founding treaties. The Amsterdam IGC was one such meeting, as was the Strasbourg meeting in 1989 which discussed the draft Social Charter and the meeting at Maastricht in December 1991 that adopted the EC Treaty.

Council meetings are chaired by the member state holding the *Presidency* at the time and the Heads of Government summits are almost always held in the country of the current Presidency. The Presidency rotates on a six-monthly basis, according to an agreed timetable which gives each member state the role every seven-and-a-half years, given the current number of member states in the Union. In addition to chairing the meetings, the Presidency usually has a significant input into determining the Agenda and priorities of the Council for the period concerned. The role of the President is in essence to progress matters as far as possible and to do so by searching for consensus. The individual national interests of the country holding the Presidency are to some extent subjugated to the role of President during the incumbency.

Much of the detailed work and intergovernmental negotiation is undertaken within the auspices of a body known as the Comité des Répresentants Permanents (COREPER) which is made up of ambassadors and senior diplomats from each of the member states. This group tends to meet on a regular weekly basis.

THE EUROPEAN PARLIAMENT

The only directly elected institution within the EU, the European Parliament (EP) has a history of little power and influence. Until recently, the roles of the Parliament in the formulation of EU policy and the passage of legislation have been limited to lobbying and being one of the bodies that had to be consulted as part of the specified processes. As part of this consultation process, the Parliament can put forward amendments but without any means of ensuring that they are accepted by the Council. They can delay but they can't stop or force change.

More recently, as part of the Maastricht Treaty, and after quite a hard fight, the Parliament has acquired limited powers of veto on issues put to the Council for adoption in specified areas of subject matter which include:

- measures directed at harmonisation in readiness for the single market;
- general action programmes for the environment;
- research and development; and
- proposals concerned with the free movement of workers.

The name given to this new procedure was the Co-Decision Procedure (*see* Chapter 8). The IGC at Amsterdam agreed both an extension of the subject matter to which this procedure could apply, and a simplification and shortening of the procedure. In both instances it has been argued that this represents an increase in the power of the EP.

It is important to note, however, that when the member states at the Maastricht Treaty summit, with the exception of the UK, agreed to give the Social Partners via the Social Dialogue a more influential role in EU decision making (*see* Chapter 8) they did not give the Parliament any rights to be consulted or involved in the process. It therefore became possible for the Council to give legal effect, via a decision, to an agreement between the Social Partners without the Parliament having any input to the process, let alone a veto over the decision. It is easy to read into this decision, whether deliberate or not, unflattering assessments of the influence and importance of the Parliament as far as the Council and Commission are concerned. As already noted, there are influences within the Union that have resisted and will continue to resist any substantive enhancement of the power and influence of the EP. The Commission has subsequently indicated that it will consult with the Parliament on such agreements between the Social Partners; it did so with the first such agreement – the one on parental leave.

Each of the member states has allotted to it a number of Members of the European Parliament (MEPs) and the allocation is intended to be roughly proportional on the basis of population. For example, the Unified Germany as the country with the largest population has the greatest number of MEPs (99). The distribution of the MEPs by member state is shown in Fig. 7.1. At the beginning of 1995, when three new member states joined the Union, the total number of MEPs was increased from 567 to 626; it would seem inevitable that as the Union is further enlarged the numbers of MEPs will continue to grow. It is hard to envisage member states agreeing to a reduction in the number of MEPs that they can currently elect though it may well be that such a reduction becomes necessary from an efficiency perspective.

It is in this context that we need to consider the Amsterdam agreement to limit the size of the European Parliament to a maximum of 700 MEPs. As a matter of interest, Poland, upon accession to the EU, on the current basis of allocating seats, would be entitled to 64 MEPs; this demonstrates the potential size of the EP upon enlargement if changes are not made. In this context the decision to limit the size of the EP must be seen as the precursor to a revision of the 'weighting' system currently in use.

The MEPs tend to ally themselves in multinational political groupings. Individual MEPs may have constituency responsibilities within a particular member state (as in the UK) but they are not sent to the Parliament with a brief to look after the interests of the particular constituencies or member state from which they come. However, MEPs are usually members of one of the major political parties in their home member state and, probably unsurprisingly, there is often a proximity between the positions adopted by MEPs from a particular member state and the positions adopted by members of the same political party at national level. For example, MEPs that are members of the UK Conservative Party are likely to adopt similar positions in their role at the EP to those adopted by Conservative

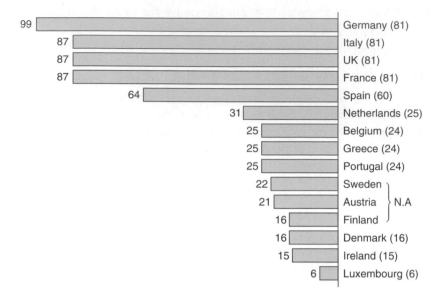

**Fig. 7.1 Number of MEPs for each member state of the EU in 1995
(figure for 1989 in brackets)**
Source: adapted from *Financial Times*, 14 June 1994.

MPs within the UK Parliament; they do after all share similar ideological positions. However, they need not and there is likely to be the greatest degree of discrepancy between them, when the national-level government or MPs of the same ideological persuasion are actually adopting an anti-Union position; most MEPs are essentially pro-EU.

The Parliament also has the right to approve the nomination of the Commission and the annual budgets and spending programmes. The Amsterdam IGC proposes that the EP will in future have the right to approve the appointment of a President of the Commission.

THE COURT OF JUSTICE OF THE EUROPEAN COMMUNITIES

The Court of Justice of the European Communities (ECJ) is the final arbiter on the interpretation and issues of European Community/Union law. It tends to deal with two different categories of case:

1 cases which are begun in the ECJ framework, for example, where the Commission is seeking to ensure that a member state complies with EU legislation or where one member state is in legal dispute with another; and

2 cases that commence within individual member states but require the ECJ's final decision on what the law means or how and when it should apply.

An example of the first category would be the UK government's allegation that the Directive adopted on working hours was improperly adopted as a health and safety issue, whereas examples of the second would include applications by individuals to the UK courts that the UK government had improperly applied the Directives on Collective Redundancies and Transfers of Undertakings or that the EU law on equal pay was not being properly applied by a particular employer. Each of these starts in the UK court system and eventually reaches the ECJ as the final arbiter. It is the Court of Last Resort.

The ECJ must be distinguished from the *European Court of Human Rights* (ECHR) which is nothing to do with the EU and has more connection with the Council of Europe than with the EU. The ECHR was established under the European Convention on Human Rights and it has been disappointing to hear members of past UK governments and the media complaining about the decisions of the ECHR as yet another example of the EU forcing unwanted law upon the UK.

The ECJ is made up of 15 judges, one from each member state, and nine Advocates-General (A-Gs). Each case that reaches the Court is allocated an A-G and he or she is expected to present the Court and the parties with an opinion on the case before it is heard by the Court itself. Very rarely are the opinions of A-Gs not followed by the Court.

There is also a Court of First Instance which was established in 1988 to hear certain cases including competition matters and European Coal and Steel Community cases.

EU INSTITUTIONS CONCERNED WITH SOCIAL POLICY

In addition to the four main EU institutions, there are a number of others that have a particular relevance to the issues and processes of the social dimension. These are the European Foundation for the Improvement of Living and Working Conditions (EFILWC), the Economic and Social Committee and trade union and employers confederations and associations that are known as Social Partners.

The European foundation for the improvement of living and working conditions

The European Foundation for the Improvement of Living and Working Conditions (EFILWC) was established by Council Regulation No. 1365/75 in May 1975. It is based in Dublin and financed via the Commission; its aims and tasks are essentially to contribute to the improvements indicated by its name and to do so by increasing and disseminating knowledge that is likely to assist in this objective. It therefore encourages and commissions research work into appropriate areas of interest and activity.

The organisation is managed by an administrative board which is comprised of representatives from and of the Commission, the trade unions, employers and representatives of the governments of the member states. The Council of Ministers appoints a committee of experts to advise the management of the Foundation.

The Foundation works on the basis of a series of four-year programmes which set out the strategy and indicate the work to be undertaken and supported. Much of the work of the Foundation is contracted out to researchers across the Union.

The last four-year programme covering the period from 1993 to 1996 identified three distinct areas of interest and activity:

● increasing economic and social cohesion and fighting against the exclusion of disadvantaged groups;

- improving the health and well-being of European workers and citizens;
- maintaining the move towards a sustainable and integrated development of the social, economic and ecological aspects of living and working conditions.

The Foundation's Annual Report for 1995 (EFILWC, 1996a) stated that a number of key principles had informed the work of the Foundation and these included:

- a concern with economic effectiveness;
- priority to prevention;
- the effective involvement and participation of those concerned;
- equality of opportunity and treatment; and
- consideration of regional disparities.

The Economic and Social Committee

The Economic and Social Committee (EcoSoc) is a consultative committee involved in the decision-making processes as one of the groups that has the right to be consulted on proposals from the Commission for policy or legislative initiatives in the areas of subject matter that concern it. The 222 members of the Committee are appointed by the Council in consultation with the Commission. Each member state is allocated a number of members and again the allocation is linked to the respective populations of the various countries so that, once again, the four biggest member states in population terms have the largest number of members on the Committee. The members of the committee are supposed to act in the best interests of the Union, and not the countries from which they come.

The members of the committee represent a number of different interests: employer representatives, people from the trade union movement, farmers, representatives of consumer groups and the professions and environmental groups.

The IGC proposes to extend the consultation rights of the Committee to encompass new provisions in the Treaty and the EP has been given the right to consult the Committee.

In the early days of the Union the EcoSoc was the main forum through which workers and employers could feed their views into the decision-making process but this has subsequently been replaced by trade union and employer organisations at the level of the Union. It is these organisations that are described as the *Social Partners* at Union level and it is the Social Partners that participate in the Social Dialogue.

The European Trade Union Confederation

The European Trade Union Confederation (ETUC) is the single representative of the labour movement at EU level. It was formed in 1972/3 and now has all the major trade union federations, national and sectoral, in Europe as members, except the Communist Confédération Générale du Travail (CGT) in France (they are expected to join in the near future). A number of ex-Communist federations have joined in the years following the break-up of the European Communist bloc and it is only really since this happened that the ETUC has been able to claim to be truly representative of European labour. The activities and membership of the confederation is not limited to the member states of the Union and ETUC is the sole significant representative of organised labour across the whole of Western Europe. As the Union is enlarged eastwards and as the countries that were formerly part of the Communist bloc in Eastern Europe become members, one would expect trade union federations in those countries to seek membership of the ETUC. In part the formation in 1990 of the European Trade Union Forum which seeks to promote cooperation between the ETUC and Eastern and Central European unions can be seen as paving the way for such developments.

The ETUC is a massively diverse organisation, however, and it would be wrong to give the impression that there is much cohesion within the movement. The nature and traditions of the many union confederations in membership vary considerably, as do their autonomy and authority in respect of their own membership. Visser and Ebbinghaus (1992) described the ETUC as 'united but fragmented and with little internal cohesion'.

The organisation has much to thank the Union for, and in particular the Commission, which has been a continuing source of both political and financial support. The importance which the Commission has attached over the years to the creation and maintenance of an effective labour movement with a voice and influence at the level of the Union has been considerably beneficial to the ETUC. It is doubtful that the organisation would be even as united and effective as it is – for example, in promoting the social dialogue (*see* Chapter 8) – at the level of the Union had it not been for this support. Again one can see this as evidence of the continuing influence of the corporatist traditions in much of the Union. This support should not be seen as a purely altruistic approach since it has long been the view of the Commission that an internal market and other dimensions of economic integration would only be possible with the support and acquiescence of European labour.

Turner (1996) takes a relatively optimistic view of the future of the ETUC despite acknowledging that in many respects the development of structures at such a transnational level seems to be at odds with the trends towards the decentralisation of decision making and collective bargaining. He suggests that the European Works Council Directive will assist the process of cross-national collaboration within and between labour movements and representatives and that while this will initially be at the level of the individual multinational organisation, the structures that do now exist within the framework of the ETUC may be both used and reinforced. He also points out, however, that the development of an effective labour movement at this EU level needs not only the structures, but also transnational rank-and-file protest and he thinks this most likely to occur in protest at some specific EU-level policy (*see* Carley (1993) and Turner (1996)).

Employers organisations

There are two main employers organisations operating at the level of the Union:

- the Union of Industrial and Employers Confederations of Europe (UNICE), which represents primarily private-sector employers; and
- the European Centre of Public Enterprises (CEEP) representing primarily public-sector employer interests.

UNICE was formed in the late 1950s and, like the ETUC, represents employers from a much wider constituency than the EU. Carley (1993) suggests that there were national federation members from 22 different countries in 1989. Buchan and Buckley (1996) state that UNICE had as members 33 industry and employers federations from 25 countries.

At the level of the EU, the organisation aims to be influential as an organisation representing a particular interest to the legislators and policy makers. Unlike the ETUC, however, the organisation has not been keen to become involved with the Commission and ETUC in policy making as a Social Partner; it is even less keen to become involved in any EU-level bargaining arrangements with the ETUC. To some extent this is no doubt due to the fact that it does not have a mandate to act in this way and it and the ETUC do not have compatible structures.

The membership of CEEP tends to be comprised of individual employers rather than federations and the geographic spread of the members of this organisation is much smaller than that of UNICE or the ETUC. As with UNICE, the direction of the organisation's activities is primarily to represent interests to the policy makers and legislators and not to participate in that process in a more direct way.

THE EUROPEAN INVESTMENT BANK

The purpose of the European Investment Bank (EIB) is to provide finance for both public and private projects inside and outside the Union. The Bank is intended to be non-profit making and it is able to raise finance on the world's money markets. The Board of Governors of the Bank comprises the Finance Ministers from each of the member states. The Bank works closely with the Commission so that its loans can be directed at activities and projects that complement the Union's policies and funding programmes. Since 1994 the Bank has been able, through the European Investment Fund (EIF), to provide guarantees for the long-term financing of major infrastructure projects – also known as Trans-European networks (TENs) – in addition to supporting the SME sector.

The activities and role of the Bank were the subject of discussion and amendment at the Amsterdam IGC and the proposals agreed there seek to widen the role of the bank. The Resolution of the European Council on Growth and Employment agreed at Amsterdam refers specifically (para 9) to the role that the Bank could play in promoting and creating employment within the Union and the Bank is urged to step up its activities in this respect.

In particular, the Bank is urged to examine its role in:

- financing high-technology projects of small and medium-sized companies;
- intervening in the areas of education, health, the urban environment and environmental protection; and
- granting very long-term loans for large infrastructure networks.

It is relevant to point out that many were sceptical of the extent to which activities of the Bank could make a significant difference to job creation in the context of an unemployment total of some 18 million within the Union (*see* Exhibit 7.1).

Exhibit 7.1

EIB cautious over its latest jobs assignment

FT

**By Wolfgang Münchau,
Economics Correspondent**

Judging by the number of jobs programmes over the past 10 years, the European Union should not have an unemployment crisis. But it does.

The jobless rate has climbed from 6.4 per cent in 1980 to 10.8 per cent last January; over the same period in the US it has declined from 7.2 per cent to 5.3.

This has happened despite a string of EU programmes focusing mainly on the demand-side of the economy. These included targeted help for regional and transnational infrastructure projects, and specifically for small and medium-sized companies.

Mr Hans-Olaf Henkel, president of the Federation of German Industry (BDI), yesterday condemned the European Union's planned jobs chapter as superfluous and said it could be accepted only because it would have no real effect.

Mr Henkel said the jobs chapter, pushed by France, was simply the deal Bonn had to accept to ensure the stability pact was passed.

Now, the Amsterdam summit has produced yet another job initiative as part of a trade-off against the stability pact for the planned single currency. Like many programmes before, it will centre on the European Investment Bank, the EU's finance arm.

As the world's largest multilateral lender, the EIB enjoys the highest credit rankings, and can therefore help finance projects in a cost-effective way. There are, however, limits to which 'off-balance sheet' financing can be pushed.

Even among bank insiders there is strong scepticism about the expectations politicians have placed in them in the fight against unemployment. This goes especially for suggestions about a possible redistribution of the EIB's profits or a stronger bank involvement in venture capital operations.

Eurojobs: in search of a programme that works

❶ Nov 85: Jacques Delors orders first jobs initiative; argues that without faster growth and lower unemployment 'the consequences would be serious for social peace, for the authority of governments and for democracy'

❷ Dec 92: Edinburgh Summit agrees on extension of the temporary lending facility. Ecu8bn made available, including Ecu7bn for infrastructure projects

❸ Jun 93: Copenhagen Summit. EIB receives extra Ecu1bn facility to create jobs in small- and medium-sized enterprises (SMEs); combined with an interest rebate of 2% financed by EU budget for five years. Goal: creation of 45,000 jobs. At the end of 1996 some 30,000 reported to have been created

❹ Dec 93: Delors White Paper for Employment and Growth

❺ Jun 94: Creation of European Investment Fund (EIF) as a guarantor for loans for trans-European networks (TENs) and SMEs

❻ Dec 95: Essen summit. EIB is asked to increase lending to TENs

❼ Jun 97: Amsterdam summit asks EIB to step up efforts further. Venture capital involvement proposed

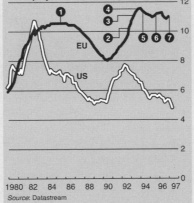

Unemployment: EU vs US (%of workforce)

Source: Datastream

As one senior official said: 'Of course, we have a role to play in reducing structural unemployment. But if you count 18m unemployed, there remains a large discrepancy.'

The EIB has been at the centre of the EU's efforts to reduce the rate of unemployment since the early 1990s. At various summits it has been given a specific remit to step up lending to small and medium companies (SMEs) and various European infrastructure projects, also known as trans-European networks (TENs).

At Edinburgh in 1992 and Copenhagen the following year, the bank was given a facility of Ecu8bn ($9bn) to lend to SMEs in combination with an EU-financed interest rate rebate of 2 per cent. The goal of this combined programme was to create 45,000 jobs. By the end of 1996, about 30,000 had been created, one of the EIB's biggest success stories in terms of job creation.

Bank officials say this is typical of the scale on which it can help stimulate the EU jobs markets. They acknowledge, though, that there is some scope for extending the EIB's remit beyond that of lender to that of an investor.

Under current arrangements the EIB could become more active in the provision of venture capital, in collaboration with the European Investment Fund, set up in 1994 to provide loan guarantees for TENs. The Fund's shareholders are the EIB, the European Commission and commercial banks.

Critics of the process say that the EU would do better to concentrate on welfare systems and labour markets, rather than relying on stoking demand in the economy.

Professor Richard Layard, director of the Centre for Economic Performance at the London School of Economics, believes the EU can play a useful role —not in devising grand schemes, but in acting as a 'transmission mechanism' that enabled positive experiences in one or more countries to be transmitted to the rest.

Source: *Financial Times*, 18 June 1997.

References

Buchan, D. and Buckley, N. (1996) *Financial Times*, 11 Nov, p. 2.

Carley, M. (1993) 'Social Dialogue', in Gold M. (ed) *The Social Dimension – Employment Policy in the European Community*. Macmillan.

European Foundation for the Improvement of Living and Working Conditions (1996a) *Annual Report 1995*. EFILWC.

European Parliament (1997) *EP News*, July.

Turner, L. (1996) 'The Europeanisation of Labour: Structure before Action', *European Journal of Industrial Relations*, 2(3), 235–44.

Visser, J. and Ebbinghaus, B. (1992) 'Making the Most of Diversity? European Integration and Transnational Organisation of Labour', in Greenwood, J., Grote, J.R. and Ronit, K. (eds) *Organised Interests and the European Community*. Sage, London, pp. 206–37.

8

LEGISLATIVE PROCEDURES AND FORMS

LEARNING OBJECTIVES

When you have read this chapter, you should be able to understand and explain:

- the main legislative forms in use in the European Union and the key differences between them;
- the four legislative procedures in operation and the circumstances under which each would be employed.

INTRODUCTION

In this chapter the differences between the main legislative forms are explained. There then follows a detailed summary of the legislative processes of the Union — the Consultation Procedure, the Co-operation Procedure, the Co-Decision Procedure and the Protocol Procedure.

LEGISLATIVE FORMS

European Union legislation comes in a range of forms and it is important to know the major differences between each of the forms.

Treaty Articles

The EC Treaty – as amended at Amsterdam and assuming subsequent ratification by the member states – forms the constitution of the Union. Treaty Articles take precedence over national legislation, customs and practice and, where necessary, they should be implemented into national legislation. Were Articles of the Treaties are clear, precise, unconditional and self-contained, however, they are said to have *horizontal direct effect* – that is, they may not need to be given effect via implementing legislation in the member states and individuals can use them as the basis for an action against another, irrespective of the member state's own legislation.

Regulations

Regulations are relatively rare but, once adopted, they are applicable directly and generally throughout the EU. They are immediately binding on member states and individuals and do not require any action at member-state level to render them effective. In cases where EU Regulations conflict with national law, the EU Regulation takes precedence. The Council can empower the Commission to make regulations.

Directives

Normally a Directive is not immediately applicable and does not have direct effect; some action is required at member-state level in order to bring it into effect, though this action need not be legislative. For example, implementation can be through agreement by the Social Partners.) Normally Directives specify an objective to be achieved and the date by which it should be achieved but leave the means to the member states. Once the implementation date is reached, the Directive becomes the law within the Union. Where the provisions of the Directive are clear, precise, unconditional and self-contained, they have what is referred to as *vertical direct effect*, which means that individuals in member states can rely upon them in actions against the member state in its role as an employer.

Decisions

Decisions can be made by the Council and in some instances by the Commission. Once made, they are binding on the parties that sought the decision in the first place. They do not automatically have general effect.

Non-binding mechanisms

There are also a range of non-binding mechanisms that can be used such as *recommendations*, *opinions*, *declarations* and *resolutions*. These are often used when one or more of the institutions want to exert influence but know that either they will not gain sufficient support for the proposal or that they don't really have the competence to act. Council recommendations, declarations, resolutions and opinions carry more weight than those issued by the Commission on its own. The ECJ may well take one or more such instruments into account when deciding a case. At the Amsterdam IGC, the Council agreed a number of resolutions – for example, one on Growth and Employment and another on the Stability and Growth Pact (*see* Chapter 9).

Having identified the main forms of legislation, we can now consider the various procedures in use in the Union.

THE CONSULTATION PROCEDURE

As already discussed, traditionally legislative intervention/action at the level of the EU has required the unanimous support of the member states; where this is the case, the decision-making procedure to be used is called the *Consultation Procedure*. This is the least complex of the decision-making procedures and is shown in outline form in Fig. 8.1. In the

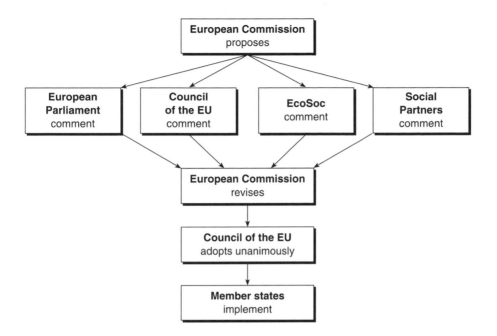

Fig. 8.1 The Consultation Procedure

early days of the Union, this was the only procedure and for many years now there has been an assumption that decisions reached using this Procedure will only be reached unanimously, irrespective of whether it was strictly required by the Treaty. As Fig. 8.1 shows, the Procedure provides for consultation with a number of fora, but only one round. The Council's decision is final; it can choose to heed or ignore the comments and amendments suggested as part of the Procedure.

THE CO-OPERATION PROCEDURE

The need to arrive at unanimous decisions as a prerequisite to action inevitably limited the ability of the Union to progress and change. It was realised that this requirement might pose very real problems to the process of creating the single market. As a result, when, in the mid-1980s, it was agreed that the single market should become a reality by the end of 1992, it was also agreed that for many of the measures necessary to the creation and effective operation of the market the principle of majority voting should apply. As a consequence, the Single European Act (Article 189c) included the creation of a new decision-making procedure called the *Co-operation Procedure* (*see* Fig. 8.2).

The two main differences between the Co-operation Procedure and the original Consultation Procedure are:

1 It arguably extended to the Parliament a greater opportunity to influence the legislative process by giving it a second opportunity, or reading, to comment and amend.

2 It specifically provides for the use of majority voting.

In cases where, on second reading, the Parliament rejects the common position adopted by the Council at the end of the first round of consultations, the Council can only overturn that rejection or proceed in accordance with its original common position on the basis of unanimity. Where the Parliament agrees to amend the Council position on second reading, those agreed amendments are passed to the Commission. The Commission can either incorporate these amendments in a revised proposal to the Council or not. If the Commission incorporates the Parliament's amendments on second reading, the Council can then act on a majority vote. However, where the Commission has not taken on board the Parliament's amendments in its proposal to the Council, the Council can only act with unanimity.

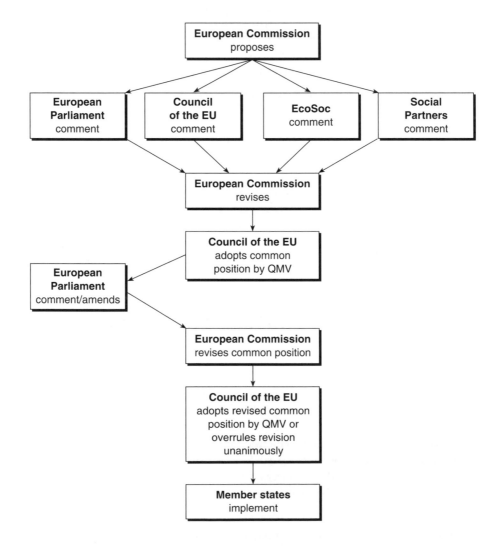

Fig. 8.2 The Co-operation Procedure

Table 8.1 Distribution of council votes

	Votes
United Kingdom	10
Germany	10
Italy	10
France	10
Spain	8
Belgium	5
Greece	5
Netherlands	5
Portugal	5
Sweden	4
Austria	4
Denmark	3
Finland	3
Ireland	3
Luxembourg	2
Total	87

This arrangement is in some respects consistent with giving the Parliament a role in the formulation and enactment of legislation, since amendments made by the Parliament can form part of the final Directive but, and some would argue that it is a big but, the final decision rests with the Council. If the member states have a mind to, they can reject the amendments and/or do nothing.

It is worth noting again that the Single European Act did not extend the Co-operation Procedure and hence did not extend majority voting to issues of harmonisation concerning tax, free movement of people and, most importantly from the viewpoint of the social dimension, the rights and interests of the employed. In practice, this meant that it was only on health and safety issues that matters of direct concern to the employed, and in the workplace, could be determined and adopted in a legislative sense by qualified majority voting (QMV).

For many within the Union, this was an inadequate outcome and, as noted earlier, there have been several arguments in the meantime involving member states and the Commission as to whether a particular proposal fell inside the appropriate definitions and interpretations of health and safety. The ECJ was required to adjudicate on this issue in 1996 with reference to the Directive adopted in 1994 that sought to protect employees from being forced to work hours in excess of 48 per week averaged out over a period of time. The decision of the ECJ was that the Directive was appropriately adopted as a health and safety issue.

The system of QMV is simple enough in that each member state has a specified number of votes in Council and these are apportioned roughly in accordance with the relative populations of the countries (*see* Table 8.1). In total there are 87 votes available and 62 are required to vote in favour of a proposal for it to be adopted via the QMV process.

Reference is sometimes made to the *blocking minority*; this figure is currently 26 Council votes. As noted earlier, the UK governments of 1979 to 1997 expressed a determination to resist the extension of QMV to more areas of subject matter; they were also determined to resist attempts to lower the number of votes (or percentage) that constitutes the necessary majority.

The 1997 IGC did not in the end deal with these problems. With relatively few exceptions, the extension of QMV and thereby the use of the Co-operation Procedure have been effectively delayed until there is another IGC and the need for reform becomes imperative, due to the proximity of enlargement of the Union.

The inclusion of the Social Protocol Agreement (SPASP) in the main Treaty may lead to an extension of the use of the Co-operation Procedure and Articles 4 and 5 of the new Title on Employment provide for the use of QMV. It also seems that Article 56(2) dealing with matters relating to the right of establishment for third-country nationals will be subject to the QMV procedures (*see* Chapter 9).

THE CO-DECISION PROCEDURE

The desire for the Parliament to have a more influential role in the legislative process can also be seen to be behind the *Co-Decision Procedure* – a new variation on the Co-operation Procedure introduced via the Maastricht Treaty (Article 189b). The Parties are required to use this new procedure in respect of measures directed at harmonisation in readiness for the single market, general action programmes for the environment, research and development and proposals concerned with the free movement of workers. This new procedure therefore applies to most of the areas of subject matter that are/were subject to QMV. As has already been pointed out, this does not include many aspects of the social dimension other than health and safety at work and certain aspects of both the free movement of people and vocational training that were added by the Maastricht Treaty (Articles 49 and 126 of the EC Treaty).

The difference between this and the normal Co-operation Procedure is important after the EP's second reading and if the Parliament intends to reject the common position already adopted by the Council (by QMV) or if the Parliament seeks to amend the common position and the Council then rejects these amendments (*see* Fig. 8.3).

- *Parliament rejection of common position.* If the position of the Parliament is that by an absolute majority of component members it intends to reject the common position adopted by the Council, the Council has the opportunity to further explain the common position that it adopted and to do so in a specially convened meeting of the *Conciliation Committee* (*see* below). If after the attempt at conciliation, the EP by an absolute majority still rejects the common position then the proposed Act cannot be adopted. This constitutes an ability by the EP to effectively veto a position adopted by the Council.

- *Parliament seeks to amend common position.* If the EP at this second-reading stage does not reject the Council position, but seeks to amend it the amendments must be by absolute majority as above and they must be put to both the Council and Commission. The Commission is required to form and deliver an opinion on the amendments. Where the Council approves all the EP amendments by QMV, the common position can be amended accordingly and adopted. Where the Commission has delivered a negative

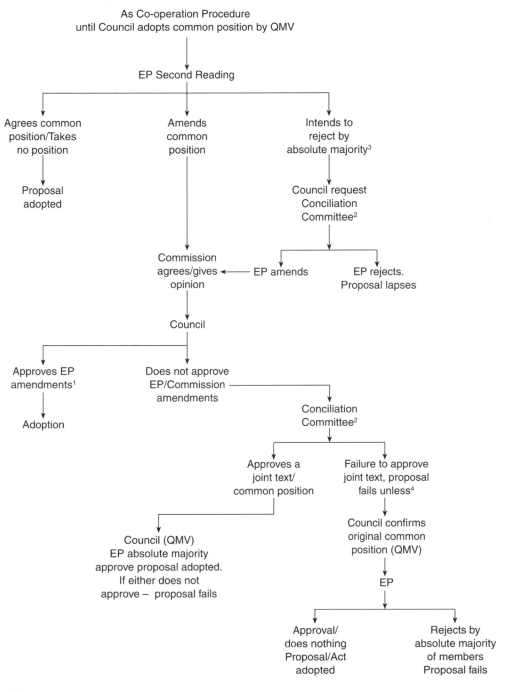

Fig. 8.3 The Co-Decision Procedure

Notes:
[1] Unanimity if Commission has given a negative view of EP amendments.
[2] Equal numbers of Council and EP members, commission acts as conciliator.
[3] Amsterdam amendments propose that if EP rejects at this stage, proposal fails.
[4] Amsterdam amendments propose that failure to approve/agree a joint text will
   cause proposal to fail, and procedure to end at this point.

opinion on one or more of the EP amendments, the Council may only approve the amendments unanimously, if it does then the common position can be amended accordingly and adopted.

- *Council does not approve proposed amendments*. In the event of the EP wishing to amend the Council position and the Council not approving these amendments, the Procedure calls for the establishment of a joint Council–Parliament Conciliation Committee with the Commission also involved as the conciliator trying to broker an agreement between the other two institutions. Where the conciliation is successful and a joint text can be agreed (by qualified majority of the Council and simple majority of the EP representatives on the Conciliation Committee), the outcome is subject to the subsequent approval of both Parliament and Council. Where there is no agreed outcome or the outcome agreed by the Conciliation Committee is not acceptable to both the institutions (Parliament by an absolute majority and the Council by QMV), the proposal lapses. In other words the act cannot be adopted and the EP has again been able to prevent legislation with which it was not in accord.

- *Post conciliation*. If, after an unproductive conciliation process, the Council (by QMV) wishes to continue with the proposal and seeks to adopt its pre-conciliation common position, possibly incorporating some of the EP's proposed amendments, the Parliament now has the right of approval and if the Parliament rejects the common position again (by absolute majority of component members) the proposal lapses. If the EP does not reject the proposal at this stage, the Council may proceed and the Act may be adopted.

Initial criticisms of this new procedure were that it was overly complex, that it would take too long and perhaps, most significantly, that in reality the voting requirements for the EP to effectively veto Council proposals (an absolute majority of all MEPs) were too onerous.

The Amsterdam IGC proposed a shortening and simplification of this Co-Decision Procedure, as well as some extension of coverage and applicability. These changes are arguably to the advantage of the EP and have been indicated in Fig. 8.3. Under the new proposals a legislative proposal will be deemed to have failed if:

- the EP rejects it by an absolute majority of component members; or if

- there is no agreement in conciliation on a joint text.

An additional change is that there will only be recourse to conciliation in the event of the EP proposing amendments to rather than rejecting the Council's common position. It has been argued that this will put greater pressure upon the Council to reach agreement through conciliation.

Furthermore, the new proposals additionally state that once the situation has reached conciliation, the Conciliation Committee should

> address the common position on the basis of the amendments proposed by the EP . . . and that, where the Committee approves a joint text, each of the institutions – the EP and the Council – shall have six weeks in which to adopt the Act in question in accordance with the joint text. If either the EP (absolute majority of votes cast) or the Council (QMV): fail to approve the proposed Act within that period, it will be deemed to have not been adopted.

Inevitably, it will be some time before it is possible to assess the extent to which the power of the EP to prevent or influence legislation has been enhanced by these proposals.

THE PROTOCOL PROCEDURE

The Agreement at Maastricht between the member states other than the UK created yet another decision-making procedure – the *Protocol Procedure*. This resulted from the desire to enhance both the social dialogue between the Social Partners at EU level and their role in the decision-making process, to include giving the Partners the opportunity to enter into contractual relations including agreements.

Figure 8.4 shows that according to this Procedure, the Social Partners can be given the opportunity to reach an agreement between themselves on a proposal for action that has come out of the Commission. If the Social Partners can reach agreement on the content of the proposal, they can further agree to seek to give effect to the agreement via collective agreements at national level. Alternatively, having reached agreement on the content of the proposal, they can ask the Commission to process the agreement through the normal Consultation or Co-operation Procedures and Decision of the Council, as appropriate, and depending upon the subject matter. The Co-decision Procedure will also be an option in future if Agreements at Amsterdam in 1997 are ratified. As noted earlier, this new Protocol Procedure does not contain a formal role for the EP.

At the time of writing, this Procedure has been 'completed' on four occasions and the variety of possible outcomes have been exemplified.

1 The Social Partners were unable to agree the content of proposals that eventually became the *EWC Directive* and the issue was returned to the Commission who issued a draft Directive and then processed it via the Co-operation Procedure. The new agreement at

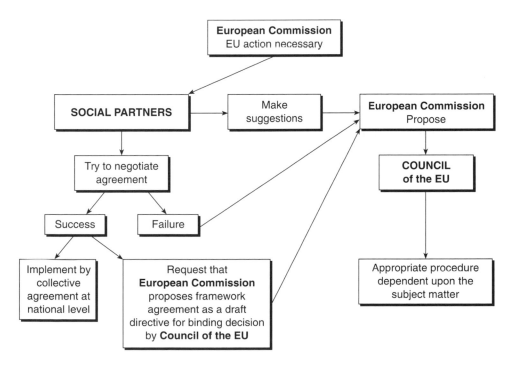

Fig. 8.4 The Protocol Procedure

Maastricht had included this subject area as one that could be dealt with this way and subject to QMV.

As noted earlier, the EWC Directive may constitute the first significant intervention into procedural relations between management and labour at the level of the firm – not that the impact in some member states of the earlier Directives requiring consultation between them on collective redundancies, the transfer of undertakings and some health and safety issues (*see* Chapters 12 and 14) can be entirely discounted.

2 The Social Partners did manage to agree proposals with respect to the issue of *parental leave* and, once agreed, the Social Partners asked the Commission to issue the agreement as a draft Directive to be processed via the normal Co-operation Procedures. At this stage, the Commission took the opportunity to incorporate 'mainstreaming' (*see* Chapter 11) into the Directive but this proposal was rejected by the Council, while it accepted the main contents.

3 The Social Partners decided against trying to reach a framework agreement on the question of the *Burden of Proof in Sex Discrimination cases* and the Commission was asked to prepare a draft Directive. The Commission intended to produce a Draft on the burden of proof that encompassed some sharing of the burden, possibly along the lines of the complainant having to first establish the facts and the employer then having to establish that there was no discrimination.

4 The Social Partners reached a framework agreement on part-time work which was then passed to the Commission to progress through the normal decision-making procedures. The Commission issued the agreement as a draft Directive in July 1997 and the Council adopted the agreement as a Directive towards the end of 1997.

There are other issues and proposals that have been diverted into the Protocol Procedures and about which the Social Partners were considering the agreement of framework directives. These include *flexibility of working time* and *security for employees* and the issue of *dignity at work* which incorporates issues of sexual harassment.

References

Council of the European Union (1997) *Intergovernmental Conference Draft Treaty*.
European Commission (1997b) *Amsterdam European Council 16–17 June, Presidency Conclusions*. SN150/97.

9

THE INTERGOVERNMENTAL CONFERENCE AND MONETARY UNION

LEARNING OBJECTIVES

When you have read this chapter, you should be able to understand and explain:

- the process of the Intergovernmental Conference (IGC) and its initial aims;
- the different agendas of the various EU institutions and individual member states;
- the main achievements of the IGC and the likelihood of the proposed changes being implemented;
- the implications of monetary union for the future of the EU.

INTRODUCTION

The Intergovernmental Conference, which opened in March 1996 and was concluded in Amsterdam in June 1997, addressed the issues relating to the renegotiation and amendment of the Treaties on European Union and the European Commission.

The various stages of the Conference are described in this chapter, as are its conclusions and achievements (although still in draft form).

The chapter ends with a consideration of monetary union and its potential impact on the countries of the EU and the other parts of the world with which we trade.

THE INTERGOVERNMENTAL CONFERENCE

The IGC opened in March 1996 and had as its objectives:

- the review of the post-Maastricht operation of the EU; and
- the consideration of how to best prepare for the expansion of the EU both to the East and the South.

Some of the potentially difficult issues have been referred to elsewhere and include an expansion of QMV and a diminution of the individual member-state veto. Allied to this in some minds is the fear that such changes will lead to a further loss of sovereignty and make a federal Union more likely. The known resistance of some interests to an extension of QMV has brought into sharper focus the issue of flexibility in the context of a twin- or multi-track Union, in that some member states pursue integration both further and more quickly than others. To some extent this became inevitable once the convergence criteria and timetable for monetary union were agreed at Maastricht, since it was always at least privately acknowledged that not all member states would achieve the qualifying targets by the first date.

In addition to the formal objectives for the Intergovernmental Conference, there were a number of other agendas, both private and public.

1 The Reflection Group

Prior to the opening of the Conference, a group called the Reflection Group was established which included representatives of the member states, the Commission and the EP. This group was charged with much of the preparatory work for the Conference and recommended in its report to the Madrid Summit in December 1995 that the IGC should concentrate upon:

- bringing the EU closer to its citizens;
- agreeing institutional reform with a view to improving decision making; and
- giving the EU greater capacity for external action.

The group had great difficulty in agreeing anything; the UK government was at the forefront of these difficulties since it was pursuing firmly its view that the treaties did not need to be changed in any major areas. Many observers saw the difficulties that the Reflection Group had in coming to agreement as an indication of what was in store for the IGC itself.

2 The Commission

The Commission's initial position was to give priority to building a citizens' Europe based on the rule of law and social justice and the promotion of a European social model. In the context of a larger Union, it envisaged the need for:

- simpler decision making;
- less use of the veto;
- a smaller Commission with one Commissioner per member state; and
- enhanced powers for a smaller EP.

3 The European Parliament

The EP position included as priorities:

- improving the employment and social components of the Union and the establishment of annual employment guidelines for the Union;
- a Commission consisting of one Commissioner per member state;
- reducing the number of decision-making procedures; and
- giving the EP the right to choose the President of the Commission from a shortlist drawn up by the Council of Ministers.

4 The Social Policy Forum

The Social Policy Forum had been created as a result of initiatives contained within the *White Paper on EU Social Policy* (1994c) and in the Third Social Action Programme of 1995 (1995c). This Forum met for the first time at the end of March 1996 and comprised a great mix of interests including among them representatives from EU institutions, member-state governments, both sides of industry and non-governmental organisations operating at grass roots level with regard to employment and social policy. This Forum made a number of detailed recommendations concerning the development of social policy within the Union. One recommendation relevant to this discussion of the IGC was that the Union should develop a Bill of Rights comprising a core of fundamental rights in the social and civil arenas and that this should form part of any new Treaty. This should include rights to:

● equality before the law;

● equality between men and women, and a ban on any form of discrimination;

● freedom of movement;

● freedom to work or study in any member state;

● freedom of association (which includes trade union membership) and collective bargaining and collective action.

This Forum also expressed the desire that the Social Dialogue should be widened to encompass interests, such as those represented at the Forum, wider than those of the two sides of industry. The intention is that the Forum meet approximately every 18 months.

5 The Comité des Sages (CDS)

This is a group established under the second Social Action Programme after the failure to gain adoption of the Social Charter. It was charged with the task of investigating how implementation of the contents of the Charter might be furthered through the revision of the Treaties envisaged as part of the IGC. This group also recommended that the revised Treaties should contain rights in the form of objectives to be achieved, including rights to education, work, social security and protection for the family. The CDS was also in favour of the Treaty containing a clause obliging member states to set a minimum income for citizens unable to find paid employment.

6 Individual member-state governments of the Conservative UK government (pre-May 1997)

The position on the objectives of the IGC was issued in the form of a White Paper, entitled *A Partnership of Nations*, and the tenor of the UK position was aptly caught by this title.

The UK government was against supranational developments at the expense of the nation state and its sovereignty and the document made a number of suggestions with reference to the Union treaties and institutions, including:

● strengthening the principle of subsidiarity so that the Commission could only act when the member states could not;

● retaining unanimous voting but with an acknowledgement that enlargement of the Union might require further discussion of majority voting;

- the creation of a two-tier Commission on enlargement with the larger states having voting members and the smaller states non-voting members;

- no enhanced role for the EP and no role for the Parliament in the IGC other than as an observer;

- reform of the ECJ so that the retrospective application of judgements is limited and an internal appeal procedure is introduced.

This sample of the different initial views within the Union on the desirable outcome of the IGC illustrates the scope for disagreement and dissent and arguably didn't present an optimistic picture since changes to the existing Treaties could only be made unanimously. As we saw at the time of the Maastricht discussions and negotiations, it only takes one member-state government to prevent progress and action.

The position of the UK government was well known and, before the IGC opened, a scenario was envisaged in which agreement was stalled or in which the UK negotiated itself a range of further opt-outs using devices similar to those devised at Maastricht. The views of the UK government and the knowledge that there had to be a general election in the UK some time around the end of April or early May 1997, allied to the apparent popularity of the opposition Labour Party, was partly responsible for an early decision by other member states to allow the IGC to continue into 1997 and beyond the date of the UK election. There was a general feeling that the UK Labour Party in government would be more amenable to some of the positions adopted by the other participants and therefore it was felt that there were potential advantages in delay.

When the IGC opened, the Heads of Government of the member states agreed that the focus of the Conference should be upon:

- an EU closer to its citizens, to include, in particular, the fight against unemployment and the strengthening of the fundamental rights of citizens;

- an examination of the role of the ECJ as part of the search for more efficient institutions;

- developing a more coherent external role for the Union in matters of security and defence;

- a closer association between the EP and the IGC.

At the first meeting of the Foreign Ministers, a majority agreed that the next Treaty should contain a chapter on employment even though it was also agreed that employment and unemployment were primarily national issues.

The Dublin Summit (December 1996)

By the time of the Dublin Summit at the end of 1996, where the agenda was primarily concerned with issues relating to monetary union and the IGC, the UK government had taken the opportunity – afforded by the ECJ decision that the Working Time Directive was appropriately adopted as a health and safety issue – to threaten that it would use its veto to stall any and all IGC agreements until it was given the opportunity to avoid the Directive. Needless to say, this confirmed the other member states in their belief that postponing the conclusion of the Conference until after the time of an election in the UK was beneficial for the future of the Union.

In a speech to the EP in December 1996, just before the Dublin Summit, Jacques Santer, the President of the Commission, criticised the UK position and implicitly alleged that their minimalist approach towards reform of the processes and institutions was in effect a block on enlargement of the Union. He argued that it was unrealistic, on the one hand, to argue for enlargement (as the UK government had) and at the same time resist reform of the way the Union works.

Leaving aside issues relating to the progress of and towards monetary union, the Irish Presidency and the Dublin Summit did make some progress towards achieving the review of existing Treaties and institutions that were seen as the objectives of the IGC. However, as already noted, the most intractable issues were left to be negotiated further by the relevant EU and national civil servants with agreement at the summit in Amsterdam in June 1997 as the objective. The issues of greater use of QMV and the weighting of individual member state votes in this process and a streamlined Commission were left, but there were agreements in principle covering the fight against crime, in particular drug trafficking, and the reduction of immigration and frontier controls. The reservations of the UK and Ireland on removing internal border controls and allowing the ECJ a greater role in the determination of immigration and asylum policy seemed likely to result in the other member states deciding eventually to proceed further down the road towards the borderless (internal) Community envisaged in the SEA without them.

In some respects the decision by the Commission and the other member states to extend the IGC beyond the date of the general election in the UK was justified by the election in May 1997 of a Labour government. This administration quickly indicated its intention to agree to the Social Protocol Agreement on Social Policy being brought back into the Treaty and to be bound by it, and to the proposal to incorporate into the revised Treaty a Title on Employment. However, there was also a continuance of the policy of refusing to concede control of asylum and immigration policy to the EU and a refusal to accede to the arrangements for removing internal controls between the member states. (This issue and the debate surrounding it are discussed in more detail in Chapter 10 on labour mobility.)

The Amsterdam Summit (June 1997) and IGC outcomes

The IGC was concluded at the Amsterdam Summit of June 1997. The main outcome was agreement on a new draft Treaty; however, it is important to point out that this draft has to be ratified by all the individual member states and that this may take some time. It is possible that one or more of them, whether the ratifying process is purely Parliamentary or whether it involves a referendum, may refuse or fail to ratify, in which case the draft may fall as revisions to the Treaty requires unanimity. The optimistic scenario expected the draft Treaty to be formally signed by the member states in October 1997.

The IGC did not agree any of the major reforms to the role, size or constitution of the various institutions and processes that had at various times been on the agenda of one or more of the interested parties. However, this may prove to be an underestimate of the significance of the changes agreed to the Co-Decision Procedure and their implications for the power and influence of the EP (*see* Chapters 7 and 8). The Commission was particularly upset at the refusal to address some of these issues and in its document, *Agenda 2000*, indicated that because of this reluctance to confront the issues, another IGC would be required prior to any enlargement of the Union (*see* Chapter 5).

The Council reaffirmed the importance it attaches to promoting employment and reducing the unacceptably high levels of unemployment in Europe, particularly for young people, the long-term unemployed and the low skilled. The IGC agreed to incorporate into the Treaty for the first time a Title on Employment.

It was also agreed to take back into the Treaty the Social Protocol Agreement on Social Policy (to form the Social Chapter). This should effectively extend the area of QMV for the whole Union. The content of the Protocol Agreement and its relationship to the Social Charter was discussed in Chapters 6 and 8. It is relevant that the Preamble to the Treaty on European Union is in the future to include as a new fourth paragraph a statement confirming:

> attachment to fundamental social rights as defined in . . . the 1989 Community Charter of the Fundamental Social Rights of Workers [The Social Charter].

These two agreements on additions to the Treaty provide the subject matter for much of the remainder of this Chapter. On the assumption that the draft Treaty is ratified, these agreements mean that there will now be a Treaty base for the Union to pursue objectives and take action in a number of the social and employment areas that was not possible before. For example, the Union can now take actions to promote employment and to combat social exclusion.

There was acceptance that it would be important prior to ratification of the Treaty that the various UK interests should be allowed to participate in the discussions that would, until ratification, continue within the auspices of the Protocol Agreement. This was in recognition of the new UK government's agreement to the accession into the Treaty of the Protocol Agreement and to be bound by the Directives already adopted via the Protocol Procedures.

The IGC also acknowledged the UK and Ireland's refusal to give up control of national borders and asylum and immigration policies.

Prior to examination of the changes to the Treaty, it is worth pointing out that the parties to the IGC reached agreement on *three main resolutions*, each of which lay down the firm commitments of the member states, acting as The European Council. Two of these were concerned with matters relating to monetary union and the other was concerned with growth and employment.

Resolution of the European Council on Growth and Employment

This Resolution spells out the general principles of the Union's economic and social policies as they relate to the issues of employment and employability. In the main, the Resolution confirms that within the context of general EU policy, responsibility for taking action remains at the level of the member state. The Commission is perceived as providing both a coordinating and monitoring role and in this context reference is also made to the new *Employment Committee*, the creation of which is provided for in the new Treaty Title on Employment (*see* below). This new Committee is expected to work closely with the Economic Policy Committee.

In terms of general principles the Resolution states that:

> . . . it should be a priority aim to develop a skilled, trained and adaptable workforce and to make labour markets responsive to economic change. Structural reforms need to be comprehensive in scope . . . so as to address in a coherent manner the complex issue of incentives in creating and taking a job . . . Economic and social policies are mutually reinforcing. Social protection systems

should be modernised . . . in order to contribute to competitiveness, employment and growth, establishing a durable basis for social cohesion.

It is argued that special attention should be given to:

labour and product market efficiency, technological innovation, the potential for SMEs to create jobs . . . training and education systems including life-long learning, work incentives in the tax and benefit systems and reducing non-wage labour costs, in order to increase employability.

This Resolution also refers to a new employment-enhancing role for the European Investment Bank (EIB), particularly through the promotion of investment projects among smaller firms, in the public services, through environmental improvement and protection projects. It is called upon to step up its interventions in large infrastructure projects and networks.

The overall objectives are enunciated in paragraph 11 of the Resolution:

. . . maximise our efforts to promote employment and social inclusion and to combat unemployment. In doing so, job promotion, worker protection and security will be combined with the need for improving the functioning of labour markets. This also contributes to the good functioning of EMU.

Finally, the Resolution asks the Social Partners to fully face their responsibilities.

Title on Employment

This new title is to be inserted into the EC Treaty after Title VI and immediately preceding Title VIII on Social Policy, Education, Vocational Training and Youth. The Resolution on Growth and Employment indicates the content of this Title. It is to contain six Articles.

- *The first two Articles* are primarily concerned with enunciating the general principles of working towards a coordinated strategy for employment. Article 1 elaborates upon the strategy by asserting that it should be:

  particularly for promoting a skilled, trained and adaptable workforce and labour markets responsive to economic change.

  Article 2 states that national policies should be devised so as to enable all member states to contribute to the achievement of EU-wide objectives and in a manner that is consistent with EU-wide economic policies.

- *Article 3* is concerned with the Union contributing to a high level of employment by encouraging cooperation between member states, and by supporting and, where necessary, complementing their action. It also stresses, however, that the competencies of the member states should be respected. The second paragraph of the Article states that:

  a high level of employment shall be taken into consideration in the formulation and implementation of community policies and activities.

- *Article 4* is concerned with mechanisms whereby the Commission and the Council (by QMV) draw up guidelines on an annual basis to guide the actions of the member states:

  guidelines which the member states shall take into account in their employment policies. (para. 2)

The Council and the Commission are to receive each year a report from each of the member states on the measures that have been taken and these, along with the views of the Employment Committee, will form the basis of an annual examination by the Council of the implementation of the employment policies of the member states. The Council and the Commission are to make a joint annual report to the European Council on the employment situation in the Union. Paragraph 4 of this Article provides the Council (QMV) with the basis for making recommendations to member states.

- *Article 5* provides the Council with the basis for adopting (via the Co-Decision Procedure and after consultation) incentive measures designed to encourage cooperation between member states and to support their action through initiatives aimed at:

  1 developing exchanges of information and best practice;

  2 providing comparative analysis and advice;

  3 promoting innovative approaches; and

  4 evaluating experiences, in particular by recourse to pilot projects.

  It is specifically stated that the incentive measures referred to in this Article are not to include harmonising laws and regulations of the member states.

- *Article 6* provides a base for the Council, after consultation with the EP, to create an advisory *Employment Committee* with the mission of promoting coordination between member states on employment and labour market policies. The role of the Committee is envisaged as both monitoring and advisory. The Committee is expected to consult the Social Partners; and the member states and the Commission shall each appoint two members of the Committee.

The potential impact of these agreements are discussed in the later chapter on Unemployment.

Social policy – revisions to the EC Treaty

The IGC agreed that the SPASP should be repealed. Articles 117 to 120 of the proposed Treaty now contain in large measure the contents of the SPASP. There are some differences and in one or two instances the proposed Articles constitute a mix of the original EC Treaty Articles and those in the SPASP.

- *The new Article 117* is a mix of Article 1 of SPASP and Article 117 of the EC Treaty. The list of objectives are those from the SPASP; the second paragraph is the second part of Article 1 of the SPASP and paragraph 3 is the original Article 117, paragraph 2. The IGC did not take the opportunity to retain from the original Article 117 the reference as an objective to the promotion of an improved standard of living for workers.

- *The new Article 118* is largely the same as Article 2 of the SPASP with the exception that the Procedure to be used is changed from the Co-operative to the Co-Decision. There is also an inclusion in Article 118(2) which adds to the list of matters on which the Council may act via the Co-Decision Procedure:

  > may adopt measures to encourage co-operation between Member States through initiatives aimed at improving knowledge, developing exchanges of information and best practices, promoting innovative approaches and evaluating experiences in order to combat social exclusion.

The term 'social exclusion' is imprecise and is presumably open to a number of different interpretations. The intention is presumably to encompass those on the margins of society including those on the margins of or excluded from labour markets, and those constituting an underclass. One can imagine a number of minority and disadvantaged groups that may be included, including ethnic minorities, third-country nationals, single mothers/parents, the long-term unemployed, the unemployed elderly, the disabled and others.

- *The new Article 118a* is SPASP Article 3 and *Article 118b* is Article 4 of SPASP. These two Articles specify the procedures, according to which matters may be dealt with by the Social Partners who, if they reach agreement, can ask the Council to implement their agreement by way of Directive. This element of the SPASP has been retained intact and there is no provision to extend the Co-Decision Procedure into this arena.

- *The new Article 118c* is a mix of the original Article 118 and SPASP Article 5. The article is concerned with giving the Commission a basis for encouraging cooperation between member states and coordination of their actions in a number of particular areas of subject matter in the social field. The list of subjects is the same as that in the original Article 118. The preamble is from Article 5 of SPASP.

- *The new Article 119* is specifically concerned with the issues of equality for male and female workers. It encompasses much of SPASP Article 6 but is not identical, the differences being quite significant. SPASP Article 6(1) refers to equal pay but only for equal work; the new Article 119(1) refers also to equal pay for work of equal value. This paragraph is concerned with the responsibilities of member states. Paragraph 3 extends the scope of the Article beyond the pay issue and provides a basis for the Council to adopt measures using the Co-Decision Procedure in order to:

  ensure the application of the principle of equal opportunities and equal treatment of men and women in matters of employment and occupation, including the principle of equal pay for equal work or work of equal value.

  Paragraph 4 of the new Article 119 is also interesting in that it can be seen as an attempt to address the issue of positive action and the difference between positive action and positive discrimination. This is not addressed directly but can be perceived from the changed wording, compared with Article 6(3) of SPASP. The new Article 119(4) states:

  With a view to ensuring full equality in practice between men and women in working life, the principle of equal treatment shall not prevent any Member State from maintaining or adopting measures providing for specific advantages in order to make it easier for the underrepresented sex to pursue a vocational activity or to prevent or compensate for disadvantages in professional careers.

  The words in italic are new. The SPASP introduction simply said that 'This Article . . .' and instead of 'the underrepresented sex', the original said 'women' only.
  This issue is discussed further in Chapter 11.

- *The new Articles 119a and 120.* Article 119a is the old 120 and the new 120 is the old SPASP Article 7 and are both of no great significance.

The new Social Chapter of the EC Treaty, since this is what the new Articles will undoubtedly be called, does go some way to dealing with some of the difficulties that have been experienced in the past as a result of not having a Treaty basis that enabled the Institutions to take the action that was felt to be required. Of particular significance may be the insertion of the reference to social exclusion, though in this context the nature of the measures referred to may be unnecessarily limited.

We have also noted that the Co-Decision Procedure in its new shortened form is to replace the Co-operation Procedure, where appropriate, although as far as can be judged at this stage, there is no intention to replace unanimity, where required in the SPASP, with the Co-operation or Co-Decision Procedure. Nevertheless, to the extent that this new Procedure provides greater opportunities for the EP to influence policy and legislation, this will also apply to much of the social policy area.

There are also evident attempts to deal with one or two particular issues in the area of equality between the sexes – namely, those concerned with the matter of work of equal value and with the difficulties surrounding positive action and the distinction between it and positive discrimination.

There appears to be no change intended to the procedure through which the Social Partners are able to negotiate an agreement and at their request have it turned into legislation via a recommendation from the Commission and a decision by the Council. The measures taken by the SPASP to enhance the social dialogue appear to have survived the renegotiation of the Treaty intact.

Equality and discrimination

In addition to the new Social Chapter, the ability of the Union in the future to pursue objectives and take action on matters of discrimination has been greatly enhanced by a new Article 6a which provides the Council, acting unanimously, with the power to take:

> appropriate action to combat discrimination based on sex, racial or ethnic origin, religion or belief, disability, age or sexual orientation.

Additionally in Article 2 of the EC Treaty the words 'equality between men and women' are to be inserted after 'a high level of employment and social protection'. This article seeks to establish the 'Task' of the Community.

Article 3 is also to be supplemented with a new paragraph which can be linked to the desire of the Commission and others to mainstream the issue of equality between the sexes (*see* Chapter 11). Article 3 sets out a long list of 'the activities' of the Community and it is suggested that appended to this list will be:

> In all the activities referred to in this Article, the Community shall aim to eliminate inequalities, and to promote equality, between men and women.

Note also the similarity between this paragraph and that referred to above regarding the promotion of employment (Article 3, para 2 of the Title on Employment). The significance of this new power to take action is referred to further in Chapter 11.

MONETARY UNION

Monetary union, although not the central issue of this book, is nevertheless important as there is a degree of interdependence between this development, policies on employment and labour mobility and the feasibility of maintaining the traditions of social protection within the Union. As a result, it is necessary to outline the process that has been agreed, the convergence criteria and timetable.

The decision to proceed towards monetary union was taken at Maastricht in 1991 and was included in the amended EC Treaty – Articles 105 to 109 being the relevant ones. In addition, a Protocol on the convergence criteria was also agreed and appended to the Treaty. The essence of the timetable – as specified in Article 109j 3 and 4 – is that currency union will commence with effect from 1 January 1999 and the decision as to which of the member states is qualified to join at this first opportunity is to be made as soon as possible in 1998 and before 1 July 1998. The decision on eligibility is effectively to be made on the basis of the countries' economic and monetary performance against a set of agreed criteria – *the convergence criteria* – in the year 1997.

The convergence criteria are:

- *Price inflation.* Over a period of one year preceding the examination, the rate of price inflation, as measured by the consumer price index, should not exceed 1.5 per cent more than the performance of the three best performing member states.

- *Long-term interest rates.* Over the period of the year prior to the examination, the member state's long-term interest rates should not exceed by more than 2 per cent the average rates of the three best performing countries in terms of price stability.

- *Total cumulative government debt.* This is not to exceed 60 per cent of Gross Domestic Product (GDP).

- *Public sector borrowing.* Here the ratio of planned or actual government deficit should not exceed (effectively for the year 1997) 3 per cent of GDP at market prices.

- *Satisfactory membership of the Exchange Rate Mechanism (ERM).* For two years preceding the examination, the member-state currency should remain within the normal fluctuation margins.

In addition to these convergence criteria, the Dublin Summit in 1996 agreed 'The Stability Pact' which is a system of penalties and fines to be applied to member states in the event that they don't maintain or adhere to the convergence criteria in the years following 1997. The details are not particularly important in the context of this work and there are a number of exceptional circumstance exemptions. One of the bones of contention at the Summit concerned the extent to which these penalties would be automatically imposed or triggered and/or whether the Council in one of its forms would make the decision and therefore have the opportunity to exercise discretion. The Pact agreed at Dublin provided the governments of the single currency members with the opportunity to vote on the application of sanctions upon members that do not comply with the monetary union rules.

Inevitably, membership of the currency or monetary union will directly limit the discretion of member states to pursue their own monetary policy. Indirectly, it is likely to affect policies regarding taxation, government borrowing and public expenditure and thereby the scale and nature of the public sector, including social security and other public provision. It is important to realise that the criteria and requirements of membership specify ratios and not absolute amounts so that national governments would still have decisions to make on issues, such as the amount of tax to raise and the size of the public sector.

The arguments in favour of monetary union tend to centre on the stability that the system will provide. With this stable base, there will be lower inflation and lower interest rates and thereby economic growth and employment growth will be encouraged.

The main arguments against monetary union are linked to issues of sovereignty, the loss of individual member-state freedom to achieve an increase in competitiveness through devaluation and to a belief that the convergence criteria require the pursuit of economic and monetary policies that will in fact harm the prospects for growth of both the economy and employment – that they are in fact deflationary and depressing. It is in the context of these fears that some have argued that the single currency experiment will in fact lock the Union into a regime characterised by high as opposed to low unemployment.

This became a particular concern in a number of member states during 1996 and 1997 as governments sought to achieve the convergence criteria through policies directed at reducing public expenditure and in particular aimed at reducing the expenditure upon various welfare programmes and benefits. In some instances, governments sought to revalue public assets, such as shares in utilities, and in the case of Germany there was temporarily a proposal by the government to revalue the country's gold reserves upwards.

In France, a left-wing government was elected in June 1997 and it is arguable that one of the main reasons for this was dissatisfaction among the electorate with the policies towards public sector pay, public expenditure (welfare) cutbacks and the shrinking of the public sector that had formed the basis of the previous right-wing government's attempts to ensure that the convergence criteria were met. The relevance of political ideology and perspective is once again demonstrated by subsequent developments in July 1997 when the new government announced that taxes were to be raised in order to ensure that the public sector deficit was reduced to a level much closer to that specified in the convergence criteria. These additional revenues were to be obtained from taxes on companies rather than individuals as this was considered to be a preferable alternative to a continuing reduction in welfare and other social benefits.

Progress towards monetary union and the Stability Pact were firmly on the Agenda of the IGC and two relevant resolutions were agreed:

1 *The Resolution of the European Council on the Stability and Growth Pact*. This Resolution commits the member states, the Commission and the Council to apply the Pact that was agreed at the Dublin Summit and, in particular, the Excessive Deficit Procedure provided for in Article 104 of the Treaty and the Protocol on the Excessive Deficit Procedure, annexed to the Treaty.

2 *The Resolution of the European Council on the establishment of an exchange rate mechanism in the third stage of economic and monetary union*. It was agreed that such a mechanism be established when the third stage of economic and monetary union begins on 1 January 1999. The purpose of the mechanism is to link the currencies of those states outside the (so-called) Euro area to the Euro and to try and ensure that there are not excessive fluctuations in exchange rates between the Euro and non-Euro currencies.

The September 1997 position regarding qualification for membership of European monetary union (EMU) and its prospects are assessed in Exhibit 9.1. In 1997 it looked as if the countries that would qualify for membership in the first wave would be Germany and France (although both countries were struggling to meet the criteria), the Benelux States, Austria, Finland and Ireland. Other countries wanted to be ready – for example, Spain and

Exhibit 9.1

Euro enters the last lap

FT

For better or for worse, Europe's leaders are too deeply committed to retreat

The race to launch the single European currency – the euro – on January 1, 1999 is entering the last lap.

The odds have shifted decisively in favour of economic and monetary union going ahead on schedule. For better or for worse, Europe's leaders are too deeply committed to retreat.

In Germany, Chancellor Kohl has staked all on the euro, brushing aside doubts within his own coalition and the opposition Social Democrats ahead of next year's elections. In France, the new left-wing government has grudgingly swung round to squeezing spending to meet the entry criteria for the single currency. In Italy and Spain, prime ministers of the centre-left and centre-right have declared their policy to be 'Emu or bust'.

Financial markets, once sceptical about the single currency, have belatedly grasped the political will behind the project. But political will alone is no enough. Other factors are at work.

Political momentum is propelling Europe towards its single currency. The fiscal targets in the Maastricht treaty may have to be blurred so that France and Germany are deemed to qualify, but the Club Med countries are performing better than expected without the need for budgetary trickery. The outcome could be an interest rate policy run by a hard-nosed central bank and an uncertain outlook for the continent's enduring unemployment problem.

The first is the economic recovery. The improvement in tax revenues will help the hard-pressed to meet the all important deficit criterion of 3 per cent of GDP.

Second, the technical preparation for the launch of the euro is largely in place, thanks to the European Commission and the European Monetary Institute in Frankfurt.

Last June, in Amsterdam, EU leaders reached final agreement on a stability and

EU government financial balances

Surplus (+) or deficit (-) as a % of nominal GDP

	1993	1994	1995	1996	1997[1]	1998[1]
Germany	−3.5	−2.4	−3.6	−3.8	−3.2	−2.7
France	−5.6	−5.6	−5.0	−4.2	−3.2	−3.0
Italy	−9.7	−9.6	−7.0	−6.7	−3.2	−3.8
UK	−7.8	−6.8	−5.5	−4.4	−2.8	−1.8
Austria	−4.2	−4.8	−5.3	−3.9	−3.0	−3.4
Belgium	−7.5	−5.1	−4.1	−3.4	−2.8	−2.7
Denmark	−3.9	−3.4	−1.9	−1.6	0.0	0.7
Finland	−7.9	−6.2	−5.1	−2.6	−2.0	−1.4
Greece	−14.2	−12.1	−9.2	−7.4	−5.2	−4.0
Ireland	−2.5	−1.8	−2.1	−0.9	−1.2	−1.0
Netherlands	−3.2	−3.4	−4.1	−2.4	−2.3	−1.7
Portugal	−6.8	−5.7	−5.0	−4.0	−2.9	−2.8
Spain	−6.8	−6.3	−6.6	−4.5	−3.0	−2.6
Sweden	−12.3	−10.3	−7.7	−3.6	−2.1	−0.2
EU average[2]	**−6.5**	**−5.8**	**−5.2**	**−4.4**	**−3.0**	**−2.6**

[1] Projected figures   [2] Excluding Luxembourg   *Source*: OECD

growth pact to govern budgetary discipline among members of the euro zone; an accord on a revamped exchange rate mechanism to regulate relations between the 'ins' and the 'outs'; and a text governing the legal status of the euro.

Third, countries have made striking progress toward meeting the Maastricht treaty's entry criteria covering inflation, interest rates, exchange rate stability, and the two most testing ones, public deficits, and government debt. EU leaders will make the final judgment in May 1998, acting on recommendations from the EMI and the Commission.

At the latest count, five countries – Denmark, Finland, Ireland, Luxembourg, and the Netherlands – met the deficit target in 1996. Belgium, Germany, Portugal, and Spain should be eligible in 1997. Sweden and, most likely, the UK will meet the deficit criterion, but will probably adopt a 'wait-and-see' attitude to Emu.

Question marks surround France and Italy. Their chances depend on the degree of latitude which EU leaders choose to use when interpreting the entry criteria. Here, the prospects for a reduction in the 1998 and 1999 deficit will count as much as the actual outturn in 1997.

In France, the post-May election revelation that the public deficit for 1997 was heading towards 3.6 per cent of GDP provided some heart-stopping moments, as did the government's threat to reopen the Stability Pact. With a robust turnaround in growth, France could end up with a deficit of 3.1 per cent in 1997, says a Brussels official. But this still leaves doubts about 1998.

France's performance in 1997 benefits from the one-off windfall created by the government's assumption of pension liabilities from France Telecom, worth around 0.4 per cent of GDP. Without additional measures, Paris could have to find savings of around 1 per cent of GDP in order to meet the 3 per cent target in 1998 – unless growth comes to the rescue.

Italy's prospects look rosier, provided it can maintain the confidence of financial markets. Convergence between Italian and German interest rates has offered Italy all the advantages of a big debtor.

The debt to GDP ratio has fallen, albeit modestly, for the first time in 18 years; the current deficit to GDP ratio is the lowest since 1971, falling from 10 per cent to 6.7 per cent between 1993–96; the annual rate of inflation stands at under 2 per cent, an 18-year low.

▶

145

Exhibit 9.1 continued

This year, Italy's deficit is likely to be just above 3 per cent. What happens next year depends on the soon-to-be-approved 1998 budget, along with associated reforms of state pensions. But a L25bn savings package is already agreed in principle between the coalition parties, and the Prodi government is wearing a confident air.

Earlier this year, central bankers and monetary officials floated the idea of a deal which would delay Italy's participation in Emu for 12 to 18 months to ensure a safe, stable launch for the euro comprised of proven 'hard currency' countries.

Italy's turnaround makes this option less likely – unless the German government calculates that the German public still needs time to adjust to the idea of exchanging, in effect, a rock-solid D-Mark for an historically weak lira.

On the other hand, singling out Italy risks triggering a north-south split in the Union.

Source: *The Financial Times*, 19 September 1997.

Italy – while others, the UK being the most apparent, were sceptical about their probable readiness and/or unsure whether they wanted to join in what they considered would be a first wave of entry.

References

Council of the European Union (1997) *Intergovernmental Conference Draft Treaty*. Office for the Official Publications of the European Communities.

European Commission (1994c) *White Paper on Social Policy*. European Commission.

European Commission (1995c) *Third Social Action Programme*. European Commission.

European Commission (1997b) *Amsterdam European Council, 16–17 June, Presidency Conclusions*. SN 150/97. European Commission.

HMSO (1996) *White Paper: A Partnership of Nations*. HMSO.

Additional reading to Part Two

Bright, C. (1995) *The EU: Understanding The Brussels Process*. Wiley.

Pinder J. (1995) *European Community. The Building of a Union*. OPUS.

Part Three

THE EUROPEAN UNION: THE KEY HR ISSUES

In this final Part of the book, we turn to six areas of HR interest which continue to dominate the Union's social agenda as it prepares to enter the new millennium – freedom of movement and labour mobility, gender and racial equality, health and safety at work, vocational education and training, employee participation and involvement in the organisation and, finally, what has arguably become the central issue facing the EU in the late 1990s, unemployment.

The author concludes with some personal reflections on the current state of the European Union and prospects for the future.

10

LABOUR MOBILITY

LEARNING OBJECTIVES

When you have read this chapter, you should be able to understand and explain:

- the factors likely to impact upon decisions concerning labour mobility;
- common barriers to such mobility;
- the initiatives taken within the Union to facilitate mobility;
- the notion of EU citizenship;
- the significance of the Schengen Convention;
- the extent to which mobility occurs and the debate concerning the need for future immigration into the Union.

INTRODUCTION

There are a number of different dimensions to the issue of the freedom with which people within the Union are able to move around, crossing national borders where they wish and living and working where they wish. In this chapter, we are particularly concerned with the process of movement across national borders and consider this from the perspective of people as human resources, engaged in an employment relationship. However, there are other economic, cultural and political dimensions.

The right to move freely within the Union can be viewed as:

1 a fundamental right attached to *citizenship* of the Union;

2 a means through which *cross-cultural development* and a degree of cultural integration may be achieved;

3 a source of *racial* and *ethnic tension* (*see* Chapter 11);

4 essential to the process of *economic integration* and the creation of the single market (*see* Chapter 14), and more narrowly as an important *adjustment mechanism* available to assist the market deal with inefficiencies and unemployment (*see* Chapter 6, social dumping);

5 a threat to national sovereignty and the maintenance of the Union as a union of nation states, since the freedom to move has generated pressures for *the abolition of internal border controls*.

As indicated above, this chapter addresses the issue of freedom of movement as a right, as well as it being a prerequisite of labour mobility. Labour mobility between jobs, occupations, sectors and regions are not the prime concern of this chapter, although inevitably such mobility often accompanies labour mobility between countries.

The chapter begins with some brief explanations of migration decision making and this entails some discussion of the barriers to mobility that may exist within the Union. The relevant Treaty articles regarding freedom of movement, the right of establishment and the notion of Union citizenship are examined. A review of the measures taken at Union level to facilitate freedom of movement follows, including those concerning mutual recognition of qualifications and experience and the issues of border controls, immigration and the position of third-country nationals. We discuss the extent of cross-national mobility in recent years in the context of the measures already taken and then discuss some of the implications for Union policies and the interventions that may be needed in order to achieve the specified objectives.

MIGRATION DECISION MAKING AND BARRIERS TO MOBILITY

Mobility from one country to another has commonly been severely restricted within the EU, the regulation of the activity being a significant potential barrier to mobility. The removal of such restrictions and the provision of an effective right of mobility have been at the centre of much of the EU activity in this area. For the moment, we shall assume that there are no legal barriers to migration and to the migrant working in the destination country.

Standard neo-Classical economic theory tends to seek to explain the process of labour migration in terms of *net advantage*. The assumption is that individuals are rational and capable and that they will act in a manner consistent with their own self-interest. They will therefore decide whether to migrate or not after calculating the net present returns to be derived from the move.

This involves a comparison of the costs associated with mobility and relocation with the present value of the additional returns (discounted) to be derived over the appropriate period of time. For example, labour shortages and/or higher wages in a different labour market may encourage someone to move to that labour market, but only if the additional returns to be derived over a period of years, discounted to present values, outweigh the costs of moving and relocating.

Included in the costs of moving may be costs associated with obtaining information about opportunities in the other labour market; an assumption is made that such information is available. If an individual doesn't know that there are appropriate vacancies and/or can't afford to find out, it is unlikely that mobility will be a possibility. The availability of such information becomes increasingly problematic where the alternative labour market exists across national borders and the information is likely to be available for some occupations and not for others.

It is in this context that mobility is perceived as an *adjustment mechanism*, coping with differential rates of unemployment in different national labour markets. Of course, this applies as much to migrants into the EU, as well as it does to those who migrate within it. In the neo-Classical model, unemployed labour in one market can be attracted into another where there is a labour shortage; in part, this is achieved through differential wage rates and the process of calculating net advantage. Labour migration is thought to be primarily a response to demand pressures (in the host country) rather than to pressures in the country of origin. If this is and remains the case, then given the high levels of unemployment in the Union in the 1990s and the decline in demand for unskilled labour, relatively low levels of inward migration are to be expected (*see* later in this chapter).

For example, after the reunification of Germany, the demand for labour in the construction industry was increased as a result of the decision to rebuild in the East. The labour shortages, allied to the high wages and the rates of unemployment in 'donor' countries, all contributed to an increase in migration into Germany. In this scenario, out-of-work construction workers in the UK were attracted to work in the construction industry in Germany as a result of decisions by the individuals concerning the fact that the net returns from the mobility were likely to outweigh the costs.

The factors associated with such mobility that imply costs are often referred to as *barriers to mobility*. These barriers may or not be overcome as a result of the decision-making processes of individuals, calculating the net advantage of one proposed set of actions against another.

Some of these factors may be relatively easy to quantify – for example, the various constituents of the costs of living in the proposed new location, such as housing, food, transport, education and health care. Indeed, various organisations produce league tables of comparative costs of living in different locations. Weighed against these costs would be the benefits package offered with the job and crucially the length of time over which these benefits would be received. This final component of the calculations is important and tends to explain the inverse relationship that commonly exists between mobility and age: the shorter the length of time that the benefits are to be derived for, the greater does the gross difference in benefits need to be to provide the necessary incentive to mobility. A similar inverse relationship appears to exist between owner-occupancy and labour mobility: the greater the proportion of owner-occupancy, the less likely is it that labour will be mobile between regions, let alone across national borders.

The problems of calculation (and adjustment) become much greater when you begin to consider other dimensions of cost and other potential barriers. Into this latter category fall:

- costs associated with the loss of entitlement to social benefits and protection;
- differences of language and culture;
- non-recognition of qualifications and experience resulting in an inability to practice or a requirement that a period of further training be undertaken; and
- emotional difficulties, such as the costs of separation in families between husband and wife and between parent and child, the loss of social networks, the costs of adjusting to different social norms and conventions, and possibly even the costs associated with exposure to racism and inequality.

These latter variables are likely to be very difficult to quantify and can all be a source of trauma and of post-migration failure.

Elias (1994) points out that the nature of training qualifications will impact upon mobility. For example, company-specific training will render an individual less mobile than training which is in transferable skills. Trade union membership may also act as a disincentive to mobility.

Van den Broeck (1996), in contrast to those who see labour mobility as an important adjustment mechanism in the context of the single market, makes the argument that labour mobility is in fact unnecessary. Classical foreign-trade theory suggests that capital is more mobile than labour and trade is a substitute for labour migration.

EU INITIATIVES

The preceding section provides indicators of the areas in which EU activity might be both necessary and productive, given the objective of enabling mobility.

Tsoukalis (1997, p. 117) summarises the preconditions for effective freedom of movement as:

> . . . not only a question of abolishing frontier controls, restrictive residence permits, and numerous other administrative obstacles for workers and their families. Free movement of labour in the context of mixed economies depends upon a much wider set of conditions . . . including the transferability of social security payments, the mutual recognition of degrees and professional qualifications, and the dissemination of information about jobs. . . .

Early interventions

Recognition that the Community had a role in facilitating mobility was first apparent in the creation of the ESF and in the determination of its role (in the Treaty of Rome 1957, Article 123):

> a European Social Fund is hereby established . . . it shall have the task of rendering the employment of workers easier and increasing their geographical and occupational mobility within the Community.

The article remains much the same today.

The ESF began to operate in 1960 and began to assist mobility through the provision of financial assistance (usually limited to 50 per cent funding by the *principle of additionality*) in respect of the costs of movement and resettlement into areas of the Community in which there were employment opportunities. Migrant workers were one of the early priority areas for the ESF. Many of those who were mobile in the early days were from the South of Italy; they often remained within the borders of Italy since there was no stipulation that the assistance applied only to cross-border mobility.

Recent changes to the ESF mean that the emphasis is now not so much upon assisting with mobility, as upon helping the young and long-term unemployed (*see* Chapter 15).

Regulation 1612/68 and Articles 48 and 49

Further developments followed in 1968 with the adoption of Regulation 1612/68 and Article 48 of the Treaty. The preamble to Regulation 1612/68 states:

> the freedom of movement constitutes a fundamental right of workers and their families; mobility of labour within the Community must be one of the means by which the worker is guaranteed the possibility of improving his living and working conditions and promoting his social advancement . . .

Article 48 specifies in paragraph 2 that:

freedom of movement shall entail the abolition of any discrimination based on nationality between workers of the member states as regards employment, remuneration and other conditions of work and employment.

This is elaborated upon in paragraph 3 and the individual is given the right to:

- accept offers of employment actually made;
- move freely within the territory of the member states for this purpose;
- stay in a member state for the purpose of employment in accordance with the provisions governing the employment of nationals of that state laid down by law;
- remain in the territory of a member state after having been employed in that state.

In summary, the individual has:

1 the right to be mobile in looking for work and accepting offers made;
2 the right not to be discriminated against on the grounds of nationality; and
3 the right to be treated the same as a national of that member state.

There are general exclusions covering the public sector and provision for the right to be limited on grounds relating to national security and public health. There is some evidence that these exclusions have been abused in order to give preference to nationals of the member state; the right not to be discriminated against does not in practice mean that it doesn't happen. The ECJ has been required to adjudicate on a number of complaints that the exclusions were being used inappropriately (Barber, 1996).

One of the most famous cases to test and demonstrate the meaning and relevance of this law was the *Bosman case* (ECJ, December 1995) in which it was established that an individual's right to free movement across national borders within the territories of the Union for the purposes of working or obtaining work was infringed by a football club in Belgium imposing a transfer fee which effectively prevented a player, Bosman, moving at the end of his contract with the Belgian club to a club in France. The Court also stated that the Union of European Football Association (UEFA) limitations upon the number of 'foreign' players that could play in a team in European competition was also against the law that outlawed discrimination on the grounds of nationality.

Article 49 provides the basis for the adoption of Directives in order to facilitate the achievement of the objectives specified in Article 48. Since the Maastricht Treaty on European Union this has to be processed via the new Co-Decision Procedure.

Specifically, Article 49 refers to the adoption of Regulations or Directives to achieve:

- closer cooperation between national employment services;
- abolition of administrative procedures, practices and qualifying periods 'the maintenance of which would form an obstacle to liberalisation of the movement of workers'; and
- the 'setting up of appropriate machinery to bring offers of employment into touch with applications for employment and to facilitate the achievement of a balance between supply and demand in the employment market . . .'.

In November 1994 the Commission established *European Employment Services* (*EURES*) as a means by which this latter objective might be achieved and this is examined in more detail later.

The issue of equal treatment for migrant workers in terms of remuneration and other terms and conditions of work has achieved a degree of prominence in recent years for somewhat different reasons. Concern has been expressed in recipient countries that incoming workers were being employed/contracted at lower rates and on worse terms and conditions than were stipulated by law or collective agreement and thereby undercutting and undermining the position of nationals of that state. This applied to migrants from other member states as well as from countries outside the Union. The latter group is frequently referred to as *third-country nationals* – a term commonly used within the EU to refer to people resident within the Union but not nationals of one of the member states. These concerns have emerged as significant in the context of generally higher levels of unemployment within the Union in the late 1980s and 1990s and have prompted proposals that such undercutting be outlawed. (This issue is considered again later in this chapter in the section on the Posted Workers Directive.)

Who is protected?

The concerns behind the original legislation, embodied in the Treaty as Article 48, were to prevent the exploitation of the migrant worker; now the concerns are more to protect the employment and standards of living of nationals of the recipient member state and also to prevent the further exacerbation of social and racial tensions in those countries.

The Treaty does not define 'worker'; the term has been given a meaning by the ECJ so that it now means (Lasok and Lasok, 1994, p. 436):

a citizen of a member state actually or potentially engaged in an economic activity for wages.

The rights to freedom of movement for the purposes of employment are limited to those who are citizens of a member state; it is up to each of the member states to determine the requirements for qualification as a citizen. It is arguable that this is too narrow and that the right to movement and associated rights ought also to be extended to long-term residents from third countries even though they have not applied for or are not qualified for citizenship of a member state (*see* later in this chapter).

Regulation 1612/68 extends the right of residence of the worker to his spouse and their descendants under the age of 21. This applies irrespective of the nationality of the dependants, so that if workers are citizens of one member state they can move to and work in another member state and their dependants, even if third-country nationals, can accompany and reside with them.

Certain other categories of person have also been provided with rights of movement and residence. Directive 90/364 provides the rights to any member-state national who does not enjoy the rights under another provision of EU law, although there are qualifications to this right of residence which stress the requirement that the individual possesses resources sufficient to prevent him or her becoming a burden on the medical and social security system of the state concerned – to all intents and purposes, in such cases the right of residence is a means-tested right.

Regulation 1612/68 also specifies that the prohibition of discrimination against workers on the grounds of nationality is extended to include such matters as social and tax advantages, the right to join trades unions, collective agreements and their contents, access to vocational training and to housing and its ownership. This same regulation also specifies that the children of a worker (in the context of this legislation a citizen of one of the member states) who are installed with the worker in the host state are entitled to be admitted into the state's educational, apprenticeship and vocational training systems on the same conditions as those applying to nationals of the member state concerned.

Treaty Articles 52 to 66 provide very similar rights of movement and residence to those who are self-employed and to the providers of services including professional services and the services provided by craftsmen.

Social security entitlements and payments

The issues of social security entitlement and the payment of benefits are addressed in Article 51 of the Treaty. The Council is required to adopt such measures as are necessary to provide freedom of movement for workers and specific provision is made for aggregation in respect of acquiring and retaining the right to benefit and calculation of the amount of benefit. It also refers to payment of benefits to people resident in the territories of member states.

The principle of non-discrimination on the grounds of nationality applies in this arena as it does in those above. Regulation 1408/71, Article 3(1) makes this clear and, in effect, this means that the nationals of one member state working and/or resident in another cannot be excluded from both the obligations and benefits of the social security system in the host country. This extends to include employers' contributions, where appropriate. This same regulation clarifies that self-employed persons are included as are the members of workers' families and their survivors.

Regulation 1408/71 also provides that certain benefits can be claimed as of right in all member states; these are referred to as *Community benefits*. These include:

- sickness and maternity benefits;
- unemployment benefits;
- old age benefits;
- family benefits;
- benefits in respect of accidents at work and occupational diseases; and
- death grants.

An example is the entitlement to retention of unemployment benefit. It is obviously important to the potentially mobile unemployed worker that in moving to seek work he or she does not lose entitlement to unemployment benefit. The provisions of the Regulation seek to ensure that in such circumstances the worker is entitled to the payment of a maximum of three months' benefit, while looking for work in another country and not available for work in the country that he or she has left. The Commission has been keen to secure agreement to an extension of this time period beyond the three months that is currently guaranteed and proposed a draft Regulation to that effect in February/March 1996. The benefit would be payable by the member state in which the individual last worked and the additional length of time for which the benefit would be payable would be based upon the least favourable of the two national schemes.

These provisions go much of the way towards removing barriers to mobility in respect of dealing with the danger of losing entitlement to state social security payments and benefits, although they do not address the issue of supplementary schemes and perhaps particularly supplementary pensions – that is, pension schemes that are additional to the basic state schemes and to which the individual and /or his or her employer contribute. In some countries there are state-run supplementary schemes; in some the trade union movement is a major actor; however, many are provided through the private-sector insurance industry. There are a plethora of different types of scheme but, in the main, they provide a variable entitlement to additional pension payments linked to contributions and the investment returns, earnings, the length of the contribution period and/or employment or some mix of these variables. A relatively common feature of these supplementary schemes is that the value of the benefits to which an individual becomes entitled increases with the length of contributory period or employment. The non-transportability of the entitlement is a potentially significant barrier to mobility to those who have built up substantial entitlement.

The Commission has shown itself sensitive to this and related problems and in the Third Social Action Programme covering the period 1995 to 1998 proposed action in the form of a Draft Directive. In January 1996, the Commission created a working group, under the chair of Simone Weil, a former President of the EP, to examine the legal, practical and administrative problems confronting people who wish to exercise their rights to move and work within the Union. One of the specific tasks was to address the means by which further labour mobility might be encouraged by provisions enhancing the mobility/transferability of supplementary pensions.

The initial intention was to introduce a Directive that would provide individuals with the right to transport their current scheme across national borders within the Union or transfer their entitlement into another scheme in the destination country. Other initial proposals sought to deal with known difficulties; for example, it was suggested that:

- people working abroad temporarily should be able to continue to contribute into a scheme in the 'home' country;
- where it was necessary to freeze the entitlement in a scheme, there should be a legal requirement that the frozen values be index-linked; and
- where it became necessary for a transfer value to be calculated, there should be some regulation of the means by which the calculation is made so as to ensure fairness to the contributor.

This would apply to the self-employed and providers of services and not only to employees.

The difficulties associated with the great variety of schemes and associated tax arrangements make it likely that the process of forming proposals that prove acceptable and workable may be lengthy.

Citizenship of the Union

The agreements at Maastricht resulted in the creation of the phenomonen of 'the citizenship of the Union'. Part 2 of the EC Treaty now states in Article 8 that 'Citizenship of the Union is established'. It goes on to state in the next paragraphs that all persons holding the nationality of one of the member states shall be a citizen and as such they shall enjoy a number of rights including:

the right to move and reside freely within the territory of the member states.

The draft Treaty revisions, agreed at Amsterdam in 1997, amend Article 8 so that it will read:

> Citizenship of the Union is hereby established. Every person holding the nationality of a member state shall be a citizen of the Union. Citizenship of the Union shall complement and not replace national citizenship.

The last sentence is new. As noted earlier, nationality is still a matter for individual member states and they have different regulations and indeed confront different problems.

Article 8b deals with rights of citizens of the Union residing in a member state of which they are not nationals to vote and stand as candidates in both municipal elections (given effect by Directive 94/80, to be implemented by January 1996) and in elections for members of the EP under the same conditions as apply to nationals of that member state. Proposals to facilitate individuals exercising these rights are subject to unanimity within the Council.

The right to citizenship and the rights to freedom of movement and residence referred to in this Article are not linked to the issue of work, whether it be as an employee, self-employed or as a provider of services.

Depending on how the term 'freely' is interpreted in this context, it is arguable that the implementation of these rights must be accompanied by the abolition of restrictive controls on the passage of individuals across internal national boundaries.

There is a larger political dimension to such rights in that if citizenship of the Union were to become a meaningful reality and if this were to be accompanied by the abolition of internal frontier controls between all of the member states, questions would inevitably be raised about the relevance and validity of the maintenance of the Union as a Union of individual and sovereign member states and about the potential longevity of such a Union.

Lasok and Lasok (1994, p. 435) refer to this Part 2 of the Treaty (Articles 8 to 8(e)) and comment that the political objective is to create a greater cohesion of the peoples of the Union through the elimination of barriers to migration and the promotion of citizenship.

Prior to the Treaty of European Union agreed at Maastricht, the decision of the member states to create a single market by the end of 1992, embodied in the Single European Act, had placed emphasis upon the issue of internal frontiers. In Article 13 of the SEA, the internal market is described as:

> an area without internal frontiers in which the free movement of goods, persons, services and capital is ensured. . . .

This phrase is repeated in the EC Treaty as part of Article 7a.

One of the issues that the Treaty does not deal with is the conditions under which the freedom to move across national borders to work or look for work may be extended to those who are legally resident in a particular member state but do not have nationality and are therefore not citizens of the Union (third-country nationals). There have been a number of attempts to address this issue. One proposal was to create a common EU-visa for non-EU nationals which would then enable them to travel throughout the Union, even though they would probably still require a work permit. However, there is considerable doubt as to the viability of the EU member states agreeing a common list of countries whose members would need such a visa (*see* the difficulties agreeing and implementing the Schengen Convention in the next section).

O'Leary (1996) is critical of the notion of EU citizenship as it exists at the moment. She feels that long-term residence ought to be a qualification for EU citizenship, even where the individual is not a national or citizen of one of the member states, and she is also critical of the means testing of the right to residence afforded to citizens that are not engaged in economic activity – a provision which she suggests may well be incompatible with the right to equality of treatment also afforded to citizens.

The Social Policy Agreement (*see* Chapter 6) provides in Article 2 for measures to be taken, in accordance with the objectives specified in Article 1 (of SPASP), regarding:

conditions of employment for third-country nationals legally residing in Community territory.

Such measures have to be adopted unanimously.

The Amsterdam IGC agreement to take SPASP into the Treaty means that these provisions of the SPASP will become Article 118(3) of the EC Treaty. At the time of writing, the wording of the provision has not been changed by the Amsterdam agreement and action remains subject to unanimity. However, as yet, the citizenship of resident third-country nationals has not been addressed.

Schengen Convention

Awareness of the importance of the abolition of internal border controls in the context of seeking to create an internal market and the disincentive effect these controls might have for labour mobility had prompted some of the member states – Germany, France and the Benelux countries (Luxembourg, Holland and Belgium) – to enter into an agreement in 1985 known as *the Schengen Convention* which initially provided that all internal border controls between them would be abolished with effect from 1990. The Convention also included agreement on an increase in cooperation between the police forces of the members and for a strengthening of the external borders. Spain and Portugal joined at a relatively early stage, compared to some of the others, and these seven countries constitute the core *Schengen Area*.

The original timescale proved to be overly optimistic and the arrangement only came into force between Belgium, Luxembourg, Germany, Holland, Spain and Portugal in March 1995. In 1996, there were still problems within and between the core Schengen members, with France being particularly reluctant to give up all passport and identity checks on people crossing its borders with Holland, Belgium and Luxembourg, although it had agreed to do so in respect of its borders with Germany and Spain.

There have been numerous difficulties and problems associated with the implementation of this agreement and its extension to include the other member states. Indeed, there were allegations that, after implementation by the core countries, controls between Schengen and non-Schengen member states became tighter. By the middle of 1996, Greece, Italy and Austria had signed the agreements but had not implemented the requirements and Denmark, Sweden and Finland had indicated their intention to cooperate but were restricting themselves to 'observer' for the time being. When Austria signed in April 1995, it was granted a two-year 'grace' period before it had to remove internal border checks. This was to give it time to develop the necessary mechanisms for effectively controlling the 1400 kilometres of borders that it shares with five non-EU countries.

Concerns regarding the Convention

The UK and Ireland have shown little intention of agreeing to the arrangements and abolishing border controls between themselves and the other member states. The two countries argue a special case because of their common travel area agreement and given the history of terrorism and their island status. The main political parties in the UK are more or less united in their opposition to the proposal that they relax their vigilance and abolish existing controls.

In the main the many reservations that individual countries have expressed have been concerned with matters largely unrelated to the creation of a single market, the rights of member-state nationals to be able to move freely, and the encouragement of labour mobility.

The dominant concerns have been with issues of sovereignty, extradition arrangements, the protection of national systems, individual and mutual arrangements with particular third countries, and with 'law and order' issues – drug trafficking, international terrorism and the freedom of movement that such arrangements would afford illegal and/or third-country nationals. This has encouraged some countries to be critical of others' arrangements for patrolling and enforcing their external borders. The Schengen core countries have agreed to cooperate on entry requirements for third-country nationals and there has been progress towards the development of a Union-wide common list of almost 100 countries whose citizens will require a visa to enter the Union.

There have also been considerable problems with the development and implementation of specific computerised information systems designed to enable the sharing of information on both people and property between the police forces of the member states.

Article 100a(2) of the Treaty appears to maintain the requirement of unanimity in respect of measures dealing with the free movement of people – as opposed to the free movement of workers or in the context of the freedom of establishment and the provision of services.

The Amsterdam IGC agreements

As indicated above, the Schengen Convention and its various ramifications were central to the IGC that was concluded at Amsterdam in June 1997. Eventually, accommodations were reached between the various parties which resulted in a new Title in the EC Treaty entitled *Free movement of persons, asylum and immigration*.

This acknowledged that both the UK and Ireland were unwilling to agree to the removal of border controls between themselves and other member states and they were similarly unwilling to give up their autonomy with respect to issues of immigration and asylum. Two Protocols (*X and Y*) were agreed and annexed to the Treaty which spelt out the position of the parties. The Title was not to apply to these two countries and with reference to the UK:

> The UK shall be entitled, notwithstanding Article 7a of the Treaty establishing the European Community, any other provision of this Treaty or of the Treaty of European Union, any measure . . . to exercise at its frontiers with other Member States such controls on persons seeking to enter the UK as it may consider necessary for the purpose . . .

This is to apply to citizens of other member states as well as to those seeking entry from other countries. The other member states retained the right to:

> exercise at their frontiers or at any point of entry into their territory such controls on persons seeking to enter their territory from the UK. (*Protocol X*)

This exclusion of both the UK and Ireland from the mainstream provisions of the new Title do not affect persons' rights to free movement, residence and the right to work that have been referred to above; it is a question of retaining controls and checks upon movement across certain borders. Nevertheless, it may be surmised that the exercising of these rights to movement may be affected by the retention of these border checks and controls.

These two countries also agreed to give up their rights to participate in the adoption procedures in respect of actions taken within the context of the new Title.

Special arrangements were also agreed with respect to the position and concerns of Denmark (*Protocol Z*).

The new(draft) Title on free movement specifies in Article A the intention of the Council to adopt within a period of five years from the entry into force of the Treaty

> measures aimed at ensuring the free movement of persons in accordance with Article 7a . . .

and in Article B the Council agrees (unanimity) within a period of five years as above to adopt:

> measures with a view to ensuring, in compliance with Article 7a, the absence of any controls on persons, be they citizens of the Union or nationals of third countries, when crossing internal borders . . .

and

> measures setting out the conditions under which the nationals of third countries shall have the freedom to travel within the territory of the member states during a period of no more than three months.

Article C, paragraph 4 requires that the Council adopt measures which define the rights and conditions under which nationals of third countries who are legally resident in one member state may reside in other member states.

EURES

One of the provisions of Article 49 of the Treaty refers to the establishment of machinery to bring employment opportunities and applicants closer together – *EURES*, a computerised transnational employment agency, was established in November 1994 as an attempt to provide the kind of machinery to which the Article refers. At the outset, the service was jointly funded by the Commission and the respective national public employment services. Prior to this there had been a system known as *SEDOC* – the Systeme Européan de Diffusion des Offres et Demandes D'emploi en Compensation. EURES replaces the old system and this was achieved through Regulation 2434/92 amending Part II of Regulation 1612/68.

The service covers all the countries within the *European Economic Area* (EEA) which comprises the member states of the Union and Norway and Iceland. In the main, it is employers who advertise vacancies free through the system, although there are some proposals to enable individual applicants to effectively advertise themselves through the network.

To some extent the scheme is an attempt to treat the European labour market as an integrated and single entity.

At the end of the first year of operation, the databank comprised some 5000 vacancies and over 30 000 applications had been handled and in excess of 5500 placements made. In addition to the job vacancy databank, there is also one which provides information for the applicant on living and working conditions in the country concerned.

There are proposals to develop further the system's information on the equivalence and comparability of qualifications, education and training within the Union and also to develop information on regional labour markets.

The Posted Workers proposals and Directives

Posted workers are people who are temporarily posted, seconded or subcontracted by their employers or a temporary work agency to provide services in another member state. There are proposals under consideration that try and ensure that such temporary assignments and periods of work are not used by employers within the destination member state as a means of gaining a competitive advantage over those employing home-based labour, by undercutting the costs of 'home-based' labour – yet another form of social dumping. It is also argued that the proposals will prevent the exploitation of labour from the relatively low-wage member states.

In the majority of member states, main terms and conditions of employment are regulated either by law or collective agreement. However, these posted workers are generally not covered by these arrangements since their place of work or employer is located in another country; they are subject to the rules that apply in the country of their employment, rather than those of the country to which they are temporarily assigned or posted. The provisions regarding the right to work in another country and to not be discriminated against on the grounds of nationality do not apply in these circumstances.

It can, of course, be argued that placing restrictions on this practice of temporary posting on parent country terms and conditions limits the role of market forces, and in particular of labour mobility as an adjustment mechanism between geographically separate markets, and therefore that they hamper efforts to enhance employment within the EU. Opponents of the proposals argue for deregulation of the markets rather than what they perceive as protective efforts to reinforce existing regulations. Nevertheless, the governments and Social Partners in the host countries view the practice as being against the interests of their citizens and, understandably, want to regulate and restrict it.

It is intriguing that given the amount of time and effort put into encouraging labour mobility, a set of proposals has been drawn up that effectively seek to discourage it. The original proposals – published as a draft Directive (COM (91) 230) and subsequently revised on a number of occasions as the many parties have sought consensus – were that national regulations and compulsory collective agreements should apply to these categories of workers regarding:

- maximum daily and weekly hours of work;
- minimum rates of pay and allowances;
- minimum paid annual leave;
- health and safety protection;
- discrimination and protection of vulnerable groups; and
- temporary work.

It was always intended that the Directive would not apply to mobile employees, such as those in the transport industry.

Efforts were made to agree on an initial period to which the provisions would not apply. The Mediterranean members, Ireland and the UK – arguably, the countries that provide the supply of such mobile workers – and the Commission tended to favour a period of up to 3 or 4 months. France, Germany and the Benelux countries as the main recipient countries tended to favour shorter periods. France and Belgium preferred no period of relief from the regulations – the zero option – and this is favoured by Germany in respect of its construction industry, but not for other sectors.

These proposals are subject to QMV but adoption proved very difficult, nevertheless.

Directive (96/7/EC) was adopted in December 1996 and is to be implemented by December 1999. The Directive is to apply to undertakings providing services which post workers temporarily to another member state where they don't have a contract of employment. The aims of the Directive are stated to be:

- to facilitate the free movement of both personnel and services;
- to remove uncertainty about the legal regime governing the working conditions of posted workers;
- to prevent unfair competition that might exist if posted workers are not governed by the same regime as other workers in the host country.

The main requirement of the Directive is that posted workers should be covered by the same legislation (as in some cases collective agreements or arbitration awards) determining terms and conditions of employment in the host country as are other workers in that host country.

Member states were given the option to exclude from implementation in their own country those postings, of less than one month's duration, but only in respect of minimum rates of pay and holidays. Other terms and conditions covered by the Directive, such as health and safety at work and provisions relating to non-discrimination would apply in respect of all postings.

Mutual recognition of qualifications

It was recognised early on that mobility between the member states for the purposes of work, including the provision of services of a professional nature, was likely to be significantly affected by the extent to which the qualifications and experience gained in one country were effectively transportable to another. The absence of mechanisms ensuring mutual recognition and comparability was potentially disastrous for such mobility.

Article 49 provides a basis for the removal of qualifying restrictions upon workers and Article 57(1) of the Treaty makes provision for action in respect of the self-employed, including the professions:

> In order to make it easier for persons to take up and pursue activities as self-employed persons, the Council shall . . . issue directives for the mutual recognition of diplomas, certificates and other evidence of formal qualifications.

Since the revisions to the Treaty at Maastricht, action in both cases is to be taken via the Co-Decision Procedure, Articles 49(2) and 57(2).

Over the years attitudes regarding this issue have changed. In the early years, the emphasis was upon agreeing, one by one, detailed comparabilities and equivalents within a particular occupation or professional field and issuing individual Directives for each one. As a result, between 1964 and 1986 Directives were adopted that covered individual sectors and occupations, including wholesale trade, food manufacturing, retail, insurance, hairdressing, dentists, pharmacists, vets, architects, nurses, midwives, general practition-ers. Rainbird (1993, p. 194) comments that the architectural agreement took some 17 years to conclude.

Furthermore, in the 1980s, *CEDEFOP* – the European Centre for the Development of Vocational Training – spent a great deal of time trying to compare jobs and qualifications in the skilled occupations and across the Union, the intention being that lists would be devised of job content and skill levels so that workers in one country would be able to demonstrate that their experience in a particular trade or job in their home country was equivalent to a particular skill level and/or job in another. Again the immensely time-consuming nature of this activity meant that very little was actually achieved from the investment.

In more recent times, and partially because of the difficulties in reaching agreement on the detail, the direction has changed and the institutions have tried to agree on equivalence between qualifications and training on the basis of time spent in acquiring the degree or professional diploma. This latter approach was given impetus by the Single European Act agreement to create a single market, allied to an awareness that continuing with the old approach was simply going to take far too much time.

The first Directive resulting from the new approach was adopted in 1989 and was con-cerned with the *Mutual Recognition of Professional Qualifications* (89/48). It was concerned to achieve mutual recognition of qualifications in regulated professions where those qualifications – higher education diplomas, certificates and degrees – were awarded on completion of professional education and training of at least three years' duration. In this context, a regulated profession referred to one regulated by the state or by a profes-sional body. Possession of such a qualification means that it should be accepted in other member states as evidence of ability to practise, and in the main should be sufficient to enable the possessor to practise. There are certain circumstances under which the individ-ual may be asked to undertake a period of supervised practice or to sit a test. This Directive, and to a lesser extent the Directive described below, imply a measure of com-parability between the educational standards in the member states. The member states reserve to themselves the right to require standards of personal conduct and character in addition to the educational/professional qualification.

A second general Directive on the *Mutual Recognition of Vocational Qualifications* (92/51) was adopted in 1992 and sought to achieve a similar state of mutual recognition for regulated vocational qualifications that were obtained after a period of post-secondary school study, lasting less than three years. If the vocation was not regulated, then evidence of two years' experience would be required.

Further proposals have been made since these two Directives, one of which sought to extend the two existing general directives to cover those occupations not covered by them and to give those with practical experience as well as paper qualifications the opportunity to demonstrate their competence and devise a mechanism by which this could then be recognised in other member states.

These proposals were initiated early in 1996 as a draft Directive (COM (96) 22). This had been trailored in the Third Social Action Programme to cover the period 1995 to 1997. At approximately the same time, the Commission began its *Simpler Legislation for the Single Market* (SLIM) initiative and, as part of the initiative, targeted for repeal some 35 Directives, dating from the 1960s and 1970s, regarding the detailed comparabilities within individual sectors and professions which were described on page 162.

Prior to this, a draft Directive on the Rights of Establishment of Foreign Lawyers (COM

(94) 572) had been proposed which sought to provide the right for foreign lawyers to gain automatic entry into the host country's profession – not just for their qualifications to be recognised, as is the current situation – without aptitude tests (a means by which freedom of movement and establishment can be frustrated). Other provisions were concerned to make joint practice easier. A common position on this was reached in the Council in May 1997.

Summary of EU support for labour mobility

The EU has made considerable efforts to counter the various barriers to labour mobility and satisfy the preconditions for freedom of movement that were identified at the outset:

- Fundamental rights to move and reside have been established.
- Despite many problems and only partial support a border check free zone or area has been created within the Union.
- Funding is sometimes available to assist with retraining and relocation.
- Measures have been taken to remove and reduce the administrative and other obstacles.
- Measures have been taken to protect and preserve rights to basic state social security benefits and entitlements.
- An information scheme has been established in tandem with a European-wide computerised databank of vacancies.
- Considerable efforts have been made to facilitate the mutual recognition of qualifications and experience and the Right of Establishment.

Often those wishing to facilitate mobility have found themselves up against others who see such mobility as a threat:

- to existing wage levels, terms and conditions and levels of employment which therefore need regulating and protecting; and/or
- to the existing ethnic and racial mix in society.

Alternatively, they have found themselves opposed by the argument that regulation is unnecessary – for example, the regulation of wages and hours of work and the granting of rights such as the right not to be discriminated against on the grounds of nationality – and that it acts as a source of inefficiency and failure in the market(s). The market should be allowed to work freely with individuals making rational responses to the circumstances pertaining in the markets. Depending on individuals' calculation of net advantage, mobility may be their response. Artificial barriers may be removed, but otherwise governments and the EU should not intervene.

In the next section we briefly examine the evidence that exists of the extent to which labour mobility appears to occur within the Union.

THE EVIDENCE OF LABOUR MOBILITY WITHIN THE EU

In 1996 the European Foundation for the Improvement of Living and Working Conditions (EFILWC) suggested that it was possible to divide the working population of the Union into five categories in terms of legal status (EFILWC, 1996d):

1 citizens living and working within their own country;

2 citizens of one member state working and living in another;

3 third-country nationals with full rights of residency and who work in one of the member states;

4 third-country nationals with leave to stay for a fixed period of time and with a revocable work permit; and

5 undocumented or illegals.

In the main, the measures and initiatives taken by the Union have been oriented towards the rights and abilities of citizens of one of the member states and in many respects the relative position of those who do not have such citizenship – categories 3,4, and 5 above – has been worsened. However, as noted earlier in this chapter, there is now specific provision within the Social Policy Agreement (to be included in the revised Treaty post-Amsterdam) for measures to be adopted unanimously to address issues associated with the conditions of employment of third-country nationals who are legally in residence.

Where people are in the Union illegally or temporarily and without the right to work, but with a need to earn money to live, there exists inevitably a group that is ripe for exploitation in the labour market, especially that sector of the market that exists outside the law.

Intra-Union mobility

Supporters of the Union's efforts to create a single market and remove barriers to the mobility of labour would no doubt like to point to evidence of enhanced and substantial internal mobility, subsequent to the implementation of the measures taken and the creation of the single market. However, there is relatively little evidence to substantiate such an impact. For example, it has been estimated that between the implementation in 1991 of the Directive on the Mutual Recognition of Professional Qualifications and 1994, at least 11 000 professional workers moved to practise their profession in another member state – 6000 of whom were from the UK (*IPD Update*, March 1996).

The vast majority of people in the labour market are geographically very static, with relatively little movement between regions within the same country and even less crossing of national borders. Rainbird (1993) quotes Bertrand (1991, p. 5):

> many workers are barely mobile beyond their local labour markets and are even less likely to be mobile beyond national borders.

Adnett (1996, p. 154) makes a similar point and comments that given the scale and persistence over time of the regional and international differences in GDP and unemployment rates:

> flows of workers between member states of the EU are surprisingly low and have been falling since the 1970s.

He quotes Commission (1993a) evidence which estimated the net degree of internal movement at approximately 300 000 per year – 0.1 per cent of the total EU population. Only Belgium and Luxembourg had more than 3 per cent of their population of working age that were nationals from another member state.

In the early 1990s, the most popular destination countries for internal EU international migrants were Germany and the UK. Ireland was notable as an exception from the norm with an exodus of labour equivalent to approximately 1 per cent of its population; the suspicion is that much of this exodus is to the UK.

In its 1996 report, *The Demographic Situation in the European Union 1995*, the Commission comments that mobility between the member states appears to have stabilised at relatively low levels (European Commission, 1996b). Overall the Commission has estimated that there may be as many as five million EU citizens that live in another member state (*European Report* 2126, 24 April 1996).

Both the pattern and the extent of mobility have changed over the years. In the 1950s and 1960s there was a considerable amount of internal mobility in terms of a net outflow from the South (much of it from and within Italy) to the North, both within and between the countries that then constituted the Community. Straubhaar (1988) has calculated that at the beginning of the 1960s intra-EC labour flows accounted for approximately 60 per cent of total labour flows within the Community; by the beginning of the 1970s this proportion had fallen to about 20 per cent. Since then the decline of intra-EU flows or mobility as a proportion of the total has apparently continued. The countries that in those days were net sources of internally mobile labour are now often recipients of labour from elsewhere.

Adnett (1996, p. 157) comments that the simple competitive models do not explain the low rates of migration both between regions within the same country and between member states. In other words, the degree of difference between wage rates, rates of unemployment and GDP in the various national labour markets would generally lead one to expect higher rates of mobility functioning as an adjustment mechanism and contributing to the kind of convergence that these competitive models tend to predict. In addition to imperfections in the market – due to the cost and quality of information on job vacancies – and associated matters relating to housing and living costs and various other institutional constraints, Adnett identifies cultural, social and language barriers as major contributors to this low level of international migration.

Generally those who are mobile tend to be the younger, better educated and qualified males, sometimes with sector-specific skills which are in demand. The other major category is comprised of those who are unemployed and move into unskilled manual jobs, increasingly in the service sector, where linguistic difficulties are likely to be less of a problem. There is evidence of a greater propensity for this mobility to be of a temporary nature with an increasing tendency for international commuting within the EU. In addition, there is an increasing mobility among students, encouraged by a number of official schemes (*see* Chapter 13).

Immigration

Tsoukalis (1997, p. 119) quotes official sources indicating that in 1992 there were approximately 10 million registered foreign residents within the EU, many of which were in Germany and of Turkish origin. It was estimated that the number of Turks resident in the EEA at the beginning of 1992 was somewhere close to 2.6 million. At the same time, the resident immigrant population in Germany was close to 3.7 million (*source*: Eurostat). Total EU population at that time was 344 million; by 1995, with the addition of the three new member states, the total EU population was approximately 372 million (European Commission, 1996b).

Salt (1996) suggests that the figures might be higher than this and concludes that there may have been as many as 16.9 million foreign nationals resident in the EU at the beginning of 1993 and that almost 5.5 million of these were nationals of other member states.

Honekopp (1996) presents a statistical analysis of new and old migration patterns into Germany and makes the point that much of the immigration into Germany since 1989 has been from Eastern Europe and has been of displaced Germans in the countries that were part of the Communist bloc prior to the collapse of the Soviet Empire.

The main countries of origin of new Europeans (those becoming nationals of one of the member states) between 1990 and 1993 were Turkey, the former Yugoslavia and Morocco. For new Europeans, the most popular destinations appear to have been France and the UK, with 233 000 and 218 000 respectively becoming nationals of those countries (*European Report* 2082, 8 November 1995).

The Commission (1996) estimates that in the period between 1990 and 1994 the rate of net immigration into the Union averaged over one million per year, compared with an average rate in the 1970s of approximately 300 000, and net emigration at the beginning of the 1980s. The political upheavals in the former Communist bloc countries were in large measure responsible for the increased immigration in the 1990s. The rate for the early 1990s is not expected to continue; in its estimates for the future demographic scenario within the Union, the Commission takes a 'medium' estimate of net immigration at 525 000 per year. However, the continuation of political difficulties in bordering countries – such as those in Albania in 1997 – might encourage a more cautious conclusion. In this demographic study, the point is made that the early-1990s rate of immigration has not had a significant effect upon the proportion of foreigners in the workforce which has remained steady over a long period. This can be attributed to the controlled immigration of workers in the 1970s having given way to the immigration of dependants of those already located within the Union.

This study also highlights the role that immigration may be required to play to combat the inevitable ageing of the Union labour force and population between the mid-1990s and 2025.

Central and Eastern Europe and North Africa look set to continue to be the main providers of immigrants into the EU over the next few years, with the exodus from Albania into Italy and other bordering EU member states in 1997 providing another example of the process begun with the demise of the Soviet Empire at the end of the 1980s – initially from the East to the West within Germany, and then from Yugoslavia. Today Italy, France and Spain tend to be the destination for migrants from the Maghreb countries of Tunisia, Morocco and Algeria, and Germany tends to be the favoured destination of those from Eastern and Central Europe and Turkey.

The UK

Figures for the UK in 1992 – compiled by both the Commission and the Office of Population Censuses and Surveys in the UK – show an outflow of approximately 227 000 people leaving the UK, of which approximately 150 000 were natives, compared with a total inflow from all sources of 216 000. Indications are that the rate of outflow to EU countries from the UK was running at about 58 000 per year in the early 1990s, Germany, France and Ireland being the popular destinations. (*The Guardian*, 1995)

CONCLUSIONS

Our discussion of the efforts made to enable and encourage the freedom of movement of labour within the Union leads us to a number of conclusions.

It is important that we remember that there are a number of dimensions to this issue. The motives and considerations are not solely economic; they are also political, social and cultural. Related to the decision to create a single market and the importance of freedom of movement to the achievement of that objective are also concerns about:

- regional imbalance;
- internal boundaries, law and order and national sovereignty;
- individual freedoms and citizenship of the Union;
- culture shock and adaptation;
- social upheaval and racism; and
- in the much longer term, concerns about the effects of demographic ageing and the extent to which considerable net immigration might be an appropriate response.

The evidence suggests that the level of intra-EU mobility between member states is very low and relatively stable, the trend having been one of decline over the last couple of decades. Labour is clearly much less mobile than capital, goods and services. There is some evidence that efforts at facilitating mobility through the mutual recognition of qualifications (only partially tackled so far), and the recent reform and improvement of the employment information services may be having a beneficial effect but, in both cases, the numbers involved are very small. Those that move are the young, enterprising and skilled; the relatively low level of movement that does occur tends to be either between the more prosperous nations or from poorer to richer. The evidence does appear to confirm that labour mobility is responsive to demand factors in the host country labour market.

There appears to be an increase in the frequency of international commuting and temporary mobility between member states. However, there remain considerable barriers to enhanced mobility of labour, including:

- language;
- social, cultural and affective ties, and concerns about the welcome that may be afforded the immigrant;
- a need to increase the mobility of occupational pensions as well as ensuring the full range of social security, health and social protections;
- the non-transportability of much work experience and the more practical qualifications; and
- the ageing of the working population which also tends to mitigate against increased levels of labour mobility, although the levels of mobility in the non-active and particularly the retired population may increase.

It seems reasonably clear that regional imbalances are not likely to be resolved through the market mechanism and labour mobility. The levels of mobility that one would expect given the differentials between regions and countries in terms of relative wage rates and levels of unemployment have not materialised. There is some evidence that labour is more sensitive to relative wage differentials than unemployment but, in addition to all the other barriers to mobility, Union labour markets are regulated and it is arguably unrealistic to expect them to generate the mobility necessary to rectify regional imbalances. We will have to wait and see whether enlargement of the Union, which is probably five years or so away, leads to a greater degree of intra-Union mobility.

There are question marks regarding the extent to which greater labour mobility is necessary given that capital is so much more mobile. There are certainly doubts about the extent to which it is genuinely desired by the peoples and governments of the Union, as evidenced by the motives and concerns revealed by some of the debates about the removal of frontier controls and the Posted Workers Directive. If mobility is to be significantly enhanced, however, then the barriers referred to above must be addressed.

Some of these barriers, such as the transportability of supplementary pensions, are being broken down. Of the others, and for reasons over and above the issue of labour mobility, concerted and further efforts should be made in the following areas:

1 *To combat racism and bigotry and enhance the understanding of different societies, their traditions and cultures.* The new Article 6a proposed at the Amsterdam Summit which provides the Council, acting unanimously, with the power to take:

> appropriate action to combat discrimination based on sex, racial or ethnic origin, religion or belief, disability, age or sexual orientation

may in the longer term help to improve this. It may also be beneficial to relax the nationality criteria that are currently the basis for attaining Union citizenship.

2 *To devise mechanisms whereby those with skills and experience can have them certified and thereby made more transportable.*

3 *To develop EU-wide schemes of vocational education and training resulting in EU-wide qualifications.* The National Vocational Qualification (NVQ) with verification in the workplace may provide an indication of the direction to be followed, even though this will meet opposition from others with traditions placing much greater emphasis upon the acquisition of qualifications via the mechanism of the written test. Any such scheme should contain an emphasis upon transferable skills, given that these are arguably the ones most consistent with the development of a high-skill, high-technology economy.

Finally, the ageing of the population and the workforce implies that a much larger level of immigration may be necessary from outside the Union in the first two decades of the twenty-first century, if living standards and levels of social protection and services are to be maintained within the EU. Immigration may increase relatively naturally, irrespective of the needs of the EU economy, if political upheaval in other parts of Europe and Africa continues. Nevertheless, it is unlikely that these levels will come anywhere near the levels necessary to compensate for the decline in the active population.

References

Adnett, N. (1996) *European Labour Markets: analysis and policy.* Longman.

Barber, L. (1996) 'Court rules on EU jobs barriers', *Financial Times*, 3 July.

Bertrand, O. (1991) 'Comparing Skills and Qualifications in Europe', in Hantrais, L. *et al Education, Training and Labour Markets in Europe: Cross-national Research Papers No. 4.* University of Aston.

Council of the European Union (1997) *Intergovernmental Conference Draft Treaty.* Office for Official Publications of the European Communities.

Elias, P. (1994) 'Job-related training, trade union membership and labour mobility: a longitudinal study', *Oxford Economic Papers,* 46(4), 563–78.

European Commission (1993a) *Employment in Europe 1993.* European Commission.

European Commission (1996b) *The Demographic situation in the European Union 1995.* European Commission.

European Foundation for the Improvement of Living and Working Conditions (1996d) *Preventing Racism at the Workplace – A Summary.*

European Report, 2082, 8 Nov 1995, European Commission.

European Report, 2126, 24 April 1996, European Commission.

The Guardian (1995) Pilkington, E. and George, R. 'Britons Look Abroad for Feelgood Factor', 9 May.

Honekopp, E. (1996) 'Old and new labour migration to Germany from Eastern Europe', in Corry, D. (ed) *Economics and European Union Migration Policy.* IPPR.

IPD Update, March 1996, p. 16.

Lasok, D., and Lasok, K.P.E. (1994) *Law and Institutions of the European Union* (6th edn). Butterworths.

O' Leary, S. (1996) *European Union Citizenship. The Options for Reform.* IPPR.

Rainbird, H. (1993) 'Vocational Education and Training', in Gold, M. (ed) *The Social Dimension: Employment Policy in the European Community.* Macmillan.

Salt, J. (1996) 'Economic developments within the EU: the role of population movements', in Corry, D. (ed) *Economics and European Union Migration Policy.* IPPR.

Straubhaar, T. (1988) 'International Labour Migration Within a Common Market: Some Aspects of EC Experience', *Journal of Common Market Studies,* September.

Tsoukalis, L. (1997) *The New European Economy Revisited* (3rd edn). Oxford University Press.

Van den Broeck, J. (1996) *The Economics of Labour Migration.* Edward Elgar.

Additional reading

Corry, D. (ed) (1996) *Economics and European Union Migration Policy.* IPPR.

Dudley, J.W. (1993) *1993 and Beyond* (3rd edn). Kogan Page.

Tapinos, G. (1994) 'Regional economic integration and its effects on employment and migration', *Migration and Development – New Partnerships for Co-operation,* OECD.

11

EQUALITY

LEARNING OBJECTIVES

When you have read this chapter, you should be able to understand and explain:

- the relevance of culture and socialisation to issues of gender or racial stereotypes and discrimination;
- the patterns of employment, participation and pay differentials between men and women and a number of the more common explanations;
- the main policy implications and choices available to deal with these differences;
- the extent and nature of the EU initiatives in the arena of gender equality;
- explanations of racial inequality and discrimination;
- the reasons for the lack of EU action in combating racial discrimination and xenophobia;
- recent developments and the reasons why the outlook may now be brighter.

INTRODUCTION

This chapter is concerned with the issue of equality between people in the context of labour markets and employment behaviour and practice – in particular equality between the sexes/genders and equality on the grounds of race or ethnic origin. In the main we will be examining issues relating to equality of opportunity, treatment and outcome.

The differences between direct and indirect discrimination will be considered, as will the various forms of labour market discrimination. The significance of socialisation, value systems and culture is covered.

We go on to examine female participation in the labour force and work patterns, rates of pay, explanations of the differences and inequalities identified and some of the policy implications. We then consider in some detail the initiatives taken within the EU to combat gender discrimination.

Until recently, the EU has shown relatively little concern about inequality and discrimination on racial and ethnic grounds and, as a result, most of this chapter is concerned with gender as opposed to racial issues and differences. Discrimination on the grounds of race or ethnic origin is discussed in a separate section.

Finally, we judge the extent to which EU-level initiatives appear to have impacted upon the inequalities and discrimination identified and consider what may still be necessary, if the objective is to be achieved, given that some initiatives may also have counter-productive consequences.

THE LANGUAGE OF EQUALITY

It is important at this point to define some of the terms that are used when discussing equality. It is possible to distinguish three dimensions of equality – *opportunity*, *treatment* and *outcome* – and some example may serve to illustrate this:

- *Equality of opportunity* may encompass pre-work experience and circumstance as well as opportunities to compete for work and for advancement within a particular employment organisation.

- *Equality of treatment* may encompass such issues as the allocation of tasks, working conditions, issues of harassment and conditions governing dismissal.

- *Equality of outcome* is likely to encompass issues of pay and other substantive terms and conditions of employment, as well as quotas of the working population.

The dividing lines between these categories of equality are blurred and in some instances they overlap.

These categories can also be distinguished by whether they are essentially procedural (opportunity and treatment) or concerned with outcomes. Jewson and Mason (1986) distinguished between equality policies that were liberal in that they sought to ensure that everyone was treated equally (*procedural*) and those that were concerned to achieve equality of outcome (which they term *radical*).

Liff (1995) argues the advantages of an alternative procedural variant, to try and ensure or create the conditions in which people can compete on equal terms – an objective she finds preferable to both the liberal and radical approaches of Jewson and Mason. She states:

> There is an alternative to the radical approach which may capture better the limitations of the liberal approach.

To ensure that such competitive equality is achieved will often require amendment of the requirements of jobs – for example, the (unnecessary) requirement that jobs be worked on a full-time basis, when the alternative of job sharing might well be feasible.

Commonly, the term '*equal opportunities*' is used to encompass all of these dimensions and, where governments have sought to intervene, they have tended to intervene in order to grant individual rights (to opportunities, treatment or outcome).

These rights are often couched in terms of a right not to be discriminated against. This is the case with many of the legislative and other initiatives taken within the EU over the years, which we examine in some detail later in this chapter. In many respects, equality and discrimination are opposite sides of the same coin, with a right to equality of opportunity or treatment implying at the same time a right not to be discriminated against.

Discrimination against or indeed in favour (usually referred to as *positive discrimination*) of a particular sex or ethnic group is possible on all of these dimensions of equality, although, as we shall see, there has recently been some concern about the legality of positive discrimination (*see* discussion of the Kalanke case later in this chapter). There has also been a considerable increase in the attention paid to the issue of *sexual harassment*, including debates about the extent to which, and how, sexual harassment cases may be already covered by the equality legislation. Harassment is most likely to be a matter of treatment at work.

Defining discrimination is difficult and unanimity is difficult to achieve. As an economist, Adnett (1996) defines it as something that only occurs when some *superficial* personal characteristic is used to restrict an individual's opportunity to achieve economic or social development and advancement. In the context of this chapter, examples of such 'superficial' personal characteristics might include colour of skin, sex and nationality.

The law tends to distinguish between *direct* and *indirect discrimination*, with direct discrimination encompassing less favourable treatment of an individual or group because of its sex or on the grounds of its race, skin colour, etc. Indirect discrimination relates to circumstances in which there may have been no intent to discriminate against a group, but, nevertheless, the reality is that discrimination occurs, with one group being disadvantaged in comparison with another. An example might be an insistence that successful applicants for a position are over 6ft tall or 'able to speak the Queen's English' even when neither of the conditions can be justified by the requirements of the job. The impact of the condition is to disadvantage one group – women or members of other nationalities or ethnic groups – in comparison with another. Selection tests, assessment centres and job evaluation and classification schemes can easily incorporate criteria and methods that result in indirect discrimination.

In defining types of labour market discrimination, Adnett (1996) identifies three:

- *pre-entry discrimination*;
- *employment* or *occupational discrimination*; and
- *wage discrimination*.

It seems to be the case that each of these types of discrimination can be detected as commonly applying to sectors of the labour force within the labour markets of the EU, including the ethnic minorities and women. There is also some coincidence between each of these types and, respectively, equality of opportunity, treatment and outcome. We return to the employment/occupational and wage discrimination in the following sections, but it is appropriate now to elaborate a little upon pre-entry discrimination in a little more detail.

Central to an understanding of pre-entry discrimination are the notions of *socialisation*, *value systems* and *culture*; in these are to be found many of the roots of *stereotyping* – that is, the tendency to perceive others as belonging to a single class or category. Examples of stereotyping are perceptions that all Jamaicans are the same, as are all women, as are other races and ethnic groups.

Socialisation, value systems and culture also explain the difference between *gender* and *sex discrimination* – two terms that have different meanings, but are frequently used interchangeably. Adnett (1996) identifies the difference between the two terms as:

> the former term [gender] encapsulates in addition to biological differences [sex], the socially constructed differences between men and women . . . labour market behaviour is influenced by perceived differences between the sexes, often reflecting norms regarding socially appropriate roles . . .

By implication, sex discrimination is that which is attributable to the biological differences only. It is gender, therefore, that is the wider concept and it is gender equality and discrimination that forms the major part of the subject matter of this chapter.

It is perhaps also important at this juncture to point out that gaps and differences are not necessarily the product or a symptom of either inequality or discrimination. For example, wage or earnings differences between men and women can be justified by differences in productivity or value added, and in a labour market context by taste and accurate stereotyping. We return to this issue later in the chapter when we look in more detail at the issue of equal pay.

CULTURE AND STEREOTYPES

As already noted, pre-entry discrimination, in particular, can be partially explained by the values and attitudes that are acquired through the process of socialisation and growing up in a particular culture and which indeed form part of that culture. These values and attitudes influence perceptions of others and behaviour and, because they are collective and shared, they tend to serve to distinguish one group or category from another. In the context of this chapter, gender and race are likely to form the basis of such groups.

In Chapter 1 we elaborated upon the relevance of national cultural difference to issues of human resource management; in this chapter we are concerned specifically with the relevance of culture to issues of equality and discrimination.

Hodgetts and Luthans (1994, p. 59) suggest that culture is:

> acquired knowledge that people use to interpret experience and generate social behaviour. This knowledge forms values, creates attitudes and influences behaviour.

and that culture is learned, shared, transgenerational and adaptive (*see* Chapter 1).

Hofstede (1991, p. 5) refers to culture as:

> collective programming of the mind which distinguishes the members of one group or category of people from another.

He continues on page 4:

> The source of one's mental programs lie within the social environments in which one grew up and collected one's life experiences. The programming starts within the family and continues within the neighbourhood, at school, in youth groups, at the workplace, and in the living community.

Hofstede (1991, p. 10) also argues that culture can be detected at a number of different levels and gender and ethnicity are two of the levels that he identifies specifically. In elaborating upon his notion of culture and level, he suggests that in any society:

> there is a men's culture and a different women's culture and that women are often not considered suitable for jobs traditionally filled by men, not because they are technically unable to perform the jobs but because they don't carry the symbols, do not correspond to the hero images, do not participate in the rituals or foster the values dominant in the men's culture; and vice versa.

Similar comments could be made about different racial and ethnic groups and in European societies the impact and consequences of 'not carrying the symbols' of the dominant racial group may be considerable, given the relatively small proportion of the populations that fall into the category of ethnic and racial minorities.

In discussing gender roles within societies, Hofstede acknowledges that there are differences between societies but that there are also common trends among most societies. He suggests that typically men are supposed to be assertive, tough and competitive, whereas women are supposed to be more concerned with taking care of the home, the children and people in general – the contrast is between the achieving male and the caring female.

In addition to asserting that there are different gender and ethnic cultures, Hofstede (1991), in devising criteria against which cultures could be measured and compared, chose as one of the four original dimensions one which he called *masculinity/femininity*. As a result of his research, it became possible to compare national cultures on this basis.

Within the EU there are notable differences in the scores on this dimension (*see* Fig. 11.1), with the Scandinavian members tending to have among the lowest masculinity scores while others – such as Germany, Austria, United Kingdom, Italy and Ireland – have relatively high masculinity scores.

Hofstede sought to explain the significance of these dimensions and scores with respect to attitudes towards and behaviour in society, the family, school and the workplace. His interpretation of the masculinity/femininity dimension (1991, p. 96) suggests that in those societies in which there is a *low masculinity score*, one would expect:

- the dominant values in society to be caring;
- both men and women to be concerned with relationships;
- both fathers and mothers to deal with both facts and feelings;
- boys and girls to study the same subjects at school;
- managers to strive for consensus;
- an emphasis upon equality, solidarity and the quality of work life.

A *high masculine score* would lead one to expect:

- the dominant values to be a concern with success and materialism;
- men to be assertive, ambitious and tough;
- women to be caring and to take care of relationships;
- fathers to deal with facts and mothers to deal with feelings;
- only girls to cry;
- boys and girls to study different subjects;
- managers to be decisive and assertive;
- emphasis upon competition and performance.

Given Hofstede's findings and their interpretation it would seem reasonable to expect clearly different gender roles in most societies and that the degree of difference would be greater in those societies that exhibit the higher scores on this masculinity index. There are also implications that the degree of pre-entry discrimination, the existence of occupational segregation and the inequalities in the treatment of the genders in the workplace will all be greatest in high masculine score societies. However, Hofstede found no correlation between femininity, in the context of a low masculine score, and labour force participation as a whole (or indeed with the recent rate of increase in female participation in work outside the home) though there was some positive correlation between high femininity and women's participation in higher level technical and professional jobs. The complexities of analysing the implications of cultural difference for employment patterns and experience are shown by the assertion that in feminine societies the barriers to progress for women may be less but so also is feminine ambition.

The characteristics of societies in which there are high masculine scores are similar in many ways to the characteristics associated with the notion of *patriarchy*. Patriarchy tends to imply a degree of domination, oppression and exploitation of women, both within the domestic and work environments. It is often also associated with capitalism and the Marxist analysis of the consequences of capitalism: that is, not only does capitalism result in the exploitation of labour, it also results in male domination and exploitation of women who serve the interests of capital by providing a cheap way of ensuring that the well-being of the labour resource is taken care of and that the next generation of labour is produced and raised (Walby, 1990; Rees and Brewster, 1995).

GENDER

Evidence of patterns of participation and pay

Before proceeding to a consideration of the potential explanations of existing inequalities and discrimination, it is pertinent to examine the evidence that inequalities do in fact exist that need both explanation and remedy. As noted above, we must not assume that the genders are homogeneous and we must not assume that all differences in workplace experience and treatment are necessarily the result of discrimination. There may be differences of outcome, for example, that are justified in market terms. As Adnett (1996) puts it:

> the existence of a gender wage gap need not indicate labour market discrimination since women may possess different labour market characteristics or tastes.

Nevertheless, there have been many allegations of gender and sex discrimination that are alleged to unfairly and detrimentally influence female participation in the workplace and the outcomes of that participation.

When examining a geographic entity as large and diverse as the EU, it is inevitable that generalisations are made and that evidential detail cannot be pursued as avidly as might be possible in a smaller arena. An indication of the scale and nature of the problem can be obtained from Rubery and Fagan (1994) who acknowledge the increasing feminisation of labour markets but highlight the following trends.

- Female participation rates are still lower than those for men (though the gap has been narrowing) (*see* Chapter 4).

- Females are more likely to be employed on a part-time and temporary basis (*see* Chapter 4).

- Occupational segregation (particular sexes dominating certain occupations and industrial sectors) is still a major feature of all European labour markets and is increasing for some groups of women (*see* Chapter 4). Adnett (1996) points out that women are over-represented in service, clerical and social work and under-represented in administrative and manufacturing occupations and among the self-employed. He comments that both occupational and industrial segregation appears to be highly stable over time. He also asserts that:

this occupational crowding of female workers in the EU prevails across member states regardless of whether activity rates are high or rapidly rising. Even in the female dominated sectors women are still concentrated in the lower occupations . . . while the skilled workers and senior professional, technical and managerial staff are still predominantly male.

● Women consistently earn less than men across Europe even in the same occupations and industries and there is a higher incidence of low pay among women than men (though there is evidence that this gender pay gap has been narrowing in recent years). Adnett (1996) asserts that the gender wage gap tends to be smaller for single women than for married women, smaller at younger ages and larger for those with children.

The Commission report (1997c) confirms that, despite the longevity of the legislation conferring rights to equal pay, there is still an average 20 per cent differential in men's favour between the earnings of men and women (*see* Fig. 11.1) This gender pay gap is narrowest in Sweden, Finland and Denmark and widest in Austria, Ireland and the UK.

This report also confirms the continuation and resistance of the other trends referred to above and in Chapter 4:

> Gender differences are very strong in the labour market and are reflected in the segregation of men and women into different kinds of work and in the concentration of women into part-time and other forms of atypical employment . . . Despite the growth of employment and the improved skill and qualifications base which women bring to employment, women continue to earn significantly less than men . . . the gender pay gap has been highly resistant to change.

In this connection the presence of minimum wage arrangements seems to beneficially affect the gender pay gap from the position of women (Sweden, France and Italy). The figures in Fig. 11.1 are for manual workers, but there is evidence that the gap is wider for non-manual workers (30 to 40 per cent) than it is for manual workers (15 to 35 per cent) (European Communities Publications office, 1996).

The above are relatively common trends and characteristics which seem to cross most national borders within the EU. Rubery and Fagan also point out, however, that there is diversity in the experience of women in the respective national and regional labour markets that make up the EU.

Women also demonstrate different patterns of lifetime employment compared to men (*see* Fig. 4.2), there is more than one common pattern. Directly associated with this are the patterns of continuous/discontinuous employment and the length of tenure, the latter being less for women than for men.

These lifetime patterns of work are affected by motherhood and the number of children in the family as well as the age of the youngest child. This is confirmed by the Commission report (1997c) which states that despite variations between the member states it is still the case overall that mothers are much less likely (compared to women without children) to engage in economic activity (though the level is rising) and such activity is more likely to be part-time.

Male participation rates vary little from one country to another, whereas those for women vary considerably and the participation profiles of mothers would seem to be differently affected by the number of children in the family. The Commission report (1997c) identifies four profiles or patterns:

1 *The participation of women in the labour force appears to be little affected by the responsibilities of motherhood.* Participation remains at a high level. This is the profile associated with the Scandinavian countries – Sweden, Denmark and Finland.

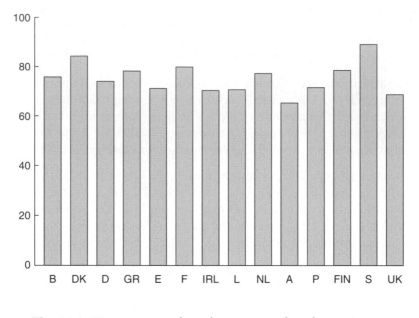

Fig. 11.1 Women manual workers average hourly earnings as a percentage of men's, 1994

Source: adapted from Eurostat – Harmonised Statistics of Earnings.
Note: Data for Austria, Finland, Sweden, 1993.

2 *The participation rate is considerably affected by the presence of children in the family.* Participation rates of mothers with one child are considerably lower than that for women with no children and as the number of children increases, participation rates fall – UK, Germany, Netherlands, Ireland, Greece and Spain.

3 *The second child seems to be the key factor.* The participation rates of women with one child are very similar to those of women with none – Portugal and Italy.

4 *Only mothers with three or more children exhibit very different participation profiles.* In France, it seems likely that this is linked in some way to the peculiarities of the French system of family benefits which favour the third child: family benefits in a three-child family equal 30 per cent of family income, compared with a figure of 11 per cent for families with two children. While only 15 per cent of French households have three children, the participation rates of mothers with three children are 49 per cent compared with a figure of 74 per cent for mothers with one or two children. Also found to a lesser extent in Belgium.

As there are variations across the Union in the impact of the number of children upon participation rates so there are also variations depending upon the age of the youngest child. In most member states, participation increases with the age of the youngest child. A comparison of participation rates for mothers shows that between 1985 and 1993 there was a considerable increase in their participation, the exception being Denmark where rates were already high. Countries in which the increase was particularly high were the UK, Netherlands, Ireland and Belgium.

Country[a]	Year/data	Publicly funded[b] services for children (%)		School-age	Length of school day in hours	Proportions in publicly funded services for children 6–10 years[c]
		0–3 years	3–6 years[d]			
Belgium	1993	27	95	6	7	–
Denmark	1995	48	82	7	3–5½[d]	62% + all six year olds in pre-primary education
Germany East West	1990	50 2	100 78	6	4–5	85% 5%
Greece	1993	3	64	6	4–5[d]	<5% (estimate)
Spain	1993	2	84	6	5	–
France	1993	23	99	6	8	±30%
Ireland	1993	2	55	6	4.40–5.40[d]	<5% (estimate)
Italy	1991	6	91	6	5½–6	–
Luxembourg	1991	6	91	6	8	–
Netherlands	1993	8	71	5	7	<5% (estimate)
Austria	1994	3	75	6	4–5	6%
Portugal	1993	12	48	6	6	10%
Finland	1994	21	53	7	4–5	5% + 60% of six year olds in welfare and education system services
Sweden	1994	33	72	7	2½–6[d]	64%+ some six year olds in pre-primary schooling
United Kingdom	1993	2	60	5	6½	<5% (estimate)

Source: A review of services for young children in the EU 1990–1995, European Commission Network on Childcare and other Measures to reconcile Employment and Family Responsibilities, 1996.

Notes:

a Information on levels of provision need to be interpreted as follows: places available in Belgium and France (for children aged 0–3, except for two year olds in pre-primary schooling), Germany, Italy (for children aged 0–3), the Netherlands, Portugal and the UK. Children attending for Belgium and France (two year olds in pre-primary schooling and 3–6), Denmark, Greece, Spain, Ireland, Italy (for children aged 3–6), Austria, Finland and Sweden.

b 'Publicly funded' means that more than half of the total costs of a service are paid from public sources, and usually between 75 per cent and 100 per cent.

c This figure does not include children in compulsory schooling; it is confined to services providing care and recreation.

d Schoolhours increase as child grows older.

– No information.

Fig. 11.2 Overview of child-care provision in EU member states

Source: European Commission (1997) *Annual Report from the Commission. Equal Opportunities for Women and Men in the European Union 1996.* European Commission, p. 56.

Difficulties with *child care* can still present a serious obstacle to women's participation in economic activity and in the main women continue to bear the main burden of child care and household chores (European Commission, 1997c). Data on child care provision is not comprehensive: the extent of state provision is reasonably easy to obtain but data on other arrangements – such as private in-home care by relatives and other non-subsidised arrangements – is difficult to obtain or does not exist. As a result, comparisons are difficult and unreliable. Nevertheless, some idea of public provision can be obtained from Fig. 11.2 which provides an overview of the situation within the member states.

Other common characteristics of female employment are that women are less likely to achieve managerial status, even in those industries or occupations in which numerically they dominate (*see* Adnett (1996) and Chapter 4), and they are more likely to be unemployed and unemployed for a long time, although this latter is by no means common to all member states (*see* Chapter 4).

Hegewisch and Mayne (1994) summarised many of these inequalities in their comment that there is a:

> . . . continued inequality of women in employment, as demonstrated in terms of their low share of managerial positions, persistent pay gaps and the rigid occupational segregation between men's and women's work across Europe . . .

Similar conclusions had already been reached by Rubery and Fagan (1993) and similar trends are confirmed by the more recent Commission report (1997c).

In a sense it is relatively easy to obtain statistical evidence of the above trends and rates; it is much more difficult to obtain evidence of discrimination or inequality at the level of the firm and in respect of aspects of treatment, such as career development opportunities, training provision, recruitment and selection and opportunities for promotion and participation in organisational decision making.

In this area of organisation-level attitude and practice, the *Price Waterhouse Cranfield Project*, as reported by Hegewisch and Mayne (1994), is a major source of information.

It has also often been alleged that women are less reliable, attend less satisfactorily and are less willing to join trade unions. These latter allegations illustrate some of the difficulties of such comparisons since it is extremely unlikely that they arise from comparing like with like. Visser (1993) argued that there is no evidence of women's lower propensity to join trade unions, but there is evidence of the unions often not seeking to recruit and not being available and visible in the sectors of the labour market dominated by women.

Over the years, there has been a great deal of debate as to what may be the major causes of the differences and general trends identified above, and indeed the extent to which they are symptoms of inequality or discrimination. In the next section, we examine some of the explanations offered by the research evidence and some of the policy implications.

Explanations for patterns, inequalities and outcomes

The overwhelming emphasis of this section is upon the explanation of gender-based inequalities and outcomes; however, where appropriate, reference is also made to those based on race.

It is extremely difficult in most of the areas of apparent inequality and discrimination to establish causal relationships; it is common that a number of factors, including the values that comprise culture, serve to explain each of the phenomena identified.

There are also moral and political dimensions to the discussion on a scale which may not be so prevalent with some other 'social' issues. It is also worth noting again that there are different types of discrimination: pre-entry discrimination, discrimination in the workplace and discrimination in terms of outcome.

One of the main difficulties in this arena is in ascertaining the extent to which differences in pay, behaviour and the distribution of employment, which may be taken as *prima facie* evidence of an inequality or unjustified discrimination, are due to and reflections of the fact that women and ethnic groups may possess different labour market characteristics or tastes.

Differences in earnings which reflect differences in tastes or education and training may not reflect discrimination if the differences in education and training are the product of *unconstrained choice* and if equal opportunity for and rewards from educational investment exist.

The conventional economic model

In terms of conventional economic theory, an *earnings gap* can be made up of a *productivity gap* and a *wage gap*; it is the latter component that is likely to be reflective of discrimination. In this context, discrimination occurs where there are differences in the terms and conditions of employment including wages (outcomes) that are not attributable to differences in the productivity of the respective individuals or group.

The earnings difference attributable to a productivity differential is consistent with the notion of economic efficiency – the market is doing its job. This productivity differential may well be the product, not of inequality or discrimination in the employment market, but of rational investment decisions by women and families (or members of racial groups), given their expectation that the return to any investment in education and training for women is likely to be diminished in comparison with the white male employee. The expectation of a lower rate of return, for example, may be the product of the expectation that they will experience discontinuous employment, an expectation most pronounced among women.

Critics of the conventional economic approach would argue that this 'efficiency' explanation begs the question of why women expect lower rates of return to such investment and whether this is itself the product of their perceptions that they are likely to be treated unequally or discriminated against.

For example, women may expect to have time out of the labour market because of their role in childbirth, the absence of adequate and convenient child care facilities, and dominant social attitudes and social customs with regard to the distribution of family responsibilities, which frown upon mothers working. In such circumstances, it may be rational for families to invest less in education and training for women and concentrate their scarce resources on investment in the human capital of husbands and sons. The market may be doing its job of efficiently allocating resources between different uses.

The question is, however, whether the 'productivity' earnings differential, that ensues as a return to the investment made, is itself the product of inequalities at one or more remove from the employment transaction? Earnings differentials that are due to differences in productivity may be a reflection of market efficiency and therefore not discriminatory; but they may also be reflections of individual and group expectations of inequality and discrimination and of inequality in the pre-entry and social environments that surround the market. In effect, we witness supply-side adjustments to an expectation of inequality or discrimination which then become self-perpetuating.

181

An alternative model is that devised by Becker (1957) which sees discrimination as a taste of the employer which is itself the result of prejudice. In the context of the competitive model, employers cease to seek to maximise profits if and when they begin to make labour-hiring decisions on grounds other than labour productivity. It is in this sense that the Becker model asserts that discrimination is the price employers are prepared to pay for the pleasure of practising their prejudices. There are a number of consequences of the employer's discrimination.

1 Employers may refuse to employ women or members of a particular ethnic group even when the value of their marginal product is greater than the wage that would have to be paid. It is in this sense that such employers are perceived to be forgoing profits in order to exercise prejudice.

2 Competition in the labour market is restricted, and 'favoured labour' earns a wage that is higher than it would be if the categories of labour that are discriminated against were active competition for the work available.

3 The labour market becomes segmented in that there are categories of labour that do not compete with one another even though there may be competition within each segment.

Under competitive conditions such discrimination would be competed away by employers not prepared to pay the price of discriminating; they would be more efficient and their costs would be lower.

We do not intend to pursue further an analysis of inequality and discrimination using the techniques and methodology of conventional competitive models of economics since as Adnett (1996) acknowledges:

> conventional economic theory provides no explanation of the origins or the persistence of discriminatory wage differentials and occupational segregation.

Models involving social, psychological and cultural factors

There are labour market outcomes that are partially the product of decisions made on the basis of superficial personal characteristics and prejudice which do not reflect value as measured by productivity and which conventional economic analysis therefore cannot explain. Understanding of such discrimination requires input from the social, psychological and cultural arenas referred to earlier and which encompass traditions, social structures and values and beliefs.

Some efforts have been made to develop non-competitive models and explanations that take into account the behaviour and prejudices of employers and existing employees as '*insiders*' (*see* Chapter 15) resisting the intrusion and non-discriminatory assimilation of the unwelcome '*outsiders*' that may be comprised of women or members of particular ethnic groups. These models tend to take as their starting position the assumption that many firms' employment policies are largely independent of competitive market forces and conditions.

Employers tend in their decision making to reflect the dominant social norms and customs and are concerned not to upset their existing labour force and employment structures. Where such firms have a well developed and structured internal market, the task of eliminating or reducing inequality and discrimination is even greater and decision-making processes are likely to serve to defend the status quo. An implication of these models is that, if insiders are racist or unwilling for whatever reason to work with women, it is unlikely that employers will voluntarily make decisions on hiring new employees that threaten existing relationships.

According to this scenario, outsiders are doomed to remain so and are therefore destined to remain within the secondary employment sectors, characterised by less favourable terms and conditions of employment, fewer opportunities, less training and investment, less security and lower expectations. The inequality and discrimination that seem central to the behaviour of firms in such models serve to confirm existing stereotypes and perpetuate the inequality and discrimination. There are similarities here with the flexibility models devised by Atkinson (1984) and others which distinguish *core* and *peripheral* workers and functions: the core are insiders and secure with good terms and conditions and prospects while the peripheral are outsiders who experience lack of security and opportunity, no career development opportunities and training and little if any attachment to the firm (*see* Chapter 2).

Factors affecting the supply and demand for female labour

Despite the weaknesses of the conventional competitive models as explanatory mechanisms, it is convenient to use the traditional supply and demand framework for identifying some of the more important influences that have been found to contribute to an understanding of gender-based differences in labour market participation, treatment and outcome.

The *demand* for female labour is likely to be influenced by the following factors:

- *Increases or decreases in the size of the service sector.* Women tend to dominate these sectors, and perhaps particularly those services that are centred around the qualities associated with caring.

- *Technological developments.* Those that remove the emphasis on the physical/strength requirements of work and maybe replace it with an emphasis on skills for which females allegedly have greater aptitude are particularly significant.

- *The degree and nature of regulation in the labour market.* For example, changes in the regulation of the labour market (such as an easing of restrictions upon the freedom of employers to hire and fire, an easing of restrictions upon the hours that can be worked, and a reduction of other employee protections), tax and social security systems (such as a reduction of the employers' taxes and social security contributions linked to each employee) may facilitate more flexible employment.

  On the assumption that women are more able to work part-time than full-time, because of the way in which domestic responsibilities are distributed within families, change of this kind may thereby enhance the demand for and the employment of women. Alternatively, demand may suffer if additional regulations and costs are introduced in order to ensure equality of opportunity and treatment between the sexes – for example, the introduction of protections and rights for pregnant workers which may render the employment of women less attractive to employers.

- *Employer and social attitudes.* These are inevitably a product of socialisation and subject to the vagaries of stereotyping. Where existing prejudices are confirmed by experience, it is likely that segregation will be the order of the day, particularly where such segregation is also consistent with the desires and prejudices of insider employees. However, where social attitudes or norms change or where experience leads to a change

183

of attitude (this may include existing employees) an increase in the demand for female labour may be the outcome.

The *supply* of female labour is influenced by the following factors:

- *The 'need' for income.* This impinges on the debate about whether women only work for pin-money and also whether they constitute a useful pool of reserve labour which can be utilised when necessary, but which can then be returned to the home when no longer needed. The greater the need for income in the family (perhaps as the result of male unemployment or short-time working), the greater is the likelihood that women will seek to work.

- *Demographic developments and trends.* These may include, for example, birth rates, the number of children in families and the proportion of single parents. In each of these instances, we can detect probable influences upon supply. If birth rates fall, we would expect supply to increase as women have fewer children to look after. A similar impact would be expected from an overall decline in the size of families (although this may be countered, if the decline means that not as much help was now available to the mother in the home). An increase in the number of single parents would seem likely to lead to a decline in the supply of female labour outside the home.

- *The age of the youngest child.* In many cultures, although not all, it is common for women to return to the labour market as their children grow up (*see* Fig. 4.2).

- *The availability of maternity leave and pay and the presence of a right to return, entitlement to paternity leave.* The expectation is that these rights take some of the insecurity, anxiety and difficulty out of seeking to combine work and family responsibilities but, as has been noted above, while there may be beneficial effects in supply terms, employers may be encouraged into further segregation and into lower levels of demand for female labour because of what they perceive as the extra costs and loss of discretion.

- *The availability and cost of child care facilities.* In this case, the existence of adequate, affordable and convenient (in terms of location and hours of opening) child care facilities would be expected to encourage an increase in the supply of labour. The reunification of Germany and the accompanying collapse of the state child care service in the East certainly contributed to a rapid and marked decline in the ability of women to take up work outside the home.

- *Legislation on equity and discrimination and the presence of an enforcing agency.* One would expect the passage and existence of each of these to encourage supply, as women become aware of their enhanced rights. However, the caution also needs to be made that employers seem adept at non-compliance and avoidance and that additional costs and reductions of managerial freedom and discretion always seem to be accompanied by warnings that demand will fall. Where demand is significantly influenced by prejudicial attitudes on the part of employers, it is unlikely that the passage of legislation will have much impact. I is notoriously difficult to change attitudes.

- *Levels and types of education and training.* As the level, type and quality of the education and training available to females is improved, the supply of female labour should become more varied and greater. As noted earlier, however, the take-up of these opportunities, and therefore their impact, will depend in part upon individual and family decisions about the expected rates of return for the investment of time and other resources and the opportunity costs. There is evidence in some member states that the lifetime working pattern of women is changing as female activity rates increase (*see* Fig. 4.2) and as a greater proportion of younger women obtain more education and training and continue to work through into their mid 20s and 30s. Figures 4.8 and 4.9 indicate the tendency for convergence in the length of time that women and men are in education and training and their levels of attainment.

- *Attitudes among society as to the legitimate distribution of domestic responsibilities and workload and the propriety of women working outside the home, especially after childbirth.*

- *An increase in relative rates of pay.* This is often brought about by the introduction and implementation of appropriate legislation and wage-fixing machinery. There is some evidence that minimum-wage legislation and centralised wage fixing generates smaller wage gaps. However, it should also be borne in mind that this might also lead to a decline in demand.

- *Technological changes and developments that render work in the home easier and facilitate other productive activity.*

Policy implications

The preceding analysis and discussion should enable the identification of policies at EU, national and organisational level that might yield benefits in terms of reducing inequality and discrimination. Such policies might include:

- work schedules and arrangements of hours that fit with the division of domestic responsibilities and workload;

- parental leave provisions that enable a more equal division of these responsibilities, where desired;

- the provision of training for women seeking to return to the labour market;

- legislation rendering discrimination unlawful and the creation of strong mechanisms for the purpose of enforcement, which does not involve the individual being left with the responsibility of pursuing justice since economic and other realities may prevent their pursuance of their rights;

- organisational-level schemes facilitating career breaks for women to facilitate the management of the consequences of childbirth;

- child care facilities that are convenient, adequate and appropriately priced;

- information gathering and monitoring mechanisms, allowing examination of the incidence and nature of inequality and the formulation of measures appropriate to the causes and incidence;

- positive action or discrimination – mechanisms whereby the under-represented group is given specific assistance (*see* later in this chapter);

- an enhanced role for women in the various decision-making processes and mechanisms.

The Commission report (1997c) comments upon the need for an enhanced role for women in the decision-making processes and presents evidence confirming that women represent a minority among political decision makers and Social Partner organisations. In the mid-1990s women hold almost 28 per cent of the total seats in the European Parliament and with variations from one member state to another the average percentage of women in national parliaments is 15 per cent. (*Source*: EC 1997c)

In commenting upon the minority representation of women, this report argues that it is not simply a numerical issue; it is a matter of bringing a wider perspective to the various debates.

The average representation of women in national parliaments is only 15 per cent (only 11 per cent in 1980) and in the EP it is 28 per cent. The Commission report (1997c) argues that this under-representation constitutes a loss for society and does not allow the interests and needs of the whole population to be catered for in full:

> Women's under-representation results in a democratic deficit, a serious loss of talent and expertise and a failure to engage with women's particular concerns and needs.

Since the appointment of the new Commission in January 1995, the Commission has come under pressure to put its own house in order and to pursue target programmes for the recruitment and promotion of women to senior positions within the Commission, where they constitute a very small proportion with only about 12 of the most senior 221 positions occupied by women. (*Source*: *Financial Times*, 8 March 1996)

EU INITIATIVES TO PROMOTE GENDER EQUALITY

Pay

EC Treaty, Article 119

When it comes to charting and discussing EU initiatives, the first thing to point out is that Article 119 of the founding treaty, the Treaty of Rome as amended by the Maastricht Treaty on European Union and now known as the EC Treaty, applies *directly*. As already explained in Chapter 8, Treaty Articles take precedence over national legislation, customs and practice and they should, where necessary, be implemented into national legislation. However, where Articles of the Treaties are clear, precise, unconditional and self-contained, they are said to have *horizontal direct effect* – that is they may not need to be given effect via implementing legislation in the member states and individuals can use them as the basis for an action against another, irrespective of the member state's own legislation. The ECJ in the case of Defrenne *v* SABENA established that Article 119 fell into this category. This Article provided that:

> Each member state shall during the first stage ensure and subsequently maintain the application of the principle that men and women should receive equal pay for equal work.

It would therefore appear that the founding members of the Union were keen to ensure that men and women should be paid equally for equal work, although there has always been the suspicion that a major concern motivating the inclusion and acceptance of this principle was related to worries that cheap female labour in one state might be used to gain competitive advantage over another. In particular, as Hegewisch and Mayne (1994) assert:

The motivation for its inclusion was less a concern with social justice and equal opportunities than an attempt to prevent social dumping and ensure fair competition by eliminating the cost advantage enjoyed by the French textile industry through paying very low and unequal wages to its female employees.

Cox (1993) argues that the motivation was twofold and that Article 119 is justified by two other articles in the Treaty, each of which specifies general objectives of the Union: the prevention of distortions of internal competition and upwards harmonisation of living and working conditions (Articles 3 and 117). Article 3(g) specified the need for:

a system ensuring that competition in the internal market is not distorted.

Article 117 stated that the member states:

agree upon the need to promote improved working conditions and an improved standard of living for workers, so as to make possible their harmonisation while the improvement is being maintained . . . such a development will ensue not only from the functioning of the common market, which will favour the harmonisation of social systems, but also from the procedures provided for in this Treaty and from the approximation of provisions laid down by law . . .

Cox (1993) quotes the judgement in the Defrenne case to illustrate the use and relevance to Article 119 of these two general objectives:

Article 119 pursues a double aim . . . to avoid a situation in which undertakings established in states that have actually implemented the principle of equal pay suffer a competitive disadvantage in intra-Community competition as compared with undertakings established in states which have not yet eliminated discrimination against women workers as regards pay [hence the relevance of Article 3 above] . . . Secondly, this provision forms part of the social objectives of the Community . . . to ensure social progress and seek the constant improvement of the living and working conditions of its peoples [hence relevance of Article 117] . . .

Pay is defined within Article 119 as:

the ordinary basic or minimum wage or salary and any other consideration, whether in cash or in kind, which the worker receives, directly or indirectly, in respect of his employment from his employer.

The Article sought to define equal pay without discrimination based on sex as meaning:

(a) that pay for the same work at piece rates shall be calculated on the basis of the same unit of measurement;
(b) that pay for work at time rates shall be the same for the same job.

While answering some questions, this Article did not adequately define the meaning of the same or equal work and much debate has followed on this and related issues of definition and meaning.

The Equal Pay Directive

The Equal Pay Directive was adopted in 1975 (75/117) and in Article 1 of this Directive, the principle of equal pay is defined as meaning:

. . . for the same work or for work to which equal value is attributed.

While the Directive elaborated on the original Article 119 and introduced the concept of equal value, it by no means resolved the issue of the meanings of equal pay or value as can be detected from the number of cases that the ECJ has had to deal with on this and related issues and from the fact that, as late as 1994, the Commission needed to issue a Memorandum on Equal Pay for Work of Equal Value (94/6) and stated its intention to produce a *Code of Practice* on the subject (*see* below).

Many of the cases that have been determined by the ECJ have been concerned to define more precisely the meaning of pay in the context of both Article 119 and the Directive. As a result of various cases it has been decided that for the purposes of this legislation, pay includes:

- redundancy payments whether statutory, contractual or *ex gratia* (Barber *v* Guardian Royal Exchange Assurance Group);
- payments under an occupational pension scheme (Barber *v* Guardian Royal Exchange Assurance Group); and
- other ex gratia payments made after the contract has ended (Garland *v* British Rail Engineering).

On the Equal Work and Value front, there have also been a number of important cases, each of which determined particular issues.

- *Macarthy's Ltd* v *Smith*. This case established that the comparable work does not have to be undertaken at the same time; the comparison could be with the person who did the job before. However, this same case also established that the comparison could not be hypothetical, it must be possible to make 'concrete appraisals of the work actually performed by employees of different sex within the same establishment or service'.
- *The Danfoss case*. As Cox (1993) points out, the ECJ has subsequently in the Danfoss case indicated that generalised pay practices within an undertaking may be covered by the legislation, even if the comparison is not with a named comparator.
- *Murphy and others* v *An Bord Telecom Eirann*. The legislation does cover circumstances in which the work of the plaintiff is of greater value than that of the comparator though such a finding of greater value cannot then be used to justify the imposition of a rate of pay that is greater than that of the comparator.

There have been numerous cases that have determined that the legislation can be appropriately used in instances of indirect, as opposed to direct discrimination. Indirect discrimination covers circumstances whereby an employer applies policies or practices which in practice disproportionately and adversely affect one sex and which cannot objectively be justified on grounds other than sex. Examples of such indirect discrimination have been found to include payment systems and arrangements that attached pay to the possession of longevity of continuous service, the completion of specified training, and an ability to work flexible hours.

It is important to note that if the practices can be *objectively justified*, then the employer will not be found to be in breach of the legislation; problems occur for the employer when such practices resulting in pay inequality between the sexes cannot be so objectively justified. In the Code of Practice (Com (96) 336) (*see* next section), the Commission suggests that each element in the make-up of pay needs to be analysed to ensure that there is an objective justification which is not affected by the sex of the workers.

There are a number of other difficulties associated with the concept of value and interventions that seek to enforce equality of outcome in terms of pay and to link this to or base it upon some measure of value. Criteria have to be set regarding the value to be used and this can itself concentrate upon either inputs or outputs. For example, the criterion could be:

● the effort, skill and responsibility put into the work; or

● the content of the work; or

● a measure of the value of the output; or

● a mix of these.

Job evaluation and classification schemes tend to be based upon a mix of input and content, rather than upon output.

Despite the fact that the Directive on Equal Pay specifies in Article 1 that job classification systems should be based on the same criteria for men and women and designed so that they exclude any discrimination on grounds of sex there are still many unresolved dilemmas in this area. There have been many criticisms over the years that traditional and existing schemes often demonstrated a bias in favour of the jobs that were 'male', as opposed to 'female', emphasising more or awarding more points to the characteristics associated with and forming part of the male jobs.

The continuing relevance of these issues and the difficulties surrounding them were demonstrated by the fact that in 1996 the Commission thought it necessary to issue a Code of Practice.

Code of Practice on The Implementation of Equal Pay for Work of Equal Value for Women and Men COM (96) 336

In the introduction to the Code, the Commission confirms the relative lack of success achieved by the prior interventions on matters of equal pay between the sexes:

> Despite these provisions of Community law having been adopted and transposed into the legislations of the member states 20 years ago, the differences in pay between women and men remain considerable.

The pay differences are confirmed to be greater for non-manual as compared with manual workers, and the Code suggests that the differences in men's and women's incomes are due to a number of factors, including:

● the vertical and horizontal segregation of jobs held by women and men;

● the numerous sectors of the economy where mainly men work offering extra pay and working time bonuses;

● the considerable differentiation in pay resulting from collective agreements linked to the recognition of skills, to the type of business and the type of industry or sector with gender-specific segregation in employment applying to each of these divisions;

● the systems of collective agreements which allow salary structures to reflect negotiating power and the fact that women are generally weaker in negotiations.

The Commission states that the Code aims, in particular, to eliminate sexual discrimination, whenever pay structures are based on job classification and evaluation systems. The Code makes two main proposals:

● that negotiators at all levels should carry out an analysis of the remuneration system and

189

evaluate the data required to detect sexual discrimination in pay structures so that it becomes possible to devise remedies; and

- that a plan for follow-up should be drawn up and implemented so that sexual discrimination is eliminated.

Interestingly, the Code states quite clearly that the prime responsibility for the avoidance of discrimination rests with the employers and in Part II it states:

> The Code is principally aimed at employers . . . because the principle of equal pay for work of equal value must in the first instance be applied by employers, who are required to pay equal wages whenever work of equal value is being carried out by male and female workers and whenever a difference in pay cannot be explained or justified other than on the basis of the worker's sex.

It is in the context of this principled obligation that it is sometimes argued that the burden of proof in such cases should be upon the employer; the obligation is upon them and of course they control much of the evidence that may be required.

The Code also proposes that governments should encourage the establishment of national-level statistical support to facilitate the appropriate and necessary analysis. The Code also identifies a number of practices and dimensions of payment systems that might be discriminatory and which should be given special attention by the Social Partners/negotiators in their efforts to avoid and eliminate discrimination. Specifically mentioned in this context are:

- basic pay;
- bonus/performance pay and piece rates;
- pay benefits, such as sick pay, pensions, low interest loans, etc.;
- part-time workers and their entitlements;
- job classification, grading, evaluation and skills/competency-based systems.

The Commission sees itself contributing by and through:

- campaigns to raise awareness and provide information;
- the training of experts;
- the greater involvement of women in the process of collective bargaining;
- the identification and dissemination of good practice.

Well intentioned though the Code of Practice and the Commission are, it should be remembered that interventions of this kind are subject to the dangers that the greater the degree of the discrimination or wage/earnings gap, the greater may be the employment impact of the interventions directed at narrowing or eliminating that gap. The greater the extent of occupational segregation, the smaller will be the impact of the equal-value interventions.

The Maastricht Treaty Social Policy Agreement

The issue of equal pay was also specifically dealt with in the Maastricht Treaty Social Policy Agreement. Article 6 of this Agreement constitutes an alternative Article 119 of the EC Treaty and was intended to replace Article 119. The differences between the two are some changes to the opening paragraph and a new final paragraph. In the first paragraph the words 'during the first stage' are omitted and member states are to 'ensure that the principle of . . . is applied'. The definitions of equal pay remain as in Article 119, but the new last paragraph (3) specifies that:

> This Article shall not prevent any Member State from maintaining or adopting measures providing for specific advantages in order to make it easier for women to pursue a vocational activity or to prevent or compensate for disadvantages in their professional careers.

Presumably, the intention is to facilitate the introduction or maintenance of payments or other benefits that would fall into the definition of pay that positively discriminates in favour of women. Into such a category might fall the costs of crèche facilities – if such a benefit was not extended also to fathers – and also paid maternity leave – if these provisions are better than would be received by a man if he were absent through illness. The intent expressed in this paragraph (the proposed Article 119(3)) is similar to the exception provided in the Directive on Equal Treatment (*see* next section). We return to the issue of positive discrimination later.

The draft Amsterdam Treaty (*see* Chapter 9) proposes to incorporate the Social Policy Agreement of Maastricht (with some revisions) into the EC Treaty as a Social Chapter and as new Articles 117 to 120. As was the intent at the time of negotiating the Agreement at Maastricht, the new Article 119 is to be the Maastricht Agreement Article 6 with some amendments. Perhaps the most significant of these are:

- the introduction into proposed Article 119(1) of the words 'or work of equal value';
- the proposal, in new Article 119(3), to extend the scope of the Article beyond the pay issue and provide a basis for the Council to adopt measures, using the Co-Decision Procedure, to:

  > ensure the application of the principle of equal opportunities and equal treatment of men and women in matters of employment and occupation, including the principle of equal pay for equal work or work of equal value,

- the substitution in the proposed Article 119(4) of the words 'under-represented sex' for 'women' as was in the earlier Maastricht Article 6. It seems likely that this is the product of recent confusion and debates around the subject of the lawfulness of positive action.

Treatment

The EC Treaty did not provide express support for the principle of equal treatment between the sexes on issues other than pay. Nevertheless, as Cox (1993) points out, the ECJ has lent support for the notion of such equality. Cox quotes another portion of the 1978 Defrenne judgement to demonstrate this:

> The Court has repeatedly stated that respect for fundamental personal human rights is one of the general principles of Community law, the observance of which it has a duty to ensure. There can be no doubt that the elimination of discrimination based on sex forms part of these fundamental rights.

Here the justification for action at a Union level is not being based on the need to achieve particular economic objectives, linked to the elimination of distortions to competition, or to the achievement of the effective operation of the single market. Justification for action is based on such equality being deemed a fundamental human right and an assertion that it is the job of the Court to safeguard and ensure such rights.

Directive on Equal Treatment in Employment

The first legislative intervention into this arena occurred in 1976 with the adoption of the Directive (76/207) on Equal Treatment in Employment. This sought to ban discrimination on the grounds of sex in respect of opportunity and a wide range of employment practices. Specifically mentioned are access to all jobs and levels of occupational hierarchies, access to all levels and types of vocational guidance and training, and working conditions including the conditions governing dismissal. The Directive covers both indirect (achieved, for example, by reference to marital status) and direct discrimination. Article 2(3) of the Directive refers to pregnancy and maternity. (The UK implementing legislation was the 1976 Sex Discrimination Act and, more recently, the Employment Act of 1989.)

There appears to be some confusion as to the Treaty Articles used as the basis for the adoption of the Directive. Hegewisch and Mayne (1994) suggest that Article 119 was used; while Cox (1993) suggests that the relevant Article was 235 and Lasok and Lasok (1994) state that both 117 and 235 were the basis. Lasok and Lasok's interpretation seems the most realistic, since 117 is concerned with the upward harmonisation of working conditions and living standards and 235 provides the Union with the means to take action where the Treaty does not provide specific justification or authorisation:

> If action by the Community should prove necessary to attain, in the course of the operation of the Common Market, one of the objectives of the Community and this Treaty has not provided the necessary powers, the Council shall, acting unanimously on a proposal from the Commission . . . take the appropriate action.

This Directive has been widely used to outlaw discriminatory practices and the ECJ and other national courts have on many occasions been called upon to interpret the Directive when presented with specific discriminatory practices. Several of the more famous cases and judgements have been concerned with issues relating to maternity and pregnancy.

One such was *the Webb case* in 1994 in which the ECJ concluded that dismissal on the grounds of pregnancy was unlawful, even when, as in this case, the individual concerned had been recruited initially to replace another member of staff who was to be absent on maternity leave. Having been recruited, Webb soon became pregnant and was dismissed. The ECJ decided that, given that the employment had been for an unlimited period, despite the initial intention that she should replace an existing employee, the dismissal on the grounds of pregnancy was indeed unlawful.

The issue of refusing to employ a women because she was pregnant had been dealt earlier in *the Dekker case* (1991), when it was concluded that this refusal to employ on the grounds that Dekker was pregnant was an infringement of the Equal Treatment Directive, since the reason could only apply to one sex and the discrimination therefore was direct.

Another example of how the Directive has been used to push back the boundaries of inequality and, by so doing, to extend the employment rights of women would be the UK Court of Appeal decision in 1995 in the case brought by *Seymour-Smith and Perez* in which the Court found that the legislative requirement that employees have a minimum of two years' continuous service prior to gaining the right to allege unfair dismissal was itself unlawful. This was because women were much less likely to be able to take advantage of the entitlement given that a much lower proportion of women worked continuously for the two-year period. The Court found that, whereas 25 per cent of men had no unfair dismissal rights because of the rule, this applied to 35 per cent of working women. The discrimination in this instance was indirect (IPD Update, October 1995).

Article 2(4) of this Directive provides for exceptions to be made in respect of measures promoting equality of opportunity for men and women, in particular through the removal of existing inequalities that affect women's opportunities. These inequalities may be in areas such as vocational training or working conditions. This provision has been taken to validate a range of affirmative action and positive discrimination programmes and was followed in 1984 by the non-binding *Recommendation on the Promotion of Positive Action for Women*. This latter document recommended that the member states should take positive action to remove existing inequalities and to encourage women to enter occupations in which they were under-represented. With the exception of Germany and Spain, the member states all enacted legislation that incorporated provisions for positive action. The sorts of areas in which it has become relatively common for positive action programmes to be adopted include adapting working conditions and hours of work, vocational training and encouraging the recruitment and promotion of women.

The lawfulness of programmes of this nature and the applicability of the exceptions provided for in the Directive have now been thrown into doubt by the ECJ decision in the *Kalanke case* (1995) (*see* later in this chapter).

Other Directives on equal treatment

There have been other Directives concerned with equal treatment in respect of specific issues or circumstances and the main ones are:

- *State Social Security (79/7)*. This sought to ensure that there should be equal treatment for men and women in respect of the scope, conditions of access, the obligation to contribute, the calculation of contributions and benefits and the conditions governing the duration and retention of entitlements to benefits (with the exception of pensions).

- *Occupational Social Security (86/378)*. This Directive excluded occupational pensions from the scope of the requirement to make occupational benefits equal between men and women. (This was effectively circumvented by the ECJ decision in *the Barber case* in 1990 which determined that pension benefits were deferred pay and that they were therefore covered by the Equal Pay Directive.)

- *The Self-employed (86/613)*. This seeks to ban discrimination in the treatment of self-employed persons.

One of the more recent interventions by the Union was the *Directive on the Protection of Pregnant Workers (92/85)* which was adopted as a health and safety measure and, as such, was subject to decision making via the Co-operation Procedure enabling QMV. In addition to some specific health and safety considerations, this Directive seeks to influence the treatment and employment, promotion and career prospects and opportunities for women by ensuring the following:

- *They cannot be fairly dismissed on the grounds of pregnancy*. This right not to be dismissed is to be irrespective of length of service, so that, once employed, the right exists (thus augmenting the original Equal Treatment Directive and various ECJ judgements, some of which were summarised above).

- *They have a right to a minimum of 14 weeks' maternity leave and a right to return to work after pregnancy and childbirth.* Again, these rights are irrespective of length of service and may be improved upon by national legislation and individual employer provision or as the result of collective agreement.

- *They have a right to minimum amounts of maternity pay while on maternity leave.* The rate of that pay is to be no less than the rate of statutory sick pay in the country concerned.

The specific requirements of a more obvious health and safety nature included:

- risk assessments of working practices and environments, to establish whether there are special dangers to new and expectant mothers; and

- alternative work or additional paid leave to be given to pregnant or breast-feeding women where the work situation might be harmful to their health.

There are other proposals currently in discussion by *all* member states and one of these is the *Draft Directive on Equal Treatment in Occupational Social Security Schemes COM (95) 186.* As noted above, the original Directive in this area sought to exclude occupational pensions from the general requirement to treat men and women equally. This proposal seeks to take account of the decision in the *Barber (1990)* and *Coloroll (1994)* cases which served to overrule the Directive. The intention encompassed within the new Draft is that occupational pensions should be included in the general requirement to treat and pay men and women equally and that contributions and benefits should both be covered. As it is outside the Protocol Agreement, this proposal requires unanimity and it would not be surprising to see it blocked by the UK and/or other interests, eventually to be taken into the Protocol Procedure where it can be adopted by QMV (*see* Chapter 8).

The Protocol Agreement and equal treatment

In addition to Article 6 of the Social Protocol Agreement (from which the UK excluded itself) dealing with equal pay, the Agreement also included in Article 2 the provision that issues of equality between the sexes:

> with regard to labour market opportunities and treatment at work

should no longer be subject to the requirement of unanimity. Initiatives within the confines of the Protocol Agreement in this area are now subject to the QMV requirements.

One of the first occasions upon which this Protocol Procedure was used and used successfully (*see* Fig. 8.4) was on a matter of equality between the sexes and the process of social dialogue resulted in a Framework Agreement between the Social Partners. They requested the Commission to implement the Agreement by the preparation of a *Draft Directive on Parental Leave.* This Directive received formal approval and was adopted at the Social Affairs Council meeting in June 1996. It is to be implemented in the 14 member states by June 1998 if the mechanism for implementation is legislative or by June 1999 if implementation is to be by collective agreement at national level. This measure will always have a special place in the history of the EU since it constituted the first occasion upon which the Social Partners at the level of the Union reached agreement through the new Social Dialogue arrangements.

The main points of the Agreement are that both parents should be entitled to:

Fig. 11.3 Overview of parental leave provisions in EU member state, 1994-95

Country	Duration		Transferability	Benefits		Flexibility		Restrictions in coverage	Conditions
	Maximum	Boundaries		Rate	Period	Part-time	Fractioning		
Belgium[a]	None	None	Individual	Flat-rate with higher payment for two and three children	Weeks	Yes[b]	Yes	On employer's agreement	12 months of service
Denmark[c]	10 weeks + 3–9 months[b]	Until child is nine years	Family / Individual	Flat-rate: 80 per cent of unemployment benefit	Weeks / Weeks	No / No	No / Yes	None	No
Germany	36 months	Until child is three years	Family	Income-related	Until child is three years	Yes[b]	Yes	None	4 wks of service
Greece	3 months	Until child is two ½ years	Individual	Unpaid		No	Yes	Companies 100 workers and eight per cent claims	12 months of service
Spain	36 months		Family	Unpaid		No	No	None	No
France	36 months	Until child is three years	Family	Flat-rate, from second child	Until child is three years	Yes	No	None	12 months of service
Ireland	None								
Italy	6 months	Following m.l.[d]	Family	Income-related 30 per cent of earnings	Weeks	No	No	Farmers/self-employed/domestic services	No
Luxembourg	None								
Netherlands	6 months part-time	Until child is four years	Individual	Unpaid		Only	No	None	12 months of service
Austria	24 weeks	Until child is four years	Family	Flat-rate[e]	Weeks	Yes[b]	No	Prov.govern. Workers and agriculture/forestry	No
Portugal	6 months Max: 24 months[f]	Following m.l.	Family	Unpaid		No	No	None	12 months of service
Finland[g]	36 months / Until child is three years	Following m.l. / Until child is three years	Family / Family	Income-related: 66 per cent / Flat-rate	Weeks	Yes	Yes	None	No
Sweden	18 months	Until child is eight years	Family	Income-related: 80 per cent (ten months) and 90 per cent (two months); flat-rate (three months)	Weeks	Yes	Yes	None	6 months of service
United Kingdom	None								

Source: Leave arrangements for workers with children, European Commission Network on Childcare and other Measures to reconcile Employment and Family Responsibilities, (1994, update 1995).

Notes:
a No parental leave, but 'career break' of 6 to 12 months per worker subject to employer's agreement.
b Only with employer's agreement.
c Leave can also be used for other reasons, such as training: workers taking leave are not guaranteed their jobs.
d M.l. – maternity leave.
e Higher for single parents or low income families.
f Portugal: maximum of 24 months to be taken in special circumstances.
g B: basic parental leave; E: extended 'child-care' leave.

Source: European Commission (1997) *Annual Report from the Commission. Equal Opportunities for Women and Men in the European Union 1996.* European Commission, p. 58.

- three months' non-transferable and unpaid leave after the birth or adoption of a child, the leave to be taken before the eighth birthday of the child;

- protection from dismissal for asking for parental leave;

- protection of the right to return to work to the same or an equivalent job after the leave; and

- provision for additional time off in urgent family circumstances, such as sickness and accident.

The agreement between the Partners leaves many of the details to be decided at the level of the member state – either by the member-state government or by the Partners operating at that level. In this case, therefore, there were no agreements at EU level on issues such as:

- what might be an appropriate length of service qualification;

- whether the leave should be full- or part-time;

- what notice periods should be given to the employer; and

- the number of days' leave that may be reasonable or allowable for the urgent family leave referred to in the Agreement.

This Agreement can be seen to be consistent with *the principle of subsidiarity* and, while it seeks to create a minimum right for employees, it does not seek to impose particular mechanisms or details; options are left open on whether the Agreement should be given effect at member-state level through legislation or through further voluntary agreements between the Social Partners. In this way, the diverse traditions and practices of each member state can be largely maintained at the same time as there is some harmonisation of minimum rights.

The potential impact of the Directive can be seen from the overview of parental leave provisions in the member states, shown in Fig. 11.3.

A number of other equality proposals have been transferred into the Protocol Procedure.

Draft Directive on Reversal of the Burden of Proof in Sex Discrimination Cases

This Directive Proposal (COM (88) 269) has been under discussion since 1988 and was stalled for some time by the opposition of the UK; like other equality proposals it required unanimity. However, the Protocol Agreement has provided an alternative mechanism and it was switched into this Procedure in April 1995.

The essence of the proposal in the draft was that employers should be assumed guilty of allegations of sex discrimination until they can prove otherwise and that the complainant should have a right of access to all the information necessary to the case. These proposals were unacceptable and for some time there were discussions on mechanisms, whereby the burden may be shared.

However, the Social Partners decided when the issue was transferred into the Protocol Procedure that they did not want to try and negotiate a framework agreement and by July 1996 they had asked the Commission to prepare another draft Directive. It seemed likely that the Commission would try and produce a Draft on the burden of proof that encompasses some sharing of the burden, possibly along the lines of the complainant having to first establish the facts and the employer then having to establish that there was no discrimination.

Another equality proposal that was put into the Protocol procedure was the:

Draft Directive on the Promotion of Employment and the Protection of Part-time and Fixed-term Employment Relationships

This Directive began as two draft Directives as part of the SAP, subsequent to the Social Charter. An attempt was made to introduce the draft Directives as health and safety issues so that they could, if necessary, be adopted via QMV. This did not work, however, and they became stalled. The Social Protocol Agreement has given them new life in that they can be proposed as equality issues and be subject to QMV. The essence of the grounds upon which they can be argued as equality issues rests on the fact that the majority of part-time (80 per cent) and fixed-term employees within the Union are female and therefore to discriminate against these categories of contract or employee is to indirectly discriminate on the grounds of sex.

Exhibit 11.1

Full deal for Europe's part-timers

FT

Andrew Bolger continues a series on employment law changes

Not all changes to the employment framework under Labour will emanate directly from Westminster or Whitehall. Earlier this month – even before the new government had signed the social chapter – an agreement was announced to give part-time employees across the European Union legal rights to match those of full-time workers.

The agreement was signed in The Hague after talks between Unice, the European employers' organisation, and the European Trade Union Confederation. Subject to ratification by the council of ministers, it will be adopted as a legally binding directive on all EU states and become law within two years.

There are 5.7m part-time workers in Britain – by 2001 one in three British employees, it is forecast, will be working part-time.

The agreement obliges states to extend to part-timers the rights that full-time workers have to equal pay and equal treatment.

The agreement is the second such deal reached between employers and trade unions in the EU, after one covering unpaid parental leave signed earlier this year. The deal on part-timers will apply to the UK once the new Labour government has signed the social chapter, as it promised to do.

Following a landmark House of Lords ruling in 1994, the British government was forced to give part-time workers the same

statutory rights as full-timers – to claim unfair dismissal and redundancy. But this did not affect contractual rights.

According to the Trades Union Congress, 60 per cent of British part-time workers do not get all the benefits full-timers receive – such as paid occupational sick leave, occupational pensions, staff discounts and share options. Many part-timers get no paid holiday. All this will now be covered by the working time directive.

Research put the cost of equalisation of part-timers' rights at 0.5 per cent of the pay bill

---

Last year research by the Policy Studies Institute put the cost of equalisation of part-timers' rights at 0.5 per cent of the total pay bill – 'significantly less than the £1.8bn-worth of perks and expenses enjoyed by company directors,' says the TUC.

The agreement applies to all part-timers with an employment contract or relationship: permanent, fixed-term contracts and temporary. This is estimated to cover about 90 per cent of British part-timers.

However, the measure has been watered down because of employer pressure to enable casual workers to be excluded

'wholly or in part for objective reasons'.

The TUC says: 'There were insurmountable difficulties in finding a definition of casual which could be applied to all states and in several languages. The transposition of this clause therefore is crucial.'

British employers take a philosophical view. 'Given the imminent ending of the opt-out from the European Union's social chapter, legislation on part-time work in the UK is inevitable,' says Adair Turner, director-general of the Confederation of British Industry. 'We believe this agreement represents the best deal on offer.'

Ruth Lea, head of the policy unit at the Institute of Directors, says her organisation is unhappy about the agreement but relieved that casual and temporary employees had been excluded from its provisions following negotiations.

The agreement has been welcomed by John Monks, general secretary of the TUC. 'This is a the kind of flexibility with fairness that offers advantages to employers and employees,' he said.

Francois Perigot, president of Unice, describes the agreement as a big step towards greater flexibility of work, needed for the restoration of European competitiveness and the creation of jobs.

'Above all,' he says, 'it contains a clause which seeks to eliminate obstacles to the development of part-time work.'

Source: Financial Times, 18 June 1997.

The Social Partners managed to reach a European framework Agreement on part-time work which was then passed to the Commission to progress through the normal decision-making procedures (*see* Chapter 8). The Commission issued the Agreement as a Proposal for a Council Directive in July 1997 COM (97) 392 and the Council adopted the agreement as a Directive towards the end of 1997 (*see* Exhibit 11.1).

The agreement reached by the Social Partners was primarily concerned to agree general principles and minimum requirements and many of the details were left to be resolved at national level. It was agreed that the purposes of the Agreement were to include:

- removing discrimination against part-time workers;
- improving the quality of part-time work;
- facilitating the development of part-time work; and
- contributing to the flexible organisation of working time.

Casual working was to be excluded from the coverage of the Agreement. The definition of part-time was broad and is to include:

> an employee whose normal hours of work, calculated on a weekly basis or on an average over a period of employment of up to one year, are less than the normal hours of work of a comparable full-time worker.

The Agreement enshrines the principle that part-time workers should not be discriminated against in terms of their employment conditions solely on the basis that they work part-time, though there is provision for different treatment to be justified on objective grounds.

Court rulings

The initiative to provide rights on non-discrimination to part-time workers had been given impetus by various court decisions since early 1994 which have ruled that to discriminate (whether by the employer or legislation) between part-time and full-time employees in terms of rights to redundancy payments, rights to join an occupational pension scheme and rights to claim unfair dismissal was indirect sex discrimination in that it affected a much larger number of women than men and could not be justified objectively on grounds other than sex.

- *Fisscher and Vroege (both ECJ Sept 94).* These two rulings established that women were equally entitled to join occupational pension schemes as men, as well as being equally entitled to benefits under the schemes. Therefore to discriminate against part-time workers (given that the great majority are female) or married women by not allowing them to join such schemes was unlawful unless there was some other objective reason. If women have an equal right to belong, so must part-time employees. These decisions required change to UK law and this was done via The Occupational Pension Schemes (Equal Access to Membership) Regulations 1995.
- *The Kalanke case.* Subsequent to the ECJ decision in the Kalanke case in October of 1995, considerable doubts were raised about the lawfulness of positive action in favour of one sex in employment.
  The Land of Bremen was operating a policy of automatically giving priority to women candidates for recruitment and promotion in sectors where they were under-

represented and where a female candidate had the same qualifications as a male candidate. The ECJ found the practice to be in contravention of Article 2(4) of Directive 76/207/EEC (the Directive on Equal Treatment) and found that rules and procedures which give one sex *absolute* and *unconditional* priority goes beyond promoting equal treatment or opportunities and oversteps the provisions for positive action provided for in Article 2(4). This allowed for action to be taken to remove obstacles to the equal treatment of the sexes as an exception from the main requirement not to discriminate. However, the ECJ found that to *guarantee* women priority went too far.

This decision appeared in the first instance to outlaw the type of *de facto* quota systems that had been the practice in the state of Bremen, and in many other places. As a result of the confusion caused by this decision, the Commission in March 1996 proposed to revise the appropriate Directive with a view to defining and clarifying what is and what is not appropriate positive action.

The object of the Commission's proposed revision of Article 2(4) in the original Directive on Equal Treatment was to permit positive action programmes and discrimination not specifically covered by the Kalanke ruling. They wanted to ensure that some relatively common measures of positive action remain lawful such as:

- plans and programmes geared towards the recruitment and/or promotion of women to achieve targets but without resorting to automatic preference in the event of individual decisions;
- the granting of reductions in employers' social security contributions when they recruit women returning to the labour market into occupations in which they are under-represented;
- plans and programmes focussing on removing inequalities in areas including vocational training, flexibility of working time and child care.

The Commission seems to want to maintain a situation in which positive action in favour of the under-represented sex is lawful as long as it falls short of the establishment and application of rigid quotas and as long as the programmes leave room for taking into account individual circumstances.

In addition to the proposals to redraft the Directive, concerns about the impact of this ruling encouraged the Commission to issue a Communication (COM (96) 88). In it, the Commission puts forward the view that the Kalanke decision only rendered unlawful measures which give absolute and unconditional rights or priority. The Commission seeks to approve positive action measures in the form of targets, in terms of quotas and time limits which express preference but which don't imply automatic preference, irrespective of qualification and which do allow for exception. The provision of incentives to employers and funding support for training, child care and the reorganisation of work so as to benefit the under-represented sex should all be considered and remain lawful.

Non-binding instruments

In addition to the Memorandum on Equal Pay for Work of Equal Value (94/6) and the 1984 Recommendation on the Promotion of Positive Action already mentioned, there are a number of other non-binding instruments relevant to issues of equality between the sexes at work and in connection with employment:

- *Council Recommendation 92/241 on Child Care* recommends that member states seek to facilitate the reconciliation of family and occupational responsibilities by providing/encouraging the provision of child care services, and encouraging the promotion of flexible working as well as a sharing of parental responsibilities.

- *Council Resolution on Balanced Participation of Men and Women in Decision-making 95/C168/02.*

- *Council Resolution on the Image of Women in the Media 95/C296/06* is concerned to encourage the presentation of a less stereotyped and therefore 'truer' picture of women in the media.

- *Commission Recommendation (92)/131* and *Code of Practice on the Dignity of Women and Men at Work* seek to address the issue of sexual harassment at work and provide policy guidance to practitioners as well as to member-state governments and the Social Partners as formal participants. The Recommendation encourages member states to use the public sector to establish practices that set an example to the private sector. The Code (which like all such documents can be taken into account by the courts) defines sexual harassment as:

    unwanted conduct of a sexual nature, or other conduct based on sex affecting the dignity of women and men at work. This can include unwelcome physical, verbal or non-verbal conduct.

  The Code also recommends that practitioners should devise appropriate policies and procedures, provide training and allocate responsibility for implementation to managers within the organisation. As noted earlier, the Social Partners are trying to reach a framework agreement on this matter.

As a general rule, resolutions and recommendations of the Council carry more weight within the Union than do those of the Commission.

Equal Opportunities Action Programmes

The Commission has also issued and sought to implement a number of *Equal Opportunities Action Programmes*; the fourth of these was issued in July 1995 and is to cover the period 1996 to 2000. The need for this Fourth Action Programme is in itself arguably a reflection of the lack of success of all the earlier initiatives.

The first and over-arching priority is '*mainstreaming*' – that is, ensuring that equality issues are taken into account in all policies and other initiatives at national and sub-national levels within the Union, as well as at EU level. The intention is to ensure that equality issues and rights are integral to all future interventions. The Commission report (1997b) comments upon this process known as 'mainstreaming' and describes it as a more global approach to the issue of equality that calls for the development of a gender perspective and gender analysis of all policies, programmes and actions.

Other priorities are:

- the encouragement of policies that will facilitate the reconciliation of professional and family life, and in the medium term the possibility of the *Recommendation on Child Care* may be followed by a framework directive;

- encouraging a better balance of men and women in decision-making positions, with the Council Resolution on this issue being followed in 1996 by a draft Recommendation that sought to give effect to some of the conclusions of the 1995 world-wide Beijing Conference on Women;

- providing women with more and better information on their rights so that they may be more widely exercised and enforced;
- the further and active promotion of the dignity of men and women at work.

Following the publication of this Action Programme, there were pressures from various groups within the Commission and the EP, as well as from other pressure groups such as the European Women's Lobby and the Social Policy Forum, to ensure that the IGC (*see* Chapter 9) incorporated a statement or Chapter that gave effect to the principle of equal opportunities. As noted in Chapter 9, the Amsterdam Treaty draft does do this.

The European Women's Lobby has also been seeking to follow up the Beijing Conference and, in particular, has been exerting pressure to ensure that a range of equality issues are addressed at the level of the Union. These include discrimination against girls, sexual harassment (where they would like a Directive) and issues of stereotyping, education and access to employment.

Amsterdam Treaty proposals

It has been noted earlier that the Amsterdam IGC proposals seek to provide a firm basis for the Community and the Council to take appropriate measures to support and complement and ensure the application of the principles of equal pay, opportunities and treatment. This is clearly specified in the proposed new Article 119. Equality between men and women with regard to labour market opportunities and treatment is also included in the proposed new *Article 118(1)*.

In addition to the new Social Chapter, the ability of the Union in the future to pursue objectives and take action on matters of discrimination (not limited to the labour market/employment scenario) has potentially been greatly enhanced by a *new Article 6(a)* which provides for the Council acting unanimously with the power to take:

appropriate action to combat discrimination based on sex, racial or ethnic origin, religion or belief, disability, age or sexual orientation.

Additionally, in *Article 2* of the proposed amended EC Treaty the words 'equality between men and women' are to be inserted after 'a high level of employment and social protection'. This article seeks to establish the 'Task' of the Community.

Article 3 is also to be supplemented with a new paragraph which can be linked to the desire of the Commission and others to mainstream the issue of equality between the sexes. Article 3 sets out a long list of 'the activities' of the Community and it is suggested that appended to this list will be:

In all the activities referred to in this Article, the Community shall aim to eliminate inequalities, and to promote equality, between men and women.

Other initiatives

The Commission Annual Report on Equal Opportunities for Men and Women in the EU 1997

This is the first of what is to be a series of annual reports and has a number of objectives:

- to give visible expression to community policy on equal opportunities for men and women (*visibility*);

- to encourage debate on the progress to be achieved and the policies to develop (*strategy*);

- to act as a reference point for the Commission, the member states and countries applying for membership (*convergence*).

The report provides a means by which it is possible to monitor progress and the implementation and implications of EU initiatives and policies in this area.

Other initiatives have been taken (usually under the aegis of the ESF) to encourage and facilitate the integration of women into the labour market. These have included encouragement and financial support for targeted vocational training and re-training programmes to enable women to return to work. In particular, the *New Opportunities for Women* (NOW) programme (*see* Chapter 15) is targeted at those who are long-term unemployed and those who seek to establish their own businesses and works towards increasing the proportion of female management. The Commission report (1997c) comments that it was the 1993 revision that enabled the structural funds to assist with issues of inequality. As a result of this revision, equality and equal opportunities became a principle running through all three funds – the ESF, ERDF and EAGGF (*see* Chapter 6) – and Objective 3 now makes specific reference to equality. The relationship between the structural funds and equality was cemented in a Council Resolution, adopted in December 1996 on Equal Opportunities and the Structural Funds.

RACISM AND XENOPHOBIA

The EU is a Union of 15 previously totally independent member states, each of which may have warred with one or more of the others in the past. It should be remembered that the maintenance of peace within Europe and between the member states was, and arguably still is a major reason for the formation and maintenance of the Union and indeed for its enlargement. There is plenty of evidence in the history of Europe of racially motivated conflicts.

The background to racism

Racism within the EU is by no means limited to that existing between the citizens of one member state and those of another. Racism and racially based discrimination occur within countries – between different ethnic groups living there and against those who may live and work within the EU but who have migrated into the Union from countries outside (regarded as third-country nationals).

As already noted in Chapter 10 when we examined the evidence of labour mobility in the EU, the EFILWC (1996d) divides the working population of the Union into five categories in terms of their legal status:

1 citizens living and working within their own country;

2 citizens of one member state working and living in another;

3 third-country nationals with full rights of residency and who work in one of the member states;

4 third-country nationals with leave to stay for a fixed period of time and with a revocable work permit;

5 undocumented or illegals.

This list can be perceived as a hierarchy of legal rights with those in Category 1 having the most rights and those in Category 5 the least. The EFILWC suggests that layered on top of this inequality is another hierarchy of inequality based upon the colour of skin and ethnicity. Even those in Category 1 above can experience inequality on the basis of the colour of their skin.

The authors of the report adopt a wide definition of race to include race, religion, colour, ethnicity and nationality and suggest that discrimination can occur on any and all of these grounds. The term 'ethnic minority' does not refer to an homogeneous group; there are substantial cultural and behavioural differences between the various minorities that may together comprise the total. There is also considerable scope for racially based discrimination between one minority group and another.

The EU is clearly and already a complex multi-racial, cultural and religious community and this complexity will be enhanced as the size of the Union is enlarged (*see* Chapter 5). Enlargement, therefore, may act as a catalyst for further tension on the grounds of race as the number of races within the Union increases. The potential for racially based suspicion, antagonism and conflict may also increase if internal labour mobility improves and as more third-country nationals enter the Union, as people from different racial backgrounds compete directly and visibly with one another for scarce resources, which in the current climate is quite likely to centre around competition for work.

There is some suggestion that there are positive relationships between unemployment, economic and social exclusion and the expression of racism. The overt and often violent indications of that racism may become more apparent with higher and longer unemployment and as the incidence of social and labour market exclusion increases. In such a scenario, racial discrimination and conflict may be seen as symptoms of a lack of social cohesion brought about by the economic and social marginalisation of those members of society who are non-active and relatively poor.

In this context, EMU, with its convergence criteria that have been designed primarily to achieve stable currencies, low inflation and thereby economic growth, may pose a threat to racial harmony if it results in high and continuing unemployment.

The creation and effective operation of the single market and monetary union may be necessary to economic growth, and the enlargement of the Union may be necessary to both growth and the maintenance of peace in the greater Europe, but in each case these desirable developments from the perspective of the economy and peace of Europe may have social consequences that include an increase in racial tensions, suspicion and discrimination. There appears a much greater likelihood that tensions of this kind will extend beyond the workplace.

Protection against discrimination

A comparison of the legislative and/or constitutional provisions offering protection against discrimination in the member states (EIRR, March 1995) suggests considerable diversity of provision and protection. Great Britain (Northern Ireland has separate provisions) and Sweden probably have the most advanced provisions with respect to discrimination on the grounds of race. Sweden defines race to include skin colour, ethnic and national origin and the British definition is similar but also mentions nationality.

Other countries tend to have various and more limited definitions or grounds upon which discrimination is unlawful, although in Germany, Italy and Portugal language is also covered.

In member states with such protections the scope of the protection also varies.

- In Sweden, the Netherlands, Great Britain and France the protection extends to recruitment, dismissal and treatment during employment, whereas in Ireland it extends only to dismissals.

- In Germany coverage extends to those employed in the establishment and in Italy any action at work is unlawful if it discriminates on the grounds of race.

- Some of the member states adopt a slightly different approach – for example, Austria, Finland and Luxembourg – in that discriminatory dismissal (including on the grounds of race) is unlawful unless it can be justified on grounds which are 'serious'.

- Portugal is the only one of the member states in which rights to equal pay are to be regardless of race or place of origin.

Most of the southern member states – Greece, Portugal, Italy, Spain – and also Ireland have different kinds of experience of racial discrimination than the others. These countries have traditions of emigration rather than immigration and in the main do not have adequate legal machinery to deal with the levels of racial discrimination suspected now that they have become countries that experience immigration. They would argue that in the past there have not been problems associated with racial discrimination in the workplace.

Incidence of racial discrimination in the EU

There is relatively little information on the incidence and impact of discrimination on the grounds of race and much of the evidence available is of the American experience and therefore not necessarily of direct relevance to the European context.

Hegewisch and Mayne (1994) assert that the evidence available within Europe supports the view that inequality on racial grounds:

> continues to be a major feature of European labour markets, as expressed, for example, in rates of unemployment and average pay levels.

This view is also confirmed by the EFILWC (1996d) report on the evidence from each of the member states and Norway in which it is concluded that the migrant and visible minority population in the EU was disproportionately represented in poor and insecure work and among the unemployed, and that this also applied to the second- and third-generation migrant descended population who had been born and had grown up within the EU.

On the question of statistical evidence, the report confirms the relative absence of such evidence but does refer to analysis of relatively large data sets in both the UK and the Netherlands which show a discrepancy between the unemployment rates of white nationals and ethnic minority groups, with only a small portion of this discrepancy being accounted for by the level of education and other differences. The conclusion drawn is that racial discrimination is the variable that most likely explains the differences in employment experience.

On the one hand, widespread and long-term unemployment among an indigenous group may act as a catalyst for the public expression of racial tension and conflict and further racial discrimination; on the other, the evidence in some countries of higher rates of unemployment among the ethnic minorities suggests that racial discrimination at work exists.

Interestingly, the EFILWC report also suggests that in the southern member states ethnic and racial minorities have a somewhat different experience of discrimination in that they tend not to be disproportionately represented among the unemployed. In these countries immigrants experience a kind of perverse positive discrimination when it comes to recruitment: they are actively preferred because they are cheaper, more vulnerable and more pliable. They are less able to resist exploitation in work and in respect of working conditions because there is a less effective legal regime and they are often 'illegals' when it comes to working.

If there is relatively little evidence in most member states of the extent of discrimination in recruitment, selection and pay, there is even less on issues relating to treatment once employed – for example, in areas such as training, career opportunities and development, promotions and dismissals.

UK experience, given that the UK is one of the countries with the most extensive and established sets of anti-discrimination legislation, would indicate that discrimination occurs in all of these areas of organisational policy and practice. Over the years, there have been many instances highlighted by the facility to take advantage of the legislation and to pursue such allegations through the system of tribunals and courts and involving the Advisory, Conciliation and Arbitration Service (ACAS).

A particularly recent and well publicised incident of this nature was the allegation in 1996 by seven Asian and Afro-Caribbean employees of Ford UK that they had been discriminated against in their efforts to secure a job in the Ford Truck Fleet operation. These jobs were regarded as among the élite manual jobs within Ford and it became apparent, once the application was made to the Tribunal, that recruitment into these positions was effectively controlled by the senior drivers. There was clear evidence of an internal labour market being controlled by insiders; the argument of the applicants was that these insiders were allocating the jobs to employees on racial and ethnic grounds. Evidence to the Tribunal in 1996 included the allegation that one of the truck fleet driver assessors was overheard saying:

It's not my fault if Pakis can't drive . . .

which, in the context of the earlier analysis, is an example of inaccurate stereotyping.

The applicants in support of their allegation submitted that some 45 per cent of shopfloor employees in the company were from ethnic minorities, whereas only 2 per cent of the truck fleet jobs were filled by people from those minority groups. An additional feature of this case was that the applicants' union – the Transport and General Workers Union (TGWU) – was in the unenviable position of supporting the applicants in a complaint about the discriminatory behaviour of the fleet truck drivers who were also members of the Union. This encouraged the truck drivers to vote in favour of leaving the TGWU to join a rival union – The United Road Transport Union (URTU).

The cultural basis of racial discrimination

Discrimination of this type is as much culturally derived and bound as gender discrimination is. Many of the explanations for gender discrimination are relevant in this instance, so that once pay differentials are greater than implied by productivity differences and labour markets are segregated, the competitive models become less relevant. Explanations for pay differentials can then be found in terms of either:

- discrimination as the product of a socially derived prejudice or taste which employers are prepared to pay for in terms of lost efficiency and profit, or
- discrimination as the product of imperfect information and insider/outsider models of economic behaviour and outcome.

Racial and ethnic minorities constitute much smaller proportions of the labour force in EU member states than do women.

Studies in the UK have tended to attribute a discriminatory earnings differential of about 10 per cent (Adnett, 1996). Hegewisch and Mayne (1994) and the EFILWC (1996d) point out that there is a tendency for the members of these minorities to also experience higher rates of unemployment. Racial and ethnic minorities are likely to be allocated into the secondary labour markets and there is a tendency for them to achieve lower levels of occupational attainment for a given level of educational attainment. Second-generation members of these groups tend to fare better in educational and occupational attainment terms, the assumption being that there are educational and cultural 'advantages' derived from being born and raised in a country even if that is not the country of racial or ethnic origin. However, as noted by the EFILWC report, there are still differentials of experience in employment and pay that are inexplicable other than as the product of discrimination.

The EFILWC report (1996d) points to some of the less obvious means through which indirect racial discrimination is effected. One of the more common of these is a reliance by employers upon an internal and extended internal labour market when it comes to recruitment. It is common in several member states for preference, either overt or covert, to be given to friends and family of those already employed – a convenient means by which members of ethnic minorities/races can be excluded. It is also common for employees and employers to blame each other where these practices are discovered, so that employers might well argue that it is their employees who are prejudiced, not themselves, and that they have to practise discrimination in this way because they would have trouble with their other employees if they didn't. Unfortunately, this is probably true in some cases (see the example in Ford (UK) already discussed).

COMBATING RACIAL DISCRIMINATION IN THE EU

The EFILWC report (1996d) identifies a number of obstacles to effectively combating discrimination which include:

- a general lack of awareness and ignorance of the problems among employers and trade unionists;

- broad ideological opposition to regulation, as for example, expressed by those who believe in the efficiency and effectiveness of the market;

- the lack of social, political and legal rights of those that make up the minorities that are discriminated against;

- weaknesses in the current legal environments at both national and EU level, both in the sense of the anti-discrimination legislation itself and in the mechanisms for its enforcement where it does exist.

The report also contains a number of recommendations as to what actions need to be initiated and encouraged at the level of the firm, at the level of the member state and also at the level of the Union. The Union-level recommendations include a Directive on Racial Discrimination, A Code of Practice, enhancement of the rights of third-country nationals to move, work and live within the Union, and investment in research and the collection of data and its dissemination. The authors of the EFILWC report expressly take the view that:

> Member States are unlikely to introduce measures which are truly effective unless encouraged to do so by a Directive at the European level.

Surprisingly, there is no legal provision (other than the catch-all Article 235) within the EC Treaty that gives the EU institutions the right to act against racial discrimination or to give individuals the right not to be discriminated against on these grounds. As a result, the central institutions, and perhaps the Commission in particular, have been and are significantly hampered in taking initiatives to promote racial, ethnic, religious and cultural equality between peoples and in the pursuit of a Union in which racial discrimination is unlawful.

Given the will on the part of the Commission and some of the member states, it is astonishing that more use has not been made of the opinion expressed by the ECJ in its judgement in the Defrenne case (*see* earlier in this chapter) to the effect that:

> respect for fundamental personal human rights is one of the general principles of Community Law, the observance of which it [the ECJ] has a duty to ensure.

The same applies to Article 235. This device/arrangement was utilised to justify the adoption of the Equal Treatment Directive (76/207).

The Declaration adopted by the Council in 1990 (*see* later in this chapter) did recognise that the right to equality on grounds of race constituted a fundamental right and confirmed that the EU and its institutions attached prime importance to the protection of such rights, but no legislative action has been taken to ensure that these rights are protected.

The closest that the existing EC Treaty comes to addressing the issue are references to discrimination on the grounds of nationality. Articles 6, 48(2) and 220 are the relevant ones; these were motivated primarily as necessary to attaining the effective mobility of labour in the single market. It was recognised that a single market and the accompanying mobility of labour could be harmed if there was discrimination within some countries against the nationals of other countries seeking to work there. Article 6 prohibits such discrimination and Article 48(2) makes the purpose even clearer:

> Such freedom of movement shall entail the abolition of any discrimination based on nationality between workers of the Member States as regards employment, remuneration and other conditions of work and employment.

It was also the case that the parties perceived this as a protection against a form of social dumping in the employment and exploitation of workers from member states in which wages and other terms and conditions are not so good. These concerns and practices are also behind the Posted Workers Directive (COM (91) 230) (*see* Chapter 10) which seeks to ensure that employees cannot be brought in from other member states and paid less than those from the home state.

The limitations of these Treaty Articles are that they refer only to nationality; and what is at issue in this section is discrimination on grounds much wider than that.

Although there have been no legislative initiatives in this area, there have been a number of non-binding Recommendations and Declarations. In 1986, the EU institutions combined to produce and issue a Declaration against Racism and Xenophobia and in 1990 the Council adopted a Resolution on the same subject though the Resolution argued action at member-state level. This latter Resolution had been preceded by the Social Charter in 1989 and the preamble to this document contains the statement:

> it is important to combat every form of discrimination, including discrimination on the grounds of sex, colour, race, opinion and beliefs . . .

Once again, no initiatives were taken to introduce appropriate legislation.

Another Declaration was made by the Council at Maastricht in 1991 and called for unambiguous responses by member states against violence and hostility that was based on grounds of race, religion, culture or national differences. However, there were no proposals for action at the level of the Union.

The 1994 White Paper on Social Policy (European Commission, 1994c) noted the problem that the treaties didn't provide an appropriate basis for action against discrimination on the grounds of race, religion, age or disability and the Commission proposed within this document that future Treaty revisions should redress this situation.

The summit meetings at Corfu, Essen and Cannes in 1994 and 1995 all discussed the issues of racism and discrimination and in October 1995 the Council adopted a non-binding Resolution (95/C296/05) on the subject of Racism and Xenophobia in employment, training and social affairs. This Resolution asked the Commission to examine existing programmes, particularly in the education and training arena, to establish whether there was any further scope within them to combat racism and xenophobia. The Resolution also called upon member states to:

- ratify any outstanding international instruments against racial discrimination;
- support democratic movements against racism;
- promote codes of practice and the like as guidance for those involved in employment and the media; and
- develop respect for diversity and tolerance in education and training programmes.

The Social Partners have also produced a Joint Declaration on the prevention of Racial Discrimination and Xenophobia and the Promotion of Equal Treatment at the Workplace in which they stress the responsibility of employers and employees. They indicate a number of the initiatives and types of measure that have been shown to be successful in the workplace.

In December 1995, the Commission issued a Communication on the subject of Racism, Xenophobia and anti-Semitism. In this document, to which was also attached a draft decision that 1997 be designated the EU Year against Racism, the Commission set out several priority areas requiring action:

- raising public awareness and combating prejudice;
- adapting EU law;
- greater international cooperation;
- promoting integration and encouraging inclusion;
- preventing racist behaviour and violence; and
- monitoring and punishing racist crime.

The Commission received a setback in late March 1996 when its attempt to apply the principle of 'mainstreaming' (*see* page 200) in the Directive on Parental Leave was effectively rejected at the Social Affairs Council (SAC). The Commission had proposed the insertion into the Social Partners agreement on Parental Leave a clause or provision that sought to outlaw discrimination that was on the grounds of race, sex, sexual orientation, colour, religion or national origin.

By the time of the opening of the IGC in 1996, many of the interested and involved institutions and pressure groups saw the IGC as an opportunity to incorporate an explicit legislative basis into the new treaties to be produced by the process. There is considerable pressure within both the Commission and the EP for the resultant Treaty to contain provisions or a Chapter on the issue of equality. This is consistent with the specified intentions of the Fourth Social Action Programme and the emphasis placed in it on the desirability of 'mainstreaming'.

However, it also became clear in the IGC discussions at the end of 1996 that the UK government was opposed to any such outcome and possibly prepared to use its veto in order to prevent the EU acquiring express authority to take action in those areas of equality not already provided for.

A further setback to EU-level action on these issues was presented in January 1997 by the UK's use of its veto to prevent the establishment of an EU centre which would have collected and analysed data, acted as the base of an information network and thereby monitored the incidence and impact of racism. The centre was to have been particularly concerned with issues of free movement of people and discrimination in employment. The UK was in a minority of one and explained its reasons in terms of subsidiarity and an opposition to the EU having such powers.

As noted elsewhere, the decision to delay the completion of the IGC until after the General Election in the UK and the subsequent election of a Labour government meant that agreement between the member states became possible on this, as on other issues. (The outcome of the IGC in terms of the new Treaty proposals has been documented earlier in this chapter and in Chapter 9.)

The main provision with respect to combating racial discrimination is a new Article 6a which provides the Council acting unanimously with the power to take:

> appropriate action to combat discrimination based on sex, racial or ethnic origin, religion or belief, disability, age or sexual orientation.

This proposal does not go as far as many wanted and it will undoubtedly be some time before any Directives are adopted via this new provision. The requirement for unanimity may yet prove to be a stumbling block to effective action being taken. Yet there are concerns, identified earlier, that the further integration of the Union, progress towards an effective single market and the planned enlargement may all make such action against discrimination on racial grounds more necessary.

CONCLUSIONS

It is possible to draw a number of reasonably firm conclusions from our discussion of equality in the European Union. European Union labour markets are characterised by inequality and discrimination on both gender and racial or ethnic grounds. The scale of this discrimination and its impact varies from country to country and between gender and race and indeed between the racial groups that make up the ethnic minorities.

In all instances, the impact of this discrimination seems to encompass:

- earnings differentials that are due to prejudice and taste, and not justified by differences in productivity;
- higher rates and longer periods of unemployment; and
- the likelihood of employment opportunities being concentrated in the secondary, poorer quality labour markets.

Women also commonly exhibit lower participation rates and various different working patterns including a greater incidence of part-time and flexible employment and a greater likelihood that the lifetime pattern of employment will include periods of discontinuity.

There are some positive indications and trends, however, such as the gradual narrowing of the gender pay gap and the trends for increased demand in the service sector and for part-time and otherwise flexible labour which all seem likely to continue and which should all help female participation rates to continue on an upward trend.

The inequalities and discrimination experienced by these disadvantaged groups does appear to be the product of stereotypes and values acquired through the process of socialisation (*see*, for example, the comments on the capabilities and characteristics of ethnic minorities as indicated in the Ford case in this chapter), and which form a significant component of the cultures of the countries that make up the EU.

There are differences between these cultures on issues such as the allocation of domestic duties and the 'proper' role of women, which are detectable in the scale and precise nature of the labour market outcomes referred to above. Even in the most egalitarian of these cultures there are detectable differences on issues such as the proportions of women appointed to senior management positions.

The EU has demonstrated a considerable interest in the issue of inequality and discrimination linked to gender but cannot demonstrate similar levels of concern and activity on the subject of racial discrimination.

It is impossible to know the extent to which inequality and discrimination on the grounds of gender have been limited or circumscribed by the actions that have been taken within the EU. It seems reasonable to assume some beneficial impact on earnings differentials and participation rates, but there is always the concern that the enforcement of equality can result in counter-productive avoiding measures being taken at the level of the organisation.

If discrimination is the consequence of ingrained values and attitudes on the part of an employer or indeed existing workers, and if there is a well developed internal market, then there is a likelihood that measures taken by the EU to enhance equality of opportunity, treatment or outcome may only result in measures being taken at the organisational level that result in further discrimination and occupational segregation. Such measures serve to confound the intentions of the legislators as well as the mechanisms created to ensure enforcement. The danger, of course, is that this somewhat sceptical conclusion can easily and quickly become a reason for doing nothing.

There is some evidence that education and training can have beneficial consequences, both in terms of creating more skilled and highly qualified racial minorities and also in counteracting ingrained stereotypes through the process of exposure. This seems to be particularly true for those that are second and third generation. This beneficial effect of education and training is also quite likely to apply to women. Other measures and interventions are more problematic in terms of the ability of the authorities to enforce them, the willingness of the employers and internal labour force to comply and their ability to devise alternative discriminatory measures.

There are measures that can facilitate the participation of women such as the availability of child care facilities in the right place at the right time and employer initiatives, such as the provision of career breaks, the organisation of work around flexibility of attendance, and positive action programmes that may involve the expenditure of resources but which do not discriminate unfairly against men or particular racial groupings. An example of such a positive action programme may be the provision of education and training schemes that seek to enhance the opportunities of women and ethnic minorities to qualify to apply for a particular position, but which leave the actual recruitment and selection process unchanged, with the emphasis remaining upon selecting the 'best' candidate.

The imposition of a minimum wage at an appropriate level could also play an important part in eliminating or at least narrowing the gender and ethnic pay and earnings gaps, since it is likely that those working in the secondary sectors where wages tend to be lowest would gain the most. As already noted, there tends to be a concentration of members of these disadvantaged groups in these sectors.

It is important that members of all these minority groups have recourse to the law and that there is a body of minimum rights and entitlements which they can rely on and use when they are discriminated against, and which gives the ECJ the opportunity to push forward the principle of equality. This has a particular relevance to the case of racial discrimination since there are no such EU-level Directives or Regulations at the time of writing. It is unwise, however, to imagine that discriminatory attitudes and values can be readily changed that way.

Enlargement of the Union, high unemployment and a requirement for enhanced labour mobility are additional reasons for trying to create a non-discriminatory Union, since these may all create the circumstances in which racial tensions and the potential for social unrest and associated violence are enhanced.

Whatever the wishes and intentions of the other member states, it is still possible for the government of any one of the member states to veto the introduction at the level of the Union of legislative and other measures concerned to combat racism and racial discrimination in society and at work. The UK was by no means the only member state with reservations in this area.

The agreements at Amsterdam in the summer of 1997 do provide the opportunity for further action to combat discrimination on both gender and racial grounds. The Union has the opportunity to commence a programme of more effective action in both areas.

References

Adnett, N. (1996) *European Labour Markets: analysis and policy*. Longman.

Atkinson, J. (1984) 'Manpower Strategies for the Flexible Organisation', *Personnel Management*, Aug, 28–31.

Becker, G. (1957) *The Economics of Discrimination*. The University of Chicago Press.

Cox, S. (1993) 'Equal Opportunities', in Gold, M. (ed) *The Social Dimension – Employment Policy in the European Community*. Macmillan.

European Commission (1994c) *White Paper on Social Policy: The Way Forward for the Union*. European Commission.

European Commission (1996a) *Code of Practice on The Implementation of Equal Pay for Work of Equal Value for Women and Men,* COM (96) 336. European Commission.

European Commission (1996d) *A Review of Services for Young Children in the European Union (1990–1995)*. European Commission Network on Childcare and other Measures to Reconcile Employment and Family Responsibilities.

European Commission (1997c) *Annual Report from the Commission. Equal Opportunities for Women and Men in the European Union – 1996*. European Commission.

European Communities Publications Office (1996) *Eur-Op News*, 5(3), Autumn.

European Foundation for the Improvement of Living and Working Conditions (1996b) *Equal Opportunities and Collective Bargaining in Europe: 1 Defining the Issues*. EFILWC.

European Foundation for the Improvement of Living and Working Conditions (1996d) *Preventing Racism at the Workplace – A Summary*. EFILWC.

EIRR (European Industrial Relations Review) 254, 'Race, Employment and the Law in Europe', Mar 1995, pp. 15–19.

Hegewisch, A. and Mayne, L. (1994) 'Equal Opportunities Policies in Europe', in Brewster, C. and Hegewisch, A. (eds) *Policy and Practice in European Human Resource Management*. Routledge. pp. 168–193.

Hodgetts, R.M. and Luthans, F. (1994) *International Management* (2nd edn). McGraw-Hill.

Hofstede, G. (1991) *Cultures and Organisations: Software of the Mind*. McGraw-Hill.

IPD (1995) *European Update*, Oct.

Jewson, N. and Mason, D. (1986) 'The Theory and Practice of Equal Opportunities Policies: Liberal and Radical Approaches', *Sociological Review*, 34(2), 307–34.

Lasok, D. and Lasok, K.P.E. (1994) *Law and Institutions of the European Union* (6th edn). Butterworths.

Liff, S. (1995) 'Equal Opportunities: Continuing Discrimination in a Context of Formal Equality', in Edwards, P. (ed) *Industrial Relations Theory and Practice in Britain*. Blackwell.

Rees, B. and Brewster, C. (1995) Supporting Equality: Patriarchy at Work in Europe, *Personnel Review*, 24(1), 19–40.

Rubery, J. and Fagan, C. (1993) 'Occupational Segregation of Women and Men in the European Community', *Social Europe Supplement,* 3/93. Office for Official Publications of the European Communities.

Rubery, J. and Fagan, C. (1994) 'Does Feminisation Mean a Flexible Labour Force?', in Hyman, R. and Ferner, A. (eds) *New Frontiers in European Industrial Relations*. Blackwell.

Visser, J. (1993) 'Union Organisation: Why Countries Differ', *The International Journal of Comparative Labour Law and Industrial Relations*, Autumn, 206–21.

Walby, S. (1990) *Theorising Patriarchy*. Blackwell.

Additional reading

Brew, K. and Garavan, T.N. (19950 'Eliminating Inequality: Women Only Training', Part 1, 19(7), 13–19 and Part 2, 19(9), 28–32.

Coussey, M. and Jackson, H. (1991) *Making Equal Opportunities Work*. Pitman Publishing.

Davidson, M. and Cooper, C. (1992) *Shattering the Glass Ceiling*. Athenaeum Press.

Ford, G. (1991) *Fascist Europe: The Rise of Racism and Xenophobia*. Pluto Press.

Ford, V. (1996) 'Equality Versus Diversity – Partnership is the secret of Progress', *People Management*, Feb, 34–6.

Hantrais, L. (1995) *Social Policy In the European Union*. Macmillan.

Humphries, J. and Rubery, J. (eds) (1995) *The Economics of Equal Opportunities*. EOC.

Jenson, J., Hagen, E. and Reddy, C. (1988) *Feminisation of the Labour Force: Paradoxes and Promises*. Polity Press.

King, C. (1993) *Through the Glass Ceiling*. Athenaeum Press.

Mazey, S. (1988) 'European Community Action on Behalf of Women: The Limits of Legislation', *Journal of Common Market Studies*, 27(1), 63–84.

McEwan, S.A. (ed) (1994) *Gender Segregation and Social Change – Men and Women in Changing Labour Markets*. Oxford University Press.

Pillinger, J. (1992) *Feminising the Market – Women's Pay and Employment in the European Community*. Macmillan.

Rees, T. (1995) *Women and the EC Training Programmes – Tinkering, Tailoring and Transforming*. SAUS Publications.

Sisson, K. (1994) *Personnel Management*. Blackwell.

12

HEALTH AND SAFETY
AT WORK

LEARNING OBJECTIVES

When you have read this chapter, you should be able to understand and explain:

- the dynamic nature of the contexts within which health and safety at work must be addressed;

- the particular relevance of the nature of work, the technology in use and the stage of industrialisation;

- the incidence and cost of industrial injury and occupational disease; particular high-risk sectors and categories of employee;

- the content, variety and changing nature of EU interventions to improve the working environment and protect those at risk;

- the range of systems and efforts at securing compliance and enforcement and the significance of employee organisations.

INTRODUCTION

Health and safety at work, the incidence and prevention of accidents, injury and occupational disease and the improvement of working conditions and environments have been the subject of many EU and national government interventions over the years. The nature of the hazards and risks are variable across industrial boundaries and over time. To some extent they are also influenced by economic and demographic contexts, as well as by changes in the technology available and its impact upon the design of the work process. The progress of science, the development of new chemicals and materials and the acquisition of knowledge on their effects are also factors that influence the nature of the risks that pertain in certain sectors.

In addition to the changing nature of the risk, we have seen a gradual change in the approach of policy makers. Initially, the subject matter of their concern tended to be protection against and/or prevention of specific risks and hazards; however, there is increasingly evidence that the emphasis is moving in the direction of seeking to achieve improvement in the work environment and towards a more general concern with health in addition to the more traditional concern with safety. New forms and patterns of work, the pressures of competition and rising unemployment have tended to emphasise the psychological effects of work and in particular there is an increasing interest in issues of stress and mental health.

We also examine in this chapter the numerous EU-level interventions, the relevant Treaty articles, and the debate that has achieved a certain notoriety in recent years regarding the location of the boundaries between health and safety, on the one hand, and employee rights, on the other.

In the final section, we consider issues of compliance, inspection and enforcement and the mechanisms that exist at national and company level. We note the temptation for employers and employees not to comply with healthy and safety practices and the particular issue of regulation in the contexts of competitive advantage and the small employer.

HEALTH AND SAFETY AT WORK ACROSS THE EU

The risks and dangers that provide the subject matter of concerns and regulation on health and safety at work vary over time with the nature of work, the technology in use and the stage of industrialisation. The dangers and risks associated with working on the land are different from those associated with work in the extractive and mining industries, which are in turn different from those involved in automated Fordist-type production systems; these are in turn different from the sort of risks to employees that may be associated with the service industries. As the nature of work changes, so does the nature and scale of the occupational risk and threat of disease.

The EU is made up of countries at varying stages in this development from agriculture, through the secondary stage of industrialisation (that tends to be dominated by manufacturing), to the tertiary stage dominated by service industries. In the early 1990s, there were considerable variations between the EU member states as to the proportions of the working populations engaged in each of these sectors (*see* Table 4.2). Greece, Ireland and Portugal each still had more than 10 per cent engaged in agriculture, while in a number of countries there were more than 70 per cent engaged in the tertiary sector – for example, the UK, Sweden and the Netherlands.

It is also the case that the nature of risk and danger in a particular sector varies over time with the development of new techniques, the acquisition of knowledge and the development of new materials. For example, agriculture has become more and more mechanised and now also uses chemicals that were unheard of in the relatively recent past. Each of these may pose its own particular and new dangers and in many respects those working in agriculture now experience many of the same risks and dangers that we have tended to perceive as typical of industry. Mechanisation of the service sector is also ongoing and we have seen new illnesses and dangers emerge with the new technology – for example, Repetitive Strain Injury (RSI) and considerably enhanced levels of stress. The industrial, technological and occupational structures and contexts are dynamic and, inevitably, those seeking to enhance protection and ensure minimum standards throughout the Union are confronted by a wide range of demands and circumstances, risks and hazards.

In most member states, the major developments in the regulation of health and safety at work were prompted by and occurred within the period of rapid growth and industrialisation in the 30-year period following the Second World War – from the late 1940s through to the late 1970s. As noted earlier, however, some member states have relatively underdeveloped industrial and protective regimes. In either case, it is possible, if not likely, that the existing regimes are inadequate and inappropriate to the requirements imposed by change.

Other contextual developments also impact upon the nature of the hazards, the incidence of accidents and illness and the preventative measures that are necessary. It may well be that the structures and regulations for the protection of people at work need in the future to focus more upon the psychological effects of new work environments and upon wider issues of employee health, rather than the more specific risks that tend to pose threats to safety.

In the case of the long-term unemployed, the effects are perhaps more upon their ability to re-enter work and the only health and safety benefit of unemployment is that there seems to be an inverse relationship between levels of unemployment and the incidence of accidents at work.

It is also important to point out that a higher incidence of unemployment appears to concentrate the minds of employees and their representatives on issues of job security and continuing employment at the expense of concern about working conditions and, in this context, health and safety. The implications of this may be damaging to EU efforts to secure an improvement in the standards of care and protection in the workplace. Similar consequences are also likely where trade union strength wanes.

There is a relative lack of data on the costs of the impact of working conditions and environments in terms of industrial injury and occupational disease. The European Foundation for the Improvement of Living and Working Conditions (EFILWC) (1996a) quotes figures for the UK that suggest that the consequential costs to companies of between £11 billion and £16 billion per year and that the cost to the economy is estimated to be between 2 and 3 per cent of GNP. Figures for other countries are not available in many instances, but industrial injury alone appears to cost approximately 3 per cent of GNP in Italy and more than that in Finland.

The relative absence of reliable data on the costs of injury and disease is echoed by inadequate and unreliable data on their incidence (*see* Table 12.1). In the Commission's Fourth Action Programme on Health and Safety at Work, it is estimated that approximately 8000 people per year die as a result of work accidents and that a further 10 million may suffer from injury or disease.

According to official statistics (Eurostat, 1997), in 1993 there were an estimated 5 million people on the receiving end of work accidents causing absence from work of more than 3 days. Fatalities from accidents at work in the same year totalled 5977. The industrial sector with both the highest rate of accidents and deaths (23.3 per cent of the total) is that of construction. Men and those under 26 experience the greatest risk.

The information that is available tends to be concerned with injury rather than illness or disease and information from an EFILWC survey (1996c, pp. 83–4) tends to demonstrate that the hazardous sectors are much the same across national borders with the construction industry and metal working topping the list in all the countries surveyed. This same survey also states that industrial injury appears to disproportionately affect males, young workers, temporary workers, foreigners and those working in small companies.

The lack of certainty surrounding the adequacy and accuracy of this information makes it difficult to measure the success of the regulatory regimes and this poses problems for those arguing the case for regulation against those that see it as a source of competitive disadvantage.

Table 12.1 Number of Injuries (latest figures presented)

Country	Fatal Injuries	Total Injuries
Germany (92)	1310	2 069 422 (55/1000)
Belgium	not provided	
Denmark (93)	61	44 247
Spain (90)	1446	700 000
Finland (91)	not provided	112 500 (of which 13.8% in transit)
France (91)	1821 (of which 40.6% in transit)	951 517 (of which 10% in transit)
United Kingdom (92)	249	168 383
Greece (92)	120	25 063
Italy (91)	1858	1 020 000
Ireland (93)	64	3606
The Netherlands	56 (91)	170 000 (28/1000) (93)
Portugal (93)	185	278 455
Sweden (93)	108	41 319
(94)	214*	39 190

*of which 129 in the Estonia catastrophe
Source: EFILWC 1996. Policies on Health and Safety in Thirteen Countries in the EU. Vol. II. The European Situation. p. 84.

EU INITIATIVES

The Single European Act of 1986, effective from July 1987, has had a significant impact upon the activity of the EU in the area of occupational health and safety and the health and safety of the working environment. The main reason for this was that the Act resulted in the amendment of the founding Treaty and specifically the inclusion of Article 118a which paved the way for measures concerned with the health and safety of the working environment to be adopted by QMV.

Prior to this and with the exception of measures concerned with the protection of workers from ionising radiation (specifically facilitated by Articles 30 to 39 of the Euratom Treaty), measures aimed at the protection and safety of workers had to be adopted via either Articles 100 or 235 of the Treaty of Rome which were general in nature and required unanimity within the Council.

A number of Directives were adopted prior to 1987 but in the main they were concerned to provide protection against certain specific risks. For example:

- the Classification, Packaging and Labelling of Dangerous Substances (OJ L259/79);

- the Use of Electrical Equipment in Potentially Explosive Atmospheres (OJ L24/76 framework and OJ L43/79 implementing);

- Safety Signs in the Workplace (OJ L229/77 and amended OJ L183/79);

- Protection of Workers Exposed to Vinyl Chloride Monomer Risks (OJ L197/78);
- Protection of Workers Exposed to Lead Risks (OJ L247/82);
- Protection of Workers Exposed to Asbestos Risks (OJ L263/83);
- Protection of Workers from Harmful Exposure to Chemical, Physical and Biological Agents at Work (OJ L327/80 and amended OJ L356/88);
- Protection of Workers Exposed to Noise Risks (OJ L137/86).

In the period prior to the SEA, there had been two Action Programmes covering the periods 1978 to 1982 and 1983 to 1988. As can be detected from the dates of the Directives listed above, there was an increase in activity during the periods covered by these programmes. The second incorporated statements of intent on a range of matters related to health and safety at work – for example, protection against dangerous substances, training and the transmission of information, ergonomics, the undertaking of appropriate research and the collection of statistics.

As James (1993) points out, however, the requirement for unanimity and the difficulties associated with determining what might be safe, allied to an increasing concern on the part of some governments with the cost impact of some proposals, all contributed to what in the end amounted to a relatively limited number of successful initiatives with relatively limited scope.

Single European Act, Article 118a

Paragraph 1 of this Article proposes that the member states should:

> pay particular attention to encouraging improvements, especially in the working environment, as regards the health and safety of workers, and shall set as their objective the harmonisation of conditions in this area, while maintaining the improvements made.

Paragraph 2 of the Article provides that the Council, in pursuing these objectives, should act in accordance with the procedure referred to in Article 189c of the Treaty which enables adoption via QMV and the Co-operation Procedure (*see* Chapter 8). However, paragraph 2 also says:

> shall adopt by means of directives, minimum requirements for gradual implementation, having regard to the conditions and technical rules obtaining in each of the member states.

Paragraph 2 also states that any such Directives should avoid imposing administrative, financial and legal constraints in a way that would hold back the creation and development of SMEs.

Paragraph 3 of this Article guards against an enforced downward harmonisation of protections and provisions in this area by protecting the right of member states to insist upon more stringent requirements and protections (than may be specified in a Directive). However, if the requirements of the Directive are less stringent than those already in force in a particular member state, and a member-state government is happy to see standards fall, then there is nothing in this Article that would prevent a member state taking the opportunity to downgrade the requirements to the level specified in the Directive.

It would seem from the contents of this Article that the intention is to encourage a general improvement in the working environment as it affects the health and safety of workers and an upward harmonisation of such conditions across the Union so that the improvements made can be maintained. However, when in *paragraph 2* the Article makes specific reference to giving the Council the legal basis for taking action in this area, reference is only made to Directives specifying minimum requirements for gradual implementation. The additional references to local conditions and technical rules and being careful not to impose constraints that will harm the interests and prospects of SMEs together tend to reinforce a suspicion that despite the new ability to adopt measures by QMV, progress of a significant nature that requires member states to uprate their current requirements so that they are closer to the 'best', may well be both slow and difficult.

The expressed intent to try and avoid impositions upon SMEs that may harm their prospects and interests does identify a dilemma, since it is arguable that it is in these companies that there is often the greatest need for protective and preventative measures to be adopted and enforced.

The EFILWC survey and report (1996c and 1996a) argues that in many respects the measures and procedures that have been introduced and encouraged by regulation tend to be more appropriate and relevant in the larger companies, partly because they tend to emphasise and rely upon action and interaction of a collective nature and between the Social Partners at the level of the company. In the smaller company it is much less likely that the necessary collective organisation and mechanisms will be available. The survey report concludes that SMEs (defined as companies employing less than 100) are the blackest point observed in every country and an indication of the scale of the problem can be obtained from the evidence that the sector appears to employ more than half and in many countries more than three-quarters of the working population. The authors of the report argue that it should be a matter of the greatest priority to conduct research into the means by which it may be possible to implement active policies on health and safety in small companies; they comment that the absence of effective policies and procedures at that level is a significant weakness throughout the Union.

The Single European Act, Article 100a

Some efforts have been made to argue that Article 100a could be used to introduce Directives concerned with health and safety of workers since paragraph 3 of this Article specifically refers to health, safety, environmental protection and consumer protection. The attraction of this Article is primarily that it also states in paragraph 3 that the Commission in making proposals 'will take as a base a high level of protection'.

This is in stark contrast to the reference to minimum requirements in Article 118a and welcomed by those who think that the standards of protection are too low and who feel that the reference to minimum standards in Article 118a inevitably means that progress will be slow. It is debatable, however, that Article 100a was ever meant to apply to matters concerning the health and safety of workers.

Since Maastricht, it is also the case that measures adopted under Article 100a have to use the new Co-Decision Procedure (*see* Chapter 8) which in certain circumstances provides the EP with an ability to veto proposals that may be acceptable to the Council.

The Social Charter

In the Social Charter – agreed by all the member states other than the UK (which exercised its veto in order to prevent the Charter being adopted in any legal sense) – paragraph 19 spells out clearly the intentions of the various parties with respect to the perceived need for employees and other workers to be protected and provided with healthy and safe working environments.

The paragraph states that every worker must enjoy satisfactory health, protection and safety in the working environment and then refers to the taking of appropriate measures to achieve further harmonisation, while maintaining the improvements made. Specific mention is also made of training, information, consultation and the balanced participation of workers as regards both the risks involved and the measures taken to eliminate or reduce them.

In the light of some of the subsequent debates concerning what is and is not a matter of health and safety and where the boundary exists between these issues and an employee right, it is interesting that in the Charter matters of working time and the protection of the young worker are dealt with in separate sections and paragraphs from that specifically concerned with the health and safety of the working environment.

This issue achieved particular prominence during the dispute between the UK and the Commission over the appropriateness of the adoption of the Directive on the Adaptation of Working Time (see later in this chapter) under Article 118a. The protection of children and adolescents is the subject matter of paragraphs 20 to 23 and the issues of working time, weekly rest periods and paid annual leave are dealt with in paragraph 7 which is concerned generally with the improvement of living and working conditions.

In some eyes, this separation may add credence to the argument that it was not the intention at the time of the preparation of the Charter that these latter issues be considered as matters of health and safety and that, had the UK government been willing to countenance regulation of these issues, the measures would have been introduced under Article 100 which requires unanimity.

The period since the adoption of the SEA has been characterised by both a greater volume of activity and by a change in the nature of the initiatives taken. There has been more concern with working conditions and particular categories of people at risk (such as pregnant and young workers) compared with the dominant concern with protection from dangerous substances that characterised the earlier period. Many of the Directives that have subsequently been adopted exhibit a greater concern with issues related to prevention, the effective management of health and safety and the enunciaton of general principles. The single most significant intervention has been the Framework Directive.

The (Framework) Directive on the Introduction of Measures to Encourage Improvements in the Safety and Health of Workers at the Workplace (89/391)

This umbrella Directive sets out some general principles concerning matters such as:

- the assessment and prevention of occupational risks;
- the training, informing, consultation and balanced participation of workers and their representatives;
- the value and necessity of formal written policies;
- the designation of competent people to be responsible for health and safety;

- the establishment of procedures for evacuation, first aid, etc.;
- the obligations of employees and their representatives to take care of their own health and safety;
- the general right of employees to leave their work station in the event of serious and imminent danger; and
- the protection of employee representatives from victimisation as a result of discharging their duties.

As was the intention, this Framework Directive has been followed by a number of 'daughter' Directives, each of which sets out to deal with a particular issue, area of risk or category of people at work. The Framework Directive sets out the general principles to apply to health and safety in the workplace, the rights, responsibilities and obligations that are to apply across the board; individual problem areas and regulations covering particular areas of risk are then dealt with in specific and relatively narrow Directives.

Article 17 of the Framework Directive also paved the way for a procedure, whereby devising and obtaining agreement on precise technical details and standards and debates are removed from the arena in which the Directive itself is determined and adopted. These details are left to committees of experts, rather than the civil servants and politicians. These regulatory committees operate at the request of the Commission and can also be called upon to advise on details and adjustments over time. Chaired by a member of the Commission, they are usually required to form and agree (via QMV) an opinion on the particular issue and present it to the Commission. If the Commission agrees with the opinion, it may then be adopted. If the Commission does not agree with the opinion of the regulatory committee, the opinion may be referred to the Council for consideration and adoption.

The establishment of these procedures for dealing with highly technical and contentious matters of standards and regulations appears to have made it considerably easier for Directives, Regulations and standards to be introduced and modified as time and new information requires (*see* below the number of Directives in the health and safety field that have been adopted since 1989). It can also be argued that they have contributed to a shortening of the timespan of decision making with respect to the adoption of Directives and to a large extent removed the determination of standards of protection and regulation from the political arena, though political considerations are likely to resurface upon consideration of the expert opinion by the Commission or Council.

These outcomes also illustrate the advantages of dealing with issues via the use of QMV, which became possible with the adoption of Article 118a.

Examples of the daughter Directives that have been adopted within the auspices of the Framework Directive include:

1 *Directive 89/654.* This was the first so-called 'daughter directive' adopted within the auspices of Article 16(1) of the Framework Directive. The Directive is concerned to determine minimum safety and health requirements for the workplace including its design. A distinction is drawn between premises being used for the first time and those already in use. The details of the Directive are concerned with matters such as:

- traffic routes to emergency exits;
- technical maintenance;

- electrical installations;
- fire detection and firefighting equipment;
- ventilation and lighting;
- temperature;
- windows, skylights, doors and gates;
- rest rooms, sanitary equipment, toilets, showers, etc.; and
- arrangements for the protection of non-smokers against the discomfort caused by tobacco smoke.

2 *Directive 89/655.* This is concerned with setting out minimum standards for the safe use of machines and other equipment at work.

3 *Directive 89/686.* This is concerned with minimum standards for the provision, use and maintenance of personal protective equipment.

4 *Directive 90/269.* This is concerned with the protection of workers from back injuries from lifting heavy loads and therefore requires the provision of training in lifting skills and lifting equipment, where possible.

5 *Directive 90/270.* This is concerned with protecting workers against some of the dangers of VDU equipment. The Directive requires the provision of free eye tests and, where necessary, free glasses, the organisation of the work station so as to avoid eye strain, the provision of regular breaks from the strains of looking at the screen and appropriate training in relevant health matters and practices.

By late 1996 a number of other Directives had been adopted using the Framework Directive and Article 118a of the Treaty. These included the Pregnant Worker and Young Worker Directives that are examined in more detail later in this chapter. Others were concerned with:

- protection against the effect of carcinogens;
- protection against biological agents;
- health and safety and the design and execution of construction projects;
- the visual and acoustic dimensions of health and safety signs and signals;
- standards of protection in the drilling and mining industries;
- health and safety on fishing vessels to include fitting, use, evacuation and the importance of training for those in command;
- protection from the dangers of asbestos; and
- safety in explosive atmospheres.

Under discussion at that time (late 1996) were additional proposals concerning:

- transport to and from work for disabled workers;
- the protection of workers in the transport industries;
- amendment of the existing directives on chemical agents and carcinogens; and
- further proposals aimed at the harmful effects of noise and other physical agents, such as vibration.

The Social Protocol Agreement on Social Policy (Maastricht 1991)

We looked at this Agreement in some detail in Chapter 6 and have commented that the contents should be perceived as an attempt at partial implementation of the Social Charter – as stated in the preamble to the Agreement.

In the arena of health and safety of workers, however, very little is added in this Agreement that was not already contained within Article 118a of the EC Treaty itself. Article 1 of this Agreement specifies as one of the objectives 'improved living and working conditions' and in Article 2 it is specified that the Community, with a view to achieving the objectives specified in Article 1, 'shall support and complement the activities of the member states' in a number of specified fields, one of which is 'improvement in particular of the working environment to protect workers' health and safety' and another of which is 'working conditions'.

Paragraph 2 of Article 2 is the one that refers to the adoption of Directives (via QMV and the Co-operation Procedure) to achieve these objectives and repeats the terminology of Article 118a concerning minimum requirements, the conditions and technical rules in individual member states and with taking care not to impose constraints damaging to SMEs.

There are some changes of emphasis and wording, although whether they are significant or not depends on personal perspectives. Certainly these provisions within the Agreement ensured that the member states other than the UK could, if they wished or needed, progress matters via this route.

The member states and institutions party to this Agreement demonstrate their awareness of the danger that their desire not to impose administrative, financial and legislative burdens upon SMEs, and thereby harm job creation, might be used as a means of avoiding appropriate regulation and protection of employees. It is also clear that the parties did not intend this, as indicated by a Declaration attached to the SPASP which states:

> . . . it was agreed that the Community does not intend, in laying down minimum requirements for the protection of the safety and health of employees, to discriminate in a manner unjustified by the circumstances against employees in small and medium sized undertakings.

However, with the benefit of hindsight and the ruling of the ECJ in the case brought by the UK government against the adoption of the Working Time Directive (*see* later in this chapter) it would seem unlikely that the protection or improvement of the health and safety of workers will often be progressed via this Protocol Agreement and the procedures described in Chapter 8. Exceptions to this may occur given circumstances in which the Commission or member states particularly want or need the Social Partners to reach agreement on an issue.

The Amsterdam IGC Draft Treaty 1997

As already noted, the draft Treaty agreed at Amsterdam in 1997 does propose to incorporate the SPASP into the Treaty. Articles 117 to 120 of the original Treaty are to be amended as a result of this decision and some changes are to be made to the contents of the Articles in the SPASP. The significance of this agreement to the provision of a basis for action to be taken on matters relevant to health and safety in the workplace is unlikely to be as great as in some other areas since this was the one area in which it was already possible to take action on the basis of QMV. Nevertheless, it is appropriate here to look at the draft proposals and consider the potential impact. The proposed new Article 118 contains pretty well verbatim Article 2 of the SPASP and, with the exception of the procedure to be used, there are no substantive changes, even the Declaration referred to above is to be retained. The procedural change is that the new shortened Co-Decision Procedure replaces the Co-operation Procedure as the one to be used by the Council when seeking to take legislative action in this area. This new draft Article 118 also retains the so-called Protocol Procedures whereby the Social Partners may make agreements which may then be incorporated into Directives by the Council.

The Directive on the Adaptation of Working Time

This Directive (93/104) was adopted in November 1993, to be implemented by November 1996, under Article 118a of the Treaty which, as noted above, facilitated the adoption of the Directive via QMV and the Co-operation Procedures.

At the time the UK government was very unhappy with the nature and contents of the Directive; it managed to secure some significant changes to the original proposals as they went through the legislative process – for example, exceptions for particular occupations and circumstances such as trainee doctors (who in the UK regularly work hours considerably in excess of the limits specified in the Directive). It also managed to ensure that the limits upon working hours could be voluntarily varied given the agreement of the parties, whether this be individuals agreeing to work longer hours or the parties agreeing a variation via a collective agreement. Perhaps strangely, given its unhappiness, the UK government did not vote against the Directive in the Council; it abstained.

In addition to the detailed content, the UK government's unhappiness with the Directive centred upon two particular issues which are of more general relevance.

Working hours are not a health and safety issue

The UK government asserted that the Directive was incorrectly adopted under Article 118a, because working hours were not a health and safety issue. So incensed and convinced was the UK government that such issues were not properly health and safety issues, that it challenged the adoption of the Directive. This challenge was ruled upon by the ECJ in November 1996 and the Court's judgement affirmed the original decision that the measure was properly introduced – in effect that there were sufficient health and safety dimensions to the notion of hours of work, rest periods and night work to justify the argument of the Commission and other member states that the Directive was properly adopted.

There are concerns that in forcing the issue, the UK government has actually engendered a situation in which, given the relatively liberal interpretation by the ECJ, it may now be easier for the EU to adopt policies and legislative measures on other issues concerning employment, utilising Article 118a. The only point upon which the Court found the legislation inappropriate on health and safety grounds was the specification that the minimum weekly rest period should in principle include Sunday; the ECJ found no health and safety reasons why this should be so.

In their judgement, the judges concluded that:

> There is nothing to indicate that these concepts [health, safety and working environment] should be interpreted restrictively, and not as embracing all factors, physical or otherwise, capable of affecting the health and safety of the worker in his working environment . . .

The Court cited the definition of health of the World Health Organisation (WHO) (to which all member states belong):

> . . . a state of complete physical, mental and social well being that does not consist only in the absence of illness of infirmity.

From a lay viewpoint it does seem reasonable to suggest that there are health and safety risks to working long hours with insufficient rest periods and breaks and that night work is likely to have additional health and safety implications. This is a view supported by Exhibit 12.1.

The regulation of working hours etc. will have a detrimental effect on competitiveness

The regulation of working hours, rest periods and entitlement to annual leave ran counter to the ideology of the UK government of that period and to the voluntarist traditions of the UK. The UK government was convinced that the key to competitiveness lay in a deregulated and flexible labour market, in which individuals are both free to and capable of entering into contracts and where this very freedom acts as a constraint upon individuals having to accept contracts of employment that they find unfavourable. It is understandable that such a government would object to something they saw as both unnecessary and damaging to competitiveness and therefore to the prospects for growth.

Adnett (1996, p. 262) points out that the proposal to limit maximum working hours to an average of 48 per week over a four-month reference period would affect only 3 per cent of the total hours worked in Britain. Taylor (1996) refers to an estimate that there may be nearly 4 million people in the UK (30.9 per cent) who work more than 48 hours per week and asserts that there is a much greater proportion of full-time employees working in excess of 46 hours per week in the UK than in any other member state (*see* Fig. 12.1) (*Source:* Eurostat).

Some will argue that by imposing a maximum upon the number of hours that can be worked by an individual there will be a job-creating effect in that if the need/demand for labour is there it will be met from the employment of more individuals, though there is little evidence to confirm that this is the effect of such measures. Another argument is that measures of this kind serve to protect those in employment rather than creating employment for those that currently are unemployed. The suggestion is that these measures – perhaps particularly those concerned with leave entitlement – like many other health and safety regulations and protections, will increase the costs of employing labour, and as a result will mitigate any positive impact upon labour demand.

As already noted, the main provision of the Directive concerned maximum working hours – that they should be limited to an average of 48 per week over a four-month reference period, although this can be extended to 12 months, either by member states or by the parties via collective agreement. Other provisions of the Directive are that workers should have or receive:

- a minimum of 11 hours' consecutive rest in 24 hours implying a maximum working day of 13 hours; and
- a minimum of 35 hours' consecutive rest per week in principle to include Sunday.

Exhibit 12.1

Health 'affected by working time'

Evidence indicates a link but experts say more research is needed

FT

By Robert Taylor

There is a link between the time people spend at work and the risk of injury and ill-health, according to a range of medical evidence – some dating back to the first world war – compiled by the European Commission.

But the experts also identify an urgent need for more research, noting that surprisingly little scientific investigation into working time has been carried out.

Medical experts – including Professor John Harrington from Birmingham University and Professor Simon Folkard from Swansea University – agree that working more than 48–56 hours a week has serious health and safety implications.

A critical review of shift work and health, published by Prof Harrington in the September 1994 edition of 'Annals Academy of Medicine argues that 'the link between shift work and increased cardiovascular morbidity and mortality has strengthened in recent years'.

'The case for an association with gastrointestinal disease remains quite good,' he adds. 'Evidence of poorer work performance and increased accidents, particularly on the night shift, is persuasive although individual factors may be as important as workplace factors.'

The review found that night work disrupts sleep patterns and likens its effect to 'a long distance traveller working in San Francisco and returning to London for any rest days'. It says fatigue – seen as 'an important, if vague symptom' – in shift work is a 'fundamental complaint' but it is 'impossible to quantify'. A California study in 1960 found increasing heart disease for males who work more than 48 hours a week.

Medical research on working hours and performance carried out on munitions workers as long ago as the first world war found a cut in working hours by 7 to 20 hours a week 'produced a substantial increase in total

---

Most west of England business leaders support government opposition to a maximum 48-hour working week. But most agree companies run more efficiently if staff do not overwork *Roland Adburgham writes*.

A survey of 150 chief executives and managing directors, showed 62 per cent were opposed to a statutory limit on working hours. The European Court of Justice is due to rule tomorrow on the government's resistance to an EU directive stipulating a 48-hour maximum week.

Excessive working was regarded as undesirable by most interviewed by Burges Salmon, a law firm, on behalf of Bristol Chamber of Commerce & Initiative. Nearly three quarters at least partially agreed 'businesses run more efficiently if staff go home at the designated time and take their full holiday allowance'.

---

output'. The survey also found 'on balance, night shift work carries a poorer performance and safety record than the other shifts'.

But the same study says 'despite the obvious circadian rhythm dysfunction there is surprisingly little evidence that working unsocial hours causes serious and widespread disease or premature death'.

The Trades Union Congress yesterday released evidence which it claimed indicated a connection between working time and health and safety. This includes a study published last year by Austin Knight, the recruitment agency, that found continual long hours affected three-quarters of employees physically and many became ill.

Some 47 per cent said their families suffered as a result.

Another unpublished study by Professor Folkard and colleagues says that accidents happen more often at night. They point to the nuclear disasters at Three Mile Island and Chernobyl, as well as the Exxon Valdez oil spill.

Four experts at the 1994 international symposium in Stockholm produced evidence that work schedules involving night activity and inadequate sleep impair health and safety. 'The absence or inadequacy of existing work hour regulations in many countries endangers public safety in industries where employee performance can affect personal or public safety,' they said, pointing to transportation and the chemical and nuclear power industries.

But the Advocate-General – in his interim judgment this summer which rejected the UK's legal challenge to the working time directive – dismissed the argument over the medical evidence, suggesting it had assumed a 'disproportionate importance'. He concluded: 'Scientific research cannot constitute the sole basis on which the community legislature can take action.'

Source: Financial Times, 12 November 1996.

These can be averaged over a two-week period. Other entitlements under the Directive include:

- a rest break after 6 hours' consecutive work; and
- four weeks' paid annual leave (three weeks for the first three years of employment) and no payment in lieu (in other words, the intention is that the leave should be taken).

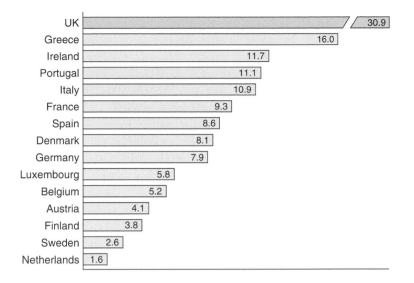

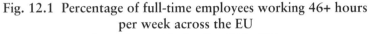

**Fig. 12.1 Percentage of full-time employees working 46+ hours
per week across the EU**

Source: Eurostat, *The Guardian*, 13 Nov 1996.

The extra provisions covering night workers seek to limit the average length of a night shift to 8 hours in 24, and propose that night workers should have free and regular medical check-ups and the right to transfer to day work on medical grounds.

As previously mentioned, there are also various exceptions and derogations. The main derogation provides that the parties can voluntarily by collective agreement introduce greater flexibility in implementing the Directive as long as adequate and appropriate compensatory rest is given (*see* above). The main exceptions cover particular 'problematic' occupations – road, rail, sea or air transport workers as well as managers and trainee doctors – and industries where continuity of production or service is required such as health, the media, post and telecommunications, emergency and public services, security services and public utilities.

In 1997 there were signs that the Commission was intending to propose that some of the occupations not covered by the Directive limits should be brought within the scope of the Directive and that their hours of work should be limited. It is clearly the intention to include junior doctors, fishermen and transport workers, but it seems as if the details of the limits might be left to be determined at the level of the member state.

In practice, it seems that the maximum hours element of the Directive becomes relevant only in circumstances where an employer is seeking to pressure an employee into working in excess of the stipulated maximum against his or her will and there is the threat of penalty if the worker refuses.

The greatest benefit to employees may come from the provisions dealing with paid annual leave; it has been estimated that in the UK there may be as many as 2.5 million workers with no paid holiday entitlement at all, the majority being part-time workers, and that more than an additional 4 million workers are entitled to less than three weeks' holiday (*see* Fig. 12.2).

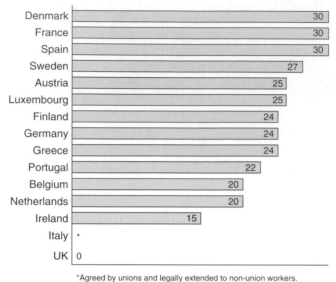

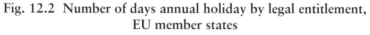

*Agreed by unions and legally extended to non-union workers.
Generally 4–6 weeks.

**Fig. 12.2 Number of days annual holiday by legal entitlement,
EU member states**

Source: *The Guardian*, 11 Nov 1996.

Directive on the Protection of Pregnant Workers

This Directive (92/85) – the tenth daughter Directive – again illustrates some of the ambiguities and difficulties concerned with seeking to distinguish between 'the rights and interests of employed persons', matters of equal treatment between the sexes and improvements as regards the health and safety of workers.

This measure was introduced and adopted as an improvement regarding the health and safety of workers using Article 118a, thereby enabling its adoption by QMV. If the proposals had been brought forward under either equal treatment or employee rights, there would have been a requirement for the proposals to be adopted on a unanimous basis. Given the concerns and positions adopted by some of the member-state governments, most notably the UK, it is likely that all or some of the proposals contained within the Directive would have been vetoed.

It is certainly arguable that some elements of the Directive have more to do with equality of treatment than with the protection of the health and safety of pregnant workers – in particular those provisions that seek to ensure that it is unlawful to dismiss someone on the grounds of pregnancy. This impression may well be enhanced by the knowledge that the ECJ had shown itself willing to use the Equal Treatment Directive as a means of protecting pregnant employees from dismissal because of their pregnancy (Hertz *v* Aldi Marked). Indeed, it had been willing to construe the same Directive as providing protection to pregnant women from discriminatory hiring decisions (Dekker).

The Directive incorporates a number of rights and protections for pregnant workers and those that have recently given birth. These include:

- the prohibition of dismissal on the grounds of pregnancy or during maternity leave regardless of length of service;
- the right to maternity leave of a minimum of 14 weeks and the right to return to work afterwards;
- the right to receive a maternity payment during maternity leave of at least the level of statutory sick pay in the member state concerned;
- protection from working conditions or hours which pose a threat to a pregnant or breast-feeding worker. A risk assessment should be undertaken and, where it is concluded that there are risks, the work should either be adapted or the worker should be offered suitable alternative employment or, if necessary, additional paid maternity leave.

The Directive on the Protection of Young People at Work

This Directive (94/33) was also adopted under the provisions of Article 118a and therefore via the Co-operation Procedure and QMV.

The rights and obligations imposed by this Directive are differentiated by three age categories and a number of the provisions will not apply to the UK for a period of four years following implementation in June 1996.

The rights and obligations include:

1 For all those under 18

- Employers are to have the responsibility to undertake a risk assessment prior to such employment; they are obliged to inform the individual and his or her parents and guardians of the risks and hazards established via the assessment.

2 For all those between 15 and 18 and no longer in full-time compulsory education

- There should be a maximum number of hours worked at these ages – not exceeding 8 per day and 40 per week; some temporary exceptions may be permitted.*
- Nightwork should be prohibited between the hours of 2200 and 0600 or between 2300 and 0700 and again, while certain exceptions may be permitted, young people in this category should never work between midnight and 0400 hours.*
- All such workers should have a daily rest period of 12 consecutive hours in every 24 hours.
- Young workers should have at least 2 days' rest in every 7 and, wherever possible, these should be consecutive days.
- Young workers should not be expected to work for longer than 4 and a half hours without a 30-minute rest break.

3 For all those under 15 or still subject to compulsory education

Here the provisions apply to those doing light work or work experience where this is allowed by the regulations in individual member states.

- Light work in term times should not exceed 12 hours per week.
- In the school holidays light work should not be undertaken for longer than 7 hours per day and 35 hours per week.
- For the over 14s only, work experience should not exceed 8 hours per day and 40 hours a week; those that are younger should not engage in work experience.
- Young people of this age should not work between the hours of 2000 and 0600.
- Daily rest periods should be at least 14 consecutive hours in every 24 and weekly rest periods should be 2 days in every 7 – consecutive, where possible.
- The maximum period of work without a rest should not exceed 4 and a half hours and the rest period should be a minimum of 30 minutes.

The provisions marked with an asterisk are those that will not apply in the UK for the first four years after implementation. Some have been referred to as the 'paperboy opt-outs'.

On balance, the set of protections in this Directive are probably less contentiously categorised as matters of health and safety, than are those in the Working Time and Pregnant Workers Directives.

Other EU initiatives

The Union also takes and supports other initiatives in the areas of training, research and the dissemination of information. 1993 was declared the European Year of Health and Safety, and in October of that year the Council confirmed the establishment of a European Agency for Health and Safety at Work.

Much of the research and information dissemination is undertaken through the EFILWC and in its annual report for 1995, the Foundation (1996a) identifies 'improving the health and well-being of European workers and citizens' as one of the three main areas of investigation for the Foundation in its four-year programme covering the period 1993 to 1996. The annual report lists a number of specific projects and publications undertaken in 1995 and these included:

- restructuring and updating the European Health and Safety Database (HASTE) so as to make it ready for computerisation;
- identification and assessment of the strategies pursued in each of the member states;
- preparation of a working paper on the subject of absenteeism and in particular on arrangements within the member states designed to reduce the incidence of ill health linked to absenteeism, including mental health;
- assessment of the cost and benefits of stress at both company and national levels;
- research into the working conditions in specific industries – meat and hospitals;
- continuation of the project of the working group established in 1993 to investigate and devise a model of economic incentives to improve the working environment; and

- the beginning of a project concerned to identify issues relating to the access into the labour market of people with disabilities.

The Commission has also been active in encouraging concern with health and safety issues outside the context of legislation. It has published four *Framework (or Action) Programmes on Health and Safety*. The fourth of these to cover the period 1996 to 2000 emphasises the need to ensure that the measures already adopted are implemented, thus consolidating existing measures rather than embarking upon a new programme of initiatives. The programme also includes a non-legislative initiative called *Safety Actions for Europe* (SAFE) which is intended to provide financial support for projects to improve working conditions, particularly in the SME sector, and to develop strategies to reduce workplace accidents and the frequency of occupational diseases. Specifically, the Programme is to:

- through a focus upon education and training, develop and promote good practice, safe workplaces and innovative approaches;
- highlight to organisations the increasingly close relationship between health and safety, economic efficiency and quality control – the suggestion being that accidents and diseases are often the consequence of a failure to apply and manage quality control procedures.

COMPLIANCE AND ENFORCEMENT

Health and safety at work seems to be one of those areas of subject matter and regulation in which the issues of compliance and effective enforcement have a particular relevance.

Some governments seem particularly loath or unable to comply with the requirements of various Directives in the sense of enacting the relevant national legislation or regulations and creating appropriate mechanisms to ensure enforcement. James (1993) points out that five out of the ten member states required to implement the noise Directive by 1 January 1990 had still not done so in the middle of 1991. He comments that, given this partial implementation, it was surprising that the Commission had not instituted infringement proceedings. The Fourth Action Programme suggests that compliance, in terms of transposing health and safety Directives into national systems, varied considerably with an overall transposition rate of about 80 per cent; and only Spain and Belgium fell below this with rates of 46 and 69 per cent respectively.

The means of enforcement within member states varies. In some states the responsibilities lie with specialist agencies of inspectors, whereas in others the responsibility for inspection and enforcement lies with more general labour inspectors. In some member states, the accident insurance associations also play an important role, both in the development of the regulations and in their enforcement. With the exception of Italy, the inspection service is attached to the Ministry of Labour; in Italy, it is attached to the Ministry with responsibility for Health. For some industries – such as the nuclear, agriculture, mining, transport and maritime industries – there are specialised and separate inspection systems.

Generally, the inspectors have complete independence and discretion as to when and where they decide to carry out inspection. They are usually able to intervene directly to require that a dangerous or otherwise undesirable practice cease. It is also common for them to impose sanctions for non-compliance, although in the case of serious offences it is more normal that sanctions are imposed through the appropriate official or judicial systems. Increasingly, the inspectors are being called upon to perform a role wider than that simply of policing the implementation of the regulations; they are being invited to advise on prevention and in some cases to act as external auditors.

At the level of the workplace, employees play an influential monitoring role through elected delegates/representatives and health and safety committees. In most of the member states, the health and safety representatives are members of, or in some other way connected to the trade unions; sometimes they are formally elected or appointed through trade union channels – as in the UK where the representative is normally nominated by the Union.

The role of the representative is usually a mix of monitor/inspector as well as acting as a source of advice and/or training to other employees and management. The representatives are required to undergo differential amounts of training in the various member states. In smaller organisations it might be relatively common for the employee representative to be better informed than management on the various health and safety issues.

The representatives usually also have a collective role as a member of a specialist consultative committee, although in some countries this role is performed within the confines of the works council. It is in this context that they are most likely to address issues associated with the impact of changes in technology and work processes. Each country tends to have different legislative requirements as regards the company size threshold, above which it is compulsory to have such consultative arrangements.

Perhaps, inevitably, it is in the smaller companies that there is the least likelihood that employees will have the opportunity to perform these representative roles.

Individual employers are sometimes loath to comply with the regulations and legislation, when and where it is adopted, and this tends to impose a particular need for and burden upon mechanisms of enforcement at the level of the workplace.

Commonly, employer compliance with new and amended health and safety regulations involves incurring costs, as working environments and equipment have to be modified, working processes and practices changed and tougher standards of care met. In the context of price competitive markets, it should not be surprising that some employers seek to avoid such additional cost burdens (which they may also perceive as unnecessary) as a means of achieving competitive advantage.

This raises the issues of practicability and proportionality. The legal system has a role in the enforcement of the obligations, standards and requirements that are imposed by way of Directive and Regulation and, where necessary, the implementing legislation at national level.

In the UK, the law governing health and safety has been a mix of common law obligations and legislation. Since the enactment of the Health and Safety at Work Act (HASAW) of 1974, this has tended to be the dominant source. This legislation imposes general duties upon employers, but subject to taking action in accordance with *the principle of reasonable practicability*. This principle is not defined in the Act but the courts have tended to interpret it in cost–benefit terms: that is, they have tended to allow employers to argue that the mix of cost, trouble and difficulties involved in taking the necessary action should be balanced in some sense against the benefit to be obtained as a result of taking the necessary protective and other measures. Only where the benefits obviously and significantly outweigh the costs might the employer be forced to take the necessary action.

Throughout the rest of the Union it is common for the courts to use the *test of proportionality* in similar circumstances. In effect, this test allows employers to argue the test of reasonableness, if it is alleged that they did not fulfil their obligations.

There has been some debate about the extent to which both of these tests are consistent with the Health and Safety Framework Directive and the obligations imposed within it, since the Directive seems to impose absolute requirements and obligations, which cannot be avoided if the cost is too much in the context of the benefits to be derived.

Here again the potential for conflict arises between the desire for and need of social policy, protection and regulation, on the one hand, and the need to be competitive, on the other. Unfortunately, it is often all too easy for employers and member-state governments to use cost as the reason for not implementing more effective regulation and ensuring compliance with those that have already been adopted.

In the context of this chapter, it would appear that in these arguments little attention is paid to the costs to companies and countries of industrial injuries and occupational disease. We noted earlier in the chapter some estimates of the costs incurred and they are substantial. Of course, not all of these costs are avoidable by the introduction and maintenance of regulatory and educational systems that achieve improvements in both protection and prevention. Nevertheless, it would seem that decisions concerning the desirability of regulation and a generally greater concern with the health and safety of people at work are subject not to a proper cost–benefit analysis, but to short-term considerations of how much might be directly added (or alternatively avoided) to production costs.

This is not an issue that is limited to the field of health and safety; similar arguments and objections are raised in respect of regulation in other areas of the social dimension. One of the ongoing issues confronting the Union and indeed member-state governments is the extent to which protection is affordable and, of course, answers to this question vary according to perceptions of the dangers, ideological positions and beliefs and the dominant values that exemplify national cultures.

At the time of writing, and as is discussed further in the final chapter, there seems to be some evidence that those arguing against regulation and for employer flexibility are beginning to win the argument.

In this context, it is interesting that there is some evidence that the courts (certainly within the UK) have recently begun to adopt an approach by which they seem more willing to find against an employer in respect of the employer's general duty to provide a healthy and safe working environment, even in the absence of specific regulation. As a result, in the UK, recent court decisions – particularly those concerning employer liability in respect of asbestos laden environments and the creation of stress-related ill health through work overload – have given employees hope that redress may be more readily available than has been the case in the past.

Employees are often confronted by insecurity and the apparent threat of unemployment if employers do have to incur extra costs in satisfying the requirements of regulation and it is again not surprising that employees often acquiesce in workplace non-compliance with the regulations. Compliance also sometimes requires working practices that are both less convenient and comfortable and, for reasons of this nature, employees are sometimes at least as willing as employers to avoid the regulatory requirements. Relatively obvious examples would include the putting on and use of safety clothing and other equipment when in a hurry or the temperature is very high or where payment is linked to the quantity of output and the safety regulations, if applied, make it more difficult to achieve output targets.

Another factor that has undoubtedly contributed to the creation and maintenance of poor standards of health and safety at work is the longitudinal nature of the effect of certain work environments and practices with the damage to health – sometimes not apparent for years after the event and with causal links difficult to establish. Similarly, it is common for the dangers of certain practices, substances and environments not to be realised at the time; it is only with the benefit of hindsight, modern technology and enhanced levels of knowledge that we are able to state today that particular historical practices and substances were hazardous and what the nature of the hazard was.

As is noted in the EFILWC report (1996a, p. 85):

> . . . the occupational diseases identified today reflect the working conditions of the past. The lists of recognised diseases are probably obsolete and this obsolescence is a serious handicap in the implementation of effective preventive policies.

In this context the need for expert informed regulation, inspection and enforcement becomes even greater and reliance upon the market and/or the voluntary decisions of the main actors within the workplace can be seen for the dangerous folly that it is.

CONCLUSIONS

The changing scientific, technological, economic and demographic environments imply that it has become imperative that regulatory frameworks are kept under constant review in order to assess the relevance and effectiveness of existing regimes and in order to anticipate as much as possible the impact of change. It does seem to be the case that health and safety risks and occupational disease, perhaps particularly the latter, are not always easy to see and sometimes only reveal themselves after the event. This adds to the continuing need for vigilance, and particularly to the need for vigilance in the developing sectors of industry and the economy.

There is a moral obligation on those concerned with the invention and implementation of innovatory techniques and materials to consider in the development processes the effect that they may have upon the immediate work environment and the people who work in it. The rapidity and scale of these changes does tend to add to the force of the arguments in favour of the approach more recently adopted by the Union – that is, to legislate in order to impose minimum rights and general principles and obligations relevant to the effective management of health and safety in work environments.

The absence of reliable and adequate data as to the costs and incidence of accidents, injury and illness imposes an imperative that the Union as far as possible should encourage member states to initiate and supervise the collection of appropriate data so that policy and action can be better informed.

The scale and rate of change also add weight to the argument that people need to be sensitised to issues of health and safety at an early age, in school, so that when they find themselves in a work environment they more naturally pay attention to and notice hazards, risks and other potential influences upon health. Such sensitising could be incorporated into educational initiatives relevant to the wider environment.

One of the major difficulties in achieving improvement is in the fact that improvements almost invariably incur costs and, in a world of increasing global competition, additional costs may have a significant impact upon competitive advantage. Understandably both employers and employees engaged in price competitive markets will often seek to avoid the requirements. In the case of employees, the incentive for acquiescing or conspiring in non-compliance is quite likely to be derived from concerns about job security.

The evidence would appear to indicate that non-compliance at the level of the company is particularly a problem among the smaller firms. This is not helped by the fact that many of the regulations in any event exclude from their coverage the smaller companies. If only a minority of people worked in smaller organisations this would be less of a problem, but this is not the case with in the region of 70 per cent of the working population within the Union working in these circumstances.

Inspection at the level of the company tends to be part of the role of elected employee representatives and these are usually appointed through the formal trade union channels. Where this is not the case, there is a tendency for the representatives to be at least partially reliant upon the information, advisory and educational facilities and services of the unions. Decline in the influence of the trade union movement therefore poses a considerable threat to the effectiveness of these mechanisms and in many EU member states there is evidence of such decline in recent years (*see* Hollinshead and Leat, 1995). It is important not to equate too closely trade union membership levels and trade union influence, whether this be at the level of the firm or at national level.

Formally, inspection of the measures taken to ensure the health and safety of workers in the workplace, and therefore to some extent compliance with the regulatory requirements, is in most countries in the hands of state-employed inspectors, although the insurance companies also have a significant role in some of the member states. The EFILWC studies suggest that the manpower available for the performance of these functions is already inadequate and that the inspectors' burden is already onerous; any further decline of funds for the maintenance of these roles is likely to have an impact upon the ability of the inspection services to perform their role adequately. These inspectors also act as advisers to many organisations, positively encouraging prevention as well as checking upon compliance with the rules. Downward pressure upon public expenditure – for example, as exerted by the convergence criteria for EMU, the desire to control inflation and remain internationally competitive and the wish of some governments to reduce the burden of taxation – poses significant threats to these services and to the health and safety of people in the workplace.

Many of the above arguments also apply to the need for and funding of research into these issues; it seems likely that the Commission will need to initiate, commission and fund more of the activities in this area.

The decision of the ECJ on the question of whether the Working Time Directive was properly adopted as a health and safety measure does seem to have determined that the Union institutions and member states acted appropriately in adopting a wide definition; this has been reinforced by the Court's reference to the WHO definition. However, in 1997, it seemed that this decision had not encouraged a further spate of legislative proposals; the tendency seemed to be to consolidate and to try and ensure compliance with those measures already adopted and, where necessary, to update them.

The process of adoption and updating of detailed standards of protection does appear to have been facilitated by the adoption of the Framework Directive (with the opportunity it provides for the adoption of daughter Directives) and the decision to create committees of specialist advisers to devise and advise upon the detailed standards. This should also serve to counter the argument that the processes of adoption are too time consuming and often lead to a situation in which the regulations are almost out of date before the member states are required to implement them. As a result, the standards should become enforceable.

Enforcement does still seem to be at the mercy of the national and European courts, however, when it comes to weighing up the requirements of the law against the costs and practicality of implementation.

References

Adnett, N. (1996) *European Labour Markets: Analysis and Policy*. Longman.

European Commission (1995) *Fourth Action Programme on Health and Safety at Work* (to cover the period 1996–2000). European Commission.

European Foundation for the Improvement of Living and Working Conditions (1996c) *Policies on Health and Safety in Thirteen Countries of the European Union. Vol II: The European Situation*. EFILWC.

European Foundation for the Improvement of Living and Working Conditions (1996a) *Annual Report for 1995*. EFILWC.

Eurostat (1997) *Statistics in Focus: Population and Social Conditions*, 2.

Hollinshead, G. and Leat, M. (1995) *Human Resource Management: An International and Comparative Perspective*. Pitman Publishing.

James, P. (1993) 'Occupational Health and Safety', in Gold, M. (ed) *The Social Dimension – Employment Policy in the European Community*. Macmillan.

Taylor, R. (1996) 'Health "affected by working time"', *Financial Times*, 12 Nov, p. 12.

Taylor, R. (1996) 'Impact upon employers and employees', *Financial Times*, 13 Nov, p.10.

Additional reading

European Commission (1994b) *Europe for Safety and Health at Work*. European Commission.

Barrett, B. and Howells, R. (1995) *Occupational Health and Safety Law* (2nd edn). M & E Handbooks, Pitman Publishing.

13

VOCATIONAL EDUCATION AND TRAINING

LEARNING OBJECTIVES

When you have read this chapter, you should be able to understand and explain:

- the major issues in the debates about whether the market mechanism is an adequate means of determining the allocation of resources to vocational education and training and the implications for the role of government;
- the relevance of the issues of competitiveness and employment to the debates on the role of vocational education and training;
- the vocational education and training systems and traditions in three member states;
- the various objectives that initiatives may pursue;
- the thrust of the many EU initiatives taken.

INTRODUCTION

Vocational education and training (VET) has been identified by many authorities as one of the factors influencing employability and employment levels. The majority of prescriptions for the resolution of the 'unemployment problem', involve some element of enhancement or expansion of, or change to, existing VET policies and provision. Such interventions are variously referred to in terms of seeking to influence the supply-side of the labour market, or as part of an active labour market policy. Chapter 15 will address unemployment in greater detail.

It is important that we define the term 'vocational education and training', as used in this book. There is little consensus regarding the meaning of the term, but in this book it encompasses a number of processes and mechanisms resulting in modifications to the behaviour, attitudes, knowledge, skills and competence of individuals in the context of the performance of work tasks and responsibilities. There are individual, organisational and societal dimensions to the concept.

This chapter examines a number of the key debates and issues relating to vocational education and training, before describing the measures taken at the level of the EU, the motives and, where possible, the outcomes.

Member states and other interest groups exhibit different perspectives on key issues such as:

● the contribution which vocational training can and does make to a company's or nation's competitiveness, to rates of productivity and economic growth;

● the effectiveness and/or efficiency of the market as the mechanism through which resources are allocated to education and training;

● the legitimacy, value and nature of government's role and, perhaps particularly, the question of whether government should perform a role in this area at all, this being inextricably linked to perceptions of the efficiency of the market;

● the legitimacy and practicality of the central institutions of the EU having a role and the nature of that role in the context of the creation of a single market;

● the extent to which education and training are public or private goods, the benefits are derived by the individual or society or both, and, if the latter, in what proportions;

● the capacity of individuals to make rational choices with respect to expenditure upon education and training given the shortcomings in the availability of information on individual costs and benefits, particularly when the benefits are commonly spread over a number of years, are difficult to quantify and may be of both a consumption and investment nature.

As is noted in other chapters, these perspectives, allied often to particular cultural characteristics and traditions, have implications for the institutional arrangements at both national and EU level, for the diagnosis of problems or weaknesses, as well as for the policies advocated and pursued.

These debates when undertaken at the level of the Union both illustrate and reflect different perspectives and traditions and commonly the discussions centre upon the respective merits of different national systems and institutions which are frequently jealously protected by the member-state governments. It will therefore be relevant to briefly detail the more stereotypical of these national systems, contrasting the neo-corporatist approach that characterises many of the national systems with the more laissez-faire, market-oriented approach of UK governments in recent years.

It must also be borne in mind that VET may be an instrument used for the achievement of social and political objectives – for example, to empower people and to advance the cause of equality and welfare – as well as labour market and economic objectives.

ISSUES AND DEBATES

Competitiveness

The essence of the debate on competitiveness is that, given the kind of high-wage economies with developed welfare institutions and post-Fordist production systems (*see* Chapter 2) that characterise late twentieth-century Europe, the key to international competitiveness is in the quality of the output rather than its price. As Streeck (1989, p. 91) points out, this implies or necessitates a reservoir or surplus of labour which is highly skilled, but which is also in possession of a broad skill base, linked to work experience and supported with theoretical underpinning. The surplus required is both qualitative and quantitative. He argues that this combination is provided by the 'dual' German system of vocational training/apprenticeship. This system combines skills training with the necessary theoretical support and seeks to provide the individual with both work and non-work based training; it produces large numbers of workers with highly developed and broadly based skills. The danger that employers may try and 'freeload' – that is, take advantage of the surplus created through the efforts of others and make no contribution themselves – may have to be countered with appropriate legislative and institutional support and structures.

Another danger is that a system apparently successful in one set of circumstances will be taken as the blueprint for the design of systems that are required to operate in different circumstances and perhaps achieve different objectives. Attempts to directly transpose the German arrangements to other member states with different traditions, cultures and maybe even different production systems and strategies may not be at all successful.

According to Regini (1995) (see also Chapter 2), there is indeed more than one way to produce the kind of technical–vocational skill mix that is implied by the Streeck analysis. He cites as alternatives the French and Italian systems with their reliance upon internal labour markets and in-firm training on top of the basic theoretical knowledge provided by the secondary school system.

Regini also questions the assumption that all firms in post-Fordist scenarios seek to compete on quality and need the kind of highly skilled and broadly based technical–vocational mix of labour that is implied by the above analysis. There are other post-Fordist production strategies that have very different implications for the type of labour required to satisfy the demands of the system in place; intellectual and social skills – such as diligence, adaptability, problem solving, social and relational skills and the ability to take initiatives – may be equally crucial.

There are similarities here with the analysis of Soskice (1993) who suggested that in a post-Fordist service- and client-dominated economy, the key skills required by employers are social, organisational, problem solving and computing. Holt Larson (1994, pp. 107–8) points to the 'increasing importance of organisations based on knowledge, service and hi-tech' in the post-Fordist European Community and stresses the importance of personality characteristics, computer, planning, negotiation and other interpersonal skills.

Regini suggests that post-Fordist firms remain concerned with price and, while they may choose to compete primarily on the basis of quality, it is unlikely to be in the complete absence of a concern with price. However, he also suggests that there are dimensions other than quality upon which firms may seek to compete – for example, product diversification, design, and flexibility in terms of adjustment to changes in demand and changes in the requirements of the customer. The firm's choice of appropriate production strategy in the circumstances will have implications for the type and quantity of labour required and thereby the outputs required of the VET arrangements.

Regini identifies five types of organisational strategy, each of which involves a different pattern of human resource utilisation. These are:

1 *Diversified quality production.* Competition is based on both quality and product diversification, thereby avoiding competition on price with low-wage economies. Often this takes the form of a high level of customisation of the product and requires the kind of labour resource that Streeck identified as being produced by the German system – that is, a mix of high and broad-based skills. In this scenario the requirement is for a labour

force that is adaptive, willing and able to learn new tasks rapidly and capable itself of contributing to innovation and product development. Value is placed upon both vocational and other problem-solving and interactive skills.

2 *Flexible mass production.* This strategy involves the mass production of a number of different goods, the firm thereby competing in a number of different markets and doing so on price, if necessary. There can be extensive automation of production and the organisation tends to require a mix of labour – low and unskilled at the production end and highly skilled middle-management, marketing, sales and technical staff. Again at the high-skilled end of the labour force, there is a need for interactive and problem-solving skills, as well as those which can be perceived as directly vocational.

3 *Flexible specialisation.* Here the emphasis is upon the organisation's ability to adapt to changes in demand. Regini suggests that this strategy is more common among small firms. The requirements of the labour involved are both functional and temporal flexibility, allied to broadly based social and interactive skills. The small firm sector rarely has a significant capacity for in-house training so that it relies upon others to provide the labour resource with the skills needed; this may be other employers, suppliers of equipment or external training agencies of one kind or another.

4 *Neo-Fordist.* There are still many firms that operate in a largely traditional Fordist fashion, relying upon Taylorist techniques of organising production with the traditional emphasis, so effectively described by Braverman (1974), upon fragmentation, deskilling and mass production of standard products. The requirement of such systems is for labour that is largely unskilled other than in operations-specific skills, that exhibits little desire to contribute to the decision-making processes and is not required to be flexible.

5 *Traditional small firm.* Small firms seek to compete on price, not through the economies that may come from mass production, but by keeping down costs, including labour costs. (The veracity of this assertion is supported by the furore in this sector that is occasioned in the UK every time there is mention of a national minimum wage.) Such organisations are not likely to provide their employees with training and many exist only because they operate in product markets that make few demands upon the skills of the labour resource, thereby enabling the employment of cheap unskilled labour.

These five different production strategies suggest that:

● they require different types, levels and mixes of skill;

● they each impose their own demand features upon the labour market; and

● the existing supply of labour in a particular country or region will impact upon the kind of production strategy that is likely to be successful/feasible.

Regini is challenging the dominant assertion that within the EU competitiveness depends upon the ability to compete on quality and, arguably more importantly given the purposes of this chapter, he is highlighting the relationship between production strategies and VET. Production strategies are both influences upon and constrained by the outputs of VET systems; they contribute to the determination of the demand for labour but they will also be constrained by the available supply. It is also important to bear in mind that these strategies are at least to some extent the product of strategic choices on the part of employers and managers and that these will be contextually bounded. One of the implications of this is that organisations may well (or may be well advised to) seek competitive advantage through searching for an appropriate match or fit between their production strategy and the available labour supply. These strategic decisions therefore impact upon the efficiency of a VET system which can be interpreted as the degree of match or mismatch between the supply and demand of skilled labour.

Market mechanism

One of the economic explanations of labour market behaviour with respect to investment/expenditure upon VET is referred to as *Human Capital Theory*. An underlying assumption of this explanation is that individuals through education and training enhance their productive capacity and thereby their earning power and they will therefore invest in education and training up to the point at which the additional or marginal benefits derived just exceed the marginal costs.

In this context, the costs of such investment need to include both the direct and indirect costs, the latter being the opportunity costs of undertaking the training as represented, for example, by the earnings forgone and/or the returns that may be derived from putting the funds into some alternative investment. The rate of interest/return on alternative investments of comparable risk therefore plays a part in the decision whether to invest in further training and education. In theory, the rational investor would continue to invest in the latter only as long as the rate of return exceeds the rate of return available from the former. The length of time over which the benefits can be derived is a factor in this equation and this in part explains the generally inverse relationship between age and a willingness to invest in further education or training.

The assumed relationship between VET, enhanced productivity and earnings is predicated on the argument that it is the marginal productivity of labour that effectively constitutes the demand for labour; the greater the marginal productivity, the greater will be the wage at which the employer is willing to acquire the labour. This explanation also contains the seeds of the explanation of wage differentials since the ultimate prediction is that in a competitive economy differences in earnings are derived via market equilibrium wage differentials which reflect differences in education and training investment.

The underlying assumptions of this argument are:

- that individuals are motivated by the desire to maximise their wealth;
- that they are rational;
- that they have access to the information necessary to enable them to make rational decisions; and
- that they are capable of pursuing their own interests in the market.

No account is taken of differences in individual ability or of differences in the quality of the training obtained. There is also the issue of the availability of funds to finance the acquisition of education and training. It is also assumed that individuals pay the cost of their own training and education. If these funds have to be borrowed, it is likely that the rate of return necessary to render the investment worthwhile will be greater than if the source of the funds is internal. The implication of this is that the rich will invest in more education and training than the poor.

Where the individual does not pay for the training directly, as for example when it is provided by an employer, it is consistent with this explanation that they pay indirectly via lower wages. Becker (1975) pointed out, however, that there is a difference between firm-specific training and training in transferable skills, such as those of a problem-solving or interactional nature referred to in the preceding section and identified by Regini (1995) as crucial to particular production strategies. Where the training is in transferable skills, these will have a market value; firm-specific skills may not and the rational investor will take this into account when deciding whether to undertake/invest in the training concerned. If the training involves transferable skills with a market value in terms of higher future earnings, the individual will have an incentive to invest, to work for lower wages; however, if the skills are not transferable in this sense there will be no market value and there may not be the same degree of incentive.

From the viewpoint of the employer, the incentive to provide training is also linked to the anticipated returns in terms of enhanced productivity and again, as with the rational consumer, the calculations need to take into account the returns available from alternative investments. Other factors influencing the willingness to invest will include rates of labour turnover and thereby the duration of the expected benefits; premature turnover represents returns forgone.

It should be reasonably clear from this that there is usually a much greater incentive for firms to engage in providing firm-specific training than training in transferable skills; equally there is a greater incentive for employees to invest in their own transferable education and training.

Proponents of this explanation argue that with appropriate modifications to eradicate the imperfections, it forms the basis of an efficient market in education and training – with individuals demanding general/transferable training which has a market value and for which they pay, and firms/employers providing and paying for firm-specific training which does not have the same degree of value in the marketplace. Organisations would emerge to cater for the transferable skills and general educational demands of the individuals and there is no necessity for government intervention or provision.

Critics of this viewpoint argue that many of the assumptions underlying this explanation are unrealistic. They do not take into account issues such as discrimination against particular sectors of the labour force – ethnic minorities and women – and the imperfections of wage setting in markets constrained by trade unions and institutional, social and cultural barriers to free movement. The critics also highlight the distorting influence upon the model of the preference of firms for internal labour markets, in which the policies pursued may be largely independent of the external pressures that are supposed to determine wages, employment levels and, indirectly, expenditure upon education and training. The model's critics also assert that education and training produce public and social benefits and utility and, by implication, decisions influencing their provision should not therefore be left solely to the interaction of market forces.

The role of government

The debates regarding the justification for government regulation, encouragement and/or provision of education and training tend to centre around a number of specific issues:

1 An educated population produces political, social and economic benefits/externalities which transcend individual benefits – for example, in areas such as the feasibility of effective democracy, greater awareness of dangers to health, birth control, reduced rates of crime and greater social cohesion.

2 Education and training contribute to economic growth through their impact upon the stock of knowledge and the base that it then forms for development and innovation.

3 Individuals are not able to take these externalities into account when making investment decisions.

4 Education and training may be integral to the achievement of particular government objectives. Training initiatives of particular kinds are widely perceived as essential to the achievement of greater employment.

5 Various market imperfections exist. For example, in the capital market, lending institutions have been relatively unwilling to finance the development of human capital which they have viewed as more risky than alternative investment opportunities. The reluctance in the UK of the private sector banks to take on the risk of higher education student loans is a case in point. As noted above, the need to obtain external funding makes it less likely that individuals will undertake the investment and this tends to add to the persistence of inequalities in that those who can finance such investment from their own resources are in a position to further boost their earning power, assuming that there is at least some positive earnings benefit linked to the acquisition of additional knowledge and/or skills. There is therefore an equity argument for government intervention.

6 The need for government regulation of training provision is enhanced by the relative inability of consumers to judge the quality of what they purchase; in many cases those most in need will be the least able to make such judgements.

7 Employing organisations are much less likely to provide/pay for education and training involving general and transferable knowledge and skills even though possession of these skills may be a prerequisite to the effective acquisition of organisation- and/or occupation-specific skills.

8 Employers are less likely to provide training of a transferable skill nature if the traditions in the external labour market include the poaching of trained and skilled staff by organisations that do not engage in training.

9 It is likely that imperfections and rigidities introduced into wage-fixing processes and structures – whether the product of institutional regulation, internal markets or trade union bargaining behaviour – will reduce the flexibility of wages and it is this flexibility which acts as the means by which the market signals to individuals that there are shortages or surpluses of particular skills.

10 Small firms find it more difficult to finance training given that they are more likely to be pursuing a product strategy of price competition and training costs are likely to form a larger proportion of total costs.

11 Any tendency by the parties to adopt a short-term approach to investment returns is also likely to hamper investment in training since the returns are likely to extend over a relatively long timescale.

It is usually for one or more of these reasons that people argue there is a need for governments to intervene to influence both the quality and quantity of the education and training provision and consumption in a community. Implicit in the arguments for government intervention are assertions that training markets left to themselves will not produce socially desirable or optimal levels and types of training provision. The nature and form which this intervention can take are varied and within the EU there are examples of many of the different means available. There are also examples of different approaches and assessments of the 'problems' posed by a reliance upon the market; some governments have a greater degree of belief in the efficiency of the market and are prepared to allow the market a greater role than others.

There are a range of ways in which governments can seek to intervene and regulate:

1 They can confer upon individuals statutory rights and obligations – for example, to full-time education between certain ages or to a certain standard, or to continuous vocational training – and then leave resource allocation decisions to the operation of the market.

2 They can leave provision and/or consumption to individuals and employers in the market and simply seek to control quality through the determination of content, creation of standards, inspection and the regulation of qualifications.

3 They can encourage or require the Social Partners to participate in the determination and/or implementation of VET policy; this may be at a national or sectoral level.

4 They can rely upon the market but seek to mitigate the impact of imperfections – for example, through the provision of incentives, both to employers and employees, such as by the provision of cheap loans with long pay-back periods or through the provision of vouchers or credits which individuals can use to 'pay' for the training or which can be used by the employer or other training provider to partially or wholly finance the provision.

5 They can act as provider, funded from public revenues derived from taxation and directly controlled by them and/or their agents.

6 They may partially provide and/or regulate. For example, they may seek to provide and fund basic education and transferable skills leaving the provision of job- or organisation-specific provision to the market.

7 They may target particular disadvantaged groups or regions or they may seek to promote the acquisition of particular skills/knowledge – for example, those associated with information technology, or those skills indicated as being in short supply at any point in time.

8 They may impose upon employers an obligation to provide or fund particular levels, forms, quantities and quality of VET for their employees.

Governments decide upon their particular approach and strategy in the context of their political, economic and social agenda and their beliefs concerning the efficiency of the market. The significance of belief is arguably enhanced by the absence of definitive quantitative evidence of the costs and benefits of the various options. Economists have still to find really satisfactory means of calculating externalities.

As was noted earlier, Regini (1995) has pointed out the significance of achieving a fit between competitive and production strategies and VET systems. There is no universal best approach and the dominant production strategies being pursued in a particular country or region constitute part of the context within which governments determine both their approach and their agenda. It is important to bear in mind that perceptions of future strategies should also form part of the context within which these decisions are made. The significance of competitive and production strategies can be illustrated through the following hypothetical example.

In a country or region dominated by a mix of traditional small firms and firms engaged in neo-Fordist mass production, both engaged in cost minimisation and competing on price, the requirement for labour is likely to be dominated by a demand for labour of low skill and low cost so as to facilitate national and international competitiveness and maximise short-term returns.

In such a scenario, if one also had a government that was ideologically committed to the market as the most efficient mechanism for allocating resources between the various and competing uses, and which was also committed to the reduction of public expenditure and taxation, and whose concerns were primarily short to medium term, it would be quite reasonable for the government to pursue a policy of non-intervention – that is, for it to rely upon the market.

However, critics would no doubt point out that the pursuit of such a policy in the given context would result in a downward spiral of wage competition, allied to a determination on the part of employers to reduce expenditure upon training, it being perceived as a short-term and dispensable cost rather than as an investment. Reliance upon the market in this scenario would lead to the perpetuation of a low-skill, low-cost labour force, enhanced poverty and inequality and, if there is a global decline in the demand for low and unskilled labour, such a policy seems likely also to result in greater unemployment.

It would become extremely difficult for the country or region to make the transition from this position to the different competitive and production scenario dominated by firms engaged in the high-tech sector, competing on quality, utilising production strategies characterised by Regini as diversified quality production and requiring a highly skilled and flexible labour force. Regini (1995) suggests that this latter scenario requires an education and training policy which he characterises as oriented to redundancy or surplus, a policy that results in the provision of an excess of skilled labour compared to actual demand.

There is an obvious danger that such a regime would become self-perpetuating with innovation stifled by VET that produce a labour force unequipped with the body of knowledge and the kind of general and transferable skills necessary to prime such innovatory activity. In a sense, it would be doomed to continue driving costs down (including both wages and training) in order to continue competing on price with those countries entering the market and with cost advantages.

Regini's (1995) thesis implies that competitive and production strategies have implications for both the supply of and demand for labour in terms of its body of knowledge and skill mix and this provides part of the context within which governments determine their role with respect to the country's VET system.

Generally throughout the EU there has been and still is a willingness for the state to undertake a regulatory and supportive role, even if not directly responsible for provision. Commonly, this is a response to concern both that employers will prefer to 'poach' or recruit already trained and skilled employees rather than incur the expenditure on training themselves and that state intervention is essential if the economies' requirements in terms of both quality and quantity of training are to be met. In a number of member states, there is a statutory requirement to provide, or a right to, training of a vocational nature as well as to basic education.

Furthermore, in many of these states the trade unions as Social Partners have a legislatively supported role in decision making – usually justified on the grounds that employers left to their own devices will tend to concentrate upon relatively short-term and to some extent parochial needs and interests. It is envisaged that the unions introduce the longer term dimension and address training from a less firm-specific direction. It needs to be recognised that it is likely that the interests of the employers and trade unions will not coincide and that the determination of policy is likely to be the product of negotiation and compromise.

The government-inspired and supported devolution of policy determination to the Social Partners also has the advantage that they should be in possession of better information as to the requirements than government; as a result the policies so determined should be relevant to the current and future needs of the employers, workers and society at large. Furthermore, the institutional involvement of the Social Partners should assist in the implementation of the decisions made since their members responsible for implementation should be in agreement with the policies jointly arrived at, and, when this is not the case, there will at least be a moral obligation upon them to comply. It is also often argued that the involvement of the unions in the determination of training policy and provision will assist the transition necessary when skill requirements change – the well rehearsed argument that involvement aids change by breeding a sense of ownership and even commitment.

The case for government intervention and the corporatist-style arrangements relatively common in the EU are predicated upon, justified and necessitated by the shortcomings and failings of the approach that preaches reliance upon the market.

NATIONAL SYSTEMS OF VET

In this section, three of the national systems within the EU are described – the UK, Germany and France. These systems have been chosen because they illustrate different and particular governmental approaches and degrees of reliance upon the market, roles for the Social Partners, combinations of education and vocational training, mixes of internal and external labour markets and training provision, and *outcomes* in terms of participation rates, expenditure and qualification and skill mix. Given the above discussion of the interaction between production strategies and demands for labour, each national system can also be seen to produce outcomes that either do or do not lend themselves to the pursuit of competitiveness in international markets on the grounds of quality and high-tech skill level inputs.

Detailed descriptions of these systems are beyond the scope of this chapter and the reader is advised to consult alternative sources such as the works of Burgess (1993) or Hendry (1995) if they need further information on a particular system.

Figure 4.11 shows the proportion of EU GDP spent on training and Fig. 13.1 gives an idea of the variations in public expenditure on training from one country to another over the period 1990 to 1995, and the distinction between the expenditure upon training for the employed compared to that for the unemployed. This shows that the countries spending the most are Denmark and Sweden and that they also spend more in relation to the numbers unemployed. Greece, Spain, Portugal and the UK all spend less than 0.1 per cent of GDP per 5 per cent unemployed.

Education attainment levels by age and sex are shown in Figs 13.2 (men) and 13.3 (women). The overall participation rates of men and women, aged between 16 and 29, in education and training are shown in Fig. 4.9 and education and training participation rates for 15 to 24 year olds in EU member states are shown in Table 13.1.

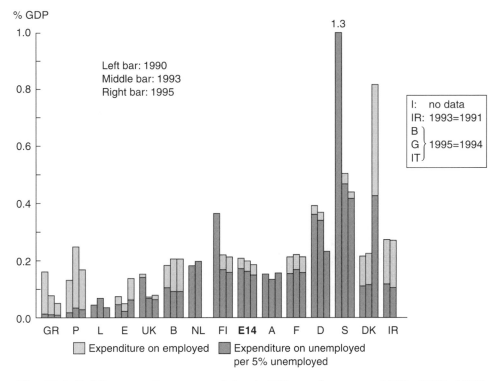

Fig. 13.1 Public expenditure on training in EU member states, 1990, 1993, 1995

Source: European Commission (1996) *Employment in Europe 1996.*

Table 13.1 Education/Training participation Rates, 1995 (%)

	Aged 15–19	*Aged 20–24*
Belgium	87.5	37.5
Denmark	82.3	50.0
Germany	93.0	39.1
Greece	80.0	29.2
Spain	79.1	41.8
France	93.2	42.5
Ireland	83.7	30.1
Italy	74.1	35.1
Luxembourg	38.8	36.5
Netherlands	88.1	49.8
Austria	81.1	32.8
Portugal	73.4	40.2
Finland	87.2	42.9
Sweden	n.a.	n.a.
UK[+]	71.2[+]	23.6[+]
E15	**82.5**	**36.9**

[+] 1994 figures

Source: Derived from European Commission (1996) *Employment in Europe 1996.*

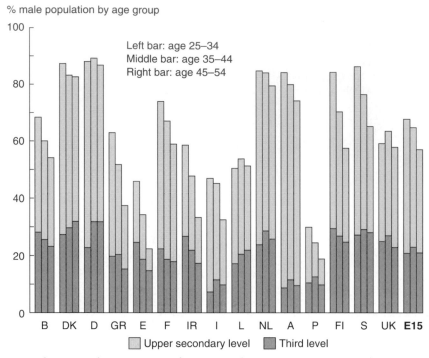

Fig. 13.2 Educational attainment of men, aged 25 to 54, in EU member states, 1995

Source: European Commission (1996) *Employment in Europe 1996.*

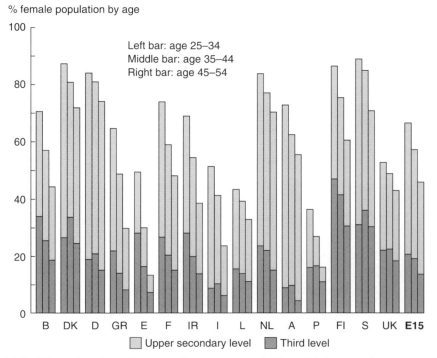

Fig. 13.3 Educational attainment of women, aged 25 to 54, in member states, 1995

Source: European Commission (1996) *Employment in Europe 1996.*

It is important to avoid implying too much from international comparisons on the basis of relatively crude statistics. To some extent these measures will obscure differences in the institutional systems, differences of definition, the impossibility of knowing whether you are indeed comparing like with like.

Hendry (1994, pp. 99–101), for example, points out that company expenditure on training will to some extent reflect the attitude of government towards state provision versus employer provision and/or whether there is government compulsion for companies to spend a percentage of wages and salaries on training as is the case in France. Other particular difficulties identified by Hendry (1994) are related to definition: what activities count as training and what elements of cost are taken into account?

The UK

Keep and Rainbird (1995) point out that the market model dominated governmental approaches to vocational training in the UK before 1964 and has done so since 1988. In the intervening period, there was in place a legislatively supported structure of tripartite *industrial training boards (ITBs)*, initially financed by the imposition of a levy upon employers. This levy could be reclaimed or, alternatively, companies could be exempted from it, if they undertook or financed an appropriate amount of training for their employees. The system organised on a sectoral basis. The Manpower Services Commission, a government agency, was responsible for overseeing the system and administering public training programmes. Trade union interests were incorporated into the policy decision-making processes. Hendry (1995) points out that one of the advantages of the levy system was that it encouraged many companies to establish training functions for the first time as a mechanism for recouping the levy.

The return of a Conservative government in 1979, however, resulted in trade union interests being removed from positions of participation and influence and eventually the ITBs were abolished – many in 1981 and the remainder in 1988.

The belief of the Conservative governments between 1979 and 1997 was that market forces were the best means of determining the type and amounts of training undertaken; in this context it is primarily the responsibility of employers (and to a lesser extent individuals) to make decisions regarding investment in training. In a survey conducted by Grant Thornton International and reported in the *IPD European Update* in July 1994, it was discovered that 19 per cent of UK employers saw no need for training and gave as the two most important reasons the cost and the time taken. The UK government view was that if the state has a role, it is limited and should be directed at exhortation and supporting provision for the disadvantaged – for example, the long-term unemployed. This UK government position has been summarised as (Keep and Rainbird, 1995):

> VET should be employer-led and employer-controlled with the influence of educationists and trade unions being sharply reduced.

This approach can be seen to have dominated government policy during this period and is reflected in the system of local training bodies established in 1991 – *the Training and Enterprise Councils (TECs)*. To some extent, these can be seen as replacements for the ITBs, but the TECs are in fact very different creatures with different funding arrangements and management structures. The TECs were local in their remit, established to deal with the requirements of local labour markets, funded from the centre and managed by a board modelled on private-sector lines and made up of employer representatives. Trade unions were formally excluded from this new structure, as were human resource professionals.

The TECs also have responsibility for administering the government's special schemes for the young and long-term unemployed, as well as the accreditation of the 'Investors in People' scheme which since 1991 has been the major mechanism by which the government has sought to encourage and raise the standards of in-company training.

Research by the Institute of Employment Studies (Hillage, 1996), covering 1800 employers confirms that the majority of employers who had participated in training expected benefits of a financial nature to emerge from their participation in terms of enhanced productivity and/or quality of production and/or service. Nevertheless, the most common direct benefit acknowledged by employers appeared to be improvements in training systems with skills and morale in second and third place.

Hendry (1995) suggests that the TECs may be the last chance for employers to justify the government's faith in the voluntary approach – an approach that was so roundly criticised by the House of Lords Select Committee on the European Communities (1990) when it said:

> the long history of failure which has marked the voluntary approach to training in this country, the committee consider that some form of statutory underpinning is needed to act as a catalyst for change.

Traditional criticisms of the UK system also included:

- There was inadequate transferability and coordination between education and vocational training systems with the educational system not providing students with the appropriate transferable skills that would form an appropriate basis for vocational training and the necessary adaptability and continuous learning.

- The system did not assist in the development of a learning culture.

- The apprenticeship system that dominated vocational skills training prior to the 1980s did not provide rigorous assessment of outcomes, relying instead on time serving.

- There were no externally determined standards of competence that had to be achieved.

- It was occupation specific.

- It was relatively static and did not assist the acquisition of transferable skills, the introduction of new technologies, or individual or collective adaptability.

The *youth training schemes* that the government initiated in the 1980s, partially as replacements for the flawed apprenticeship schemes, did try to accommodate some of these criticisms and did partially copy the German dual system by seeking to combine in-company training with time off-the-job in an educational environment with an emphasis upon more transferable skills. However, the early attempts and schemes were criticised as:

- merely a means by which government sought to artificially reduce the youth unemployment figures;

- failing to be matched by genuine job opportunities in which acquired skills could be utilised; and

- a scheme perceived by many employers as providing cheap labour consistent with employers' desires to cut costs and compete on the grounds of price rather than upon degree of skill, quality, flexible specialisation or flexibility of response.

Hendry (1994) compared 1987 data relating to labour costs and unit labour costs in the various member states. Assuming these costs reflect skill levels, training and the capitalisation of industry, he concluded that the UK, with its below-average labour costs and its above-average unit labour costs, showed definite signs of being a low-wage and low-skill economy. Hendry suggested (1995, pp. 426–7) that the UK government had been deliberately pursuing a policy of international competitiveness via low wages and pointed out that such an approach was short sighted, fundamentally wrong and that it was likely to undermine the incentive to innovate and invest in new technology skill and new work practices.

The *National Vocational Qualification (NVQ) initiative* started back in 1986 with the creation of the National Council for Vocational Qualifications (NCVQ). The intention was to create a system that offered a means by which vocational experience and skill could be acquired, demonstrated and acknowledged through performance and assessment at work; various levels of achievement and progression can be demonstrated. The emphasis was to be upon the assessment of individual competence.

The GNVQ, introduced in 1992, represents a largely college-based and full-time education route to the acquisition of competence-based vocational qualifications. It also represents a more concerted effort to encourage the widespread provision and acquisition of more transferable and flexible skills. The compulsory core skills of the GNVQ scheme include communication, presentation, numerical, keyboard and IT skills.

These schemes do provide for and incorporate a range of changes and developments to previous arrangements. The GNVQ, in particular, provides a more vocational alternative to the traditional academic approach and qualifications while in full-time education. It is claimed that over time the initiative will develop into a system of continuous training that encompasses the later stages of formal and compulsory education, initial and adult vocational training. Complementing this initiative the government has also decided to fund a number of new 'modern apprenticeships'.

There are, of course, criticisms and alleged deficiencies:

- Assessment at work is potentially a massive and unrealistic task.

- National standards are likely to be too broad and not sufficiently specific for companies' requirements.

- The standards and criteria of assessment are likely to be too closely related to jobs and work as it is currently performed and inappropriate to dynamic circumstances.

- There is insufficient theoretical underpinning.

- The administration and control of the scheme is overly dependent upon employers; there is still too small a role for educationalists in the determination of standards and direction.

- The trade unions are still largely excluded.

It may be too early to make an assessment of changes of direction or emphasis consequent upon the return of a Labour government in May 1997. However, a couple of months after the 1997 election, the Institute of Personnel and Development (IPD) produced a report entitled 'working to learn' compiled by eight independent academic experts which was highly critical of the reliance of previous governments upon the market mechanism as the means through which VET is provided. The report is particularly critical of the schemes devised to provide education and training for the young. It argued:

1 that few of the national targets for education and training were likely to be met;

2 that youth training and similar programmes had been stigmatised through their association with government efforts to reduce the claimant unemployed;

3 that these programmes were characterised by high drop-out and failure rates (a criticism also made of the GNVQ/NVQ schemes).

The report calls for companies to be required by law to provide quality education and training for their teenage employees. The current system of youth training should be replaced by a system of work-based trainee ships whereby under-18s are guaranteed at least two days' education and training per week. What is envisaged is a programme of integrated academic, vocational and practical learning that also incorporates the transferable and core skills referred to in other parts of this chapter. Every trainee should be accorded a mentor and a programme tailored to his or her needs. The two-year programmes would also provide opportunities for both academic and vocational qualifications to be obtained.

This report encapsulates many of the arguments and debates that form the context of this chapter and it will be interesting to see the extent to which it is picked up by the Labour government. Among the issues to be addressed would be the question of cost, who is to meet it, where the in-company trainers and mentors are to come from, how realistic it is to envisage individually tailored programmes and whether such a compulsion would also apply to SMEs.

Germany

The German system has traditionally exhibited a twin-track or dual approach to both education and vocational training. The formal educational system is comprised of both academic and vocational schools.

At the heart of vocational training is the *apprenticeship scheme*; this comprises training on the job as well as continuing basic education in subjects such as maths, general studies and German as well as in the relevant technical subjects. The apprentice is required to spend approximately two days a week at the vocational school. The system is regulated nationally by statute and administered locally by the local chambers of commerce. Major changes to syllabuses require the agreement of the government and the Social Partners. There is a tripartite Federal Vocational Training Institute which guides and to some extent coordinates the work of the Social Partners locally or, in particular occupational groupings, in updating this vocational training content and provision.

The overwhelming majority of the costs of this initial vocational training has traditionally been borne by employers, who have been obliged to pay by government. The output of qualified personnel has been considerably greater than in either of the other two countries whose systems are described here. This output has included a technically qualified labour supply that also has a greater resource of transferable skills.

However, these costs are considerable and there are suspicions that, confronted with global competition and the highest labour costs in the EU, employers in Germany may become increasingly reluctant to continue funding vocational training on such a grand scale. An alternative strategy arising from the opportunities presented by the single market is to relocate some production elsewhere within the Union, where training costs may not be so high, thereby also reducing employment opportunities within Germany itself. As noted by Regini (1995), there is still scope for competition via production strategies that do not demand the high and transferable skilled labour force that the German system produces. In the late 1990s, unemployment in Germany was at record levels compared with the preceding four decades.

In addition to the initial vocational training system, *the Meister system* of advanced vocational training has also played a major part in the development and competitiveness of German industry. Here the focus is on advanced technical skills. The system again involves local administration by chambers of commerce of nationally determined syllabuses and examinations and applicants must have two years' post-apprentice work experience. The Meister provides technical leadership in the workplace and one of his or her major roles has been the workplace-based training of apprentices – a training role for which training is received as part of the Meister programme.

Hendry (1995, pp. 424–5) concludes that one of the advantages of the Meister system has been that it has enabled German industry traditionally to manage with fewer layers of supervision because of the higher quality of this post-apprentice level. In referring to the vocational training system as a whole, including continuous development, he suggests that the German system better facilitates the kind of high-skill and quality-based production strategies that are commonly assumed to provide the greatest scope for competitiveness, growth and prosperity in the EU of the future.

Opportunities for training and re-training are made available to individuals (and also to employers in certain circumstances) hit by restructuring or unemployment, via grants or subsistence allowances from the Federal Labour Institute. Since re-unification, this organisation has also been called upon to make a major contribution in terms of job creation and training in the East.

Within organisations, the effective Social Partner representing the interests of the employees is the Works Council and the Works Constitution Act of 1972 provides these Councils with various rights which include the right of co-determination (*see* Hollinshead and Leat, 1995, pp. 160–1) in respect of the implementation of workplace training.

Few, if any, observers would question that the German system has been comparatively preferable to most others and beneficial for the development of a learning culture and in its provision of a labour force that is relatively skilled and flexible (at least in terms of skill and ability). It has provided a resource that is more productive and is itself the basis for future development. Nevertheless, there was evidence in the late 1990s that the system was coming under strain from the impact of rationalisation and restructuring and unemployment. Employers were finding it more difficult to find and to fund the training specialists and opportunities traditional to the system. This was particularly a problem for initial vocational training and employers were beginning to look for greater contributions from the state.

France

Perhaps the most notorious feature of the French system – at least to the UK employers and government – is the requirement that tax is levied to finance vocational, and in particular on-the-job, training. In 1993, this tax was increased to 1.5 per cent of the wage and salary bill. All firms employing more than 10 employees are covered by the legislation and the tax is collected if the employer is unable to document that at least the amount of the tax has been spent on appropriate training activities.

Since the introduction of the tax in 1971, there has been an increase in the quantity of training. It is more difficult, however, to ascertain the impact upon quality of the measure and indeed whether the effects of the tax are desirable in terms of the skill areas and levels of training that are financed in this way. The employers are required to devote 0.3 per cent of the tax to the training of young workers (or it is paid to the Treasury) and a further 0.2 per cent is to finance the external training of employees on individual training leave. The remainder need not be spent on the company's own staff: it can, for example, be used to finance training for the unemployed and initial on-the-job training is excluded from these calculations.

Another of the individual features of the French system is the right to individual training leave. All employees are entitled to continuous vocational training and employees with 24 months' general work experience (which need not be consecutive) and 12 months' employment with their current employer are entitled to paid absence of up to one year for full-time training outside the company. It is sometimes alleged that employers, particularly those who are relatively small, prefer to pay the tax rather than provide their employees with the means to acquire transferable skills that effectively make them more attractive to other employers.

Much of the initial vocational and technical training is provided within the state educational system and there has been relatively little use made of the apprenticeship system. There are a group of vocational training schools within the state sector and a series of recognised, graded and national initial vocational qualifications. The main initial vocational qualification is the vocational training certificate (CAP). The apprenticeship system was overhauled in 1992 with the intention of enhancing its value and use. Apprenticeships are intended to combine both on- and off-the-job training, as well as both general practical and theoretical training. It is also the intention that the apprentice training should result in the acquisition of a vocational qualification, the majority of which are industry specific. Employers pay the apprentice a percentage of the legal minimum wage (SMIC), and employers are exempted from social charges in respect of their apprentice employees.

There is a major problem of youth unemployment in France and there are some schemes for enhancing and ensuring the provision of vocational training to this group. Many of these fall into the category known as sandwich courses which seek to combine practical in-company experience with a more formal and general training. These are usually for a fixed period and are often combined with incentives to the employers, such as arrangements enabling them to pay below the SMIC and an exemption from the payment of employee-related social security charges.

The French government took a number of additional initiatives in this area in 1995/6 with a view to reducing the levels of unemployment. These and similar schemes have also been extended in some instances to the long-term unemployed. Observers sometimes comment that these and similar schemes suffer as training initiatives and experiences because they are taken for other non-training motives.

The representatives of employees do have a legislatively supported right to consultation at company level through the Works Council as well as through their trade unions to engage in collective bargaining. The right to collective bargaining is also extended to the level of the industry or sector. In addition to the obligations already referred to, companies are obliged by the Labour Code (Articles L. 932–6) to produce an annual training plan and to consult with the Works Council on its contents and its implementation. Many of the collective agreements reached at company level concern training matters and at industry level the parties must engage in collective bargaining on a range of training matters at least every five years.

EU POLICY AND INITIATIVES

The Treaty of Rome requires that the Commission develop a common vocational policy and the European Social Fund was established in 1960 in accordance with this requirement (Adnett, 1996, p. 126). Although this is examined in detail in Chapter 15, it is perhaps worth noting at this point that there are pressures from within the Commission in 1997 to again reorganise these structural funds so as to produce a simplified form in which there are only two main sets of objectives:

1 assistance to the poorer regions and areas with problems of industrial adaptation; and

2 the issue of human resource development as a whole within the EU.

The Social Affairs Commissioner also feels that it may be time to drop the additionality requirement for funding programmes.

As already noted, EU initiatives in the area of VET have not always been motivated by the desire to achieve a well educated and trained labour force, desirable though that may be. For example, particular VET initiatives have been advanced with the objective of:

- reducing levels of unemployment;
- assisting in the reduction of inequalities between regions and sectors of the population including genders;
- alleviating poverty and/or social exclusion;
- easing the path to cultural awareness and empathy; and
- providing a mechanism for the achievement of greater mobility of people and ideas.

This section examines in more detail the policies and initiatives pursued at the level of the Union, the underlying assumptions, objectives and, where possible, the outcomes.

Before proceeding, however, it is relevant to refer again to the thesis of Regini (1995) which has considerable implications for the pursuit of VET policies at the level of the EU. If, as is suggested, the dominant competitive and production strategies differ between regions, let alone between countries, within the Union and if these strategies have significant implications for the organisation and utilisation of human resources, in that they influence the demand for labour/skills in terms of both quantity and quality, the scope for and desirability of effective action at the level of the Union is placed in some doubt. This also has implications for the prospects for convergence between the systems operating within the various member states.

Such a thesis tends to reinforce arguments for an approach, policies and initiatives that are consistent with *the principle of subsidiarity* – with action at the level of the Union limited pretty much to the drawing up of appropriate frameworks, the expression of non-legislative recommendations, the formulation of appropriate joint opinions and perhaps the creation of some very basic and common legislatively supported rights.

There is some evidence that the Commission realises this, although it has tended to cite cultural, tradition and institutional differences as the reason for not seeking to pursue policies aimed at the harmonisation of systems. The Commission seems to perceive Union policy to be concerned with specifying the desirability of achieving particular objectives, but leaving responsibility for their attainment largely in the hands of national authorities (*see* Rainbird, 1993, p. 186).

Rainbird (1993) argues that behind the Commission's policies and initiatives on training lie three main *assumptions*:

1 *A competitiveness assumption to the effect that in order to compete in world markets the Union and its member states will need a well trained and educated labour force.* There are similarities between this assumption and that of Streeck (1991). This assumption can be seen to underlie much of the recent activity of the Union institutions and the revisions of the Treaty agreed at Amsterdam in 1997.

2 *An assumption that differences between the systems of qualification in the various member states are a significant barrier to the mobility of labour within the Union.* This is particularly the case since the creation of the single market although there are arguments that labour mobility is much less necessary than the mobility of capital.

3 *An assumption that the restructuring of industry and regions encouraged by the single market and other forces can be alleviated by the use of active labour market and regional policies that encompass initiatives in the area of VET.*

In addition to these main assumptions, Rainbird (1993, p. 188) also notes that underlying the approach of the Commission to the determination and implementation of VET policy is the assumption that it is desirable to involve the Social Partners in the decision-making and implementation processes. At Union level this is to be achieved through the Social Dialogue (*see* Chapter 6). As already noted in Chapter 1, this assumption that neo-corporatist arrangements are beneficial lies behind many of the initiatives taken by the Union in areas other than VET. It is an assumption that reflects the values, approach and institutional arrangements in many of the member states but which tends to be at odds with the neo-Classical approach to education and training markets.

Contained within these main assumptions are a number of implied objectives, the achievement of which can be assisted by the pursuit of appropriate VET policies. These *objectives* include:

● enhanced competitiveness and, by implication, economic growth;

● enhanced freedom of movement and mobility of labour;

● mitigation of the consequences of the operation of the market, including unemployment and mismatch between demand and supply.

Rainbird (1993) suggests that the initiatives taken by the Union can be categorised into three groups, each of which can be seen to relate to one of the main assumptions and implicit objectives listed above:

● measures aimed at increasing the skill levels and adaptability of the labour force overall (and thereby competitiveness and growth);

● measures aimed at the removal of institutional barriers to the free movement of labour;

● active labour market policies aimed at reducing unemployment and countering regional disadvantage.

There is the potential of overlap between these categories with particular measures perhaps achieving more than one of these general objectives. For example, measures that fit into the first of the categories above may well also enhance employment levels, if the causes of the unemployment include a shortage of the skills concerned or if the assumptions about competition on the basis of quality are appropriate.

Hendry (1995) describes EU policy in the area of skills and training as directed at achieving both efficiency and quality: *efficiency* through the encouragement of labour mobility and *quality* through improved education and training. He suggests that the second of these has so far been the more important. Arguably the mid-1990s has seen a shift in importance from issues of quality to objectives related to reducing levels of unemployment.

Despite this and in the context of this chapter, we are particularly interested in the policy issues and initiatives taken that would fall primarily into the first of these categories – that concerned with the objectives of raising skill levels and labour's adaptability generally so as to enhance competitiveness and economic growth. (The measures relating to the other two groups of initiatives are discussed in Chapters 10 and 15 respectively.)

The measures are discussed in chronological order, with the relevant Treaty Articles identified that provide the basis for institutional action, as well as specific initiatives.

The Treaty of Rome

The founding Treaty provided the Commission and other Union institutions with the right and responsibility to take initiatives in this area. Prior to the redrawing of the Treaties at Maastricht in 1991 (*see* later in this chapter) there were two main Articles – relevant to the objectives of generally raising skill levels and labour flexibility – Articles 118 and 128.

Article 118 provides that:

> the Commission shall have the task of promoting close cooperation, between member states in the social field particularly in matters relating to . . . basic and advanced vocational training.

This article was substantially unchanged by events at Maastricht.

Article 128 provided that:

> The Council shall, acting on a proposal from the Commission and after consulting the Economic and Social Committee, lay down general principles for implementing a common vocational training policy capable of contributing to the harmonious development both of the national economies and of the common market.

In summary, these articles gave the Commission the role of promoting cooperation between the member states and of initiating (remember it is the Commission that has the right of initiative with respect to legislation at Union level even though it is the Council that takes the decision) a set of general principles to guide the implementation of a common vocational training policy that was directed at the development of the economies of the member states and the Community.

It was in the context of these articles that the Council adopted a Resolution on Continuing Vocational Training in 1989. This Resolution effectively invited the Commission to draw up an action programme to develop this; the action programme was devised and adopted later in 1990 (156/90). This resulted in the *FORCE programme* which included among its objectives:

● encouraging investment in vocational training;

● supporting innovation in training techniques and methods;

- promoting schemes that take explicit account of the completion of the single market; and

- contributing to the capacity to respond to changes in the EC labour market.

The FORCE programme also stated the right (not a legal one) of workers in the Community to access vocational training throughout their working lives and that the public authorities, firms and /or the two sides of industry should establish permanent systems to achieve these objectives. Specific attempts were made to encourage the participation of SMEs in these schemes and by 1993 around 80 per cent of partner companies fell into this category.

In addition to the FORCE programme, there were other programmes initiated in the late 1980s including those known as COMETT and PETRA.

- *COMETT (The Community Programme in Education and Training for Technology).* This programme was devised to encourage cooperation between industry and the universities, so as to develop initial and continuing training in technology and to meet the needs of industry for a qualified labour force. The first phase of this programme began in 1987.

- *PETRA (Action Programme for the Vocational Training of Young People and their Preparation for Adult and Working Life).* This is another programme that started in 1987 and it had a number of objectives:

  1 to ensure that all those young people who wanted to could receive vocational training upon leaving compulsory full-time education;

  2 to raise the standard of initial training and ensure that it leads to recognised qualifications;

  3 to increase the capacity of training schemes to adapt to social, economic and technical change; and

  4 to develop a European dimension to initial vocational training.

The Community Charter of the Fundamental Social Rights of Workers 1989

This document remains as a statement of intent only – a non-binding Declaration – since, as noted elsewhere, the UK government refused to agree its contents. As a non-binding Council instrument, it can be relied upon by the Courts when interpreting related legislation and taken into account as evidence. However, it has acquired a significance beyond that since it represents the desires and intentions of the majority of the member states; it formed the basis of the Social Action Programme that followed in 1989–1990. Perhaps equally importantly, it also formed the basis for the development of the draft Social Chapter that was initially included in the Maastricht Treaty on Union and, when it was rejected by the UK, formed the basis of the Agreement on Social Policy between the eleven under the aegis of the Social Protocol. The preamble to this Agreement specifically states that the eleven member states had made the Agreement with the desire to implement the 1989 Social Charter on the basis of the *acquis communautaire* (*see* Chapter 5).

The Charter refers to education and training in several of the main contexts already identified in this chapter. It proclaims the rights of workers to:

- freedom of movement which also implies the elimination of obstacles arising from non-recognition of qualifications;

- access to vocational training throughout a person's working life and, in order to facilitate this, the establishment of continuing and permanent training systems enabling every person to undergo retraining to improve or acquire new skills particularly in the light of technical developments;

- equality (between men and women) of access to education, vocational training and career development;

- for young people, following the end of compulsory education, initial vocational training to enable them to adapt to the requirements of their future working life.

The Second Social Action Programme 1989–1990

This constituted an attempt by the Commission and the member states, other than the UK, to give effect to some of the rights/proposals contained in the Charter described above. Specifically it contained proposals for the following items:

- *An instrument on access to vocational training.* A Recommendation on Access To Continuing Vocational Training was adopted by the Council in June 1993 (93/404) and it recommends various measures that member states should take to promote access and thereby improve EU training levels in the light of technological developments, increases in competition and demographic trends. Specific measures included in-company training, the achievement of recognised transferable qualifications and increases in state provision for particularly disadvantaged groups.

- *Updating of a 1963 proposal to give effect to Article 128 of the original treaty.* This Article was removed from the founding treaties as part of the negotiations at Maastricht.

- *A communication on the rationalisation and coordination of the various community action programmes concerned with initial and continuing vocational training.* This was issued in August 1990 and proposed that vocational training programmes at community level should be grouped into three categories: initial, higher and continuing. The basis for this once again was Article 128.

- *Exchange schemes for young workers and youths.* The scheme known as PETRA was initially concerned to enhance vocational training for young workers but, upon its re-adoption as PETRA II (214/91), it was extended to encompass the 'exchange of young workers programme'. The PETRA programme achieves these exchanges through the formation of transnational training partnerships and these are consistent with one of its objectives – the development of a European dimension to initial vocational training. Youth exchanges are covered by the 'Youth for Europe' programme as amended (175/91) which was originally established in 1988 and is concerned primarily with social and cultural exchanges. The third phase of this programme covers the period 1995 to 1999 and contains proposals relating to the formation of modular programmes of higher education and apprenticeships so as to facilitate the aim of improving the mobility of students and trainees/apprentices within the Union.

- *The enhancement of progress on the comparability of vocational qualifications.* A Resolution on the Comparability of Vocational Qualifications was adopted late in 1990 (109/91). As noted in Chapter 10, there are two Directives concerned with the mutual recognition of professional (89/48) and vocational qualifications (92/51). In the late 1990s there are proposals (COM (96) 22) to extend these advantages of mutual recognition to a range of occupations not covered by existing Directives.

The Treaty of Rome as amended by the Treaty on European Union (Maastricht) and by the Treaty of Accession

Title VIII of the current Treaty is concerned with Social Policy, Education, Vocational Training and Youth.

The original Article 118 was left largely unchanged by the amended Treaty. However, one of the outcomes of the negotiations at Maastricht was the effective repeal of the old Article 128. There is now arguably a more limited role envisaged for the Commission and more limited scope for action by the Council at the level of the Union. There are now two Articles, 126 and 127, which seek to encourage cooperation at the level of the Union but which also explicitly refer to the autonomous rights of member states.

- *The new Article 126* is concerned with matters of education and seeks to encourage cooperation between member states with a view to developing quality education while preserving member state responsibility for the content of teaching, the organisation of education systems and their cultural and linguistic diversity.

- *The new Article 127* is concerned with vocational training and proposes that a vocational training policy is implemented that supports and supplements the action of the member states and aims to:

  > . . . facilitate adaptation to industrial changes . . . through vocational training and re-training . . . improve initial and continuing vocational training in order to facilitate vocational integration and reintegration into the labour market

  It should preserve member-state responsibility for the content and organisation of national systems.

There would appear to be a much greater degree of coincidence between the purposes of the ESF and these Articles than was the case before. The purposes of Union-level action on vocational training may seem to be more limited, if compared to the original Article 128, but there is undoubtedly room for debate as to what precisely might be covered by the term 'industrial changes'.

The *Amsterdam 1997 Treaty* revisions do not impact upon Articles 126 and 127 except in that the adoption procedure referred to in 127(4) is to be changed from the Co-operation to the Co-Decision Procedure.

Social Protocol Agreement on Social Policy

In the case of the SPASP, one can detect again references to elements of the former and less restrictive role and interests.

Article 1 of this Agreement states that the Community and the member states shall have a range of objectives including:

> . . . the development of human resources with a view to lasting high employment and the combating of exclusion.

This phrase is retained verbatim in the draft revised Treaty agreed at Amsterdam in 1997 as part of the new Article 117.

The Community and the member states are both also reminded that any measures taken should take account of:

. . . the need to maintain the competitiveness of the Community economy. Again the new Article 117 contains these words in paragraph 2.

The notion that Union-level policies and initiatives on VET might be specifically targeted at providing benefits in terms of competitiveness was omitted from the Maastricht Treaty revisions and therefore from the explicit role of the Commission. However, it is doubtful that this was due to a widespread revision of the view that a highly skilled labour force is essential to the competitiveness of the economies of the member states on the world stage (the assumption being that competition is inevitably going to be based on production strategies geared towards competing on quality, flexibility and diversification rather than on price). The omission may well have more to do with debates within the Union concerning subsidiarity (*see* Chapter 6) and the division of responsibilities between the Union institutions and those residing within the member states.

The White Paper on Growth, Competitiveness and Employment

This document, published in December 1993, has stimulated a considerable amount of discussion within the EU. The main thrust of this debate has been concerned with finding solutions to the 'problem of unemployment' but integral to it are also the concepts of competitiveness and growth.

In this section we have tried to distinguish those education and training initiatives that fall into the arena of active labour market policies directed primarily at easing the difficulties associated with restructuring and the creation of a single market and reducing unemployment levels, from those that are directed more at the general improvement of skill levels with a view to assisting competitiveness and economic growth.

This White Paper, in linking the three concepts together, highlights the difficulty of separation and indicates that there is the potential for overlap and incongruity between policies and objectives. It also demonstrates the complexity and lack of certainty as to the nature of the relationships between skill level, competitiveness, productivity and economic growth.

The White Paper proposes that education and training are of strategic importance in enhancing the EU's competitiveness in the 'Global Economy' and that the future development and success of the EU is dependent upon the exploitation of advances in technology which in turn relies upon the knowledge of the labour force. It is not just a question of trying to reduce current unemployment levels.

Referring back to some of the discussions earlier in this chapter, the proposals in the White Paper are consistent with the following notions:

1 competing on the dimensions of quality, design, diversity, flexibility and the utilisation of appropriate production strategies rather than competing primarily upon price and the utilisation of neo-Fordist mass production systems that require relatively unskilled labour;

2 a positive and interventionist role for government where individuals and employers are

unable to provide for themselves – as, for example, among the uneducated and unskilled poor and small employers without access to the necessary capital and other investment resources; and

3 the tripartite determination of VET policies and interventions compared with a reliance upon the market.

However, in the White Paper the Commission also acknowledges the apparent world-wide decline in the demand for unskilled labour. This raises the possibility that generating a more employment-intensive growth model – one that is employment friendly to unskilled labour – may provide solutions to the levels of unemployment, but it may have negative implications for labour productivity. This appears to sit uncomfortably with the dominant notion that the future competitiveness, growth and prosperity of the EU is inextricably linked into the hi-tech, high productivity, innovation and quality end of the global market and the resulting need for greater EU resources to be diverted to the provision of VET directed at the general improvement of skill levels.

This apparently uncomfortable juxtaposition of remedies may be perceived, of course, as nothing more than the identification and separation of short- and long-term problems and solutions. The short-term solution to the current problems posed by the decline in demand for unskilled labour is to deliberately generate labour-intensive patterns of pro-duction, perhaps even to substitute labour for machinery and technology, where possible, although to do so in a manner that is economically viable would seem likely to involve neg-ative consequences for the price of unskilled labour.

In the longer term, the solutions to both a lack of competitiveness and to unemployment are perceived to involve enhanced investment in VET, resulting in improved skills gener-ally. With a more extensive and higher skill range, even labour at the bottom end of the skill range would become more adaptable and flexible (although this will obviously depend upon the nature of the skills that are targeted and enhanced, bearing in mind the impor-tance in this context of transferable problem-solving and interpersonal skills). Such unskilled labour would also be more productive and demand should therefore be greater. In the same longer term, enhanced skill levels at the top end would be perceived as essen-tial to competitiveness at the high-tech, quality end of the market.

As Rainbird (1993) points out, there is a widespread perception that it is impossible on any significant scale for European industry to compete in international markets on the basis of low labour costs, and, by implication therefore, knowledge, skill and labour flex-ibility constitute the more fruitful battlegrounds.

The Commission's report on *Employment in Europe 1994* (European Commission, 1994b) arguably highlights again these difficulties and apparent inconsistencies. In refer-ring to growth, the report emphasises the importance of the White Paper's analysis of the long-term structural problems in the EU which include:

- inadequate investment in education and training to improve the skills and capabilities of the Community labour force upon which long-term competitiveness ultimately depends; and
- the failure to achieve a sufficiently employment-intensive pattern of growth.

The report also refers to the decisions taken at the Corfu Council meeting in June 1994 and comments positively on the seven key areas identified as requiring action, one of which was improving education and training systems, especially continuous training.

It is interesting to note that the response of UNICE, the private-sector employers association, to the Commission's analysis and its proposals for action as presented in the White Paper concentrated upon reducing what were perceived as unnecessary regulatory burdens upon employers and the reduction of labour costs. There was no evidence in the employers' remedies of the Commission's view that greater investment in education and vocational training was an essential prerequisite to greater competitiveness and economic growth.

The LEONARDO action programme

The FORCE, COMETT and PETRA programmes all came to an end in 1994 and the guidelines of each were subsumed into the *LEONARDO* action programme. This was developed and introduced in the context of the White Paper on Growth, Competitiveness and Employment. The new programme was to last from 1995 to 2000 and it was given a budget that was twice that for the vocational training elements of the previous programmes. It was envisaged that by incorporating all of these programmes into LEONARDO, a more coherent EU-wide policy would emerge. Consistent with the Treaty changes made at Maastricht, the LEONARDO programme was explicitly concerned to uphold the principle of subsidiarity (*see* Chapter 6). Priorities for this programme included:

- encouraging and enabling young people to enter the workforce through the acquisition of the appropriate skills;
- the promotion of core skills and competencies; and
- the effective investment in training by both employers and individuals.

In the main funding is matching and it is up to individuals to apply for support. Criticisms have been made of the length of time that it takes to obtain decisions and payment.

The Year of Lifelong Learning

Late in 1994, it was announced by the Commission that 1996 was to be the official Year of Lifelong Learning in the EU. The year was to have four main objectives, two of which were to be:

- raising public awareness of the importance of lifelong learning, encompassing both education and training, thereby assisting in the development of an employment-intensive competitiveness and growth model in Europe; and
- improving communication between education and training bodies and business, especially SMEs.

This was another initiative taken in the context of the White Paper on Growth, Competitiveness and Employment.

Third Social Action Programme

The Commission's Third Social Action Programme, published in April 1995, promised a White Paper on Education and Training and measures to improve the quality of training but little else in the area of the subject matter of this chapter.

The White Paper Teaching and Learning: Towards the Knowledge-based Society

This was first issued for consultation towards the end of 1995. It proposed action at both EU and national levels and had a number of explicit objectives:

- to expand knowledge;
- to prepare for future change;
- to strengthen the sense of belonging and combat the sense of exclusion; and
- to foster innovation.

To achieve these objectives the Commission envisaged action at the level of the EU that encompassed:

1 the creation and establishment of an EU-wide accreditation system covering basic, technical and vocational skills;
2 the development of a skills record card that would be individual and recognised throughout the Union;
3 investigation of the possibilities for the development and introduction of a basic legal right to access to continuing vocational training;
4 the development of apprenticeship schemes that might allow for exchange across national boundaries within the Union; with the existing LEONARDO and SOCRATES schemes giving priority to the acquisition of complex technological skills.

Within the SOCRATES programme of educational cooperation, educational exchanges have developed at a rapid rate. By the middle of 1997, demand was outstripping the financial resources allocated to the scheme. Requests for grants totalled over 700 million Ecu in 1996 and this compared to a budget of only 173 million Ecu for the year and 850 million Ecu for the five-year programme. Over 1600 higher education institutions had applied to the programme for contracts to run appropriate European activities and programmes. The Commissioner Cresson claimed that the programme had been an outstanding success and that it had a vital role to play in developing high quality education and preparing young people for life in a wider European context. (The second proposal was picked up early in 1996 by the EU Council of Education Ministers who suggested that such a card could hold general information on the educational background and attainments of the individual. This would help individuals to be mobile across and within the EU as it would provide evidence of ability and training and could be treated as a basis upon which individuals could make application for additional training.)

The proposals for action within the member states include:

- greater emphasis on the practical teaching of science and technology;
- greater use of distance learning and information technology to enhance knowledge and skills at all levels;
- encouragement of self-employment and small business start-ups as sources of innovation;
- investigation of changing taxation regimes and accounting practices to allow trained labour to be viewed as an asset, as human capital;

- greater efforts to give those from deprived backgrounds a second chance to acquire qualifications;
- the greater integration of science and technology students into the industrial research environment.

The objective to give people from disadvantaged backgrounds a second chance to gain qualifications was to be achieved through the creation of so-called 'second chance schools' and by the middle of 1996 this had been translated into an initial target of one in each member state. The first was established in Marseilles in December 1996 and by the middle of 1997 four others were about to open in Bilbao, Athens, Catania in Italy and Hameenlinna in Finland. By this stage, over 40 towns had applied to open schools – all in areas of high unemployment. The emphasis was to be on the provision of training in areas such as computer skills and other new technologies.

All the proposals listed above appear to rest upon the underlying assumption that by raising skill levels generally, labour productivity, the value of the marginal product and hence demand for labour will be increased. The proposals are seen as a means by which employment-intensive growth will be generated.

The proposals also acknowledge the fact that employers need incentives to invest in vocational training; by implication, the market on its own has not produced an adequate and appropriate match between the supply of and demand for skills. It is not efficient. There is no significant evidence of a disposition to require that employers demonstrate a greater commitment to VET.

It is difficult to avoid the conclusion that it is the 'problem of unemployment' that is driving these proposals rather than a more specific concern with issues of competitiveness and growth. This conclusion would seem to be supported by the Amsterdam Treaty revisions which perpetuate in Article 117 the emphasis upon the development of human resources *'with a view to lasting high employment'*. It is certainly consistent with the recommendations of the EU's Competitiveness Advisory Group (sometimes known as the *Ciampi Group* after the first Chairman).

Relatively few of the Ciampi recommendations are concerned with issues relating to VET. The group saw reform of the European social model, wage restraint, the reduction of employment costs and the encouragement of part-time and generally more flexible working patterns as means of generating greater competitiveness. Training was only significantly mentioned in connection with trying to improve the employment prospects of the long-term unemployed (*Source: Financial Times*, 12 June 1996).

To some extent, this conclusion is also reinforced by UNICE's response to the White Paper on Teaching and Learning which was itself primarily concerned with the link between education and training and employment. They suggested that long-term unemployment could be significantly avoided by providing training and education that gave the young the necessary skills, implied by the jobs available in the market. As part of their response they were critical of education systems in many of the member states for being too classical in orientation and, by implication, insufficiently concerned with the provision of skills. It is unclear whether they are referring to general transferable skills or those which are more commonly considered 'job or occupationally specific'.

The employers through UNICE indicated that they were prepared to give a higher priority to vocational training but there is no clear indication of the extent to which they perceive it as their role to provide it, or the extent to which they perceive themselves, the recipient or the state as bearing the costs.

Eurostat did report in 1997, however, that some 60 per cent of employers employing 10 or more workers were conducting some form of continuing vocational training in 1993. There were country variations with those in the North more active in providing such training than those in the South. The figure was over 80 per cent of employers in this size category in Denmark, Germany and the UK. In the Southern states, the figure was below 30 per cent and only 13 per cent in Portugal (*Journal of European Industrial Training*, 1997). The proportion of workers engaged in such programmes was also greater in larger firms and overall it was reported that 28 per cent of EU workers were engaged in continuing training activities conducted by their employers in 1993. Banking and insurance led the way as a sector.

Commission Report on Employment in Europe 1996

Given the focus of this report by the Commission (1996a) it is not surprising that it emphasises the employment/employability benefits of greater investment in VET. It is clear that the Commission perceives a link between competitiveness, economic growth, job creation and employment/unemployment and between all of these and investment in VET. However, there is still the impression that it is jobs and unemployment that are the major driving force behind the emphasis afforded the need to enhance skill levels.

Included in the conclusions and recommendations is the following:

> The skill level of the European workforce is a critical element in the potential development of future jobs.

However, the report (European Commission, 1996a, p. 8) also recommends that:

> The challenge posed by . . . new technology demands an urgent response to the upskilling of the workforce. A quantum leap in investment in education and training is required . . .

Approval is given to the notion of lifelong learning and updating of skills both as the means by which organisations can protect themselves and enhance their ability to adapt to change and become learning organisations, and as the means through which individuals can maintain their employability.

The report comments upon the apparent inverse relationship between the educational level attained by individuals and the propensity for them to lose their jobs, and the likelihood that the lower the educational level, the greater the likelihood that the individual will be left behind and at greater risk of social exclusion.

There are recommendations with respect to the redesign and provision of training which, the report argues, should be based on a partnership between business and government, and exhortations are made to business to play a role in training provision. It is asserted that the revolution in information technology requires an overhaul of education and training and particular mention is made of the need to transform the emphasis from one of teaching to one based upon learning. It is also recommended that enterprises should offer more learning by doing.

Various other recommendations are made regarding the unemployed (*see* Chapter 15).

Commission Green Paper on Partnership for a New Organisation of Work

This paper, published in April 1997 is an interesting document in that it is specifically concerned with the issue of adaptability as an essential element of the kind of new work organisation deemed necessary to enable European companies to be competitive internationally (*see also* Chapters 1 and 14). The authors make clear their assumptions that the road to competitiveness requires:

a better organisation of work at the workplace, based on high skill, high trust and quality.

The paper is relevant in this context because it poses some of the important questions such as

is it possible to establish a new partnership for a more productive, participative and learning organisation of work?

and

how to organise the necessary training and retraining, so that the workforce can meet the increasing need for skills and competence.

Considerable emphasis is placed upon the development of human resources as a potential knowledge-creating resource rather than as a cost to be reduced. This is again linked to productivity and competitive advantage, both for countries and companies.

The implication of the new organisation of work is made apparent and contrasted with the traditions of mass production (1996a, p. 4):

In the new decentralised and network orientated organisations workers perform a range of tasks, rather than pass the job from one to another. The skill structure is changing. Good skills in numeracy and literacy as well with computers, the ability to interact with new technology . . . becoming more and more important. This is a need not only for higher skills but also for broader skills.

The authors further support the conclusions and recommendations of the White Paper on Teaching and Learning and in particular the need for schools and business to more closely complement each other.

The assumptions underlying this paper and the stereotypical organisations and skill mixes, presented as essential to future competitive success, do need to be set in the context of the debate prompted by the Regini findings (1995) and identified earlier in this chapter and also against some of the implications of this kind of work organisation (*see* Chapter 1).

CONCLUSIONS

In accordance with the primarily corporatist and tripartite traditions of many of the member states, the central EU institutions do consider that there is a legitimate role to be played at the level of the Union. It is also reasonably clear, however, that in recent years, if not before, the tendency has been towards this role being consistent with the principle of subsidiarity. The central institutions:

● initiate debate;

● prompt member states and other interest groups into action;

- seek to involve the Social Partners;
- suggest initiatives and objectives;
- coordinate action;
- provide partial/additional funding;
- undertake and encourage research and development;
- undertake transnational activities; and
- issue non-binding instruments, opinions, recommendations and declarations,

but they have not usurped the autonomy of the member states to preserve their traditions and systems in this area of VET. There have been no statutory rights or obligations for employees/employers created at this level and no significant moves in the direction of enforced convergence of national systems, although there are pressures for systems to borrow ideas and mechanisms from each other.

There are undoubtedly individuals and interests that would welcome a more directive and interventionist role from the central institutions but, as noted earlier, Regini's analysis and thesis (1995) raises considerable doubts about the scope and wisdom of such an interventionist role, if its purpose is to press for convergence or universality.

It is also clear that these central institutions do not accept the view that VET is primarily the responsibility of employers and that it should be driven by them; in more recent publications and policy statements there is an increasing degree of exhortation to action through partnership. They perceive the market as a flawed and imperfect mechanism for the determination of resource allocation in the VET market. Individuals often have both insufficient funds and information and are incapable of taking investment decisions that take into account the public and social costs and benefits – such as the creation of a learning culture or an employment-intensive growth model. It is also arguable that labour markets are too regulated to allow the flexibility necessary for an efficiently operating market in vocational education and training.

It is difficult to avoid the conclusion that the central institutions believe that not only are individuals unlikely to make market decisions in accordance with the perceived requirements of the Union, but so also are employers. Without regulation many employers seem willing to rely on a kind of poaching free for all, pleading poverty and regarding VET as a cost rather than as an investment. According to the central institutions, employers perceive competition primarily in terms of lowering costs rather than improving quality, concentrating upon the short-term rather than the long-term outlook and ignoring the fact that the long-term solutions require regulation for the benefit of all. One suspects that these views and perceptions of market imperfection and the need for regulation may be common centrally, but that the political tide has turned against centralism, regulation and indeed against the trade unions. In the context of the late 1990s, these central institutions are responding to political if not economic and social realities.

In recent years the Commission and other Union-level institutions and interests have commonly espoused a belief in the value and necessity of greater investment in VET – whether it be to reduce unemployment, enhance labour mobility or assist in the creation of a more competitive, quality and employment-intensive growth model within the Union and in a sense against the rest of the world. It is therefore unsurprising that in many instances the central institutions put forward proposals that envisage a tripartite approach, involving a variably active role for member-state governments in support of or in conjunction with the Social Partners. In some instances, the member-state governments are perceived as the main provider and funder whereas other proposals envisage a role for government as the creator of standards and the provider of coordinating and/or regulatory mechanisms, such as accreditation and inspection.

An examination of the documentation and debates leaves little doubt that greater investment in education and vocational training is perceived as a necessity, primarily because of the contribution it promises to make to resolving the problem of unemployment, although, as we have seen, competitive and production strategies are not uniform and influence the type of labour required. There are potential benefits in terms of competitiveness and growth, but they are not guaranteed; they are probably longer term and certainly difficult to measure and realise. There is overlap between the motives for enhancing the commitment to VET and, as a result, initiatives are likely to have more than one form of outcome.

Regini's contribution to the debate (1995) serves to highlight the interrelationship between competitive and attendant production strategies, their implications for the utilisation of human resources and thereby the demand for labour. At the same time the supply of labour is a product in part of the form of VET in place and acts as both a facilitator of and constraint upon competitive and production strategies. Influences upon the VET system therefore are also influences upon realisable competitive strategy. Given the dominant belief among the central institutions and most member-state governments in the advantage to be gained from the pursuit of competitive strategies focusing upon quality, diversity and flexibility of response, it is logical and reasonable for the EU institutions to encourage VET systems in this direction. The systems should then produce as an output labour with the appropriate mix and level of theoretical and practical, occupationally specific and transferable knowledge and skills.

It is also arguable, however, that far too little has so far been achieved and that this objective has been consistently undermined by governments and employers. Governments have jealously guarded their autonomy and their national systems and institutions in the belief that they are the best and have insisted upon the implementation of the principle of subsidiarity. They have practised a laissez-faire policy relying upon the market. Employers have taken the easy way out; they have utilised neo-Fordist production strategies and sought to continue to compete on price by forcing wage costs down. They have relied upon the market to provide large amounts of unskilled and cheap labour and have resisted the exhortation and regulation that would halt the emphasis upon cost reduction and encourage investment in VET – investment that is necessary in order to produce the type and quality of labour supply that would facilitate the appropriate change of production strategy.

If one accepts the assertion/assumption that the future competitiveness and growth of the EU does lie at the high-tech, innovatory, service-oriented and client-dominated end of the global market a number of conclusions follow:

1 there is no long-term future in European economies and companies seeking to compete globally on the basis of price, implying low wages and continual downward pressures upon costs.

2 future competitiveness and growth is therefore likely to depend upon the production of a high-skilled, high-quality labour force with both the technical and vocational skills and the transferable interpersonal, organisational, computing and problem-solving skills that are necessary.

In this context, subsidiarity and a reliance upon the market mechanism can be perceived as constraints upon the development of an appropriate labour supply, which then itself acts as a constraint upon competitive and production strategies and thereby future development.

Effective action of a statutory and regulatory nature at the level of the Union does seem unlikely given the current political make-up and agendas of the member-state governments. Exhortation alone is unlikely to make significant inroads into eliminating the shortages and changing deeply ingrained perceptions of the efficiency and effectiveness of the market.

Of the suggestions so far made by EU institutions, there would appear to be scope for initiatives aimed at providing incentives to both employers and individuals to provide and acquire targeted skills and which are not geared primarily to the reduction of the unemployment total. Incentives may be in the form of soft or cheap loans to finance the acquisition or provision, or changes to the tax and accounting treatment of expenditure upon appropriate education and training. There is scope also for the financial encouragement of training providers and for the introduction of incentives for employers, perhaps particularly those in the SME sector, to adopt and develop competitive strategies that do not depend upon the employment of unskilled labour, low wages, cost reduction and low prices.

References

Adnett, N. (1996) *European Labour Markets: analysis and policy*. Longman, Chap 4.

Becker, G. (1975) *Human Capital: a theoretical and empirical analysis*. NBER.

Braverman, H. (1974) *Labour and Monopoly Capital: The Degradation of Work in the 20th Century*. Monthly Review Press.

Burgess, P. (ed) (1993) *Training and Development* (European Management Guides). Institute of Personnel Management and Incomes Data Services.

European Commission (1993b) *White Paper on Growth, Competitiveness, Employment*. European Commission.

European Commission (1994a) *Employment in Europe 1994*. European Commission.

European Commission (1994c) *White Paper on Social Policy*. European Commission.

European Commission (1995d) *The White Paper: Teaching and Learning: Towards the Knowledge-Based Society*. European Commission.

European Commission (1996c) *Employment in Europe 1996*. European Commission.

European Commission (1997d) *Green (Consultative) Paper. Partnership for a New Organisation of Work*. COM(97) 128, European Commission.

Hendry, C. (1995) *Human Resource Management: Strategic Approach to Employment*. Butterworth–Heinemann, Chap 19.

Hillage, J. (1996) Institute of Employment Studies. . . .

Hollinshead, G. and Leat, M. (1995) *Human Resource Management: An International and Comparative Perspective on the Employment Relationship*. Pitman Publishing.

Holt Larson, H. (1994) 'Key Issues in Training and Development', in Brewster, C. and Hegewisch, A. (1994) *Policy and Practice in European HRM*. Routledge.

House of Lords Select Committee on the European Communities (1990) *Vocational Training and Re-Training*. HMSO.

IPD European Update, July 1994.

IPD Report, 'Working to Learn', July 1997.

Journal of European Industrial Training (1997) 21(4), vi.

Keep, E. and Rainbird, H. (1995) 'Training', in Edwards, P. (ed) *Industrial Relations: Theory and Practice in Britain*. Blackwell.

Kirkbride, P. (ed) (1994) *Human Resource Management in Europe*. Routledge.

Rainbird, H. (1993) 'Vocational Education and Training', in Gold, M. (ed) *The Social Dimension: Employment Policy in the European Community*. Macmillan.

Regini, M. (1995) 'Firms and Institutions: The Demand for Skills and their Social Production in Europe', *European Journal of Industrial Relations*, 1(2), 191–202.

Soskice, D. (1993) 'Social Skills from mass higher education: re-thinking the company initial training paradigm', *Oxford Review of Economic Policy*, 9(3), 101–13.

Streeck, W. (1989) 'Skills and the Limits of Neo-Liberalism: The Enterprise of the Future as a Place of Learning', *Work, Employment and Society*, 3(1), 89–104.

Streeck, W. (1991) 'On the Institutional Conditions of Diversified Quality Production', in Matzner, E. and Streeck, W. (eds) *Beyond Keynesianism: The Socio-Economics of Production and Employment*. Edward Elgar, pp. 21–6.

UNICE (1994) *Making Europe More Competitive – towards world class performance*. UNICE.

Additional reading

Addison, J. and Siebert, W. (1994) 'Vocational Training and the European Community', *Oxford Economic Papers*, 46, 696–724.

Finegold, D. and Soskice, D. (1988) 'The Failure of Training in Britain: Analysis and Prescription', *Oxford Review of Economic Policy*, 4(3), 21–53.

Holden, L. (1991) 'European Trends in Training and Development', *International Journal of Human Resource Management*, 2(2), 113–31.

Holden, L. and Livian, Y. (1993) 'Does Strategic Training Policy Exist? Some Evidence From Ten European Countries', in Hegewisch, A. and Brewster, C. (eds) *European Developments in Human Resource Management*. Kogan Page.

Lane, C. (1989) 'New Technology and Changes in Work Organisations', in Lane, C. (ed) *Management and Labour in Europe*. Edward Elgar, pp. 163–95.

Lane, C. (1990) 'Vocational Training and new production concepts in Germany: some lessons for Britain', *Industrial Relations Journal*, 21(1), pp. 247–59.

Mabey, C. and Salaman, G. (1995) *Strategic Human Resource Management*. Blackwell, Chap 3.

Marsden, D. and Ryan, P. (1991) 'Initial Training, Labour Market Structure and Public Policy: Intermediate Skills in British and German Industry', in Ryan, P. (ed) *International Comparisons of Vocational Training for Intermediate Skills*. Falmer Press.

Prais, S. J. (1991) 'Vocational qualifications in Britain and Europe: theory and practice', *National Institute Economic Review*, May.

14

EMPLOYMEE PARTICIPATION
AND INVOLVEMENT

LEARNING OBJECTIVES

When you have read this chapter, you should be able to understand and explain:

- the differences between the various concepts and in particular the meanings of the terms involvement, participation and democracy in this context;

- techniques and mechanisms associated with each concept;

- the motives and the objectives of the various parties;

- the various EU initiatives in the arena of providing employees with rights to information and consultation;

- the particular significance of the EWC Directive and its implications for the development of Euro-level collective bargaining;

- the process known as the social dialogue;

- the debates surrounding the notion of employees having a financial stake in the performance of the business;

- recent statements and positions adopted by the Commission and the potential implications for employee participation in the form of information, consultation and co-determination.

INTRODUCTION

Within the EU, there is a history of Commission-inspired attempts to introduce legislation requiring employing organisations to create formal institutions for the purpose of enhancing employee participation. The early Commission initiatives, which began in the 1970s, were in part prompted by the political and social unrest apparent in a number of member-state countries in the late 1960s. The prime objective of this chapter is to trace these early initiatives and their subsequent development, along with other more recent interventions, and to critically appraise them.

It would be inappropriate to examine the record of the EU in stimulating employee participation without also bearing in mind some of the contextual influences and constraints discussed in Part One of this text. Examples of relevant contexts would include the globalisation of markets, the increasing freedom and influence of the multinational organisation, the different ideological and cultural traditions within the EU, the varying interests and influence of trade unions and the labour movement, and technological development and change, including the radical developments in information technology.

It is also important that the issues of terminology, definitions and interpretation are addressed to provide answers to questions such as:

- What does participation mean?
- What, if any, is the difference between participation and involvement?
- Where does industrial democracy fit into the picture?

The motives behind the various initiatives will be examined. This will include the perceived advantages of requiring organisations to introduce formal arrangements, or formalise existing informal arrangements to enable employee participation. Many of the initiatives have met with hostility from other interest groups – in particular, employers and their associations – and the reasons for this opposition will also be examined.

To some extent attitudes towards encouraging employee participation can be seen to reflect different ideas about the kind of Community or Union that participants want. These different attitudes and expectations can be seen to be rooted in ideological and cultural differences as well as reflecting different models of corporate governance, ownership and investment which imply managerial roles, ranging from acting as agents of the shareholders first and foremost to acting as trustees of the business and the various stakeholding interests. These models have different implications for the legitimacy of managerial prerogative or exclusivity of control and hence for employee participation.

Finally, the chapter contains an attempt at crystal-ball gazing to include the prospects for employee participation within the EU both within employing organisations and at wider sectoral and inter-sectoral (EU) levels.

DEFINITIONS AND INTERPRETATIONS

In any study of employee participation in the EU, problems arise regarding terminology, definition and interpretation; these surround the use of the terms *'participation'*, *'involvement'* and *'democracy'*. In some instances the terms are used interchangeably and in others they are distinguished and distinct. In the UK in recent years there has been an increasing tendency to use the terms 'employee participation' and 'employee involvement' interchangeably and to thereby blur distinctions between them. Similar, albeit less serious difficulties arise with these two terms and 'industrial democracy'.

Undoubtedly, this involves genuine difficulties in that there are areas of overlap between the concepts, with a number of the practices or arrangements associated with the terms fitting into more than one of the categories. For example, the arrangements associated with and exemplifying the term 'industrial democracy' are all likely to be participative in nature; some of the practices associated with the term 'employee participation' are both democratic and involving; however, many of the practices associated with the term 'employee involvement' are arguably not participative and have nothing to do with notions of democracy.

There are certainly many attempts at definition and distinction in the literature and it is probably at least partially because of the capacity for particular practices often to fit into more than one category that practice has failed to provide a meaningful basis for definition and distinction.

The more useful and durable definitions seek to distinguish the concepts in terms which encompass intent, motive, prime initiator and outcome.

Industrial democracy

Marchington (1995) suggests that there are both political and moral dimensions to the notion of industrial democracy and points out that it:

> . . . commences from the standpoint that employees ought to have the opportunity to become *involved* [my italics] in decision-making at work in much the same way as political democracy refers to their rights as citizens.

and

> . . . industrial democracy has its source in the right of the governed to exercise some control over those in authority.

Schregle (1976) also suggests that the concept has political and ideological overtones but is critical on these grounds arguing that they contribute to it being of an emotive and ill defined nature.

Unsurprisingly, schemes which fit with this definition are unlikely to be initiated by management since they have as an objective a form of organisation inconsistent with notions of managerial prerogative, acknowledging as they do employees' right to exert at least some control over management activities. Examples of schemes to which the label of industrial democracy might reasonably be put include mechanisms such as employee representation on supervisory boards of directors and self-management schemes such as producer cooperatives, which need to be distinguished from wholesale and retail co-operatives.

Farnham and Pimlott (1995, pp. 144–5) discuss Chamberlain and Kuhn's (1965) model of collective bargaining which broke down the process of collective bargaining into three stages. Farnham and Pimlott (1995) suggest that the third of these which is depicted as a system of 'industrial governance' can be appropriately viewed as providing a mechanism through which employees, through their representatives, are able to participate in the determination of those policies most affecting their working lives. As the area of joint determination expands, so also does the participation of the employees, through their trade union, in the management of the enterprise. Farnham and Pimlott (1995) also suggest that:

> Underlying the concept of collective bargaining as a process of industrial governance is the principle that those who are integral to the running of the enterprise should have some voice in determining the decisions of most concern to them.

They further suggest that:

> . . . this 'principle of mutuality'. . . correlates with the concept of political democracy . . .

and that collective bargaining (in this form) becomes a means for establishing its workplace equivalent – industrial democracy.

There are clear similarities between these views of the nature of collective bargaining, if it achieves its potential, and Marchington's (1995) notion of industrial democracy referred to above: in each case there is the underlying belief or moral principle that those to be affected have a right to participate in the decision making.

Employee participation

Employee or worker participation is perhaps the term used most widely and, as already indicated, it is often used to encompass notions of industrial democracy as well as some of the means used to seek or achieve employee involvement. Again there are different perspectives apparent in the many attempts at definition.

For example, Walker (1974) argues that worker participation in management occurs when workers take part in 'the authority and managerial functions of the enterprise' – areas of decision making that had previously been the preserve of management and indicating a change in the balance of decision making. This interpretation of the term, which some may see as restrictive, coincides reasonably closely with one of the four competing paradigms of participation identified by Marchington *et al* (1992), each of which can be seen to represent a particular strand of thought. The four paradigms are:

1 *The control/labour process paradigm.* This depicts a situation in which employee participation results in a transfer of control of the labour process from management to employees.

   The other three paradigms, however, serve to further illustrate the multiple and often confused use of the terminology since they separately refer to notions of participation with quite different underlying assumptions, motives and intended outcome.

2 *The satisfaction/QWL paradigm.* This assumes a link between employee participation and job satisfaction, the assumption being that enhanced participation leads to enhanced satisfaction – a notion that has much in common with quality of working life programmes which focus upon job design and self control of the task and immediate task environment. The participation envisaged in this paradigm is job centred with employees deriving satisfaction from an expansion or enrichment of their role, the latter yielding them greater responsibility and authority.

3 *The cooperation/industrial relations paradigm.* This links participation with conflict resolution and cooperation. This paradigm focuses upon collective bargaining and consultation as mechanisms through which cooperation can be enhanced and conflict reduced or resolved. By implication, this is a paradigm which acknowledges a plurality of legitimate interests within organisations and between workers and employers/managers. The notion or model of collective bargaining inherent to this paradigm is not limited to the advanced or mature stage of the Chamberlain & Kuhn (1965) typology; here collective bargaining is seen as an efficient and effective mechanism for resolving conflict rather than as a means through which employees pursue their legitimate rights to participation in process such as decision making.

4 *The commitment/HRM paradigm.* Positive relationships are perceived to exist between participation and commitment and between commitment and performance. It is this which provides management with its motive for encouraging or facilitating the participation. Commitment in this context is commitment to the employing organisation and employers or their agents may or may not acknowledge that employees are frequently confronted by multiple and often competing commitment demands and scenarios.

It is clear that Marchington *et al* (1992) are using the term 'participation', as Fenton O'Creevy and Nicholson (1994) point out, as an umbrella term covering all the ways:

> . . . in which employees may purposefully influence managerial decision making.

However, it is also arguable on a number of dimensions that paradigms 2 and 4 are more appropriately described as involvement, rather than participation paradigms.

Strauss (1979) refers to three different participation models, each being distinguished on the dimension of the depth or the degree of workers' influence or control over management:

- consultative participation;
- co-management or decision making; and
- workers' self-management.

Consultative participation gives workers and/or their representatives the right (or opportunity) to be informed and to give a view or to raise objections, but crucially the right to decide remains with management; their prerogative remains intact. Sparrow and Hiltrop (1994, p. 616) suggest that this is the most common form of participation practised in Western Europe.

With *co-management*, employees share the right to decide; they have joint decision-making powers with management and this may well translate into an effective right of veto – the consent of both parties being required before action can be taken.

Self-management by workers describes a scenario in which it is the employees individually or through representatives that alone have the role of decision making – perhaps by virtue of the employees being the owners of the enterprise.

Strauss (1979) concentrates upon the depth of participation, the degree of control over or influence in managerial decision making. This represents concern with a narrower perception of participation than Marchington *et al* (1992) – an interpretation much more consistent with that of Walker (1974), and indeed with notions of industrial democracy. It is an interpretation consistent with only one of the Marchington *et al* (1992) paradigms and arguably represents only one of a number of dimensions upon which employee participation can be distinguished and compared.

Part of the value of this concern with the depth or degree of influence or control is that it highlights the significance of power – the ability to influence. There are many potential sources of power and many influences upon them. Traditionally, employees and their representative associations have sought to gain power through a collective control over the supply of labour and thereby the job. Examples of the latter may be the pace of work, the degree of fragmentation, quality and the allocation of work. In many developed countries, including many of those in the EU, the mechanism used to exert this power has most commonly been collective bargaining. In the event of a failure, it has not been uncommon for the employees to further exhibit their power through the use of industrial action and the imposition of sanctions upon the employer. It has already been noted that collective bargaining can afford employees a means through which they can participate; in its more advanced form, it may yield industrial democracy. In either event the depth of participation achieved through collective bargaining is likely to be a function, at least in part, of the relative power of the parties. Power is a factor in determining both the nature and extent of employee participation in any particular organisation, country or time.

Employee involvement

When addressing the issue of employee involvement (EI) specifically, the areas of difference between this concept and that of employee participation begin to emerge with greater clarity. Marchington *et al* (1992) use the term 'employee involvement' to indicate the range of managerially inspired, designed and initiated processes at the level of the firm which:

> . . . are intended to improve communications with employees, to generate greater commitment, and enhance employee contributions to the organisation.

Such processes may or may not be participative in nature in the context of the 'depth' perceptions already referred to; certainly such a definition of involvement enables the inclusion of devices and mechanisms that have very little connection with notions of democracy.

The central role given in this definition to the generation of greater employee commitment implies that EI encompasses a set of practices and intentions that are consistent with models of human resource management, such as those of Beer *et al* (1984). These prescriptively place organisational commitment at the centre of the outcomes that should be achieved as a result of HRM initiatives. Mowday *et al* (1982) have highlighted three components of organisational commitment:

- identification with the goals and values of the organisation;
- a desire to belong to the organisation; and
- a willingness to display effort on behalf of the organisation.

In this context, EI can be seen as an attempt to win the hearts and minds of employees and to motivate them. One of the factors influencing the success of such initiatives, however, is the compatibility of the organisational goals and values with those of the individual employees and those of the other organisations, institutions and people that effectively constitute alternative and often competing focuses for commitment. Relevant examples of the latter may be the workgroup and the trade union.

Marchington (1995) refers to EI as a relatively new term which appears to represent the latest attempt by employers to find participative ways in which to manage their staff and which:

> . . . has for the moment replaced other variants, such as workers' participation and industrial democracy.

This comment, while acknowledging a reality, is also misleading in that it implies that EI practices are participative – an implication which requires a much wider perception or definition of participation than would find favour with Walker (1974) or Strauss (1979).

It is also possible to distinguish the various terms and concepts according to whether they are seen primarily as ends in themselves or as means to another end. Industrial democracy can most comfortably be defined as an end in itself with its undertones of moral imperative. EI, on the other hand, fits clearly into the latter category – as a means to some other end. To the extent, that employee participation encompasses both of the others (or at least partially in the case of EI) it will straddle both ends and means.

TECHNIQUES, PROCESSES AND FORMS

The discussion in the previous section has already implied a range of participatory and involving processes and the task of this section is to identify and elaborate upon the more common of them.

The notion of a continuum of participation is useful here (*see* Fig. 14.1) in that it facilitates the association of process or techniques with degree of participation in decision making and control. This continuum can be seen as an elaboration upon the three models of participation developed by Strauss (1979) and the control/labour process paradigm identified by Marchington *et al* (1992).

At one end of the continuum are processes which equate with total employee control, such as self-management schemes and producer cooperatives, while at the other extreme are processes which yield employees no influence in decision making – processes which are synonymous with unilateral management control. Between the two extremes are processes affording employees varying degrees of influence/control including both collective bargaining and mechanisms for joint consultation.

The works council – a technique or process particularly common in some member states – is indicated in this figure as providing employees with a measure of limited joint decision making, thereby falling into the second of the three participation models identified by Strauss (1979). Works councils do have powers of co-management or co-decision on issues such as hours of work, vocational training and health and safety in a number of member states (for example, Holland, Germany, Italy and Sweden) but in many or most instances their powers are more limited and fall more accurately into the category of bilateral communication and discussion/joint consultation – the first category of Strauss (1979).

Some forms of participation are *direct* and others *indirect*, the difference being in whether it is the individual employee that participates in the decision making or whether this participation is achieved through representatives. The scale of the modern employing organisation is usually such that direct participation is logistically difficult on issues other than those that affect only a relatively small number of employees. As a result, decisions concerning workgroup matters – such as the allocation of work, output quality or job redesign – may lend themselves to determination through mechanisms that enable employees to participate directly and individually even if this is done within the forum of the workgroup. Decisions of a wider or more strategic nature are much more likely to be made through indirect or representative participatory mechanisms.

Many years ago Michels (1966) identified the incompatibility between large-scale and direct democracy or participation, although it is important that we bear in mind not only the revolution in information technology that may make the words of Michels less relevant, but also the extent to which the employee is being required or invited to participate actively or passively. If the participation envisaged extends only so far as the one-way passage of information, then scale and direct participation may not be incompatible. At the same time, the question should be posed as to whether passive participation constitutes participation at all in any real sense?

Regalia's (1996) study of the views of the Social Partners towards direct participation uses a slightly different definition again. It is derived from that devised by Geary and Sisson (1994) and encompasses both consultation and delegation of decision making. However, there are clear areas of coincidence between this definition and the simple notion of

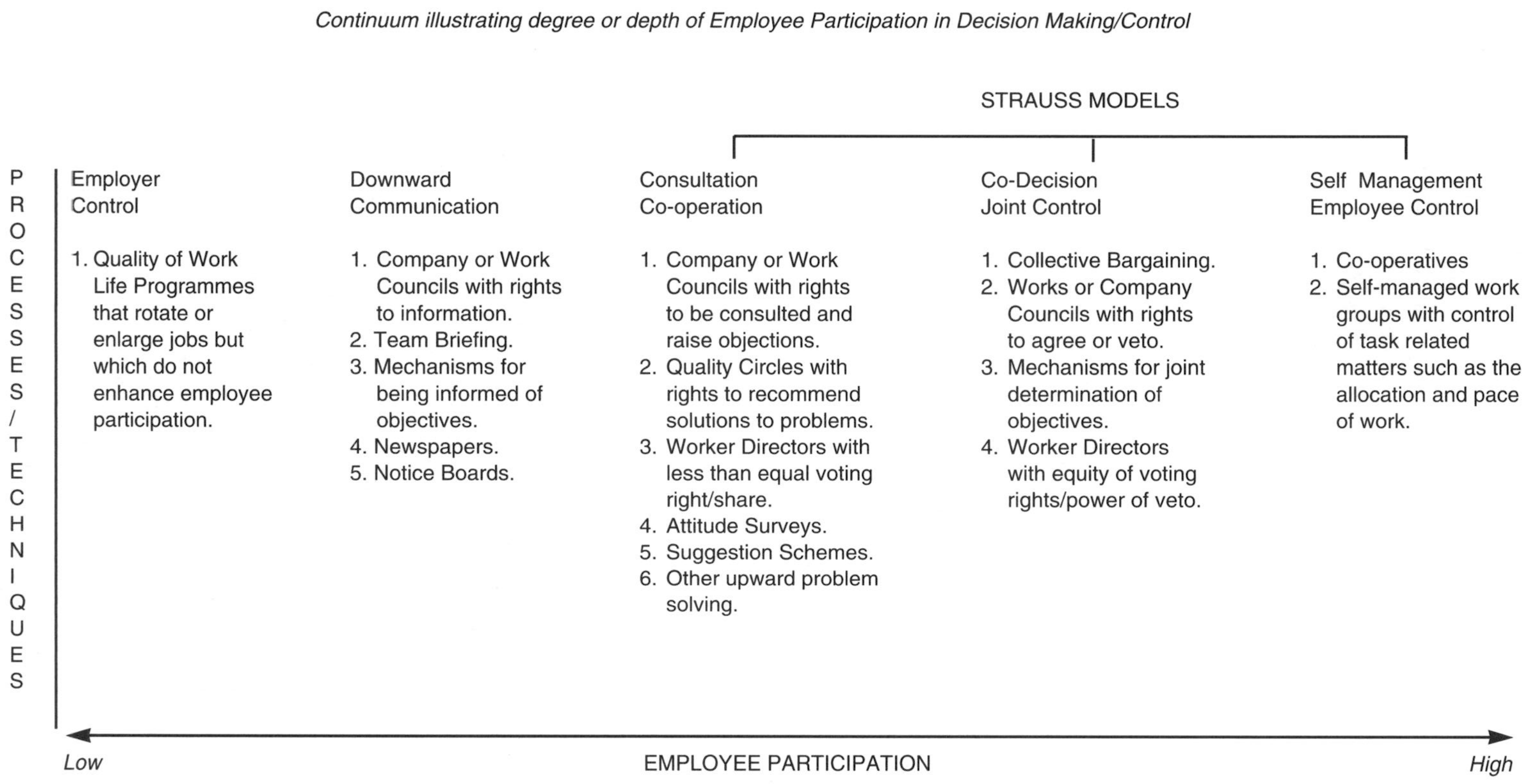

Continuum illustrating degree or depth of Employee Participation in Decision Making/Control

STRAUSS MODELS

	Employer Control	Downward Communication	Consultation Co-operation	Co-Decision Joint Control	Self Management Employee Control
	1. Quality of Work Life Programmes that rotate or enlarge jobs but which do not enhance employee participation.	1. Company or Work Councils with rights to information. 2. Team Briefing. 3. Mechanisms for being informed of objectives. 4. Newspapers. 5. Notice Boards.	1. Company or Work Councils with rights to be consulted and raise objections. 2. Quality Circles with rights to recommend solutions to problems. 3. Worker Directors with less than equal voting right/share. 4. Attitude Surveys. 5. Suggestion Schemes. 6. Other upward problem solving.	1. Collective Bargaining. 2. Works or Company Councils with rights to agree or veto. 3. Mechanisms for joint determination of objectives. 4. Worker Directors with equity of voting rights/power of veto.	1. Co-operatives 2. Self-managed work groups with control of task related matters such as the allocation and pace of work.

P
R
O
C   Low ──────────────────────────────── EMPLOYEE PARTICIPATION ──────────────────────────────── High
E
S
S
E
S
/
T
E
C
H
N
I
Q
U
E
S

Fig. 14.1 A continuum of employee participation in Decision Making/Control

direct participation already described. The subject matter is confined to the task, the organisation of work and the reasonably immediate surroundings and, while the definition embraces both individual and group activity, the implication is that the participation is dominated by individuals rather than by any form of representative arrangement. This study exemplifies many of the differences of perception and meaning associated with these concepts. One of the findings was that direct participation was conceived by both sides as being complementary to representative participation, rather than the one displacing the other.

Recently in the UK the tendency has been to devise and distinguish categories and typologies of involvement rather than participation.

Ramsay (1992, p. 214) devised a system or typology of form which is fourfold:

- task and workgroup involvement, to encompass quality circles, job redesign, enrichment and enlargement, teamworking and total quality management programmes;
- communication and team-briefing schemes;
- consultative arrangements, to include various forms of joint arrangements;
- financial participation – a form and notion of participation which is examined in its own right later and which may have considerable potential, if linked to changes in corporate governance and employee shareholding.

Marchington (1995) uses a fivefold classification system of form:

1 Downward communication

The most common purpose of such communication from management to employees is to educate employees so that they are more willing to accept management plans and proposals. No doubt these mechanisms have a further role in encouraging employees to experience or feel the commitment to the organisation already discussed. Marchington refers to a number of specific techniques that are common and fit into this category. Examples include:

- written and unwritten briefings which may be either group or individual, formal or informal, regular or *ad hoc*; and
- house journals and other news vehicles – for example, in some organisations video recordings.

2 Upward problem solving

These techniques are to be seen as efforts on the part of management to 'tap into employee knowledge and opinion' and to some extent both depend upon and seek to encourage a spirit of cooperation between employees and management – an integrative approach which is often claimed to have the potential for yielding benefits for both 'sides', akin to a variable and positive sum game. One of the most common and famous technique of this type is the *quality circle*; suggestion schemes and attitude surveys also fit into this category as, he suggests, does total quality management (TQM). In a similar vein, schemes of continuous improvement could also be included in this group. Upward problem-solving schemes of this nature are held to be consistent with the effective management of change and notions of employee empowerment.

Not surprisingly, those of a more radical perspective see these and similar schemes as mechanisms through which management seek to exploit the knowledge and skills of the workforce for its own ends and in order to maintain the status quo in terms of the distribution of authority and power in capitalist systems. It is almost as if management is deliberately trying to create among its workforce an appearance or illusion of participation, enhanced feelings of concern, involvement and trust which it can then use to disguise the imbalance of power in the favour of capital and its interests. This is a theme to which we return later when examining the relevance of perspective in greater depth.

3 Task participation

This encompasses issues of job design and re-design. These schemes are commonly linked to or motivated by the belief that employees gain satisfaction from individual or group participation in terms of a widening of the scope of jobs, whether this be vertical or horizontal. It may involve a simple horizontal addition or enlargement of tasks or the enrichment may be of a vertical nature extending the job into new areas of responsibility or activity. In addition to the enlargement of tasks, this category also encompasses some of the teamwork schemes which extend to the team an enhanced role in organising the work. These techniques are based upon the reverse of the Taylorist principles upon which much of the developed world based the design of production from the 1920s onwards. Rather than de-skilling, these examples of task participation arguably represent a re-skilling of the workforce.

4 Consultation and representative participation

This category is immediately differentiated from the other three categories in that the participation takes place through representatives of the employees – that is, the participation is indirect. The representative structures that tend to be formally erected in order to facilitate the effective operation of such schemes may or may not be trade union dominated and this can be demonstrated by examination of the various works council schemes that pertain in some member states. For example, in Germany and Holland, the works councils are not trade union bodies and are made up of employee representatives, not elected on a trade union ticket, but who may be union members. In France, the works councils are joint management – employee bodies and the arrangements are such that the first ballot for electing the employee representatives is restricted to union nominees (Hollinshead and Leat, 1995, pp. 158–62). Often these arrangements provide the mechanism through which employees are able to raise and resolve grievances.

Marchington (1995) excludes collective bargaining from his discussion and typology of participation, no doubt in part because it is different in nature from these other representative schemes. Collective bargaining in the UK certainly has a conflictual as opposed to a cooperative history and is a power-based political process with the nature of the bargaining being distributive rather than integrative or cooperative. It is the latter approach and mindset that consultation rests and depends upon. However, much of the collective bargaining in other member states does have a more cooperative and integrative tradition and this is certainly the category of participation into which many of the major European schemes and EU initiatives fit.

5 Financial participation

This category encompasses a considerable range of schemes designed to erect or maintain a relationship (which may or may not be direct) between individual or group reward and group or organisational performance. These arrangements are intended to encourage employees to identify with the organisation and, in particular, its commercial success. Presumably, the hope and assumption are that the traditional conflicts will disappear and employees, once they have this financial stake in the organisation, will become in some sense more cooperative and responsible. They will work harder and more efficiently and thereby contribute to even greater commercial success. There are a large number of assumptions and unanswered questions underlying these schemes, with relatively little evidence to confirm some of them. As we note later, however, there is an increasing body of research, though still small in number, that there is an association between participation schemes of this kind and enhanced productivity.

In the UK, the vast majority of such schemes so far introduced have been either relatively simple and straightforward bonus/share of profits schemes or they have rewarded employees with shares in the company. In the UK and in some of the other member states, share-ownership schemes have been encouraged by government, usually by way of specially favourable tax treatment of the income or gains made. The PEPPER report (Promotion of Employee Participation in Profits and Enterprise Results) (European Commission, 1992) concluded that France was the EU country in which financial participation schemes had proliferated the most, there being at that time some 17 000 in existence covering 18 per cent of the workforce. The compatible figures for the UK were 7000 and 8 per cent.

Financial participation of this kind has very rarely been directly combined with participation of a more traditional nature – with influence in or control over managerial decision making – and it is perhaps in this area that there is scope for development.

There are clear points of contact between Marchington's (1995) typology of forms and the paradigms of participation discussed earlier (*see* p. 275). It is also clear from this typology that there are perceived differences between the notions of participation and involvement. Participatory forms or mechanisms that may have more in common with notions of control and democracy – for example, collective bargaining, worker directors and mechanisms for co-decision or determination – are excluded from the typology of involvement. Fenton O'Creevy and Nicholson (1994) also seek to distinguish these latter forms of participation from EI strategies and suggest that the formal co-determination systems of Germany and Austria should be viewed more as:

> . . . methods for resolving the competing interests of industrial stakeholders through governance procedures and decisional frameworks than as strategies designed to enlarge the scope of employee control over the management of tasks so as to enhance motivation, commitment and performance.

MOTIVES, OBJECTIVES AND PERSPECTIVES

The expansion of EI practices, discernible in the UK in the 1990s, can be explained as management responses to a set of developments and circumstances that may have both encouraged and facilitated these initiatives.

1 *The pressure to adapt to organisational, environmental and technological change.* All of these changes can be seen to be exerting pressures in the direction of a need for greater labour cooperation and flexibility with involvement programmes again perceived as the

means through which the objective can be achieved – a combination of communications and job redesign yielding greater employee satisfaction, greater commitment and a greater willingness to be cooperative and flexible (*see* the Commission Green Paper (1997a) discussed later in this chaper.

2 *Pressures in the product market encouraging an emphasis upon customer service or quality.* Involvement programmes are perceived as the means through which employees can be encouraged to adopt these values.

3 *Difficult labour market conditions.* These may well place a premium, for example, upon retaining staff, particularly if they have skills which are relatively scarce. This can encourage employers to adopt QWL-type (Quality of Working Life) involvement programmes in the belief that employees will respond with loyalty.

4 *The desire to bypass or avoid trade unions.* Involvement programmes are perceived as the means through which direct communications can be achieved with the labour force. Alternatively, employees can be encouraged into a level of commitment to the organisation that effectively negates the desire for or perceived need to have their own interests represented by and through a trade union.

5 *The apparent success of management techniques from other parts of the world.* Involvement type programmes which appear transportable – for example, the quality circle, job redesign, total quality management, self-managing teams and consultative management, among others – are examples of this trend.

6 *Social and political change.* This may involve the encouragement of new values of individualism and enterprise combined with an antipathy towards collective organisation and the regulation of labour markets and employer freedoms.

The expansion and adoption of employee involvement practices has almost certainly been greater in the UK than in the other member states, although there is evidence from the Price Waterhouse Cranfield Project (Brewster and Hegewisch, 1994, Chap. 10) that across Europe there has been a general increase in communication with employees over recent years – with a particular increase in communication with employees as individuals. The increase in the UK is due in part to the Conservative governments between 1979 and 1997 acting in a positively encouraging role.

The perspective and underlying assumptions of EI are predominantly consistent with these governments' liberal individualist, laissez-faire, ideology (*see* Chapter 1) – an ideology that encouraged individualism, enterprise and deregulation, based on a belief in the legitimacy of capitalism as a system of economic organisation and the justified unilateral prerogative of employers/management (the owners of capital and their agents). Conservative governments openly espoused EI as an integral part of their strategy to improve the flexibility and efficiency of the labour market, to increase the productivity and competitiveness of British industry and, at least initially, also as part of the strategy to create a shareholding democracy. It was not part of their approach to require organisations to introduce such arrangements.

Consistent with this approach was their constant opposition to initiatives within the EU to legislatively impose upon employers requirements to provide mechanisms through which employees could participate in managerial decision making and thereby create rights to participation for employees. The UK governments thought that employee participation should clearly be at the discretion of the employer and on their terms.

It is arguable that the apparent preferences of Conservative governments and employers for participation in the form of EI programmes on the employer's terms serve only to perpetuate the low-trust relations that it has been argued bedevil employee relations and explain the essentially conflictual tradition. As Crouch (1982) pointed out:

> It is usually employers' representatives who bemoan the idea of two sides of industry and who call upon workers to cooperate in the common good. But it was not workers who instituted the rigorous distinction between those who make decisions and those who receive instructions.

At the heart of EI is the objective of a satisfied, committed and cooperative workforce and yet the lack of inclination on the part of both management and government to extend to employees rights to participate above the task level are potentially counter-productive to the achievement of the central objective. The success with which managements appear to have been able to resist and constrain pressures from employee groups for an extension of participation above the level of the task may be another indicator of the uneven distribution of power between the main actors and reflective of a broader management desire to retain control.

As Poole and Mansfield (1992) discovered:

> Managers appear to support most employee involvement practices so long as these do not radically affect their control function within the firm. In other words they tend to prefer a unitary rather than a pluralist approach to employee participation in decision making.

Governments and employers throughout the EU do not appear to be anything like so reluctant to afford employees and their representative associations rights to participate in control terms, in areas that in the UK would be considered to be management's prerogative and at organisational levels that again would normally be barred to employees in the UK. Arguably, the employee relations traditions in many of these other countries are cooperative and integrative and consistent with this are the notions of social partnership and corporatist decision-making mechanisms that are pervasive. We shall see in the next section that these are at the root of the participative initiatives that the Commission has proposed over the last quarter-century.

It is important that we note that not all the other member states have these traditions and exhibit quite the equable approach to employee participation that the above might suggest. There are other member states in which employee participation has not been embraced with quite this degree of gusto, just as there are other member states in which managements have sought to achieve similar objectives through the introduction of EI initiatives as have employers in the UK. France, for example, has seen the greatest implementation of quality circles and a drive towards the individualisation of the employment relationship.

Nevertheless in many of the other member states employees do have participative rights including rights to information and consultation buttressed by the law. Brewster and Hegewisch (1994, p. 156) have categorised member states into three groups according to the degree of legislative regulation.

They distinguish between countries such as Germany, Denmark, the Netherlands, Finland and Sweden which they categorise as being highly regulated, France, Italy, Portugal and Spain which they put into a medium regulated category and Ireland and the UK which they put together in a 'less' regulated category. The other member states were not included in their survey but in each of Luxembourg, Austria, Greece and Belgium there is some degree of legislative regulation. The UK is almost certainly the member state in which employee participation is buttressed by the law to the least extent and what rights there are in the UK to consultation are largely the product of EU level initiatives, for example those regarding 'the rights' of Health and Safety Committees and representatives, and the rights to consultation in the event of collective redundancies or the transfer of an undertaking.

Legislative support has been found to be an important explanatory variable of the cross-national differences in the extent and type of employee participation/industrial democracy (IDE, 1981). There is evidence in the follow-up study (IDE, 1993) that participation systems that are buttressed by legislation seem to be more resistant to negative contextual developments that might undermine the stability of employee participation. An example of this might be the considerable increase in unemployment that has occurred in the EU in recent years and which might have been expected to have resulted in a diminution of labour's bargaining power and ability to enforce the maintenance of employee participation.

We cannot assume that the existence of legislative support for employee participation mechanisms that curb managerial prerogative – for example, the system of co-determination in Germany – are exclusively motivated by a normative belief in the desirability of industrial democracy. In the case of Germany, the legislative curbing of managerial control was also prompted by the political motive of preventing the future rise of another Nazi party; the unions, in particular, were determined to try and prevent a situation in which industrialists would once again be able to finance an extremist party. The cooperative relationships between employee and employer, epitomised in the exchange of information and consultation in the German works councils, is also set against a background of corporate financing and ownership which has been both long term and low cost. Banks and insurance companies take large, often majority, equity stakes in companies which they hold long term and the emphasis is not so much upon short-term financial return as upon long-term growth and long-term relationships.

From the viewpoint of employees/trade unions the promotion of participation within the employment environment may be related to and part of a transformational strategy in society at large; industrial democracy may provide a stepping stone to political democracy. This is unlikely to be the case in many, if any, of the current member states but, as the EU expands to the East, it is much more likely that we will come across scenarios in which this is indeed the case – situations in which EU-initiated requirements that employees have rights to participate in organisational decision making are used to promote and preserve political democracy.

We must also not make the mistake of assuming that trades unions/employees necessarily have an equal enthusiasm for all the various forms of participation or indeed for legislative support. For example, we might expect employees to be more amenable to EI initiatives than trades unions since in some instances, as already noted, these initiatives have specific union bypassing or avoidance objectives and for employees to reject the opportunity to participate, even if the nature of the participation offered may be limited in terms of its depth or scope, is arguably tantamount to them saying that they prefer an authoritarian regime. It is also likely, or at least it might not be surprising, if employees preferred direct as opposed to indirect (representative) participation since direct participation affords them a tangible role – a visible opportunity to influence.

However, in each of the last two instances, we assume that employees don't have a purely instrumental approach towards work – an approach that might militate against an interest in participation and influence and which would certainly raise doubts about the attractiveness of participation/EI schemes designed to provide employees with opportunities for deriving intrinsic job satisfaction on the way towards becoming committed employees.

In reviewing the survey evidence, Marchington (1995) concludes that

> In principle, employees are keen to have more say within their establishments and to find out more about actions which are likely to impact upon their own jobs and activities at work . . . the common view is that employees are not satisfied with employers acting without some effort to keep them informed.

It could be suggested that these conclusions don't represent the substance of a major challenge to notions of managerial control and prerogative nor do they constitute a claim for industrial democracy.

There may be ideological underpinnings to the attitudes and behaviour of employees and their representatives. For many years the trade union movement in the UK was opposed to the statutory creation of rights to participation, preferring to rely upon the voluntaristic tradition and the development of employee participation through voluntary collective bargaining. The attitudes of the Italian trade union movement have had similar consequences in that there has been a reliance upon participation through collective bargaining even though the radical elements of the movement have often been resistant to participation in management through any forum. The system of legislatively supported co-determination in Germany, on the other hand, rests upon common consensual, integrative and interventionist traditions with the parties at the workplace required to collaborate with each other and with the legislation providing the order and authority that reduces uncertainty.

IMPACT

As noted earlier, there is some evidence that employees are interested in receiving information about issues and participating in decisions that are close to them, particularly where they are directly affected, but there is also evidence that in respect of other areas of subject matter, employees are often reluctant to enter into participatory arrangements perhaps because they are simply not interested, not willing or because they are incapable. Brewster and Hegewisch (1994, pp. 162–3) quote Heller (1992):

> . . . participation succeeds or fails on the basis of employee competence and that the conditions for successful participation are motivated competence . . .

Bean (1994) refers to studies of arrangements for employee participation in management decision making in a number of different countries and concludes that the effectiveness of the participation seems to be contingent upon the nature of the subject matter, with the employee representatives tending to be both most interested and most influential in decision making on personnel and social matters. While some of these arrangements gave the employee representatives a more influential role in decision making on these topic areas – for example, the right of veto as opposed to a right to be informed and consulted – it also seems likely that the relative lack of effective influence on wider business issues is a function of interest and perceptions of competence and confidence. Bean (1994) cites Poole's (1986) assertion that:

> In general the pattern is for management decision-making powers to be left largely unimpaired by representative bodies and for no fundamental transformation of actual influence to take place.

Interestingly, given the debate that the proposals have generated within the EU and between member states, the PWCP study (Brewster and Hegewisch, 1994) produced evidence indicating no correlation between legislative provision for communication and consultation of strategic and financial information and actual provision, there is apparently no simple link between the provision of information and communication and national legislation.

One of the major management motives for the introduction of EI schemes is the belief that they will assist in the development of a committed workforce and yet Marchington (1995) cites evidence in respect of the introduction of team briefing that the vast majority of the respondents indicated that they felt there had been little or no change on their understanding of management decisions, in the quality of upward communication or openness, or in their commitment to the organisation.

Other inquiries have produced similarly sceptical conclusions about the impact of EI interventions upon employee attitudes, their commitment to the organisation and the impact upon performance and Marchington's (1995) general conclusion is that:

> . . . it [EI] has only a limited impact upon employee attitudes and commitment, and even less on behaviour and performance.

It should be borne in mind, however, that there are many factors that may influence the extent to which these schemes achieve the objectives intended, included in any such list would be the competence and commitment of management, particularly perhaps management at supervisory levels who are likely to have front line responsibility for implementation. This is an area that Fenton O'Creevy and Nicholson (1994) examined and their conclusions include the view that it is crucial to the success of any EI initiative to enlist the commitment of middle managers and supervisors and yet their researches indicate that these very categories of employee often resist these initiatives.

EU INITIATIVES

As noted in the previous sections of this chapter there is a history stretching back to the late 1960s early 1970s of EC/EU initiatives of various kinds designed to provide legislatively supportable rights for employees and their representative institutions to participate more in the activities and decision-making processes of their employing organisations. In general these initiatives have sought to encourage participation across a range of strategic and financial business issues, however there have also been initiatives that have sought to target very specific issues. It is probably fair to summarise these initiatives as proposing participation of a representative and downward communication/consultative nature, although, as we shall see, some of the earlier proposals were more ambitious and proposed to introduce schemes consistent with notions of co-management and co-decision.

More recently, there have also been efforts to encourage various forms of financial participation for employees.

Above and outside the level of the employing organisation, there have been initiatives to encourage collective bargaining at a sectoral level within the boundaries of the Union and at the level of the Union itself. It should be remembered that the decision-making and consultative processes at Union level have long provided for the participation of employee representatives and interests as one of the Social Partners, commonly via the Economic and Social Committee.

Within the terms of the Social Protocol to the Maastricht Treaty there has been a strengthening of the potential role of the Social Partners and the scope for collective agreements in the determination of EU policy. The proposals at Amsterdam in the summer of 1997 to incorporate these procedures into the Treaty would appear to indicate both some satisfaction with the procedures as they have operated since 1993 and an intention on the part of the major institutions and member states to seek further cooperation of the Social Partners in the decision-making process (*see* Chapter 8 for more details of this procedure and its use).

As already noted, many of the EU initiatives over the years can be seen to be rooted in an ideological position that runs counter to the voluntarist tradition of the UK and is even more at odds with the neo-laissez-faire, liberal individualist position adopted by Conservative governments between 1979 and 1997.

Cressey (1993) points out that the debate within the EU should be seen not simply as a dispute between the UK and the rest but as a clash of philosophies on how best to regulate a modern capitalist market economy. This can be taken further since there is clearly a difference of perception as to the desirability and acceptability of outcomes as well as the degree and mechanisms of regulation.

At one level the community view, as expressed by the Commission initiatives, can be seen as an expression of the desire for and belief in a community founded on consensus and harmony with undertones of equity and democracy (this latter being one of the general principles underlying the Union), participation rights providing a counter to the otherwise unfettered rights of capital. At another level, however, the Commission initiatives should be viewed as a reflection of the position that providing employees with the right to participate is central to achieving enhancement of the efficiency and competitiveness of the economies of the member states – a means by which competitive advantage can be obtained through the contribution and commitment of the labour force, their knowledge, skill, problem-solving capacity and innovation. On yet another level, employee participation is viewed as a means by which the increasing autonomy and influence of multinational companies might be countered or at the least mitigated and some EU initiatives have specifically targeted the multinationals while others have sought to enhance employee participation within national undertakings.

Clearly the motives of the Commission are a mix of those identified in the earlier sections of this chapter and are based on the belief that greater employee participation has the potential to yield benefits for employees, employers, national economies and the economy and social fabric of the Union as a whole. They can be seen also to represent acceptance of several of the participation paradigms identified by Marchington *et al* (1992).

Consultation and Information

The Draft Fifth Directive on the Harmonisation of Company Law/Company Structure and Administration in the EC

This Draft Directive was the first significant attempt by the Commission and some member states to harmonise community-wide provisions with respect to the participation rights of employees and their representatives. The earliest draft dates from 1972 and reflects very clearly the German system of co-determination. The original proposal was that all public companies employing over 500 employees should be required to establish and operate a two-tier board system with employees having the right to have their interests represented by a number of full members of the supervisory board. In this form of two-tier structure, the supervisory board, while non-executive, has the right to appoint and supervise the management board. Supervisory boards often also have responsibility for longer term planning and strategy formulation. The management board is the decision-making forum with responsibility for day-to-day management and operational issues.

These first proposals were not adopted and by the time another draft was produced in 1983 and put to the Council for adoption considerable changes were apparent. It must be remembered that between these two dates the EC had been enlarged and the political complexion of the Community had been transformed.

The second draft no longer proposed a single obligatory system or format and, while the notion of employee directors was still encompassed, it was as one of several alternatives from which the parties would be able to choose. This step back from seeking to impose one best method of participation was in part a response to the enlargement of the Community and the increased diversity of experience and tradition as well as preference. This second draft also restricted the catchment area of companies by proposing that it should apply to only those companies that employed more than 1000 employees.

Under the revised proposals there were three main options available:

1 a system of employee or worker directors on a supervisory board or as members of a unitary board (with precise proportions and role varying);

2 a system of works or company councils made up of employees and/or their representatives which would then have certain specified information and consultation rights; or

3 a system of voluntarily and jointly agreed arrangements that nevertheless complied in their broad respects and principles with the other two above.

In all cases the purposes were to impose upon management an obligation to inform employee representatives regularly about the company's progress and its prospects and also to consult with the employee representatives prior to major decisions that would be likely to affect their interests.

This second proposed draft was also never adopted by the Council. There were further and subsequent revisions to the text of the 1983 draft in 1988, 1990 and 1991 but the various interests have as yet been unable to agree.

The Draft Directive Accompanying/Complementing the European Company Statute

In 1975, the first significant proposals were made to enable the incorporation at a European level of a range of employing organisations including companies, cooperatives, mutual societies and non-profit-making organisations. Once adopted, the proposed company law regulations would enable such organisations at their own discretion to incorporate. They would then be able to operate across the EU without needing to form separate subsidiary organisations in each country; they would also gain certain tax advantages. In return for this, the organisations would be required to provide employees with information and opportunities for consultation. Unlike the proposals in the Draft Fifth Directive, these proposals were clearly aimed at multinational organisations. The original draft Directive proposals required the obligatory establishment of a supervisory board with employee representatives as full members and a European-level works council of employee representatives. The works council was to have co-determination rights in certain areas of subject matter concerned with employment and consultation rights on important management board issues with rights to information in other areas. These proposals were again very much influenced by the German system. The draft statute was not adopted.

Another attempt to provide for European-wide incorporation was made in 1989 when another draft Regulation was proposed. Again it was accompanied by proposals for a draft Directive pertaining to employee information and consultation. As with the 1983 version of the Fifth Directive, these latter proposals were less restrictive and provided the parties with a number of very similar choices. The range of choices once again included:

- employee representatives on a supervisory board within a two-tier board system;
- employee representatives as supervising, non-executive directors on a unitary board;
- an employee-only company level representative body

or jointly agreed alternative but analogous arrangements. The rights were to include information and consultation, but not co-determination. Companies choosing to incorporate in this way would be required to regularly inform employees on progress and prospects and consult with them, or their representatives, before taking major decisions affecting employees' interests. As Cressey (1993) points out, this 1989 draft can be seen as a choice between systems of participation derived from the arrangements in a number of the member states:

> ... choices effectively between the German model of worker directors, the French/Italian model of separate works committees/councils or a collectively agreed form of participation such as is popular in Denmark and other Scandinavian countries.

In 1991, further amendments were made to these proposals after the first round of consultation. The major amendment to be made at this stage was the addition of the choice to implement the system operating in the member state in which the head office is located. This raises the question of quite what the requirements upon an incorporated company might be if the head office member state has no such system and arrangements between the parties are of a purely voluntary nature. Logically, this latter option would only be available if the system were broadly compatible with the general thrust and criteria of the other options.

As with the Fifth Directive, the parties have so far been unable to agree and the proposals have not yet been adopted.

The Draft Vredeling Directive

This proposal is otherwise and more formally described as the Draft Directive on Procedures for Informing and Consulting Employees in Undertakings with Complex Structures, specifically multiplant and multinational organisations. The arguments upon which this proposal was based were very similar to those underlying the EWC Directive adopted in 1994 (*see* later), namely that as organisations become increasingly complex structurally and multinational, it is more and more often the case that decisions affecting employee interests in a substantial way are taken both without much regard for those interests and by people and at locations considerably removed from the place of impact.

The original proposal was made in 1980 and amended in 1983. The provisions of the later amended version were to apply to companies (parent and subsidiaries combined) with over 1000 employees in the EC. The purpose was:

1 *To provide employees with statutory rights to be informed regularly on overall company progress and prospects*. This included information relating to company structure, the financial situation, employment and investment prospects. This information was to be provided annually to employees in subsidiary companies through their representatives and by management of the subsidiary.

2 *To give employees and their representatives in subsidiary companies rights to be consulted about proposals by the parent company that constitute proposals for major change affecting one or more subsidiaries*. The employees/representatives in those subsidiaries were to be consulted at least 30 days in advance of the decision and the aim of the consultation was to reach an agreement on the measures.

3 *To give employees a right to by-pass local management and gain access to the company's ultimate decision makers*.

This set of proposals has suffered much the same fate as those already described – the draft Fifth and the draft European company statute – in that the member states have been unable to agree on both the need for EU-level legislative intervention in this area and/or the nature and content of any such intervention. Many multinational employers and employers associations have also expressed opposition to the proposals.

In recent years the emphasis within the EU was transferred from these three sets of proposals to those of a similar nature contained within the Social Charter and the subsequent Second Social Action Programme and, in particular, the proposals concerning the establishment of European Works Councils in community-scale undertakings (*see* later in this chapter). Having secured adoption of these latter provisions by the 11 member states (excluding the UK) using the Social Protocol Procedure (*see* Chapter 8), the Commission has recently signalled its intention to return to these stalled proposals.

The Third Social Action Programme

The most recent developments were in 1995 and 1996. The Third Social Action Programme published by the Commission in April 1995 (COM95/134) indicated that the Commission had not given up in its determination to implement measures that would give employees at both a European and national level certain limited rights to participate in the management of their employing organisations via information and consultation, if no longer via membership of a company-level board. It should be noted that the Commission had come under considerable pressure from the European Parliament to resurrect these proposals.

The Action Programme contains two specifically relevant, non-legislative proposals: one is for examination of the EWC Directive (*see* later) to see if it might be useful in assisting the adoption of the revised proposals for European-level incorporation; the other proposal is for consultation with and between the Social Partners on the future direction of EU initiatives on employee consultation in national undertakings.

In November/December 1995 the Commission invited the various interested parties to comment upon some alternative routes for dealing with these stalled draft Directives (Company Statute, Fifth and Vredeling). In particular, the Social Partners have been asked to consider whether action under the Social Protocol/Policy Agreement (SPASP) is possible or appropriate. Prior to the agreement at Amsterdam in 1997, in this latter event agreement/action would have excluded the UK.

The alternative routes identified by the Commission were:

1 to continue trying to negotiate an agreement between the member states;

2 to replace the existing draft Directives with other instruments – for example, a Regulation or a Recommendation;

3 to drop the existing drafts and prevent companies from taking advantage of EU-level incorporation, if they are based in a member state not covered by the EWC Directive;

4 to withdraw all the drafts referred to above leaving the EWC Directive as the only EU-wide measure requiring employers to inform and consult with their employees/representatives.

Member-state reactions to these proposals were discussed at the Social Affairs Council meeting in June 1996 and the responses were generally cautious with respect to taking further steps at the EU level; they were more sympathetic to the notion of enhanced rights to employees at a national level. The UK government predictably was the main dissenting voice arguing its view that voluntarism was best and that further legislation was both undesirable and unnecessary. It was particularly critical of the option that the 14 proceed and facilitate EU-level incorporation for companies covered by the EWC Directive (option 3) (*see* later in this chapter). The election of a Labour government in the UK and a 'Socialist' government in France in the summer of 1997 may in the medium term influence these developments, as may the proposals contained in the Commission Green Paper (1997) (*see* later).

So far in this section dealing with EU initiatives, we have looked only at proposals that have met sufficient opposition to prevent their adoption. In the remainder of this section we examine action that has been taken to provide employees with rights to participate in decision making. With the exception of the EWC Directive, these initiatives have been subject specific and are concerned with collective redundancies, transfers of undertakings and health and safety.

The Directive on Collective Redundancies (75/129 extended by 92/56)

This Directive, which was adopted in 1975, provides that employee representatives should in appropriate circumstances have the right to be both informed and consulted.

The information requirement specifies that employers/management should give in writing all relevant information including the reasons for redundancies, the numbers to be made redundant, the numbers usually employed and the time period over which they are to take effect. This same information has to be given to the 'competent authority' and a copy of this notification should be given/sent to the employee representatives. The redundancies should not take effect until at least 30 days after the competent public authority has been so notified.

The consultation should take place before the redundancies take effect and should be at the workplace where the redundancies are to occur, even if the decision has been taken elsewhere, including in another member state. Consultation should be by local management. The object of the consultation should be to agree on ways of avoiding or mitigating the number of redundancies and their consequences. The legislation applies only where specified minimum numbers of people are to be made redundant within a specified timescale.

The weaknesses of this legislative requirement were amply demonstrated by the actions of the French multinational, Renault, in 1997 when, with little, if any, prior consultation, it announced its intention to close one of its factories in Belgium, thereby concentrating production more upon French sites.

The Belgian employees and the Belgian government protested; industrial action was taken but in the long run to no avail. Matters were made worse when it subsequently came to light that the company was at the same time negotiating with the Spanish government and the Commission for funding assistance to open a new plant in Spain.

To a very large extent, the EU Directive was demonstrated to be of little value to employees confronted by an employer that is determined and prepared to flout the law in the pursuit of its perceived interests. This example demonstrates many of the reasons why it is important that the Union seeks to counter the power of the multinational and why it is important that the interests of labour and their participation in strategic decision making are supported further. This particular incident may also act as a catalyst for pressures for much harsher sanctions (although it is difficult not to be pessimistic about this as a route for remedying the situation) and also for the further harmonisation of living and working conditions within the Union (*see* section on the debate about social dumping in Chapter 6).

Directive on the Transfer of Undertakings (77/187)

This Directive, which is also known as the Acquired Rights Directive, is primarily concerned with the protection of employees' rights and terms and conditions of employment on the sale or transfer of a business. As part of the strategy for ensuring that these acquired rights are protected, however, the Directive also provides employees and their representatives with rights to be both informed and consulted.

The Directive requires that employee representatives are informed 'in good time' of:

1 the reasons for the transfer;

2 the legal economic and social implications of the transfer for the employees;

3 measures envisaged in relation to employees.

They should also be consulted, again 'in good time', on any measures that are envisaged by either the transferor or the transferee. The obligation to consult seems to apply to employers in respect of their own employees, so that the transferee appears able to avoid consulting with employees of the transferor until after the transfer occurs. However, there is an obligation upon the transferee to inform the transferor of measures proposed and, where the transferor is aware of measures proposed by the transferee, it should inform and consult its employees.

In September 1994 a draft was proposed which revises the 1977 Directive. The new draft is called the Draft Directive on Safeguarding Employees' Rights in the Event of Transfers of Undertakings, Businesses or Parts of Businesses. The main thrust of these proposed revisions does not concern the information and consultation procedures, although there are some relevant proposals:

- The minimum threshold for the requirements to apply should be 50 employees; undertakings employing less than 50 should be exempt from the requirement to consult employee representatives.

- Where there are no employee representatives, the workforce would have a right to be informed in advance that a transfer is to take place; it is unclear whether the requirement will extend beyond notification that there is an agreement to transfer.

- It was clarified that the obligation to inform and consult is to apply wherever the decision is taken, even if in another state.

These proposals appeared to be relatively uncontentious.

In the UK, there has been considerable debate over the years concerning the way in which the original Directives on Collective Redundancies and Transfers of Undertakings had been implemented and in particular there was concern that the implementing legislation provided for information and consultation to be with the representatives of recognised trade unions rather than as specified in the Directives with employee representatives. As the density of trade union membership declined throughout the 1980s and 1990s, the legislation had become less and less relevant and binding upon employers since in the absence of recognised trade unions there was arguably no obligation to inform and consult. As a consequence of concern, the Commission challenged the UK government's interpretation and in June 1994 the ECJ ruled that the requirements of the Directives applied to non-unionised workplaces. As a result of this ruling the Collective Redundancy and Transfer of Undertakings (Amendment) Regulations 1995 (effective on 1 March 1996) require that UK employers carry out the following procedures.

1 They must choose whether to consult with a recognised and independent trade union or with elected representatives of the employees that are affected by the events in question, with elected representatives being employees of the employer and the consultation being on an 'as necessary' basis. There is no requirement that permanent or standing arrangements be created in order to satisfy these new requirements.

2 They must give elected employee representatives similar rights and protections as would be enjoyed by the representatives of an independent recognised trade union.

3 They must consult 'in good time' and not at 'the earliest opportunity' as was the prior terminology.

However, these new regulations do not define 'elected representative' and do not appear to require employers to inform their employees that they are entitled to elect representatives to be consulted.

The 1989 Health and Safety Framework Directive

This Directive again provides employees and their representatives with rights to information and consultation. The requirements for information are concerned with health and safety risks in the enterprise, in the job and at the workstation and give employees access as of right to risk assessments and recommendations for protective measures. Consultation, which must be 'in good time', should cover all questions relating to health and safety at work including training for employees. Health and safety representatives are afforded protection by the Directive from being penalised by the employer in respect of the performance of their representative duties. Further discussion of the significance of this Directive can be found in Chapter 12.

The EWC Directive

The correct title of this Directive is the Council Directive 94/45/EC on the Establishment of a European Works Council or a Procedure in Community-scale Undertakings and Community-scale Groups of Undertakings for the Purposes of Informing and Consulting Employees.

This Directive was adopted by the 11 (excluding the UK) member states under the Social Protocol Agreement (*see* Chapter 8) in September 1994. It was the first Directive to be adopted under this Agreement and utilising the Procedures agreed via the Protocol. The Social Partners did not take advantage of the opportunity this Agreement gave them to conclude an agreement between themselves on the Commission's proposals and so the Directive was adopted via the Co-operation Procedure (*see* Fig. 8.2) and by the Council of the EU (excluding the UK). The Social Protocol Agreement had extended qualified majority voting (QMV) and thereby the Co-operation Procedure to proposals concerning the information and consultation of workers. The Amsterdam agreement proposes to take these procedures into the EC Treaty and the information and consultation of workers are to be subject to the Co-Decision Procedure, though action in support of co-determination remains subject to unanimity (*see* Chapter 8).

This Directive is often referred to as the EWC Directive and has been effectively adopted by all the members of the EU and the EEA (Norway, Iceland and Liechtenstein) with the exception of the UK, although the intention is that the Directive will apply in respect of UK employees and UK-based companies once the Amsterdam proposals are ratified. Implementation was in September 1996.

This Directive can be traced back directly to the Social Charter and indirectly to the earlier initiatives already mentioned and, in particular, to the Vredeling proposals. Cressey (1993) refers to this Directive as 'son of Vredeling'. Paragraph 17 of the Charter specifically referred to the intent to provide rights to information, consultation and participation for workers in companies or groups of companies having establishments in two or more member states and the Commission published proposals to give effect to this intent in January 1991. The proposed Social Chapter of the Maastricht Treaty was intended to give effect to more of the Charter than had been possible, given both the UK's veto at Strasbourg in December 1989 and its subsequent opposition to specific proposals such as these. The Agreement on Social Policy annexed to the Social Protocol states quite clearly the parties' intention to implement the 1989 Social Charter.

It must be remembered that the Directive is aimed only at transnational or Community-scale undertakings and is to be viewed as a response to concerns about the autonomy and power of the multinational to take decisions in one member state, or indeed in a parent country that is outside the EU, which affect employees in one or more other member states.

The intention of the Directive is to ensure that all employees in the same community-scale undertaking/group are both properly and equally informed and consulted about such decisions. The Directive is in part therefore a response to the increase in the number and scale of multinational activities and undertakings that accompanied the creation of the single market, their ability to divert capital investment from one member state to another, and the absence of alternative employee representative arrangements and structures. (For discussion of these matters and issues, *see* Chapter 3.)

This is a Directive that is consistent with the principle of subsidiarity since it is only at EU level that action could effectively be taken, although whether action is necessary is another issue.

As is indicated clearly in the title of the Directive, it is to apply to community-scale undertakings and groups of undertakings; for the purposes of the Directive a community-scale undertaking is one:

- that employs at least 1000 employees in member states covered by the Directive; and
- that employs at least 150 in each of two such member states.

Both of these workforce size criteria have to be satisfied and the calculations are to be based on the average labour force over the preceding two years. The Directive is also applicable in EEA member countries (*see* Chapter 5).

It is important to note that the Directive applies to companies of any nationality; there is no requirement that the company/undertaking be domiciled in or originate from one of the member states. Once covered by the Directive, all an undertaking's establishments within the member states should be covered by the one procedure.

Both the UK employees and establishments of community-scale undertakings were initially exempt, but not UK companies. If their non-UK EU activities qualified them as community scale, then they had to comply with the Directive in respect of all their employees and activities within the other member states, not just those in which they employ in excess of 150.

Early estimates suggested that in excess of 1150 companies qualified as being of community scale and were therefore covered by the Directive. Among them were companies domiciled in 25 different countries. Germany topped the list with 274 qualifying companies followed by the USA with 187, France with 122 and the UK with 106 (ETUI, 1996). There were 101 companies that qualified which were based outside the EEA, but had their largest European operation in the UK. Other non-EU countries with significant numbers of companies covered in respect of their EU operations include Japan and Switzerland.

Another measure of the potential impact of the Directive in the UK was the estimate by the Engineering Employers Federation (EEF) that among its members in the UK there were nearly 900 companies that were subsidiaries of companies likely to be of community scale in respect of their non-UK activities (*Financial Times*, 7 December 1995). Estimates are that in excess of 300 UK companies would be required to comply with the Directive if/when UK operations and employees are not excluded from coverage.

One of the issues raised by the UK's non-participation as one of the countries in which employees and activities are subject to the Directive has been whether both UK and non-UK companies subject to the Directive in respect of their non-UK activities would voluntarily choose to include their UK activities and employees in the arrangements established in order to comply with the Directive. Many UK companies indicated their intention to do so and all of the first dozen to conclude voluntary arrangements in advance of the implementation of the Directive included their UK activities – ICI, British Telecom, National Westminster Bank, Pilkingtons, United Biscuits, Coats Viyella, BP Oil,

Courtaulds, GKN, Zeneca, T&N and GEC-Alsthom. The EEF research referred to above indicated that none of the 66 companies in membership covered by the Directive in respect of their EU/EEA activities intended to not include their UK operations and employees in procedures introduced in order to comply with the Directive. Japanese-owned Panasonic has also indicated that it intends to include its 3500 UK employees. Of the first 100 plus companies creating EWCs or other similar arrangements, only one had taken the opportunity to exclude its UK operations and employees (ING, the Dutch finance group that includes the UK Barings Bank) where these were significant (*The Guardian*, 15 May 1996 and *European Works Council Bulletin*, May/June 1996).

Naturally, trade unions and their officials have generally welcomed the Directive. However, some have expressed concerns that the mandatory model of an EWC outlined in the Annexe to the Directive – the model that would be imposed in the event of the parties failing to agree between themselves – specifies that the EWC members are to be employees of the company and that this will result in their own role and influence being diminished relative to the role of lay trade union and other employee representatives.

The Directive provides for groups or undertakings to be exempted from the detailed requirements, if on the date of implementation of the Directive (22 September 1996) they had in force transnational information and consultation agreements which covered the entire workforce. This provision has led to other trade union concerns, namely that some managements might try and use it to bypass the trade unions. Certainly early efforts by Marks and Spencer to establish a EWC were criticised by trade unions who felt that the company was seeking to establish arrangements which were not adequate substitutes for the arrangements specified in the Directive and which were at least in part inspired by the desire to avoid an anticipated approach from trade unions on behalf of their employees.

The Coopers and Lybrand (1995) survey of eight companies that had voluntarily established EWCs might well reinforce any such suspicions, since in the majority of these companies works council membership was the product of employee election rather than election or nomination by trade union means. Union officials attended EWC meetings at only one of the companies. The survey also suggested that companies with an EWC were less likely to consult with trade unions than those without, although it should be noted that the survey involved a relatively small sample and conclusions need to be drawn with caution.

It was estimated that by the early summer of 1996 (just prior to the date of implementation) substantially in excess of 100 voluntary agreements had been reached in and by companies to whom the Directive would apply and that a number of others were in the process of establishing such voluntary arrangements.

Rivest (1996) studied the first 59 agreements establishing voluntary EWCs in the decade preceding September 1995 and came to somewhat different conclusions as to the role and influence these arrangements had on both national and international trade union organisation. This analysis indicated that national and international trade union organisations were involved as signatories to the agreements in 47 per cent and 44 per cent respectively of the cases surveyed. Other findings of this analysis are that where trade union organisations have been party to the agreement it is likely that the employee representatives on the EWC will normally be nominated by the trade unions and it is more likely that trade union officials will have rights of participation or attendance. However, there is also evidence that country of origin traditions play a part in the constitution of the EWC and the method of selection of employee representatives, as does industrial sector. In some sectors –

food and construction in particular – the sector appears to have greater influence than country of origin and the tentative conclusion is drawn that this is a product in part of the strength and effectiveness of international trade union organisation in these particular sectors. A further assumption is made that these voluntary agreements are likely to establish precedents and models of organisation and structure that will be followed by others.

One of the first UK companies to agree an arrangement with the trade unions was United Biscuits. The company and the unions agreed in November 1994 to establish an EWC covering operations in eight countries (including the UK) and comprising 20 employee representatives. A management representative stated the company's position (in *The Guardian* of 10 November 1994) as a belief that:

> A workforce that understands the objectives of a business and the pressures on it is better able to respond appropriately to necessary operational changes.

The responsibility for organising the process of implementation and/or compliance with the Directive rests with the central management of the organisation and may be undertaken at their own initiative or at the request of employees. Employees and their representatives can initiate the process by submitting a written request on behalf of 100 employees in each of at least two member states. Only in the event of the employer refusing to negotiate within six months of such an employee initiative, or in the event of the parties being unable to agree upon voluntary arrangements within three years of the original request for negotiations, will a particular form of information and consultation arrangement be imposed. In this sense, this Directive is consistent with the later versions of the earlier employee participation initiatives – the draft Fifth, Vredeling and European Company Statute Directives – in that the intention is to allow the parties to choose systems that are consistent with various national traditions as well as their own wishes as long as certain basic conditions are complied with. The Directive refers to self-determined EWCs and alternative procedures and only if there is a failure to introduce such an arrangement do the 'subsidiary requirements' or mandatory model of EWC become applicable.

The detail of the Directive provides that central management has the responsibility to set up a Special Negotiating Body (SNB) of employee representatives and to convene a meeting with it to 'negotiate in a spirit of co-operation with a view to reaching an agreement' (Article 6. 1). The SNB should comprise between 3 and 17 members who may be employees or their representatives and elected or appointed in accordance with the requirements of the respective member states. The intention is that the constitution of the SNB should be representative of the distribution of the labour force of the undertaking within the EU. The Directive specifically provides that employees in establishments without employee representatives should be given the right/opportunity to elect or appoint members to the SNB.

There are a range of possible outcomes of the negotiation process:

1 The SNB, once convened, may decide that it doesn't want to continue the negotiations, although it must do so by a vote of 66 per cent.

2 Central management and the SNB may reach a written agreement to establish an EWC – a self-determined EWC. The Directive requires that any such EWC agreement would have to include details of:

- the undertakings and/or establishments to be covered;
- the composition, size and term of the EWC;

- the functions and procedures for informing and consulting;
- the frequency, venue and duration of meetings;
- the financial and material resources to be allocated to the EWC;
- the duration of the agreement and the procedure for its renegotiation.

3 There may be a written agreement on a different information and consultation procedure, although any such alternative would need the majority support of EWC members.

4 Central management and the SNB could decide to set up an EWC which meets the 'subsidiary requirements' that are applicable if the parties are unable to agree a self-determined EWC or an alternative procedure.

These subsidiary requirements specify a model of an EWC and are included in an annexe to the Directive. The main points of the model are:

- The EWC must have between 3 and 30 members.
- The EWC should be comprised of employees of the undertaking or group elected or appointed by them and in accordance with the national legislation or practice.
- The competence of the EWC should be limited to information and consultation on matters concerning the undertaking or group as a whole or at least establishments or undertakings in two different member states.
- The composition of the EWC should include at least one member from each member state in which the undertaking or group has an establishment with the remaining membership determined on proportionate grounds.
- Such an EWC is to be reviewed after four years and the parties may choose to allow it to continue or to negotiate an alternative.
- The EWC has the right to an annual meeting with central management to be informed and consulted on the basis of a written report provided by management and on:

   . . . the progress of the business of the Community Scale undertaking or . . . group of undertakings and its prospects.

The subject matter of the meeting is then detailed. It relates:

   . . . in particular to the structure, economic and financial situation, the probable development of the business and of production and sales, the situation and probable trend of employment, investments and substantial changes concerning organisation, introduction of new working methods or production processes, transfers of production, mergers, cut backs or closures of undertakings, establishments or important parts thereof, and collective redundancies.

- There is also provision for additional meetings at the request of the EWC in exceptional circumstances.

It is clear that the EWC/similar arrangements envisaged in the Directive is not going to provide employees and their representatives with rights and a role that imply an element of co-decision or co-determination. Using the terms of Strauss, the Directive is imposing only rights to bilateral communication and discussion. In terms of employee participation, the proposals are therefore quite limited. Nevertheless employers are to have their unilateral 'right to manage' curtailed by the Directive, although, as indicated earlier, in many of the member states the notion that management should have any such rights would appear strange.

Employer concerns and opposition

At this stage it is unclear what penalties or sanctions may be available in the event of an employer refusing to comply even with these limited employee rights to information and consultation. Penalties and sanctions are left to the member states and all the Directive stipulates is that there should be adequate administrative or judicial procedures available to enable the obligations to be enforced.

It is too early yet to ascertain the extent of employer opposition to the Directive. It is also too early to estimate the number of companies that will wait for their employees to take the initiative and institute the proceedings culminating in the establishment of the SNB and how many may then choose to do no more than specified in the subsidiary requirements described in the annexe to the Directive which effectively provides a mandatory model EWC. There are attractions to employers in adopting this approach if they are opposed to the intent of the Directive; they can delay implementing the information and consultation for three years and there are cost advantages.

Many employers may also find the arrangements in the annexe preferable in that they are relatively limited and probably the least that they can reasonably expect to get away with, particularly where they are confronted by a trade union actively representing their members and seeking to widen the scope of the information and consultation arrangements, as many undoubtedly are. The annexe provides a ready-made set of arrangements and the employer can be certain that employees will have no grounds to appeal against the arrangements as not being adequate or satisfactory when measured against the requirements of the Directive. Against this, of course, is the argument that in choosing to allow a system to be enforced, control and flexibility are lost. The employer is not going to be able to design and implement a system that fits with the requirements and structure of the organisation.

Employers express concern about the need to ensure confidentiality in respect of some of the information that the Directive suggests should be given to the employee representatives. The authors of the Directive have sought to counter these concerns by again placing upon the member states the duty to ensure that the members of the various bodies that may be established under the aegis of the Directive are not authorised to reveal information that is expressly given to them in confidence and this obligation is to remain even after their term of office expires. The Directive also gives member states the duty to make provisions which ensure that central managements situated within their territory are not obliged to transmit information that according to objective criteria would seriously either harm the functioning of the undertakings or would be prejudicial to them. It is again as yet too early to establish the extent to which these protections for employers are either necessary or adequate, although it is clear that managements are concerned at the possibility – as evidenced by the case of United Biscuits insisting that breach of confidentiality would be treated as a serious disciplinary offence.

Article 11 of the Directive provides that employee representatives should be given administrative or judicial procedures enabling them to appeal against decisions to withhold information on confidentiality grounds.

Other management criticisms of informing and consulting employees are that the process is inevitably time consuming and expensive and damaging to performance. However, it would appear from the research of Fernie and Metcalf (1995) that not only is there no general evidence of unfavourable relationships between formal joint consultative committees and economic and industrial relations outcomes but on two particular counts – productivity growth and industrial relations climate – such arrangements are favourably associated with performance. They cite German research which similarly found no adverse association between works councils (stronger bodies than the UK joint consultative committees) and productivity, profit and investment. The authors urge that UK employers should throw off their blinkers and work in harmony with unions or employees to improve performance, although to do so through the mechanism of formal joint consultative committees would require a reversal of the trend identified by the 1990 WIRS. The WIRS research indicated that less than 25 per cent of establishments in private-sector manufacturing had such arrangements in 1990, compared with 36 per cent in 1980.

The likely impact of the Directive

There are a number of different views of the likely impact of the Directive upon the conduct of industrial relations and perhaps in particular upon the prospects of the Directive encouraging the development of collective bargaining at the level of the Euro-company.

The achievement of the Directive (notwithstanding the dangers of not being able to effectively enforce the Directive as demonstrated earlier in respect of Renault's alleged failure to comply with the Collective Redundancies Legislation) concerns the level at which the consultation is to take place and in the 'strategic' nature of the subject matter. For the very first time, many multinational organisations are to share information with employees at a supranational, sometimes corporate level and there is an obvious potential in these arrangements for the further development of joint arrangements and trust.

If relationships between management and employees do improve and trust levels do rise then it is certainly not beyond the bounds of possibility that over time the arrangements may develop into something more akin to collective bargaining and joint regulation. The UK is certainly not the only member state in which the two processes – joint consultation and collective bargaining – sometimes merge or overlap and while the intention of the Directive is to create consultative arrangements, it is possible that drift will occur once the arrangements are up and running.

The trends in collective bargaining over recent years, however, tend to have been in the opposite direction of decentralisation rather than the centralisation that might be implied by the developments postulated here as possible outcomes of the formation of the EWCs.

Marginson and Sisson (1994) took the view that there seemed little prospect of the Directive leading to the extension of collective bargaining at the level of the transnational or multinational organisation since:

- companies would lose the opportunity to seek competitive advantage from the existence of different national labour market conditions and regimes;
- such a development would run counter to the trend of decentralisation of both operational and collective bargaining decision-making structures;
- companies are likely to want to continue with the separation of consultative and bargaining institutions that was common in many member-state systems;
- trade unions at national level may also have reasons for preferring to keep the existing national or sectoral multi-employer bargaining structures, in that their roots and power bases are in national systems and they may well be reluctant to cede any of their autonomy to European-level organisations.

Nevertheless, they do acknowledge that EWCs will provide opportunities for the development of contacts and the exchange of information among employee representatives.

Rivest (1996) includes the calculation that if the average employee representation on an EWC is 30 then there are going to be somewhere in the region of 36 000 employee representatives engaged in cross-national meetings every year and it is suggested that they are bound to make comparisons of rates of pay, working conditions and systems of representation and bargaining.

Marginson and Sisson (1994) suggest that it is possible to envisage the development of a kind of pattern bargaining, whereby the employee representatives may seek to extend concessions won in one country or division to others within the company. Such a development would impose a greater pressure upon the management of transnational companies at group or division level to exert effective control over the decisions taken in individual business units so as to prevent the creation of dangerous precedents. This can be construed as a reason to centralise.

Activity of this kind by the trade unions may combine with a number of other pressures to encourage a degree of centralisation in the conduct of industrial relations within the Euro-company, even if there does appear to be an inconsistency between this and the trends towards decentralisation already noted.

By 1996, Marginson and Sisson confirmed that in many Euro-companies the decentralisation of operational and industrial relations decision making to individual business units had also been accompanied by some centralisation to the Euro level. They argued that, though apparently contradictory, these trends may be mutually reinforcing. As decision making and collective bargaining are decentralised, there is an internal need to coordinate and control at or from the centre. It is therefore possible to conceive an enhancement of collective bargaining at the Euro-company level, even if this bargaining may be geared more to the production of framework agreements or joint opinions than to the contractual arrangements that are the tradition in the majority of EU national systems. These developments may well be facilitated or encouraged by the creation of EWCs at this Euro-company level.

Schulten (1996) takes a somewhat different view in that he suggests that EWCs may in future lead to a new transnational micro-corporatism helping to stabilise the emerging Euro-company while at the same time reinforcing the contemporary trend of undercutting national, regional and sectoral bargaining through decentralisation of decision making.

In examining existing voluntary EWC arrangements, he concludes that there is considerable diversity but also a basic minimalist model which consists of annual information giving and little in the way of consultation and genuine participation in management decision making, let alone co-determination.

In most cases the pressure for the creation of the EWC came from the employees and/or their trade unions, but the Directive's provisions enabling the parties to agree their own arrangements might be expected to encourage some managements to take the initiative so that they can keep control.

Schulten refers to the arrangements in Danone, the French food company, which is at the forefront of these developments and which is one of the very few to have concluded collective agreements at this transnational company level. It has reached four framework agreements on the issues of training, womens' equality, basic information rights for employees and trade union rights in each Danone subsidiarity. He concludes that the company constitutes the first example of a company-specific 'European Collective Bargaining System'.

Schulten proposes a matrix of the various models or stages in the development of EWCs along two dimensions:

- the level of independent labour–labour cooperation and
- the level of labour–management cooperation.

Where the cooperation on both of these dimensions is high, it is possible that the EWC becomes the forum for the spread of best practice learning within the company. In such circumstances it might be that management itself takes the initiative in the formation of the arrangements which Shulten refers to as 'micro-corporatism'. However, he warns that even in such circumstances of micro-corporatism, managements would still look to go regime shopping and, where advantageous, seek to use the social dumping approach.

Where the Euro-company does seek to conduct industrial relations at the Euro-level (as, for example, in the case of Danone) there is a danger that individual subsidiaries may well become detached from their national and multi-employer systems.

Another development emanating from the implementation of the Directive may be an enhancement of the degree of trust and joint arrangements at national and lower levels – the notion that if relationships and trust can be improved at a supranational level, it might be possible to cascade these improvements downwards. An early example of this potential was the creation by the Danish multinational, ISS, of a UK works council as a branch of its EWC (*The Guardian*, 4 July 1995). In a survey of eight companies already operating EWCs by January 1995, all were also found to be operating works councils at a national level (Coopers and Lybrand, 1995).

EMPLOYEE PARTICIPATION AT EU LEVEL AND THE SOCIAL DIALOGUE

Employees are able to participate in decision making at the level of the EU through their trades unions via a number of formal consultative arrangements and specifically through the European Trade Union Confederation (ETUC) (*see* Chapter 7) in its role as a Social Partner in the Social Dialogue. These roles in the EU decision-making process have been detailed elsewhere in this text, in particular the recently enhanced potential for the Social Partners to participate in a form of collective bargaining on Commission proposals for EU-level initiatives and intervention (*see* Chapter 8). Inevitably, these roles provide individual employees with only the most indirect of forms of participation and many would no doubt argue that these particular mechanisms constitute employee participation in name only. The alternative view is that this is an argument that can be extended to any form of representative democracy and that, indirect and distant though it may be, the ETUC, and the confederations that are members, as a Social Partner is there to act as a pressure group and to both represent and actively pursue the sectional interests of its membership.

The partners did not succeed in reaching agreement with regard to Commission initiative put before them – the EWC proposals covered earlier in this chapter – but early in 1996 they reached their first agreement under the Protocol arrangements; this involved the Commission initiative regarding the reconciliation of professional and family responsibilities (often known as the Parental Leave Proposals/Draft Directive) (*see* Chapter 11). This framework agreement was then returned to the Commission for progress; formal adoption by the Council followed later in June 1996. This first agreement was greeted warmly by proponents of the enhanced role as evidence that it could work and that it was possible for employers through their organisations and trade unions to reach meaningful agreement at this level. The Social Partners have been invited to reach framework agreements on a number of other matters since this first agreement.

One of the potential spin-off effects of these new EU-level arrangements is that experience at this level may encourage the further development of employer–employee relationships at a lower transnational level – that of the industry or sector – and that this may lead in the future to limited collective bargaining at this level. There is a history of dialogue at sector level which in some sectors pre-dates developments at the higher EU inter-sectoral level. However, formal arrangements are limited in number; this has been partly due to the difficulty of identifying employers associations at this sector level. Trade unions have been more able to establish relevant and representative European Industry Committees (EIC) to engage in dialogue at sector level.

The Commission has successfully encouraged some joint committees at sector level, mainly in those industries in which the Community has sought to establish common policies – for example, coal and steel, agriculture, sea transport and sea fishing, railways, road transport, civil aviation and telecommunications. The purpose of these joint committees is to assist the Commission in devising and implementing Community policy aimed generally at improving and harmonising living and working conditions in the respective sectors.

The Commission has also sought to establish informal dialogue in a number of other sectors, often doing so via the mechanism of establishing working parties on particular issues of concern to the industry.

It is probably a fair assessment that it is the employers that have been the more reluctant and less able partner in dialogue at this level and that at least in part this is a product of organisational/structural inadequacies, though it should also be noted that there is often less desire on the part of the employers.

Carley (1993) points out that there are significant obstacles in the way of the development of collective bargaining at sector level and that to some extent these mirror difficulties at the inter-sectoral level and are connected to the following factors:

- the partners' lack of a mandate to bargain;
- the partners' less than full representativeness of the industry, both employers and employees;
- the partners' inability to control their members' actions.

They are also linked with the generally significant divergence in economic well-being and living standards across the EU and particularly between North and South. This last factor may well increase rather than decrease in significance if the EU expands to the South and East.

Schulten (1996) also notes a number of significant obstacles to the creation of effective collective bargaining arrangements at the European or sectoral level:

- There is an absence on both sides of appropriate institutional, organisational and political structures and mandate.
- Both sides are still required to cope with and satisfy the national interests of their members.

- There are still fundamental differences between the attitudes of the two sides on issues such as the need for an integrated social policy within the EU.
- There are no appropriate structures at the multi-state level of the Union to encourage, let alone enforce, the development of such pan-European collective bargaining structures from above.

As was noted earlier, there are some instances of international trade union organisations – particularly in the metals, chemicals and food sectors – reaching agreements with individual employers on the creation of voluntary EWCs and these again are relationships and outcomes that may be built upon. However, it is difficult not to conclude, that if such arrangements are to develop it is likely, in the absence of legislative intervention, that the trade unions will have to provide the driving force and overcome many obstacles, not the least of which is the apparent reluctance of the employers.

This assertion applies equally to the development of Euro-company level collective bargaining outside the EWCs. There are few if any reasons to imagine that the development of such arrangements would be at the behest of the employers.

In reviewing EU initiatives in the arena of employee participation, Hall (1994) makes the point that the fate of the range of employee participation proposals that have been initiated by the Commission over the years amply illustrates the difficulty of seeking to harmonise member states' representation or participation arrangements and procedures. He argues that the only successes have been with measures:

- requiring information, consultation and participation procedures in respect of certain specific social issues; and
- which accommodate member states' existing employee representational arrangements rather than specifying particular institutional forms.

The examples of successes are:

- collective redundancies;
- transfer of undertakings; and
- the Framework Health and Safety Directive.

He suggests that collective institutions and procedures are seen as integral to national social and political power relations, hence the reluctance of member states to see these interfered with or regulated from outside.

It has been easier to 'harmonise' individual rights and substantive outcomes than collective or procedural arrangements and requirements. To some extent, the different traditions and systems render this both inevitable and intractable. He reinforces this point by noting that the EWC Directive is aimed at the creation of transnational, as opposed to national arrangements and while particular procedural forms may be an outcome, this will be at a transnational level and therefore not so potentially dangerous to the maintenance of national arrangements and traditions.

The Social Dialogue arrangements described in Chapter 8 and discussed in the previous section of this chapter also fall into this transnational and thereby less threatening category.

FINANCIAL PARTICIPATION

There have been many schemes devised to enable employees to participate relatively directly in the economic and financial success of their employing organisation. Commonly, these schemes range from individual and group bonus and other performance-related payment arrangements through to various forms of share option and ownership deals including producer cooperatives.

The faith of employers and governments that have promoted and implemented such arrangements is in its essence predicated upon the simple assumptions that offering employees some form of tangible and visible financial stake in the success of the organisation will:

- enhance their commitment to the organisation and its goals and activities;
- motivate them to work harder and more effectively;
- lead to improvements in productivity;
- reduce labour turnover and other symptoms of dissatisfaction;
- encourage employees to become more cooperative and traditional conflicts will either disappear or at least be more easily resolved;
- result in the company prospering and management's job becoming in some senses easier.

The Commission has sought to encourage the development of both profit- and equity-sharing arrangements and in 1992 the Council adopted a non-binding Recommendation (92/443) on Equity Sharing and Financial Participation that encourages member states to themselves support such schemes via the creation of sympathetic legal and fiscal environments and regimes and provides advice on the issues and criteria that those seeking to encourage and introduce such arrangements should consider.

Sparrow and Hiltrop (1994) review the incidence of such schemes in the EU and conclude that they are not common in many member states and, where they have been introduced, they rarely provide employees with the opportunity to participate significantly in either profit sharing or in share ownership – with the percentages rarely exceeding 5 per cent in each case. As noted earlier, the two member states in which the legal and fiscal environments have been most sympathetic and/or encouraging are France and the UK; it is in these two member states that the frequency and popularity of such arrangements have been greatest. In France, there have been legislative requirements on firms employing more than 50 employees and in the UK tax incentives have been used to encourage profit sharing by employees.

More recent evidence reported by the Commission (1997b) suggests that other member-state governments have begun to encourage such schemes – for example, Ireland, the Netherlands and Finland – and in Germany, Spain and Italy the Social Partners have been encouraged by government to promote such schemes.

The Commission is still very much in support of these arrangements and in its 1997 report it encourages their establishment and support. The Commission refers to research evidence, all of which supports the assertion that the introduction of profit-sharing arrangements is associated with an increase in productivity. This appears to be the case irrespective of the precise method used. It is also asserted that these schemes have beneficial effects upon levels of employment.

The Commission is sufficiently persuaded of the potential of these arrangements to encourage the Social Partners at Union level to consider reaching an appropriate Framework Agreement through the Protocol Procedures (*see* Chapter 8). The temptation is to see this Commission support as being a product of the beneficial effects upon productivity and employment claimed rather than as an indication of its commitment to notions of employee participation or democracy.

The Commission does warn employers against the practice of taking advantage of opportunities to offload stock at times when the company or economy is in trouble.

Robinson and Perotin (1997) confirm that a review of the research evidence does support the contention of an association between share-ownership schemes and productivity improvement, but they take a more cautious view of the inevitability of the association and the causal nature of any relationship. The magnitude of the improvement in productivity seems to vary between the studies in the range of 3 to 13 per cent. They suggest that the higher rates seem to be achieved when the employee profit sharing is combined with other initiatives consistent with the culture change that they argue is advisable/necessary. They argue that profit sharing should be accompanied by other measures that give employees influence. On the relationship claimed between these schemes and a reduction in unemployment, the authors assert that at best it remains unproven.

In the UK, the John Lewis Partnership, Unipart and the National Freight Corporation are well known examples of different variations on the theme of employee participation through financial partnership/share ownership.

In the case of the John Lewis Partnership (*see* Exhibit 14.1), employees are partners and collectively own the organisation. In addition to an entitlement to a share in the profits, they have a range of mechanisms through which they can seek to influence management and decisions, including the direct opportunity to comment and question anonymously via letters to management which must be answered via the in-house newspaper. There are also forms of indirect representative participation, a structure of employee committees/councils that have constitutional rights of information and consultation and whose overall consent is required before certain decisions can be taken, such as changes in trading hours.

The National Freight Corporation example involved a different form of financial participation. The employees owned shares with double voting rights – an attempt to prevent dilution through the need to raise capital in the market – but over the years this proved to be insufficient protection as financial problems led to a situation whereby in 1995 employees owned only 11 per cent of the shares and the ability of the employees and their shareholder director to influence management decisions was inevitably limited.

The problems of the NFC are symptomatic of those experienced by many organisations that seek to give employees a financial stake in the organisation for which they work. The investment market seems reluctant to provide funds to organisations in which there is an employee participation regime of this kind and private companies in the service sector where employees are highly qualified and able to generate sufficient earnings to continue to fund expansion would appear to stand the best chance of continuing in this form long term. Exhibit 14.2 illustrates some of the difficulties firms with substantial employee share ownership face with the city as a source of finance for investment.

It is clear that the majority of schemes in existence give employees at best a financial

Exhibit 14.1

Goodwill store

FT

The John Lewis partnership goes beyond the purely commercial,
writes **Christopher Brown-Humes**

Enlightened, caring and progressive? Or paternalistic, old-fashioned and eccentric?

It is a debate the John Lewis Partnership continues to inspire nearly 70 years after John Spedan Lewis launched a unique experiment in business ownership by handing over the company to a trust for its employees.

For many, the retailer is a model employer, sharing the fruits of its success with its 35,000 staff, or 'partners', and giving them a say in how the group is run. For others it belongs to the world of the 1970s television sitcom *Are You Being Served?*: an anachronism, weighed down by bureaucracy, that stifles individualism and entrepreneurship.

What seems unarguable is the group's ability to combine commercial success with high-sounding principles. It is heading for record profits this year lifting first-half profits by 72 per cent to £78.1m. Department store sales in the 13 weeks to October 26 were 16 per cent higher than a year ago – comfortably outstripping the market average.

These figures are not exceptional. In the words of a rival department store retailer: 'They've been producing excellent results for years and years and years. It is a tremendous business: the brand is so strong their advertising is virtually non-existent.'

The performance stands out all the more at a time when House of Fraser is planning to close up to 20 per cent of its stores amid falling profits and lost market share and when the department store concept is being questioned due to the rise of out-of-town retailing and 'category killer' specialists.

It also perplexes those who feel capital markets should be better than employees at keeping companies on their toes. But some argue that not being quoted has been an advantage because it has allowed the group, which has 23 department stores and 113 Waitrose food stores, to take a longer term view than competitors.

Partnership works in a variety of ways.

One of the main aims is to hold managers accountable to staff through an elaborate network of councils and the weekly staff *Gazette*. Branch councils scrutinise management decisions at store level while a 135-strong central council acts as a group-wide forum. More informally, employees writing to the *Gazette* – anonymously, if they so wish – are entitled to a written response from a relevant manager.

Another element of the concept is what the company calls the 'best profit-sharing scheme in the country'. Last year it gave staff a bonus equal to 15 per cent of their salary, and this year they should do even better.

Senior managers also get the bonus, but they do not get the long-term incentive schemes or options common in many boardrooms. And basic salaries in an era of fat-cat excess are below those found in other big retailers. The chairman, Stuart Hampson, earned £343,000 last year, including partnership bonus. But this is £160,000 less than the maximum allowed under partnership rules.

Partnership is not just about pay and perks. For one employee it is about 'not letting the side down'. For another it is about 'decency and honesty' – meaning you wouldn't use your store discount card to buy goods for your sister. It aims to benefit everyone it comes into contact with, ensuring suppliers are paid promptly and the shop is 'never knowingly undersold'.

But critics say the bureaucratic council system smacks more of the Soviet era than the modern one while the paternalism is reminiscent of Japanese corporate culture. The rigidities are certainly not to everybody's taste. 'People discover fairly quickly whether they like it or not, and if they don't they leave,' says one employee.

It also carries costs that many other groups would consider an extravagance. These include the councils, registrars (a discreet breed of advisers to partners and local managers), private country clubs and the cost of funding a raft of other benefits. The

group clearly believes these ultimately pay for themselves in terms of employee motivation.

David Young, deputy chairman, says the group's structure has resulted in lower levels of staff turnover and staff theft. The stability extends from the shop floor to the boardroom. He adds: 'If we were targeted by a Hanson, some of the partnership overheads would be regarded as fat to be blown off. Short-term profitability would improve; long-term, it is more questionable.'

There are times when the caring concerns of a partnership fly in the face of purely commercial considerations. Earlier in the decade the group held open two run-down stores – Pratts in Streatham and Jones Brothers in Islington – so that they did not close before a new store in Kingston opened. This was to avert job losses, but meant the group was briefly overstaffed. 'Commercially it was a strain but the loyalty and commitment we generated will have produced a long-term return,' says Hampson.

He also implies partnership could also restrict the group's freedom when it comes to making acquisitions. A big acquisition, in particular, could dilute the group's culture, he believes.

Hampson believes an increasing number of companies are recognising the benefits of involving their employees in their business.

Marks and Spencer and Asda are among the retailers who have gained a reputation for looking after staff well. But no big company has gone anything like as far as John Lewis in the array of benefits or degree of employee involvement.

This seems odd given that the group seems to offer a spectacular example of successful capitalist and communist co-existence. Numerous businesses contact the group, eager to learn about its organisation, but very few, if any, end up copying it.

The fact is that it takes an unusually enlightened person to hand over a successful business for no financial gain.

Source: *Financial times*, 6 November 1996.

Exhibit 14.2

Unipart rules out flotation

FT

By John Griffiths

Mr John Neill, chief executive of Unipart, yesterday ruled out a flotation for the foreseeable future, despite the automotive car parts and accessories group breaking through the £1bn sales threshold last year and the soaring value of directors' and employees' equity holdings.

Sales last year were £1.1bn, up 17 per cent on the previous year's £864m, and pre-tax profit rose 5.2 per cent to £34.3m.

The group, privatised from the Rover Group 10 years ago, is 50 per cent owned by its managers and nearly 4,000 employers and 30 per cent by institutions. Rover retains a 20 per cent stake.

Its share price last year reached 2.3p, compared with 0.05p at privatisation. The £7.1m dividend share-out is a 9.2 per cent increase over 1995's £6.5m.

Mr Neill, a fierce critic of the City's 'short-termism', pointed to Unipart's smaller profits growth relative to turnover as one reason for ruling out a flotation.

He said: 'It arises from the heavy investments we're making in new business and joint ventures for which the pay-offs are in the longer term. We are taking a 10-year view of this business and we have to be free to manage it for long-term growth and development. We cannot be beholden to the short-term concerns of the stock market.'

Investment is running at about £100m a year, targeted mainly on four motor components manufacturing joint ventures. Three are with Japanese component suppliers to Honda. The fourth is with German group Kautex. All four ventures, creating about 400 jobs, are due to come fully on stream next year.

Unipart has also formed a joint venture with TVS, an Indian components group, to distribute car and truck parts across Europe. Mr Neill disclosed yesterday that s part of an increased drive into continental European markets it had been setting up aftermarket parts and accessories operations in countries including Hungary, Poland and Russia.

My Neill warned that to develop these businesses would continue to require 'significant levels of investment'.

Source: *Financial Times*, 4 April 1997.

stake in the organisation, very rarely does this also involve or imply an influence in the management or control of the company.

For employee share ownership to yield real influence in corporate decision making, various changes would be required in the UK model of corporate governance that go beyond the current EU proposals. There are those who argue, however, that this is precisely the direction which holds out the greatest potential for employee participation of a real and positive kind – that, as stakeholders in their employing organisation, employees should share with other stakeholders the decision-making capacity and that this can be best achieved by creating circumstances and an external environment that both encourage and do not discriminate against employee share ownership of a significant scale. This share could be accompanied by internal mechanisms through which employees and their representatives participated along with the representatives of the other stakeholder interests for the benefit of all. Without this stake in ownership, employee interests will always be subservient to those of the other stake/shareholders and management will be in the position of giving priority to these other interests.

The innovative scheme at Levi Strauss described in Exhibit 14.3 recognises the interests of employees as stakeholders in the company but this comes after the repurchase of employees' shareholdings and the ending of an employee stock ownership scheme. There is doubt as to whether such an arrangement would have been possible had the company not been returned to private ownership in 1985 and there is no indication that the scheme envisages any enhancement of employee participation in any decision-making sense.

Exhibit 14.3

Levi Strauss offers £500m cash bonus to employees

By Diane Summers and Richard Donkin

Levi Strauss, the US company which makes one of the world's leading brands of jeans, aims to spend £500m ($760m) giving every member of its global workforce a year's extra pay.

Each of the group's 37,000 employees – from senior managers to cleaners – will receive the bonus in 2002 if a cash-flow target is met.

The payout could be even higher than £500m if the target, considered by unions and management to be readily achievable, is exceeded. The scale of the deal is thought to be unique.

Levi Strauss is a privately owned company, founded in 1850, with its headquarters in San Francisco. It was recently valued at more than £8.40bn and had sales last year of £4.4bn. Mr Robert Haas, its chairman, is a great-great-grandnephew of the company founder, Levi Strauss, who was a Bavarian-born immigrant to the US.

Mr Haas said that ever since the company was founded it had sought to conduct business 'in ways that are consistent with our values, which include recognition – both psychic and financial – for those who contribute to our success'.

Union leaders in the UK and US are holding up Levi Strauss's scheme as a model for other employers to follow. Mr Des Farrell, clothing and textile national secretary of the GMB union in the UK, where Levi Strauss has two factories and a finishing centre in Scotland, described the promised payment as 'ground-breaking'.

It was a practical example of stakeholding, with employer and union working together, he said. 'Many other companies, rather than paying out large dividends to their shareholders, should be looking at this kind of scheme.'

Mr Jay Mazur, president of Unite, the US textile union, said it was 'consistent with the times' that employees should share in profits.

Independent pay specialists emphasised that it might be possible for employees to gain an extra year's salary over a six-year period through share schemes, but a simple cash payment on this scale was highly unusual. Mr John Gilbert, a director of Monks Partnership, the pay consultant, said: 'It really is clean and simple, and beautifully packaged.'

Levi Strauss returned to private ownership in 1985. Earlier this year, it completed a financial restructuring, including the repurchase of shares held by employees and the ending of an employee stock ownership plan. These shares accounted for about 4 per cent of all outstanding shares and ownership is now concentrated in a few family hands.

The cash-flow target which will trigger the extra year's salary is £4.9bn by the end of the 2001 financial year. Ms Janie Ligon, general manager of the company in the UK, described the target as 'pretty cautious'. Employees have to stay for at least three years to benefit.

About 28,000 of Levi Strauss's employees are in North America, with about 7,000 in Europe, 2,000 in Asia-Pacific and a small workforce in Latin America. The company has been carrying out a phased withdrawal from China and Burma for human rights reasons.

Source: *Financial Times*, 13 June 1996.

European Commission 1997 Green (Consultative) Paper – Partnership for a New Organisation of Work

The subject of this consultation document (European Commission, 1997d) is not specifically that of employee participation; however, the proposals within it touch upon the contents of this chapter and are arguably revealing of the current direction of Commission views.

The authors of this document are very keen to emphasise the importance of partnership between employees and employer to the achievement of the high-skill, high-trust and adaptive workforce which, they argue, is necessary to facilitate and take full advantage of the new forms of work organisation that are considered to be the key to the achievement of competitiveness in the new global marketplace. Competitiveness is perceived as the key to resolving the problem of unemployment. The authors talk of inviting:

the social partners and public authorities to seek to build a partnership for the development of a new framework for the modernisation of work. Such a partnership could make a significant contribution to achieving the objective of a productive, learning and *participative* organisation of work.

There is clearly a danger that what is envisaged are initiatives and arrangements under the banner of partnership and participation that in fact have very much more in common with the notion of EI than with concepts of industrial democracy or employee participation, in that the latter terms confer upon employees rights to take part in and influence decision making outside the confines of the task and the organisation of work. Forms of financial participation are approved.

The authors acknowledge that:

> The new organisation of work will challenge industrial relations . . . Industrial relations will require, in a new organisation of work, to be built on a basis of co-operation and common interest. Therefore, new forms of industrial relations have to be developed, including, for example, greater participation by employees, since efficient production requires enhanced levels of both trust and commitment in firms.

It is argued that there are potential advantages to employees in developing this approach:

> . . . the new organisation of work can offer workers increased security through greater involvement in their work, more job satisfaction and the possibility of developing skills and long-term employability.

Employers are offered a more stable, versatile and contented labour force.

The willingness of the employees and their representative organisations to wholeheartedly enter into the forms of partnership envisaged in the report might be considerably enhanced if there were also some proposals to extend employees' rights to information, consultation and co-determination. The European Union will have an appropriate legal basis for relevant initiatives, once the Amsterdam Treaty proposals are given effect. The new Article 118 gives the Council the power to act on information and consultation using the Co-Decision Procedure and on co-determination via unanimity. There is evidence of an awareness that these rights and appropriate arrangements are an issue since the authors do state:

> The role of workers in decision making and the need to review and strengthen the existing arrangements for workers' involvement in their companies will also become essential issues.

They go on to indicate the need to consult with the Social Partners on the

> advisability and direction of Community action in the field of information and consultation of employees at national level.

There is therefore potential within the consultative paper for discussions to ensue on matters of employee participation and democracy in addition to the developments of an EI nature that are promoted.

However, the sceptic observer might argue that giving employees the right to join a trade union and for that union to be given rights to represent its members and engage in collective bargaining at the level of the firm is an alternative route to providing employees with security; such an approach might well better engender the constructive cooperation, partnerships and high-trust relationships considered by the authors of the report to be essential to the development of new forms of work organisation and enhanced competitiveness. Nevertheless, this begs the question of the extent to which it is realistic to consider that there is enough common interest between employers and employees to justify the perception of work organisations as partnerships.

CONCLUSIONS

It is clear that employee participation means different things to different people. There are various perspectives on the concept, each of which is likely to be influenced by culture and ideology, as also are support for or opposition to the practice. There are obviously different perceptions of the interests served by such participation. Employee participation can be participation in ownership, profit, control of the labour process, managerial decision making, and/or the organisation of the task.

There is some ambiguity of meaning and interpretation between the various terms commonly used to describe the subject matter – participation, involvement and democracy. *Employee participation* seems to readily encompass industrial democracy and the latter seems to be commonly perceived as an end in itself and as a matter of right with both moral and political associations. *Employee involvement* is less easily and comprehensively subsumed within employee participation since some of the practices often associated with the term are not genuinely participatory. Examples would include downward-only mechanisms for information and communication, which may seek to involve employees, may seek to gain their commitment, and may even enhance their satisfaction levels, *but* do not provide employees with an opportunity to participate in any form of decision making at any level, nor do they provide an enhanced role in ownership or profit sharing.

The increasing number of EI schemes may well be reflective of a shift in the balance of power in favour of employers/capital. Involvement programmes are commonly motivated by the desire/need to improve profitability, performance, flexibility, etc. and thereby competitiveness; they are not seen as a desirable end in themselves.

The EU initiatives over the years have mostly been motivated at least in part by the belief that employees have the right to participate in managerial decision making, that they are stakeholders in the organisation and that they therefore have some form of moral right to participate along with the other stakeholders. This view is a reflection of cultures and traditions that are different from those of the UK and are to varying degrees often characterised as being corporatist. It would be a mistake, however, to think that these are the only reasons for the initiatives. Employee participation has also been perceived to be:

- an efficient means of resolving, if not eradicating conflict between the interests of owners, managers and employees;

- a means by which efficiency and productivity can be improved with employees being encouraged to use their knowledge, skill and ingenuity to achieve such improvements; and

- a means by which the power of capital may be counteracted, particularly the power of the multinational to move funds and hence also employment and wealth around the single market at will, without necessarily any concern for the welfare of employees.

It must be remembered, however, that the research evidence indicates a somewhat negative assessment of the success of legislative initiatives to encourage employee participation of the information and consultation variety and it is this area that the EU initiatives have predominantly covered.

There is evidence of a 'watering down' of the early initiatives, each successive draft seemingly representing less of an incursion into what in the UK has been traditionally viewed as areas of managerial prerogative.

The impact of the subject-specific initiatives – providing rights to information and consultation in the event of collective redundancies and the transfer of undertakings – has been limited in the UK by the restriction of the rights to trade union representatives. As a result, where there were no trades unions recognised, the rights intended by the Commission and other member states were for many years and in many organisations and workplaces unenforceable. It is too early yet to ascertain the impact of the amendments contained within the Amendment Regulations of 1995 and reservations have already been noted.

The EWC Directive is in many senses the most significant initiative taken so far. It is aimed directly at the multinational and has as one of its objectives the achievement of greater equity between the treatment of such an organisation's employees across national borders. The fact that the UK operations of multinationals are excluded from the scope of the Directive, until the new 1997 agreements at Amsterdam involving the Labour government are implemented, does not appear so far to have persuaded organisations otherwise covered by the Directive to exclude their UK employees from the arrangements being constructed. It is again too early to draw conclusions from the operation of the Directive since it became effective only in September 1996.

It must be remembered that the provisions for participation in the Directive are relatively limited in that they are only concerned with information and consultation and do not imply any extension of rights to co-determination or joint decision making. Nevertheless, the Directive may inspire companies and employees/trade unions to enter into voluntary agreements that go beyond the specific requirements of the Directive.

There are some grounds for believing that there will be positive effects on cross-national relationships between employee and trade union representatives and that new liaisons and relationships might yield a potential for the labour force to more effectively combat the power of the multinational and secure greater security and benefits for employees – perhaps through a form of Euro-company level collective bargaining.

It has also been argued that the Directive and the arrangements that it generates will over time lead to an improvement of relationships and trust between employers/managers and employee representatives and that these will assist a progression from informing and consulting to processes more akin to joint regulation, at least on some issues of a company-wide relevance.

However, there are also reasons for being sceptical about the prospects for the creation of collective bargaining arrangements at Euro-company level. Outside the organisation, at the level of the industrial sector and at the multi-sector level, there do seem to be major obstacles to the development of effective employee participation in managerial decision making whether by consultation or collective bargaining, not the least of these being the lack of a mandate and suitable representative structures.

Progress in both of these areas is likely to be very much linked to effective trade union organisation and persuasion; there is little reason to assume that initiatives will be taken by employers.

At EU level, there are perhaps grounds for greater optimism since the Social Partners have already managed to reach a couple of framework agreements within the procedures agreed at Maastricht with the likelihood that more will be arrived at in the foreseeable future. However, it must be borne in mind that this is employee participation of a very indirect kind – about as far removed from the level of the firm as is possible. It is reasonable to expect employers to be attracted to schemes for employees to participate in the financial success of the firm the more the research evidence indicates an association with improvements in productivity.

Significant extension of the use of such schemes might be dependent upon the adoption of a European Company statute which includes governance requirements and stipulations that would require companies to give greater weight to the interests of a wider range of stakeholder interests than is currently required by many of the national systems. Developments in this area would seem to necessitate more than a sympathetic tax/fiscal regime. If such changes did come about, then there are grounds for arguing that they could provide the scope for the most fundamental of developments in employee participation.

It does not seem at all likely that the EU will try to impose a particular model or form of employee participation throughout the Union or to harmonise existing national arrangements. This would seem to be confirmed by the Commission Green Paper on partnerships and new forms of work organisation (European Commission, 1997a). Nevertheless, this document does provide cause for concern in that there appears to be much less emphasis in it upon moral and democratic justifications for employee participation and a much greater emphasis upon the encouragement of EI schemes with a view to facilitating greater productivity and efficiency and thereby employment. This does constitute a departure from the early justifications and is evidence of the shift in sentiment that would appear to have been encouraged by the threat of unemployment and by the arguments of capital and business interests. It may well also be indicative of a shift from the traditional social capital and social protection models traditional in many EU member states (*see* Chapter 1), despite the rhetoric.

There are reasons to believe that the interests of capital and labour are not the same. Exhortations to labour to cooperate and enter into partnerships are likely to be directed at the achievement of managerial objectives and interests rather than those of labour. If genuine partnership is the intent, then initiatives should be directed at the encouragement of means of employee representation and mechanisms providing the means for labour to participate on an equal footing with other stakeholders. In many respects, the Commission and other Union institutions used to occupy the moral high ground on the issue of employee participation; this has been cast into doubt as it seeks also to satisfy the interests of multinational capital.

References

Bean, R. (1994) *Comparative Industrial Relations* (2nd edn). Routledge.

Beer, M., Spector, B., Lawrence, P., Mills, D. and Walton, R. E. (1984) *Managing Human Assets*. Free Press.

Brewster, C. and Hegewisch, A. (1994) *Policy and Practice in European HRM*. Routledge pp. 154–67.

Chamberlain, N. and Kuhn, J. (1965) *Collective Bargaining*. McGraw-Hill.

Carley, M. (1993) 'Social Dialogue', in Gold, M. (ed) *The Social Dimension – Employment Policy in the European Community*. Macmillan.

Coopers & Lybrand (1995) *European Works Councils. Consultation and Communication in European Companies – A Survey*. Coopers & Lybrand.

Cressey, P. (1993) 'Employee Participation', in Gold, M. (ed) *The Social Dimension – Employment Policy in the European Community*. Macmillan.

Crouch, C. (1982) *The Politics of Industrial Relations* (2nd edn). Fontana.

European Commission (1992) *PEPPER: Promotion of Employee Participation in Profits and Enterprise Results*. European Commission.

European Commission (1997d) *Green Paper, Partnership for a New Organisation of Work.* European Commission, COM (97) 128.

European Commission (1997e) *PEPPER II: Promotion of participation by employed persons in profits and enterprise results (including equity participation) in member states* (COM (96) 697). European Commission.

European Works Council Bulletin, 3, May/June 1996, IRS/IRRU.

Farnham, D. and Pimlott, J. (1995) *Understanding Industrial Relations* (5th edn). Cassell.

Fenton O'Creevey, M., and Nicholson, N. (1994) *Middle Managers: their contribution to employee involvement.* Employment Department Research Series No. 28. HMSO.

Fernie, S. and Metcalf, D. (1995) 'Works Councils are the Future, but there is no need to be afraid'. *The Guardian*, 22 May.

Geary, J. and Sisson, K. (1994) *Conceptualising Direct Participation in Organisational Change: The EPOC Project.* European Foundation for the Improvement of Living and Working Conditions.

Hall, M. (1994) 'Industrial Relations and the Social Dimension', in Hyman, R. and Ferner, A. (eds) *New Frontiers in European Industrial Relations.* Blackwell.

Hegewisch, A. and Brewster, C. (1994) *European Developments in Human Resource Management.* Kogan Page.

Heller, F. (1992) (ed) *Decision Making and Leadership.* Cambridge University Press.

Hollinshead, G. and Leat, M. (1995) *Human Resource Management: An International and Comparative Perspective.* Pitman Publishing.

I D E Research Group (1981) *Industrial Democracy in Europe.* Clarendon.

I D E Research Group (1993) *Industrial Democracy in Europe Revisited.* Oxford University Press.

Marchington, M., Wilkinson, A., Ackers, P. and Goodman, J. (1995) 'Involvement and Participation', in Storey, J. (ed) *Human Resource Management A Critical Text.* Routledge.

Marchington, M., Wilkinson, A., Ackers, P. and Goodman, J. (1992) *New Developments in Employee Involvement.* Employment Department Research Series No. 2. HMSO.

Marginson, P. and Sisson, K. (1994) 'The Structure of Transnational Capital in Europe: the Emerging Euro-company and its Implications for Industrial Relations', in Hyman, R. and Ferner, A. (eds) *New Frontiers in European Industrial Relations.* Blackwell.

Marginson, P. and Sisson, K. (1996) 'Multi-national Companies and the Future of Collective Bargaining: A Review of the Research Issues', *European Journal of Industrial Relations*, 2(2), 173–97.

Michels, R. (1966) *Political Parties.* Free Press.

Mowday, R. T., Steers, R. M. and Porter, L. W. (1982) *Employee-Organisation Linkages: The Psychology of Commitment, Absenteeism and Turnover.* Academic Press.

Poole, M. and Mansfield, R. (1992) 'Managers' Attitudes to Human Resource Management: Rhetoric and Reality', in Blyton, P. and Turnbull, P. (eds) *Reassessing Human Resource Management.* Sage.

Poole, M. (1986) 'Participation through representation: a review of constraints and conflicting pressures', in Stern, R. and McCarthy, S. (eds) *International Yearbook of Organisational Democracy 3, The Organisational Practice of Democracy.* Wiley.

Ramsay, H. (1992) 'Commitment and Involvement', in Towers, B. (ed) *The Handbook of Human Resource Management.* Blackwell.

Regalia, I. (1996) 'How the Social Partners View Direct Participation: A Comparative Study of Fifteen European Countries', *European Journal of Industrial Relations*, 2(2), 211–34.

Rivest, C. (1996) 'Voluntary European Works Councils', *European Journal of Industrial Relations*, 2(2), 235–53.

Robinson, A. and Perotin, V. (1997) 'Is profit sharing the answer?', in *New Economy*, 4(2).

Schregle, J. (1976) 'Workers' participation in decisions within undertakings', *International Labour Review*, 113, 1–16.

Schulten, T. (1996) 'European Works Councils: Prospects of a New System of European Industrial Relations', *European Journal of Industrial Relations*, 2(3), 303–24.

Sparrow, P. and Hiltrop, J. (1994) *European Human Resource Management In Transition.* Prentice-Hall.

Strauss, G. (1979) 'Workers participation: symposium introduction', *Industrial Relations*, 18, 247–61.

Walker, K. F. (1974) 'Workers' participation in management: problems, practice and prospects', *Bulletin of the International Institute for Labour Studies*, 12, 3–35.

Additional reading

Cotton, J. L. (1993) *Employee Involvement*. Sage.

Fernie, S. (1995) 'Participation, contingent pay, representation and workplace performance: evidence from Great Britain', *British Journal of Industrial Relations*, Sept.

Gold, M. and Hall, M. (1994) 'Statutory European Works Councils: The Final Countdown?' *Industrial Relations Journal*, 25(3), 177–86.

Hall, M. (1992) 'Behind European Works Councils Directives: The European Commission's Legislative Strategy', *British Journal of Industrial Relations*, 30(4).

Hall, M., Carley, M., Gold, M., Marginson, P. and Sisson, K. (1995) *European Works Councils – Planning for the Directive*. Eclipse Group and Industrial Relations Research Unit, Warwick.

Hyman, J. and Mason, B. (1995) *Managing Employee Involvement and Participation*. Sage.

Keller, B. (1994) *Towards a European system of collective bargaining? Perspectives before and after Maastricht*. Leverhulme Public Lecture. Industrial Relations Research Unit, University of Warwick.

Knudson, H. (1995) *Employee Participation in Europe*. Sage.

Lawler, E. (1986) *Higher Involvement Management*. Jossey Bass.

Moye, A. M. (1993) 'Mondragon: Adapting co-operative structures to meet the demands of a changing environment', *Economic and Industrial Democracy*, May, 251–76.

OECD (1995) 'The incidence of profit sharing in OECD countries', *Employment Outlook*. OECD

Pickard, J. (1993) 'The Real Meaning of Empowerment', *Personnel Management*, 25 Nov, 28–33.

Rogers, J. and Streeck, W. (eds) (1995) *Works Councils: Consultation, Representation and Co-operation in Industrial Relations*. University of Chicago Press.

Streeck, W. (1994) European Social Policy after Maastricht: The Social Dialogue and Subsidiarity. *Economic and Industrial Democracy*, 15(2), 151–77.

Wall, T. D. and Lischeron, J. A. (1977) *Worker Participation: A Critique of the Literature and some Fresh Evidence*. McGraw-Hill.

15

UNEMPLOYMENT

LEARNING OBJECTIVES

When you have read this chapter, you should be able to understand and explain:

- different definitions of unemployment and their significance for the international comparison of data;
- the scale, impact and nature of unemployment within the Union and the groups affected;
- the differences between the different types and causes of unemployment;
- the main elements of the major different diagnoses, explanations and models;
- their implications for the policy choices available and what these policy options are;
- the initiatives taken within the EU and their location in terms of the above;
- the continuing debates within the Union and their respective implications.

INTRODUCTION

From the outset it was realised by the architects of the European Community that the removal of tariff barriers to facilitate the promotion of free trade within the community would in all likelihood have positive, negative and differential employment consequences. It was determined very early on that remedial actions and interventions might be necessary, and so the Social Fund (ESF) was established in 1960 in accordance with Article 123 of the Treaty of Rome which required that the European Commission should seek to render the employment of workers easier and enhance their occupational and geographic mobility.

The decision in 1986 to create the single market gave further impetus to these concerns. The research undertaken under the auspices and sponsorship of Paolo Cecchini (1988) suggested that while in the longer term the employment effects of the creation of the single market would be positive – possibly to the extent of 5 million jobs created – in the immediate and medium term the effects would be negative – possibly to the tune of 500 000 jobs lost (European Commission, 1988). The role and scale of the ESF were subsequently enhanced.

The issue of unemployment was given even greater importance by the recession of the early 1990s and the job losses associated with it and the reunification of Germany. As demonstrated in Hollinshead and Leat (1995, p. 42) the reunification of Germany and the subsequent restructuring had serious implications for unemployment in the East. Since then the European Union – its members, institutions and officials – have probably given more attention to the 'problem' of unemployment than to any other single issue.

The European Commission (1993b) produced a draft White Paper on the subject for the summit meeting of the Council in December 1993 and all subsequent six-monthly summits have to varying extents had the subject on the agenda. The global significance of unemployment in the 1990s, in the EU and elsewhere, is indicated by the attention given to unemployment at the May 1994 and subsequent meetings of the Group of 7 (G7) major developed countries – United Kingdom, Germany, France, Italy, Japan, United States and Canada. In the main, both these sets of meetings have been concerned to identify and agree upon both causes and cures, informed both by their members' experiences (which as we shall see later vary widely) and of course by their own beliefs and perspectives.

This chapter examines definitions of the phenomenon of unemployment and presents evidence of the scale of the 'problem', including evidence of its variable impact upon nations, regions, industrial sectors and groups of people differentiated by skill level, occupation, age, and gender. The scale and costs of unemployment are usually presented *quantitatively* – the percentage of the labour force in work and not in work, or annual unemployment costs of so many million or trillion pounds or dollars in terms of lost production, transfer payments, forgone tax revenues, etc. It is important that we also appreciate that there are considerable *qualitative* implications – personal and social costs and consequences. Unemployment has an impact upon the quality of human experience at both individual and community levels, and throughout this chapter the intention is not to lose sight of these latter dimensions of the costs of unemployment.

There is substantial room for disagreement on the causes and cures of unemployment and the third part of this chapter seeks to examine the main schools of thought regarding causes and explanations of the phenomenon and their respective implications for preferred solutions and remedies.

In the remainder of the chapter we examine the debate at EU level between the representatives of the member states and other interest groups, particularly as it has been encouraged by the Commission and the 1993 White Paper. It is also intended to examine the various initiatives and programmes that have been taken and adopted at EU level, including the proposals agreed at Amsterdam in 1997, and discuss, where possible, evidence of their impact. In conclusion, we shall reflect upon the extent to which it seems likely that these initiatives and programmes are appropriate given the nature of the 'problem' and its diagnosis.

DEFINITIONS OF UNEMPLOYMENT

There are a variety of ways in which the term 'unemployment' can be defined and, as is the case with any attempt to undertake cross-national comparisons of statistical material, it is important that efforts are made to try and ensure that we are comparing like with like. Consistency of definition and methodology are essential.

Eurostat – the central statistical office within the EU – revised the methods used to calculate unemployment rates early in 1995, the adapted methods being based upon new and more reliable surveys and designed to produce statistics more consistent with the recommendations of the International Labour Office (ILO). This new method was first used to collect and present the data for February 1995. It does seem that the ILO definition is becoming the most popular for undertaking such cross-national comparisons, although it is important that we realise that not all national statistics are collected in accordance with this methodology.

The Organisation for Economic Cooperation and Development (OECD) also produces statistical series which provide a basis for international comparison and, since 1984, both the ILO and OECD series have used similar definitions and methodologies. In essence, both seek to ascertain by means of survey the numbers of people:

1 who are without work (by which is meant both paid employment and self-employment) and;

2 who are available for work; and

3 who are actively seeking work, specific evidence of which may be required.

These are then expressed as a percentage of total labour force, including members of the armed forces.

Superficially, this may seem relatively straightforward but there are many differences and nuances of interpretation and meaning and unanswered questions that can make even the collection of these data problematic. In particular, one can envisage difficulties over the following concepts:

1 *Paid/Payment*. What does and does not constitute payment? Are there to be limits upon the level of such payment? For example, does payment of a wholly inadequate or even unlawful amount nevertheless qualify and render the individual employed, as opposed to unemployed?

2 *Available*. Does this mean that someone must be able to accept or begin paid work? Must this availability be within a specified period of time and, if so, what should this time period be? (I spent part of my adulthood as an unemployed/without paid work single parent and remember vividly being informed that I was not eligible to be classified as 'unemployed' because I was not able to start a job at three hours' notice!)

3 *Work*. What does this mean? Is it any work or work for which the individual is qualified? An illustration of the complexities inherent in these questions might be the solicitor working as a waiter: is he or she unemployed, or not? Perhaps more crucially, would refusal of an offer of such work be taken as an indication that he or she was not actively seeking work and therefore take him or her out of the ranks of those classified as unemployed?

4 *Actively and seeking*. There is considerable scope for differences of interpretation of both these concepts. Does reading the situations vacant columns in a newspaper constitute 'actively seeking'? If not, what would?

Partly because of these and other issues, some national governments have been keen to be more specific in their definition and interpretation of the term 'unemployment'. In particular, governments have sought to limit the description and hence the calculation to those people who qualify to and do claim some form of unemployment or social security benefit. The United Kingdom Conservative governments between 1979 and 1997 fit into this category. Such a system provides a number of advantages:

● It generally produces unemployment totals that are lower than they would be using the ILO/OECD basis of computation.

- There is scope in such a system for governments to manipulate the totals by varying the tests or criteria that have to be met in order to qualify for the claimant benefit.

It must also be acknowledged, however, that there is scope in such a system for the unemployment totals to be overstated to the extent that the benefits are fraudulently claimed and/or those claiming and in receipt are not actively seeking work.

There are other dilemmas surrounding the definition and calculation of unemployment totals. Some of these are concerned with the distinction between unemployment and under-employment; perhaps, the easiest illustration of this is the part-time worker who is working part-time not out of personal preference, but because he or she had no option. Is such a person unemployed or under-employed? Even if this constitutes under-employment, should efforts be made to include a measure of this under-employment in the statistics since they are presumably intended to facilitate measurement and act as an indicator of the under-utilisation of the labour resource within the economy. Similar problems of inclusion or exclusion apply to groups such as:

- the long-term sick;
- the discouraged searcher;
- the single parent with no access to child care but who would otherwise work;
- premature retirees; and
- those who continue in full-time education because they would be unemployed otherwise.

In order to at least partially tackle this problem, the OECD in its Employment Outlook series has started since 1995 to augment the unemployment statistics with statistics which seek to quantify both the discouraged and the involuntary part-time working population. In some economies, these groups are substantial.

As we shall see later in this chapter, economists tend to have other definitions of unemployment. In some instances they argue that unemployment is the relatively simple measure of the difference between the supply of and demand for labour in a price-adjusting market, with the excess supply comprising active searchers and the excess demand represented by unfilled vacancies. However, economists also define unemployment as a measure of immediately available workers willing to accept market-clearing wages, or as the difference between employment levels at a market-clearing equilibrium wage and employment at the prevailing market wage, where the latter is greater. The use of these and other definitions is likely to be influenced both by perspective – which particular beliefs and assumptions the user holds – and by the purpose to which the measure is to be put.

THE SCALE, IMPACT AND COST OF UNEMPLOYMENT

This section should be read in conjunction with Chapter 4, which gives detailed statistics on demography and labour market trends.

As noted in the introduction to this chapter, the scale of unemployment throughout the EU in recent years has meant that unemployment has been described as the single greatest problem or issue confronting the Union. This was clearly still the feeling among the authors of the Commission report (1997c, p. 36) who express this view quite unequivocally:

Unemployment is the major challenge faced by the Union and the Member States.

At the time of the publication of the Commission's White Paper in December 1993, the gross unemployment rate within the Community as a whole was 10.9 per cent, representing approximately 17 million people (European Commission, 1993b). It is perhaps surprising to realise that this degree of unemployment was not in fact substantially higher than rates dating back to the early and mid-1980s. Figure 4.5 shows that the EC rate hovered at or just below the 10 per cent mark throughout the period from 1984 to 1988, fell to a subsequent low point of 7.7 per cent in 1990 and then rose again, breached the 10 per cent mark in 1993 and then remained at or about the 11 per cent mark well into 1996. This final figure represented approximately 18 million people (taking into account, union enlargement in 1995).

Despite the attention given to the issue since 1993 there has been no substantial and general improvement in the rate in the intervening years and Table 15.1 shows that the OECD does not envisage the rate falling below 10.8 per cent before 1999.

It is also clear from Table 4.5 that there are considerable variations in the unemployment experience of the member states with some demonstrating consistently high or low rates and differences also in the direction of movements and trends. Much work has been undertaken in an attempt to understand these variations in experience and considerable interest has also been shown in seeking explanations for the differential experiences of Europe compared with Japan and the USA. Both of these countries have exhibited considerably lower rates of unemployment over the same period of time compared with the EU, the Japanese rate varying only between 2 per cent and 3 per cent and the USA rate varying between 9.5 per cent and just over 5 per cent. (*See* Fig. 4.5)

One of the suggested explanations of these latter variations relates to the apparent abilities of the respective economies to create jobs. The EU economies have a much lower apparent capacity for job creation and certainly, in comparison to the USA, a much greater ability to create jobs in the public, as opposed to the private sector. Between 1970 and 1992, the cumulative rates of economic growth in the USA and the EU were approximately the same at between 70 and 75 per cent and yet, while in the USA this was accompanied by 45 per cent job creation, in the EU the overall rate of job creation was only 7 to 8 per cent. Perhaps significantly, most of the jobs created in the USA were in the private services sector, whereas in Europe the majority were in the public sector. In the USA over this period average real wages fell while in Europe they rose. To some extent this is what might be expected as the greater levels of employment in the USA drove down the marginal product of labour and the majority of the jobs created were in low added-value service sectors.

These generalisations mask a number of other possible explanations concerned with the respective inflows into and outflows from labour markets and the respective regulatory regimes and associated perspectives – issues to which we return later.

It should be noted that the same unemployment rate can be the product of quite different patterns of movement and duration. In the USA, the inflow and outflow rates tend to be relatively high and the incidence of long-term (*see* later in this chapter) unemployment relatively low whereas, in Europe and Japan, the inflow rates tend to be low in comparison. In Europe, there is also a tendency for outflow rates to be low and for duration to be higher.

In addition to the above cross-national variations in unemployment experience, it is also clear from Table 4.5 that there are differences by gender, with women experiencing higher rates in most countries than men, the UK being an exception in this latter case. Figure 4.7

Table 15.1 Unemployment as a percentage of the labour force according to the OECD

	1996	1997*	1998*
Austria	6.2	6.4	6.2
Belgium	12.9	12.7	12.3
Denmark	8.8	8.1	7.4
Finland	16.3	14.7	13.7
France	12.4	12.6	12.2
Germany	10.3	11.1	10.9
Greece	10.4	10.4	10.5
Ireland	11.3	10.8	10.5
Italy	12.1	12.1	11.9
Luxembourg	3.3	3.3	3.2
Netherlands	6.7	6.2	5.6
Portugal	7.3	7.1	7.0
Spain	22.7	22.1	21.2
Sweden	8.0	8.1	7.5
UK	7.4	6.1	5.6
Total EU	**11.3**	**11.2**	**10.8**

*projected figures
Source: adapted from OECD Economic Outlook, No. 61.

shows that age also appears to be a factor in that in many countries the under-25 age group exhibits higher rates than others. There are also significant regional variations both within the Union as a whole and within countries. It is more difficult to provide statistical evidence of these variations throughout the EU. Over time, however, some indication can be detected from European Report 2134 of May 1996 in which it is stated that throughout 1995 the unemployment rate was consistently above the EU average in a third of its regions, the worst affected being Andalucia and the least affected being Luxembourg. The widest differences within countries were in Germany (particularly between the new Länder and some of those in the South, such as Tübingen and Bavaria), Spain and Italy.

Another group that tends to experience particularly high rates of unemployment is the manual unskilled, reflecting perhaps a decline in the demand for unskilled labour as robotics and other new technologies render that labour less necessary and less viable at the real wages that in many European countries have to be paid. Lone parents also tend to experience greater than average rates of unemployment (OECD, 1995) and often membership of these groups also coincides with longer term unemployment.

The duration or length of time that someone is out of work is another dimension upon which there is considerable variation between countries within the EU and again between the experience of the EU and that in the USA and Japan. In particular, there has been considerable concern about the proportions of the unemployed who remain unemployed for a period exceeding one year; commonly, this is taken as the threshold beyond which someone is classified as 'long-term unemployed'. Table 15.2 shows that there are considerable variations between countries in the proportion of the unemployed that fall into this category. There are a number of explanations for these variations, each with a slightly different emphasis on the role of demand and supply factors.

Table 15.2 Percentage of labour force unemployed that have been unemployed
for 12 months or more, 1995

	Men	Women	Total
Belgium	61.5	63.5	62.4
Denmark	31.8	24.8	27.7
Germany	45.9	51.3	48.7
Greece	42.2	58.1	51.3
Spain	49.0	60.0	54.6
France	39.2	41.1	40.2
Ireland	66.7	52.4	61.3
Italy	62.7	64.4	63.6
Luxembourg	50.0	33.3	40.0
Netherlands	52.4	41.1	46.7
Austria	25.0	31.3	28.0
Portugal	48.1	53.5	50.8
Finland	42.3	31.6	37.2
Sweden	23.4	15.9	20.2
UK	49.6	32.3	43.5
EU15	48.3	50.0	49.2

Source: Derived from EC Rep. Employment in Europe 1996.

Demand factors might include:

- industrial decline (in Europe this applies to employment in both agriculture and manu-facturing);
- changes in the industrial impact of new technologies;
- a regulatory regime;
- associated costs discouraging the employment of labour, such as high real wages for unskilled labour linked to the presence of a minimum wage and/or high social security; and
- other non-wage labour costs.

On the supply side, explanatory variables might include:

- hysteresis effects generally rendering the unemployed more and more 'unemployable' as the length of their unemployment increases and the value of their skills decreases;
- the failure to adequately train and retrain;
- the social security and benefits regimes and their impact upon incentives to work; and
- other problems associated with barriers that there might be to labour mobility, such as language, culture and property laws (*see* Chapter 10).

Debates about long-term unemployment tend to touch more than others upon the issue of voluntary, as opposed to involuntary unemployment. In societies and cultures imbued with the Protestant work ethic, the latter is in some sense far more 'acceptable' than the former. In some European economies there is still a feeling that adults ought to work and that long-term unemployment is the product of sloth and an unwillingness to work – that it is voluntary, rather than involuntary. The belief that idle hands make mischief has by no means disappeared. We return to these issues later.

With regard to the costs of unemployment, the estimates obviously vary according to how widely the net is cast. If only those costs that can be directly attributed are included – for example, lost production and unemployment benefits payable – an estimate of costs is arrived at that is considerably lower than if less direct costs were included, such as those incurred owing to a higher incidence of ill health and unemployment-related crime. The European Commission (1993) estimated that unemployment in the Union in 1993 implied total costs of 210 000 million ECU – a total roughly equivalent to the GNP of Belgium. The costs allowed in this calculation were relatively comprehensive and included lost output, benefits payable, lost tax revenue, increased social and health services costs and the costs of increased crime.

These costs in the main represent costs to society but there are also costs to the individual, some of which have been implied by the costs included in the EC calculations – for example, those related to poorer health. There are other individual costs, however, some of which are relatively easy to calculate – for example, lost income and consumption. The quantification of others poses considerably greater difficulties – for example, the loss of self-esteem and confidence which while bad enough on their own often contribute in the longer term to other costs associated maybe with behavioural problems, alcoholism and marriage break-up. The relationship between occupation/employment and social status has long been on the agenda of social scientists with unemployment generally implying a diminution or loss of both social status and self-esteem, and contributing to feelings of alienation and social exclusion. The term 'underclass' is sometimes used to refer to people in this position.

These costs to the individual and to society are often long term and in some instances permanent. Topel's (1993) research indicates that unemployment often results in a permanent decline in earning capacity; the longer the duration of the unemployment, the greater the indirect costs are likely to be. There has been considerable debate over the years as to the extent to which it is possible and reasonable to argue a causal link between unemployment and crime, other incidents of social unrest and disruption and even premature death. The research evidence is by no means conclusive and particular self interests are likely to impinge upon the interpretation of events and research evidence. It is not surprising, therefore, that a government that is under criticism for pursuing policies that have led to an increase in unemployment seeks to deny any causal connection between unemployment and increased crime or social unrest.

In the next section, the various forms of unemployment are examined and this is followed by a review of models and explanations.

FORMS OF UNEMPLOYMENT

Over the years, a number of different forms of unemployment have been identified and particular labels have been attached to them in order to facilitate differentiation. In the main, there is a broad consensus on the use and application of these terms and the main criterion of distinction tends to be cause. Commonly, a distinction is drawn between the following forms:

- frictional or search unemployment;
- structural unemployment; and
- cyclical or demand-deficient unemployment.

Sometimes reference is also made to a fourth category – technological unemployment – though this form is also often subsumed within either frictional or structural.

Frictional or search unemployment

Frictional or search unemployment comprises those looking for their first employment and those in between jobs, having left one and about to begin another. As already indicated, some definitions of frictional also include unemployment caused by and comprising those losing a job because of technological change (Parkin and King, 1992).

It is sometimes suggested that, if the only unemployment is frictional, then the economy is experiencing 'full employment'. It is also sometimes the case that frictional unemployment is equated with the 'natural rate' of unemployment although this definition in some models also includes those who choose to remain in unemployment. Frictional unemployment has often also been perceived in essentially temporary terms; it is a form of unemployment that does not last long, although this particular association has become less common in recent years in Europe as the average duration of unemployment has increased.

Structural unemployment

This form of unemployment tends to be longer term than frictional and is the product of one or more of a variety of different causes. Examples include unemployment that is due to the decline of traditional industries and/or skills. This may be caused either by a straightforward decline in the demand for the product of the industry – perhaps because a substitute has become available or is cheaper – or because competition from low-wage economies means that the product can no longer be produced on a price-competitive basis in the current location – changes in comparative advantage.

The relatively high labour and social costs of employment in Europe, compared, for example, with those in South-East Asia, are often alleged to contribute to this kind of unemployment. Increasingly, we may see this process occurring within and between regions in the EU as the process known as 'social dumping' takes hold. It is already the case that some of the historically high unemployment in Germany and to a lesser extent in France is the product of this process of relocating investment and production facilities.

Commonly, this type of unemployment has skill implications in that as the industries decline so may the demand for a particular skill. Of course, some skills are industry specific, as in the case of coal mining, so that a terminal decline in the industry may also present a terminal decline in demand for the skill.

Governments in Europe have on many occasions sought (and in some instances are still seeking) to protect particular industries and regions from the full consequences of this type of unemployment. Much of the effort of the EU over the years has been directed towards mitigation of these kinds of pressures and consequences.

Technological unemployment

This form of unemployment is often due to an inability to adapt quickly to technological change, but can also occur as a result of the substitution of technology for labour or as a result of new technology causing the expansion of one sector often at the expense of another. As has already been pointed out, there are areas of overlap between this and both some frictional and structural definitions; some technological change leads to the decline of industries and some of the unemployment that results is of a frictional nature.

Cyclical or demand-deficient unemployment

Unemployment of this kind is a product of the periodic fluctuations in demand within the economy that are associated with the notion of the business cycle. While there is some fluctuation within the cycles, it seems that there are greater fluctuations between the same point of successive cycles than within. In Europe in recent decades unemployment has tended to demonstrate an upward trend from the peak of one cycle to the next and this trend fluctuation is greater than that between the peak and trough of the one cycle. Much less attention is paid now to this phenomenon of cyclical unemployment than hitherto, owing to an erosion in the minds of governments of confidence in the Keynesian theory on which the notion is founded.

Of these various forms of unemployment most attention is paid these days to structural unemployment – its explanation and measures that may be taken to alleviate its effects.

MODELS AND EXPLANATIONS

In this section it is not practicable to give detailed and specialised treatments of all the common models of labour market behaviour mentioned in the introduction to this chapter. Nevertheless, it is important that the basic elements and implications of the various positions are explained since this will mean that when policy options and prescriptions within the EU are examined later in this chapter, it will be easier for the reader to understand the current debates and to weigh up the evidence and arguments between the various groups and positions.

The simplistic model of unemployment in the EU, implied in an earlier section of this chapter, suggests that the reasons for the higher levels and greater duration of unemployment compared with the USA and Japan are to be found at the output end of the process. Inflows into unemployment are not noticeably greater given the same structural and technological developments and rates of positive or negative growth; the difference is primarily in the outflows from unemployment – the levels of job creation and hirings – and maybe also in the job search behaviour of individuals and their propensity to be both geographically and occupationally mobile.

It has become relatively common to leap to the conclusion that the low outflows in Europe are the product of employers confronted with regulated labour markets, relative wage rigidity and high non-wage labour costs being reluctant to employ additional labour and choosing to substitute technology for labour or to simply relocate production outside the Union.

It was noted earlier that the levels of job creation in the EU appear low in comparison with the USA and this was confirmed in the OECD Jobs Study of June 1994 and charac-terised as a contrast between the weak employment growth and high productivity growth of Europe against the USA's record of creating a high level of low-skill and low-produc-tivity jobs. The OECD approved neither of the patterns. However, as noted in Chapter 4, the Commission in its 1996 report casts some doubt upon the presumption that the EU problem stems from a lack of job creation. It concludes that the poor overall performance of the European economies in expanding employment, relative to the USA and Japan, owes much more to the scale of job losses in the primary and secondary sectors than to the low rate of net gains in services – the expanding sector.

The classical view of unemployment

The classical viewpoint places reliance upon the market as a price-adjusting forum and mechanism that ensures that unemployment does not occur. In a competitive and essen-tially free market – that is, without regulation – the demand for labour and the supply are rendered in equilibrium through adjustment of the price. Wages adjust in order to clear the market. As can be seen from Fig. 15.1, when the market is in equilibrium at A, demand and supply are matched at the equilibrium price – real wage W – and there is no unem-ployment (frictional). The willingness to employ as represented by unfilled vacancies and the willingness to work as represented by active searchers are equated at the equilibrium real wage.

However, at the prevailing equilibrium price, some labour is voluntarily choosing not to actively seek work and this is represented clearly by the supply curve LS in Fig. 15.1 which indicates that at prices above the equilibrium of W_1 more labour would be supplied.

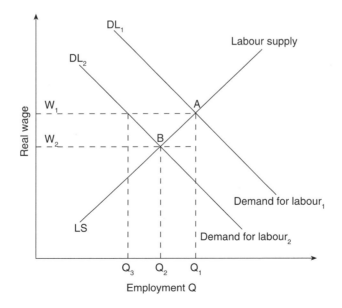

Fig. 15.1 The Classical view of the demand and supply of labour

Similarly, it is clear from the demand curve DL_1 that at higher prices there would be fewer vacancies – that is, fewer opportunities for employment.

This classical, market approach assumes that, once in equilibrium, the market will remain so until there are developments in either supply or demand that effectively result in a shift of either to the left or right (DL_2 in the figure). There are then new levels of active searching and/or unfilled vacancies at all price levels. The figure illustrates a contraction of demand from DL_1 to DL_2 – the sort of contraction that arguably many markets in Europe have experienced in recent years. As can be seen, the contraction of demand results in fewer vacancies at each wage or price level and this sets off the process of adjustment that eventually results in a new equilibrium at a price real wage of W_2. At this new equilibrium again there is no unemployment since job seekers and vacancies are matched at Q_2.

In this context there may be some temporary or frictional unemployment while the market/price is adjusting to the new demand or supply conditions. The market is some-times described as being self-regulating with an inbuilt tendency towards low unemployment.

In this model individuals are deemed to be free to exercise choice and are assumed to be rational and capable of rational choice; they are therefore capable of looking after their own interests. It should also be remembered that in this model it is assumed that the var-ious parties act individually and that the market equilibrium is the product of all the participants exercising their roughly equal power in their own interests. No single indi-vidual is capable of influencing the market.

If the market were not unregulated or self-regulating and free, as assumed above, then unemployment may well exist at the prevailing market price. This can be demonstrated using Fig. 15.1 by introducing the assumption that when the demand conditions change, market price remains at the original equilibrium level. In other words, there is a measure of price/wage rigidity which may be due, for example, to the influence of legislation on minimum wages or trade union negotiated minima. As can be seen from Fig. 15.1, such rigidity would result in an excess of active searchers over job vacancies ($Q_1 - Q_3$) at the prevailing wage of W_1.

In Fig. 15.1, the maintenance of real wages at the original equilibrium rate W_1 can be argued to result in 'classical unemployment' ($Q_2 - Q_3$), this being the difference between the quantity of employment at what would have been the new equilibrium (B) and the actual, lower level that is the result of wage rigidity.

We already see in this model the seeds of the arguments that unemployment is voluntary and that unemployment is the product of wage rigidity owing to the influence of the trade unions and/or statutory minimum wages above the market-clearing equilibrium and that deregulation of labour markets in Europe is a precondition for the reduction of unemployment.

The Keynesian view of unemployment

The essence of the Keynesian viewpoint implies a rejection of many of the assumptions underlying the classical model and was a response to the apparent inability of the model to explain the high and persistent levels of unemployment of the 1920s and 1930s. Keynes rejected the explanation that unemployment was the product of wages persisting at too high a level to enable market clearing and he also rejected the view that unemployment was voluntary. He argued that unemployment was primarily structural and the product of an inadequate aggregate demand for labour. The implication of this analysis was a role for governments in managing aggregate demand so as to reduce unemployment to more socially acceptable levels (given that there was always likely to be a need for a pool of unemployed labour to be available to take up vacancies as they emerged in response to the dynamic nature of product markets and structural change).

However, managing aggregate demand in the economy as a whole has an effect both upon equilibrium prices and upon employment levels. One would expect both employment and wages to rise in response to an increase in aggregate demand. Other prices are also likely to rise in response to these demand pressures and it is in this that the pressures for an upward spiral of both wages and prices emerge. The relationship between prices and unemployment can be perceived to be inverse.

For many years in the 1950s and 1960s when governments in Europe were adopting an essentially Keynesian approach, it was accepted that there was a trade-off between employment and inflation and in a sense the art of successful management of the economy was to achieve a socially optimal combination of the two via the management of aggregate demand. This relationship is depicted in Fig. 15.2 which shows the short-run Phillips curve. The figure shows an economy in which the natural rate of unemployment is 5 per cent and expected inflation is 8 per cent. If unemployment were to be less than 5 per cent, the expected rate of inflation would be higher than 8 per cent. If the rate of unemployment was greater than 5 per cent, the expected rate of inflation would be less than 8 per cent.

Towards the end of the 1970s the Keynesian model became discredited as it failed to produce the promised land of coincident low unemployment, controlled inflation and economic growth. Critics emphasised the inflationary role of trade unions and/or minimum wage legislation, which ensured that money wages never fell, allied to the difficulties of

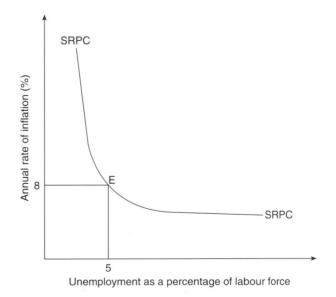

Fig. 15.2 The short-run Phillips curve

management and coordination, imperfections in the flow of information and communications and the difficulties of forecasting and coping with the respective time lags inherent in the process.

The neo-Classical/monetarist view of unemployment

This approach denounced Keynesianism and argued that steadily rising unemployment was the product of:

● inflation;

● excessive growth in the money supply;

● high wages and trade union power;

● generous unemployment benefits which reduced the incentive to work; and

● other supply-side problems typified by occupational and locational immobility and a mismatch between skills available and skills required.

The neo-Classical viewpoint constitutes a reassertion of the classical model with the exception that it seeks to take account of recognised imperfections in the market. The tendency for the market to perform a clearing function was restated but associated with equilibrium would be a *'natural rate of unemployment'*. In other words, there would be a tendency towards a market-clearing equilibrium but the imperfections in the market would ensure that this would not occur at a price at which there was full or no unemployment. At the market-clearing level of wages, there would be a pool of unemployment (the natural rate) comprising those in transition (in the past referred to as experiencing frictional unemployment) and those who choose not to work at the prevailing wage level. This natural rate would be high, if unemployment benefits (the replacement ratio) or trade union power were high.

This can be reasonably simply shown diagrammatically, and is depicted in Fig. 15.3. Here we have two supply curves shown: one (SL_2) represents the total supply of labour and the other (SL_1) represents the supply in terms of the labour actually prepared to accept jobs offered at the various prices/wage rates. Demand in this instance is defined to exclude vacancies and therefore represents existing employment. At price real wage W_1, the numbers willing to accept jobs equals existing employment and the market would be in a kind of equilibrium, but with the natural rate of unemployment measured as the difference between Q_2 and Q_1.

Clearly factors which lead to a shift of SL_1 to the left – such as an increase in unemployment benefits which facilitate voluntary unemployment, or an increasing mismatch of searching labour with vacancies – will lead to an increase in the natural rate. Solutions to unemployment in this context then are likely to include:

● improving mobility;

● improving the match between labour required and labour available;

● reducing wage rigidity and dispensing with any artificial wage floors; and

● making it less comfortable to be unemployed.

Pursuing Keynesian solutions of expanding aggregate demand so that the DL_1 curve shifts to the right in Fig. 15.3 would in this analysis tend to produce inflationary increases in wages and have little significant effect upon employment.

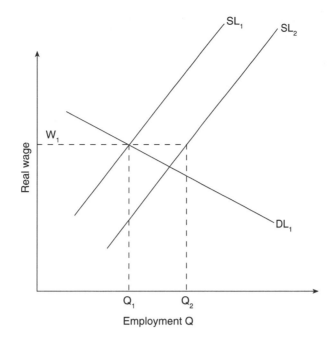

Fig. 15.3 The neo-Classical, natural rate of unemployment model

In recent years a variation on this basic neo-Classical, natural rate position has been developed which is referred to as the non-accelerating inflation rate of unemployment (NAIRU) model. The NAIRU is also sometimes referred to as the sustainable rate of unemployment. The essence of this position is that there is one level of unemployment that is consistent with stable inflation.

Probably the most common version of this explanation that is used is that associated with Layard and Nickell (1987). The model seeks to encompass within the general competitive model some of the imperfections of both product and labour markets and seeks to explain unemployment in terms of the behaviour of price setters and wage bargainers. The conclusion is that there is a non-inflationary equilibrium position at which the feasible real wage implied by the pricing behaviour of firms equates with the target wage of wage bargainers. The rate of unemployment at this equilibrium position is the NAIRU and is sustainable.

Shocks which influence the price-setting or wage-setting behaviour of the respective participants will influence the equilibrium position. In this model there is a negative relationship between real wages and employment, so that an increase in real wages will imply or require a reduction in the level of employment at equilibrium and hence a larger NAIRU.

The hysteresis view of unemployment

This viewpoint rejects the notion that there is any such thing as a natural rate of unemployment; the essence of the hysteresis model is that current unemployment causes/encourages further and future unemployment. The higher the level and the greater its persistence, the greater is the likelihood that unemployment will continue to rise; the greater the duration of unemployment, the higher will future levels be. Unemployment tends to breed future unemployment.

The hysteresis explanation produces a somewhat pessimistic prognosis for many of the European economies, in comparison to countries such as the USA and Japan, since both the level of unemployment and the average duration are relatively high, as is the proportion of the unemployed that has been continuously unemployed in excess of one year, thereby falling into the category of 'long-term'.

Keynesian methods and solutions which involve managing the level of unemployment through aggregate demand are ineffective in the context of this explanation. Central to the model is the assertion that when external shocks cause greater unemployment, labour markets respond and adjust to them only slowly, so that a shock that results in unemployment will have a relatively long-term effect. There are both partial and full hysteresis models with full hysteresis implying no adjustment back towards the earlier lower levels of unemployment, while partial models allow for slow adjustment. Central to these models is analysis of wage-setting behaviour: partial hysteresis implies that wage-setting behaviour does slowly respond to the new lower levels of employment, thereby facilitating an increase in the equilibrium level of employment at a lower wage, while full hysteresis implies that there is no such adjustment in wage-setting behaviour and the market remains in equilibrium at the post-shock level of unemployment.

Wage-setting behaviour is influenced, of course, from both the demand and supply sides and it takes place in an institutional context. On the supply side, trade unions and those still in work may resist a decline in real wages preferring unemployment of non-members and outsiders to a lowering of their own wages (the insiders). This is also likely to be influenced by institutional regulation of wages, particularly if this has a statutory basis, and also by the attractiveness/ relative comfort of unemployment which is influenced by the level of unemployment benefits. On the demand side, wage-setting behaviour may be influenced by the costs to employers of hiring and firing and other elements of employee protection and job security. Where these are high, the incentive for employers to increase employment and exert downward pressure upon wages may be lessened.

Insider–outsider membership models which demonstrate that insiders do not appear to take outsider interests into account in wage bargaining may not only explain why wages do not fall post shock; they may also explain why, if demand increases again, the response of the insiders is to seek to bargain up wages rather than employment levels. In such circumstances the unemployed (outsiders in this context) are hindered from competing with insiders for work. On one level, they cannot price themselves back into work because the insiders and institutional regulation will not let the wage rate fall. Allied to this is the additional disadvantage that the value of their skills may diminish with the length of their unemployment rendering them less productive and competitive.

If, as is agreed by many observers of labour markets in Europe (see later), those most prone to unemployment in developed economies are low skilled in the first instance, and, if the relevance and value of skills decline with unemployment duration, then the implications of these insider–outsider and duration models tend to complement and support the assertions of the partial hysteresis thesis and explain the high levels and persistence of unemployment in Europe.

The hysteresis model gives much less credence to the view that unemployment in Europe is largely voluntary, since the unemployed are in many respects unable to compete with those in employment. Once they become unemployed, they are arguably relatively passive participants in the labour market. Often low skilled at the commencement of their unemployment, the value of their labour declines even further with its duration. Their employment prospects depend very much upon the interests and behaviour of both employers and those currently in employment.

Many of the recent initiatives and prescriptions are consistent with this diagnosis in that they are concerned to raise the skills of the unemployed through training and through work experience and to provide employers with incentives to employ those currently unemployed.

In this section we have looked briefly at the major models, viewpoints and explanations of unemployment. All of the models have implications for the role of government and policy prescriptions and initiatives. Inevitably, these different positions are to some extent themselves in competition, each having their advocates and achieving transitory prominence over time.

There is still considerable scope for debate and disagreement between different protagonists and interests and this will become apparent in the following sections when we examine policy options and the initiatives undertaken within the EU in the context of the current debate and the many solutions proposed.

POLICY OPTIONS

Governments and inter-governmental organisations and institutions have available to them a range of policies and instruments that they can use to address issues, problems and to achieve particular objectives. Governmental and inter-governmental approaches and initiatives, in this case towards unemployment, will be influenced by their diagnosis of the problem and its causes and in part by their perspective and ideology. Political considerations also play a role, as do issues of national interest.

In this section, most of the more common options are introduced and brief explanations are offered regarding how they are perceived to influence the level and duration/persistence of unemployment.

It should be remembered that the willingness to intervene in the operation of the market and the perceived potential and value of such intervention are likely to be influenced by political ideology and belief.

The most obvious and in a sense extreme example of this phenomenon is the laissez-faire, classical, liberal individualist position which implies no role for government on the grounds that the market is the most efficient mechanism for allocating resources between different uses and thereby the organisation of production. Where there are imperfections in or hindrances to the free and efficient operation of the market, then government may be justified in intervention in order to cure the market of these impediments to its efficient operation and to create an environment that is as conducive as possible to the market. For example, if the view is that trade unions by their very existence and activity pose a threat to the free and efficient operation of the market – that is, they pose a threat to the achievement of a 'no unemployment' equilibrium at a market clearing price – it is legitimate for government to seek to constrain that existence and activity.

Governments with a different perspective, whether it be liberal collectivist, corporatist, socialist or Marxist, will have formed different impressions and judgements of the market, its efficiency and the desirability of its consequences. These will influence their diagnosis, preferred policy options and outcomes.

It is convenient to categorise the options into those essentially concerned with demand-side influences and management, supply-side factors and the institutions.

Demand management

The Keynesian analysis led to policies geared towards the management of aggregate demand so as to achieve economic expansion and thereby full employment. A range of mechanisms was available for use to stimulate demand, including fiscal and monetary instruments – for example, public expenditure, taxation, government borrowing, monetary conditions, interest rates and the exchange rate. With the increasing acceptance of the diagnosis that managing aggregate demand to achieve full employment was inflationary and therefore damaging to international competitiveness, the popularity of the Keynesian analysis and indeed the popularity of demand management has waned.

In recent years in Europe, demand management policies have been used to achieve the objective of price stability and, where necessary, deflation as opposed to the objectives of full employment and expansion. Interest rates and the control of the money supply, public expenditure and taxation have all been used to damp down demand on the assumption that this damping of demand would reduce inflationary pressures in the economy and beneficially influence a nation's international competitiveness. As a result, growth via exports would be achieved. In other words, the objective has become one of non-inflationary growth.

This overwhelming concern with controlling inflation has been at the root of much of the interest in the notion of establishing a non-inflationary model of labour markets and in particular the identification of a non-accelerating inflation rate of unemployment (NAIRU, *see* p. 332). Deflationary demand management policies have been blamed by many as significantly contributing to the increase in unemployment in Europe since the 1970s, although there is by no means unanimity on the scale or duration of the contribution.

Many countries within the EU are now confronted with a scenario in which the objectives of low inflation/price stability have been broadly achieved and, as pointed out in the introduction to this chapter, the 'big problem' is now unemployment. There has in this context been a resurgence of interest in using expansionary demand policies to try and stimulate employment. However, the currently popular labour market models, whether they be natural rate or hysteresis models – suggest still that expanding demand is predominantly inflationary and that any use of such a strategy should be both partial and targeted.

Examples of such 'approved' expansionary demand management interventions might be:

1 increased public expenditure on infrastructure schemes as was suggested in the Commission's White Paper (1993b);

2 other schemes directed at job creation in the public sector and geared towards the employment of the young or long-term unemployed, as in the creation of community work and welfare programmes; or

3 schemes to encourage job creation and/or the employment of the same target groups in the private sector – for example, as recently introduced in France, Belgium, and Ireland –

involving the subsidising of such employment either via direct payments or through devices such as a reduction of participating employers' non-wage labour costs in respect of additional employment of members of the target groups. On some occasions the effective subsidy has been linked to schemes involving the reduction of working time and partial early retirements (as in France) or linked to a minimum period of unemployment, such as the scheme in Ireland which specified a three-year minimum unemployment threshold.

Here we see adaptation of working time being used as a means of expanding employment, the assumption being that if the amount worked by individuals is reduced, this effectively creates employment opportunities for others. There is a difference between adapting working time for this reason and making working hours more flexible so as to meet the requirements of individual employees or the needs of the business.

Supply-side initiatives

Emphasis in the last two decades has been placed on neo-Classical and hysteresis explanations, implying a greater role for both supply-side and institutional initiatives. On the supply side, governments have a range of policies and interventions available by which they can seek to improve the match between labour demand and supply. In the main, the problems facing governments in Europe are not so much problems of quantity as those of quality, skill level and type. There are problems concerned with mobility – both skill/occupational and geographical – but it is the match between the skills or lack of them of the unemployed and those required in the expanding sectors and by those employers that are creating jobs and recruiting that seems to have generated the main activity.

Many of the initiatives taken have been directed at the longer term unemployed who tend to suffer a progressive skills erosion as the duration of their unemployment increases. In the main, the initiatives seek to provide training and/or re-training directly, or provide incentives to encourage employers and other bodies to provide the appropriate training, or they are directed at improving the information available and its communication to the interested parties – frequently under the aegis of the public employment services.

Many schemes have also been directed at the young unemployed – another group with particular problems in many countries. These initiatives are often concerned to provide the young unemployed with some form of vocational training, mixed with work experience. One of the more innovative of these schemes has been operating in Spain over the last ten years or so. The scheme is for 16 to 24 year olds and has a heritage focus, the aim being to provide training in skills such as marquetry, upholstery and gilding, as the participants work on renovating historic buildings. Many of the initiatives that are taken to improve the supply-side match and quality are commonly classified as *active labour market policies* (*see* later in this chapter).

Institutional initiatives

There is considerable consensus in Europe that labour market institutions need reform and much of this consensus is concerned to make the institutions less rigid and less limiting to job creation. Much of the debate in the EU over the last five years, which is examined in more detail in the next section, has been concerned with proposals for and issues of labour market/institutional reform. The arguments for such reform have much in common with debates about flexibility. However, while there may be consensus on the need for or value of reform, there is far less consensus about the detail – for example, the choice of institutions and parameters. Inevitably, these debates are influenced by social and political agendas, as well as by economic argument and understanding.

With the exception of the classical model, each of the models or explanations referred to and described earlier acknowledge institutional imperfections and rigidities in markets.

- The Keynesian analysis in particular highlights the downward inflexibility of money wages.

- The neo-Classical model points up the role of trade unions and minimum wage legislation as well as the role of unemployment benefit and other social security benefits as disincentives to employment.

- The hysteresis models identify the significance of insider resistance to downward pressures upon wages, preferring, if necessary, to bargain down employment for others, and the disincentive influence to employers of hiring and firing costs and legislative support for employment protection and job security.

Policy options then tend to fall into three main groups according to primary target.

1 Some policy options are directed at reducing the bargaining power of trade unions and other insider groups, and associated with this may be action to remove or diminish the impact of minimum wage rates and make wages more responsive to local as opposed to national labour market conditions. Examples of this may include making it more difficult for trade unions to take industrial action, encouraging local collective bargaining/wage determination and abolishing minimum wage legislation.

2 Some options comprise those that seek to make life for the unemployed less comfortable. Additional obstacles may be put in the way of claiming unemployment benefit; the value of the benefit may be reduced; the period of entitlement may be reduced; conditions may be applied to the receipt of benefit that ostensibly encourage job search; and ultimately receipt of benefit may be made discretionary.

3 Some options seek to provide incentives for employers to hire more labour. In the main, these initiatives include the provision of financial inducements which reduce the various components of non-wage labour costs and/or ease the constraints of a regulatory nature upon the freedom of employers to hire and fire and apply employment terms and conditions that increase the attractiveness of employment of labour as opposed to technology, or that encourage expansion.

This latter category might include:

- easing the regulations that protect employees against dismissal;
- making it cheaper to dismiss by reducing statutory redundancy or severance pay;
- amending restrictions upon hours of work and the use of fixed-term, temporary and part-time contracts;
- withdrawing rules that prevent or curtail the activities of private-sector recruitment agencies and consultants; and
- removing restrictions upon the employment of cheap labour, such as immigrants and children.

It should be apparent how easily proposals in this area can be confounded by opposition that has more to do with issues of equity and social and political considerations.

Passive and active labour market policies

It is quite common these days for the distinction to be drawn between active and passive labour market policies. Increasing amounts of research are being undertaken with a view to ascertaining which type is the more effective and more efficient.

In the main, policies falling into the *active* category are training and job creation schemes and policies directed at the provision or improvement of the public employment services. Whereas those falling into the *passive* category would include redundancy schemes and payments, early retirement schemes and payments not linked to health, and unemployment benefits.

The difference is in essence fairly simple in that the active schemes are those that are seeking to provide additional employment or protect existing employment or improve the matching or searching processes, whereas the passive schemes are directed more at facilitating unemployment and making it easier to bear and more comfortable for the recipient. In this respect some argue that passive policies actually encourage unemployment.

As the emphasis in the Union shifts in the direction of employment creation and improvement, a shift in the direction of active policies and initiatives and, where necessary, a shift away from passive policies would not be unexpected. Expenditure as a percentage of GDP on each category is shown in Fig. 4.10. The Commission in its *Employment in Europe* report for 1994 (European Commission, 1994c) commented that there had been a shift of expenditure in proportionate terms in the direction of active policies between 1985 and 1992 but that this camouflaged an increase in the active proportion between 1985 and 1990, when unemployment fell, followed by a reversal of that trend as unemployment increased again between 1990 and 1992. The authors of the report comment that in 1992 little more than 1 per cent of Community GDP was devoted to active measures aimed at getting the unemployed into work. Figure 4.10 also illustrates the variations in the pattern of expenditure on active and passive measures between the member states.

EU INITIATIVES

As noted in the introduction to this chapter, there have been concerns about the employment consequences of the creation of the Community and the abolition of trade barriers pretty much since the creation of the Community back in the 1950s. The significance of Article 123 of the founding Treaty and the subsequent creation of the European Social Fund (ESF) was also noted in the introduction and the initiatives undertaken under the aegis of the Fund and its objectives were outlined in Chapter 6. The objectives and activities associated with the ESF are primarily supply-side measures.

During the 1970s and 1980s, there were various demand shocks and contractions which adversely affected employment within Europe. It has already been noted that unemployment throughout the Union has been high and growing from one business cycle to the next with relatively little adjustment back towards pre-shock levels of employment.

The agreement to create the single market in 1986 led to predictions of initial job losses (Cecchini, 1988) but the long-term assumption was that the removal of barriers to the mobility of capital, labour and services would contribute to economic expansion and that there would be accompanying positive benefits for employment. By the time that the market was created in January 1993, unemployment in the Union was at near record levels and developments since have seen no substantial reduction.

Since 1993, there has been a great deal more open discussion regarding other forms of initiatives and policies. Many of these fall outside the arena of the ESF and supply-side initiatives and are more concerned with reform – usually of a deregulatory nature – of labour market institutions and in some instances the management of demand.

It is also clear that different perspectives and interests are involved among the member-state governments, the Commission and Social Partners and there has been considerable difficulty in achieving consensus. It must be remembered that legislative action at the level of the Union on many of the initiatives and policies that have been mooted as solutions either have no basis within the Treaty or require unanimity (*see* Chapter 8).

It should also be borne in mind that there are as yet no mechanisms for the determination and implementation of common fiscal and economic policy at the level of the Union. There is considerable resistance to proposals to develop such institutions and mechanisms. The UK government prior to 1997 was publicly at the forefront of the opposition to such developments, expressing concerns about sovereignty and national interest as well as concerns about the direction and efficacy of some of the specific proposals. The agreements at Amsterdam in 1997 (*see* Chapter 9) succeeded only in securing agreements on the need to coordinate national economic policies in the context of an agreed EU-wide framework, but the member states have not been willing to give up control over determining and implementing their own economic and fiscal policies.

The Maastricht proposals for a single currency and monetary union have been at the centre of many of these discussions. Concerns centre on the way in which membership of the single currency is likely to much more significantly limit an individual member state's autonomy to devise and pursue its own policies, particularly given the agreement on the Stability Pact at Amsterdam in 1997 and mechanisms for imposing penalties on those member states that infringe the rules of membership once the single currency is up and running. There is also a body of opinion that suggests that the criteria devised at Maastricht are essentially deflationary and therefore damaging to employment prospects. (*See* Exhibit 15.1 for a summary of the different viewpoints.)

It is considered that the concentration in the criteria upon price stability and strict control of government expenditure and borrowing will require member-state governments to pursue policies that rule out any expansion of demand through public-sector job-creating initiatives and supply-side measures that require government spending. It was estimated in a report to the European Parliament in July 1995 by its committee on employment, that between 1994 and 1999 some 1.5 million jobs will be lost as a result of such budgetary restrictions in pursuit of convergence. There is also evidence in some countries – for example, France, Belgium, Holland and Germany – that achievement of the criteria is promoting policies concerned to reduce social security, unemployment and other welfare benefits. Employment prospects may also be harmed through the implementation of tight monetary policy. There is certainly scope to argue that a single currency, as presently proposed, will lead to a Union in which high unemployment is effectively locked in.

It is unnecessary to examine all of the various EU-level contributions to the debate and initiatives and solutions proposed; the following concentrates upon the landmark contributions. Since Chapter 6 has outlined the initiatives taken via the ESF, we begin discussion

Exhibit 15.1

Structural reform is overdue

By Andrew Balls

Politicians have dangled European economic and monetary union before a sceptical public as a solution to Europe's unemployment which afflicts 23m people.

There are reasons to be hopeful that Emu will help to soothe Europe's unemployment ills, just as there are reasons to be more pessimistic. Overall however, the causes of high unemployment, and the structural reforms needed to remedy the plight of the jobless, are the same regardless of whether or not Emu takes place. The important question is whether Emu will help or hinder this process.

In 1997, according to the Organisation for Economic Co-operation and Development (OECD), 11.2 per cent of the EU labour force is unemployed with unemployment in Germany, France, Italy and Spain above the average.

European politicians have promoted Emu as a vital part of the fight against unemployment, increasing growth and employment levels. Much of the potential gains from the single market have been left unexploited owing to the residual exchange rate risk associated with trade within the EU. By removing the costs and uncertainties of trade, the single currency will complete the single market, allowing greater competition and arbitrage across national borders, more efficient resource allocation, higher growth and – in theory at least – lower unemployment for its members.

The European Central Bank (ECB) will provide anti-inflationary credibility where this is lacking. In countries with a history of high inflation, and high public debt, this will impose a greater external discipline on unions. Wage bargainers will no longer be able to demand excessive wages, safe in the knowledge that high inflation and devaluation will bear the pressure. The ECB's anti-inflationary credibility could help to reduce unemployment in Italy, Portugal and Spain.

However, in the short term – particularly in the event of a broad Emu involving countries with poor inflation records – the ECB is likely to keep interest rates above the level necessary to ensure price stability. By demonstrating its anti-inflationary resolve, the ECB will thus reduce economic activity and increase unemployment.

Moreover, with Emu involving more than just the core, the ECB is unlikely to be able to design monetary policy to suit the needs of all member countries in the event of localised slow-downs. This could augment Europe's regional imbalances, resulting in unemployment black spots.

The Maastricht tests concentrate on financial criteria with little attention paid to real convergence in growth rates, productivity growth and unemployment levels. A reasonable amount of real convergence has been achieved between Germany, France, Austria and the Benelux countries, but less so for others.

Politicians may not be right in promoting Emu as a weapon against unemployment

---

Emu removes interest rates and the exchange rate as policy tools for national governments. With floating exchange rates, slower productivity growth in one country leads to an exchange rate depreciation. With fixed exchange rates, prices and wages must bear the burden of adjustment in the event of asymmetric shocks, which affect some countries more than others. Deflation must take the place of devaluation. Fiscal policy could be used to cushion adjustment. However, the stability pact, if strictly enforced, will curtail room for fiscal manoeuvre.

When growth rates and business cycles diverge the labour market takes the strain. This may work smoothly in the US, where a high degree of labour flexibility and mobility, and fiscal transfers through the federal tax system speed adjustment. However, in sclerotic European labour markets, immobility, inflexibility, and downward rigidity could lead to the emergence of higher unemployment in countries affected by shocks, and even greater regional imbalances.

Europe's unemployment malaise goes beyond cyclical unemployment. An upturn in the business cycle, higher growth rates owing to the completion of the single market, or, in the long term, lower interest rates under a proven ECB, will not be enough to overcome structural unemployment. Rather than higher employment levels, higher growth is likely to mean higher wages.

High minimum wages, high taxes and generous social security and unemployment insurances funded by levies on workers increase the price of labour and non-wage labour costs. Job protection legislation to protect those in work makes it more costly to create new jobs. In addition, with greater security for those in work, the threat of redundancy fails to keep a check on wage growth.

Politicians, forced to devote their energies to tightening their macroeconomic belts at a difficult point in the cycle, have made little progress in microeconomic reform. With Emu under way, policy makers should begin to turn their attention to long overdue structural reform.

German policy makers seem to be aware of the need for greater labour market flexibility, even if little progress has been made; French policy makers seem to be less aware of this.

Disagreement between the two main countries on the fundamentals of economic policy, could undermine Emu. The stability pact, and fines if enforced, could lead to further recriminations between members. And as Emu has become entangled with budget deficit reduction to hit an arbitrary target, so the ECB risks becoming associated with deflation and unemployment, leading to a public backlash, which could undermine its political legitimacy.

The result could be instability within the EU, and pressure to strengthen the social chapter and harmonise labour regulation. Emu should be a catalyst for reform. It could lead to the further entrenchment of eurosclerosis.

Source: Financial Times, 19 September 1997.

339

of recent debates and developments with the White Paper on Growth, Competitiveness and Employment 1993.

The White Paper on Growth, Competitiveness and Employment 1993

This document (European Commission, 1993b), which is sometimes also known as the Delors Report after the President of the European Commission at the time, was produced towards the end of 1993 and discussed and to a large extent endorsed by the European Council at its meeting in Brussels in December 1993. This White Paper does represent a watershed in the Community's approach to and treatment of the issue of unemployment. The report contains a diagnosis of the European problem, identification of causes and types, and proposals for resolving some of the difficulties identified along with the establishment of a framework to guide future discussion and policy. This document did indeed spark off a substantial debate which is ongoing. It succeeded in placing the issue of unemployment firmly at the centre of the EU agenda for the remainder of the 1990s, and it also marked a substantial shift of emphasis and approach by the Commission and the Union. Adnett (1996, p. 243) argued that the White Paper:

> . . . shifted the focus of EC policy from reducing unemployment to increasing employment. It also represented a change towards supply-side policies, arguing the need for reform of impediments to job creation.

In subsequent years, however, the Commission still found itself as the mainstay of the view that economic and social policy must be coordinated and economic objectives should not disregard social cohesion and the traditions of welfare capitalism. Intriguingly, the Commission has arguably found itself pursuing contrary policies in respect of monetary union and the sanctity of the Maastricht criteria.

In the White Paper, the Commission argued that the principal types of unemployment within the Union were *cyclical*, *structural* and *technological*. However, it also acknowledged that macroeconomic policies, primarily concerned to combat and control inflation, had done little to stimulate employment and that the real wages paid in the Union were potentially a hindrance to international competitiveness. This was in a sense compounded by both the additional burden of non-wage labour costs, which was encouraging some employers to relocate outside the Union, and by regulation and employment protection which meant that those in employment were arguably being protected at the expense of job creation.

The Commission's analysis of the structural problems facing the Union were:

1 *insufficient coordination of economic policy in and between the member states*;

2 *the failure to achieve a sufficiently employment-intensive pattern of growth*, which results in underemployment (people not even bothering to actively search because they know there are no jobs) as well as unemployment;

3 *insufficient flexibility of labour markets* which has tended to slow down the adjustment necessary to maintain international competitiveness;

4 *inadequate investment in training and education of the labour force* which again hampers long-term competitiveness.

The Commission proposed an essentially two-pronged strategy to overcome these structural barriers to employment:

● the coordination of national economic policies so that faster growth can be achieved; and

● a more employment-intensive pattern of production so that the growth is translated into jobs.

The Commission acknowledged the need for a much greater rate of job creation. It was suggested in the White Paper that 5 million jobs needed to be created by the end of the decade in order to prevent unemployment rising; in order to halve the current rate, it would be necessary to create a further 10 million in the same time period.

From the moment the Commission presented this analysis and strategic response, it was clear that there would be opposition from among those who perceived proposals for the greater coordination of economic policy as a threat to national sovereignty, in much the same way as they viewed monetary union as a threat. Many argue that policy for employment and growth should remain within the competence of national governments.

In addition to the White Paper prompting another round in the above debate, it also gave further impetus to the debate between those who argue that unemployment is a major social and economic problem requiring government intervention and the other viewpoint, associated particularly with the neo-Classical position, that far from such intervention being necessary, it is positively counter-productive. This latter view held that with some obstacles removed and left alone, the market would provide the mechanism whereby unemployment could be eliminated.

The White Paper also contained suggestions as to how the Union should seek to achieve the increase in employment/ reduction in unemployment. These were presented as broad guidelines for discussion at the Council meeting and were not proposed as specific policy proposals. These suggestions included:

● significant additional investment in new technologies, information highways, and in pan-European transport, energy and environmental infrastructure – the only demand-side policies advocated;

● lifelong learning and advanced vocational training;

● enhancement of labour market flexibility through retraining and the use of more flexible working hours, easing the path for more part-time working and job sharing;

● pricing people back into work via reducing unemployment benefits but not at the expense of minimum income guarantees;

● reducing the burden of non-wage labour costs by reducing social security contributions, particularly on low-skilled labour;

● an increase in spending on active labour market measures, particularly on the expansion of public employment services for job seekers.

With regard to the additional investment, the role of the European Investment Bank (EIB) (*see* Chapter 8) was to be enhanced with additional emphasis and resources to be allocated to lending and guaranteeing loans to support job creation in small and medium-sized companies and through trans-European networks (TENs).

The Commission's continuing commitment to the preservation of social protection is apparent in these proposals and the point is made in the White Paper that wage cutting and pruning welfare payments will only depress demand even further; also apparent is an acknowledgement of the argument that European labour markets are too rigid. The proposals can be seen as an attempt to tread a difficult line between the opposing viewpoints.

The meeting of the Council at which the White Paper was presented generally endorsed the analysis and strategy outlined and identified seven key areas for particular attention by member states:

- improving flexibility within enterprises and within the labour market;
- reorganisation of work at enterprise level;
- targeted reductions in indirect costs of labour, especially statutory contributions on low-skill labour;
- better use of public funds for combating unemployment;
- developing new areas of work, new and developing industries and sectors;
- specific measures to help young people without appropriate training and skills;
- improvements in education and training, especially continuous training and development.

It is of note that the Council found it much easier to agree measures to be undertaken at member-state level than to agree action at the level of the Union.

At the time of the White Paper going to the Council meeting, UNICE – the EU-level employers organisation (*see* Chapter 8) – produced an alternative document called *Making Europe More Competitive* (UNICE, 1994) in which it put forward its solutions to the problem. It is clear from the document that the employers see the issues very much from a neo-Classical perspective, with the solutions requiring a significant measure of deregulation and an increasing reliance upon the market and employer freedom. UNICE specifically proposed:

- a reduction in high non-wage labour costs, especially employers' social security contributions on low and unskilled labour;
- restraint on real wage increases, keeping them below the rate of increase in productivity;
- a widening of wage differentials – via the cutting of minimum wage rates and marginal tax rates – providing thereby an incentive to acquire skills and an incentive to work;
- relaxation of rules on hiring and firing and working hours;
- lower unemployment benefits and more limited access to social security systems.

While the employers' agenda naturally represents their perceived interests the Commission document can be seen to be a more balanced set of proposals which are not so partially directed to the interests of business and which seek to balance the interests of business with those of social justice and equity.

As noted earlier, the White Paper signified a much greater degree of formal interest and debate at the level of the Union in the problem of unemployment and this was carried forward to subsequent meetings of the Council. Indeed the 'European' problem has also become a subject of considerable concern in wider inter-governmental forums, perhaps the most significant being the Group of Seven industrialised nations (G7) and the Organisation for Economic Cooperation and Development (OECD).

At meetings in the first half of 1994, the G7 countries discussed unemployment and came to some general agreements as to cause, but again agreement upon appropriate remedies was more difficult. There was a general agreement that there had been a permanent decline in the demand for unskilled labour and that, while it was important to try and increase this demand, it was also important that increased attention be given to lifelong training and increasing the quality of the labour supply. There was also general agreement on the need to reduce barriers to employment and flexibility in the labour market. In a sense what was proposed implied a combination of European-style investment in education and training with US-style labour market flexibility, mobility and dynamism – all encompassed by macroeconomic policies encouraging growth.

The OECD Jobs Study of June 1994

Although not an EU initiative, this report has important implications for labour markets within the EU.

In this report, the OECD puts forward an analysis that is critical of both European and American models of job creation characterising the American model as one that creates a large number of low-skill, low-productivity jobs and the European model as one that involves weak employment growth and high productivity. The authors of the report express the view that Europe has the more difficult task, due to the lack of encouragement given to high technology industries and entrepreneurial activities and because of the rigidity of its labour markets and social security systems. In the report, they suggest a fairly radical strategy for the reform of European labour markets and social security systems and traditions. It must be remembered that the OECD is a fairly orthodox body in terms of perspective and its analysis paid little attention to social and political agendas. It is impossible for all of the detailed suggestions made to be reproduced here, but the following constitutes a summary of the measures proposed:

- to promote an entrepreneurial climate;
- to increase flexibility in working time, wage and labour costs and, in particular, to make it easier for employers to employ flexibly, utilising part-time and fixed-term contracts so that they can respond more quickly to fluctuations in demand and can reduce labour costs;
- to reform employment protection so that it is easier for the employers to dismiss on economic grounds;
- to expand and improve active labour market policies, particularly those concerned with improving job search, and to tailor training programmes for the unemployed more to the requirements of the economy;
- to improve skills among the workforce, to smooth the transition from school to work and to enhance incentives for continuous development;
- to reform unemployment and other associated benefits, ensuring in particular that these benefits are not available indefinitely.

This last suggestion rests on the argument that indefinite unemployment benefit both reduces the incentive to actively search for work and, as noted earlier, contributes to the duration and persistence of unemployment and progressive unemployability. The assumption presumably is that without such support the unemployed would be forced to actively search for work at market-clearing rates, even if this involves rates of pay below the levels of unemployment benefit.

At about the same time as the publication of this study, the French and German governments produced a joint paper in which some of these and earlier suggestions were echoed but with crucial differences. The Franco–German paper recommended the reduction of labour market regulation, the encouragement of new enterprise and technologies, establishing a link between pay and productivity and the introduction of more flexible working. However, there was certainly no support in this document for the kind of far-reaching reform of employment protection and welfare systems that are central to the OECD's prescription for future prosperity and job creation.

White Paper on Social Policy 1994

In subsequent months and in the period leading up to the summit meeting in Essen in December 1994 the Commission:

● published its *White Paper on Social Policy* in July 1994;

● published its annual report on *Employment in Europe* in September 1994; and

● announced the launch of an EU-wide employment information network to be known as *EURES* in November 1994 (*see* Chapter 10).

The White Paper (European Commission, 1994c) contained a number of proposals for action in the period 1995 to 1999:

● the seeking of closer cooperation between the employment authorities in the member states;

● the development of an action plan to combat unemployment;

● the extension of apprenticeship schemes; and

● the provision of incentives for employers and individuals to invest in training and education.

In addition, the Paper contained a section concerned with encouraging high labour standards within a competitive Europe; this involved proposals for Directives on European Works Councils, the extension of employment rights for part-time and temporary workers, the provision of rights to parental leave and proposals relating to the enforcement of host-country national employment laws and standards for posted workers.

The juxtaposition of these various proposals might strike some observers as a prime illustration of the contradictions within the Commission's position since the latter proposals are symptomatic of the regulation and inflexibility that arguably mitigate against the EU being competitive, acting as disincentives to employers recruiting even part-time and temporary labour, as well as increasing the costs of employment. (The agreement between the Social Partners on this issue eventually excluded most temporary and casual workers due in part to the difficulty of definition.) The Commission viewpoint was that competitiveness should not be attained at the expense of employees and social justice and that to do so would lead to an inevitable downward spiral in wages and living standards, quality and productivity.

The *Employment in Europe* report (European Commission, 1994a) rejected the suggestions that solutions to unemployment were to be found in enhanced labour flexibility, although it did appear to lend credence to the view that the high costs of employers' social contributions were a factor mitigating against employment, particularly when in many member states the proportionate costs were greater for low and unskilled labour. It illustrated this by pointing out that in Belgium, Ireland and Germany these costs constituted in excess of 60 per cent of the overall cost to employers of an unskilled worker.

The Essen Meeting of the European Council, December 1994

Unemployment was at the top of the agenda once again at this meeting and the outcome of the meeting was agreement on an action plan, which constituted a set of non-legislative proposals seeking to shift the emphasis away from employment protection towards creating greater opportunities for the unemployed. The action plan agreed, but with no legislative support, was concerned to:

- reduce non-wage labour costs;
- increase the employment intensity of growth through a more flexible organisation of work and a wage policy encouraging investment in job creation by keeping wage rises below the increase in the rate of productivity;
- improve employment opportunities through greater investment in vocational training and the acquisition of vocational qualifications, with lifelong learning being encouraged as a means by which employees are able to adapt to technological change;
- target assistance upon the young and the long-term unemployed;
- change social security and, in particular, income support schemes to encourage reemployment and move in the direction of a more active labour market approach.

Once again these were initiatives and policies to be implemented at a national level and it was not long before interested parties were expressing concern at the relative lack of positive action.

As early as May 1995, the Commissioner for Social Affairs was complaining about the slow progress being made towards the target of creating between 15 and 18 million jobs by the end of the century. The *White Paper on Growth, Competitiveness and Employment* at the end of 1993 had indicated that this was the scale of job creation necessary to reduce the EU rate of unemployment by half.

Another outcome of this summit meeting had been agreement on a much greater willingness to consult and pool information at government level on employment issues; this was followed in March 1995 with agreement on a new system of surveillance of member-state employment policies.

The EIB was also invited to increase its lending to trans-European networks (TENs).

The 1994 Commission report on employment in Europe (European Commission, 1994b) estimated that some 6 million jobs had been lost in the EU in the period between 1991 and 1994, with the countries most affected being Italy, the UK and Spain.

European Strategy for Employment 1995

By October 1995, the Commission was presenting a very much more optimistic picture of job and employment prospects within the Union. In its *European Strategy for Employment* document (European Commission, 1995b) the view was expressed that prospects for investment-led growth were good – the best for 20 years – and that structural reforms of labour markets were beginning to make a contribution to necessary flexibility. The document projected that a growth rate of 3 to 3.5 per cent a year would yield a decline in unemployment from the then current 10.6 per cent to 7.5 per cent by the year 2000 and that could be reduced further, to 5 per cent, if the structural measures agreed as an action plan at the meeting in Essen were implemented.

In this document the Commission also argued the alternative view of the impact of the pursuit of monetary union upon jobs and warned that failure to pursue policies consistent with the achievement of the criteria on budget deficits, government debt and inflation would harm prospects for growth and thereby employment.

In this warning we can see the Commission approach as constituting a mix of tight monetary policy and control of public expenditure and inflation, allied to policies which improve labour market flexibility, lower labour costs, and enhance employers' willingness to employ an improved quality, more mobile labour force. The former create conditions in which economies achieve and retain international competitiveness, investment-led growth is encouraged and the growth is more employment intensive than has been the case in Europe since the 1970s. Underpinning these policies is a system of social protection and equity which ensures that the weakest are not exploited in the search for growth and job creation and which are a force against social unrest and disruption.

The Commission's assessment of the situation within the Union and the prospects for growth and employment were criticised by others as being overly optimistic.

Early in 1996, a head of steam built up behind proposals from a number of sources for a restatement of the Union's commitment to job creation, reducing unemployment and the maintenance of social protection. This was at least in part sponsored by increasing concerns that the Union-wide employment statistics were not improving, although there were varying trends between member states, and a fear that pursuit of the monetary union convergence criteria in a continuing climate of high unemployment was and would continue to be a threat to employment growth. EU unemployment at the end of 1995 was still at 10.9 per cent (reaching a peak of 11 per cent in February 1996) and GDP growth in the third quarter of 1995 was only at an annual rate of 2.15 per cent rather than the 3 to 3.5 per cent per annum upon which the Commission had based its projections for employment growth. By the beginning of 1996, the Commission was revising downwards its projections for growth in 1996 to only 2 per cent.

Confidence Pact for Employment

The President of the Commission sought to address some of these concerns in a speech to the European Parliament at the end of January 1996 in which he argued strongly for coordination and social partnership at the level of the Union. He argued that employers associations and trade unions (the Social Partners) should be fully involved in the coordination of member-state policies to achieve on a Union-wide basis the objectives of stimulating growth, investment and employment. These objectives were to be achieved by three main initiatives:

- greater efforts to reduce non-wage labour costs, thereby encouraging employers to take on more people;

- additional infrastructure projects of a trans-European nature funded by savings from reform of the common agricultural policy;

- inclusion of the issue of employment on the agenda of the forthcoming Intergovernmental Conference, so that the monetary pillar (EMU) is joined by an employment pillar.

The Scandinavian states and the trade unions had been promoting this final inclusion and while details were not specific, presumably this proposal was incorporated by the Commission as a trade-off in return for the retention of the Maastricht convergence criteria – the alternative perhaps being a determined attempt by these parties to use the IGC to rewrite or even abandon the convergence criteria on the grounds that they were likely to lock in high unemployment.

The President of the Union proposed that the Social Partners should meet to discuss these proposals further and at this point the proposals were being referred to in terms of a 'Confidence Pact for Employment'.

The first of these meetings took place at the end of April 1996 but achieved little as it was characterised by disagreements between the employers' and employees' representatives on the following issues:

1 *High labour costs and the effect of reduced labour costs upon employment.* On the one hand, the employers firmly argued that the burden of high non-wage labour costs was particularly detrimental to job creation while, on the other, the labour representatives disputed the significance of these costs in terms of employment levels and argued, somewhat cynically, that many employers would use any reduction in such costs to stimulate returns to investors rather than for employment-generating investment.

2 *The role of the EU in promoting job creation and fighting unemployment.* This was significant, given that the employers organisation representatives tended to emphasise action within member states.

3 *Regulating atypical work.* This included the issue of employment rights for such groups.

4 *The contribution that reducing working time could make to job creation.* This is a debate that has been a feature of discussions between employers and trade unions for a number of years, particularly in Germany. (For a comparison and evaluation of the schemes operating in France, Germany, Italy and Spain, *see* Mosley and Krupp (1996).)

Nevertheless, despite these differences of perspective, the Commission still seemed to anticipate that the Social Partners could reach agreement on practical actions to promote job creation.

The opening of the Intergovernmental Conference 1996

When the IGC opened in March 1996 employment was one of the issues on the agenda with early discussions agreeing that, while it was primarily a national issue, there was scope for benefit to be derived from EU-level coordination and monitoring. A majority of the member states supported the suggestion that there should be a chapter on employment in the final Treaty agreement. As noted elsewhere (*see* Chapter 9), agreement was achieved at Amsterdam on the inclusion of a Title on Employment in the Treaty.

As the IGC was opening, another G7 summit on employment took place in April 1996.

At this meeting, the President of the Commission reiterated the need for Europe to create more jobs and referred to this as the main objective of the 'Pact'. However, the summit achieved little and continued to demonstrate the conflicts between those with a preference for the market model and those preferring a greater role for government and social protection as constraints upon the market and in creating the conditions for social cohesion. This conflict was also apparent in the discussions concerning the USA's desire to insist on minimum labour standards as a condition of free trade in the context of the General Agreement on Trade and Tariffs (GATT) and subsequent World Trade discussions.

The President of the Commission presented his proposals for a tripartite 'Confidence Pact', entitled *Action for Employment in Europe* to the Florence Summit in June 1996. By this time the emphasis was upon tripartite commitment and mobilising the local actors (decentralised within member states at both local and national level) to work together to create jobs, and to enhance the employability of young people, through practical measures to promote education and training as the key to employment. Member states were asked to select regions or cities where work could begin on the creation of such pacts and to report back to the Dublin Summit in December 1996.

Also in June 1996, the EU's Competitiveness Advisory Group published a report echoing many of the ideas of the President of the Commission. They called for reform of the European social model, but not at the expense of social protection and insisted upon the need to press on with completion of the single market and the single currency as part of the context within which the Union could grow. They also emphasised wage restraint and the elimination of employers' social security contributions for the lowest paid. (*Source: Financial Times*, 12 June 1996).

In May 1996, the free-market OECD published the results of its Jobs Study concluding in general terms that structural causes are overwhelmingly important in explaining the phenomenon of unemployment in the industrialised world – in particular industrial relations practices and benefit structures. The authors of the study played down the role of cyclical influences and therefore argued that demand management of a traditional Keynesian nature can have very little effect. They suggested that the measures necessary to resolve the problem should involve steps to enhance employers' freedom in wage setting and reduce the disincentive effect of overgenerous benefit systems. Proposals included the following:

- to increase work pattern flexibility, encouraging temporary and short-term working;
- to remove restrictions on business ingenuity and enterprise;
- to make wage setting less restricted and increase the flexibility of wages and labour costs;
- to reform social security systems so as to encourage employment;
- to reinforce active labour market policies;
- to improve education and training in the context of lifelong learning;
- to eliminate the poverty trap by reducing unemployment benefits, thereby enhancing the incentive to work;
- to increase and encourage competition and growth;
- to encourage the creation and spread of greater technical knowledge and ability.

Employment in Europe 1996

The Commission report on employment in Europe for 1995, published towards the end of 1996, identified trends in European labour markets and propounded the strategies that would have to be followed if the Union was to combat the problem of unemployment and develop a labour force appropriate for the future.

The main labour force trends were summarised in Chapter 4; here we concentrate upon the policies and strategies that the Commission report urges member-state governments and the Union to follow.

In general terms, the objective was to encourage employment-friendly growth and the report asserted that traditional demand management through public deficits had not been effective in achieving sustainable growth performance or solutions to the structural problems. The Commission therefore recommended continuation of stability-oriented macroeconomic policies. The Commission asserted that employment-friendly growth should be achieved from a basis of offensive demand-enhancing policies that together constitute a four-pronged investment-led attack, comprising investment in:

- physical productive capacity;
- human resources;
- an entrepreneurial environment; and
- knowledge and skills.

Additionally, structural rigidities had to be addressed so as to enable the various markets to function efficiently.

The Commission report also stressed that the reforms:

> . . . respect the principles of solidarity and social justice. Combining efficiency, adaptability and security must be considered as the strength of the European way . . .

It became clear in this report that a different definition or concept of security was being developed. When the Commission talked of reform and achieving flexibility with social justice and security, it was not security in present job that was intended; it was security in terms of current and future *employability* that was at issue. It was in this context that the provision of training opportunities for those in work, as well as those out of work, could be seen to be an important element of the overall strategy. It was also suggested that the problems of the young and long-term unemployed groups could be substantially removed if they were provided with a combination of training and work experience, but it had to be appropriate to the future requirements of the labour market.

The report acknowledged that excessive non-wage labour costs had created distortions against the low skilled and, while the policy might encompass efforts to counter this, it should not be assumed that there was much scope for addressing the issue of unemployment through this mechanism. Substantial wage dispersion at that lower end of the market would be at a cost in terms of social protection and justice and in terms of fiscal implications that would render it and the maintenance of the European social model untenable.

This report confirmed that in terms of work organisation, working time and the regulatory framework the labour markets in the Union had become and are becoming more flexible, a view also expressed in Exhibit 15.2. However, the employment potential of this enhanced flexibility does not appear to have been realised. In part, this is the consequence of firms applying the new flexibilities at the margin of their workforce, through expanding the use of out-sourcing, temporary contracts and atypical work arrangements. The Commission made the point that barriers between insiders and outsiders and internal and external labour markets needed to be broken down if the full potential of the new flexibilities were to be attained.

Considerable importance was placed upon education and training in the report and it was pointed out that the training had to be targeted. The report asserted that the skill level of the workforce was a crucial element in the potential development of future jobs. There was an urgent need to upskill the workforce in the face of new technological demands and this required what the Commission referred to as a 'quantum leap' in investment in education and training. Combined with rights to lifelong learning, this investment was to form part of new active supply-side policies to raise the quality of the labour force. The initiatives were to be targeted to prepare the young for the world of work and to both prevent and combat unemployment, particularly long-term unemployment where there was a greater propensity for people to have low levels of skill and skills that were outdated. As the report stated (European Commission, 1996, p. 8):

> More emphasis must be given to training for the unemployed to combat the process of deskilling and to give them better access to jobs.

Appropriate work experience was also perceived as a crucial element of a coherent programme to assist the young and the unemployed.

> Young people . . . should concentrate on early, targeted measures of linked work experience and training.

The report gave the public employment services an important role in the achievement of these policies.

There was an obvious appreciation on the part of those in the Commission that effective action to combat unemployment in the Union required the agreement and cooperation of all member states. Reference was made to the Essen summit, subsequent to which, it was claimed, the member states were committed to a European employment strategy based on:

> interrelated measures to enhance employment creating growth, social solidarity, equal treatment and special efforts to promote access to jobs for the most vulnerable groups on the labour market.

The Commission was of the view that the initiatives recommended were consistent with this commitment.

Amsterdam 1997 – The Resolution of the European Council on Growth and Employment and the Title on Employment

In the summer of 1997 the heads of government met in Amsterdam and agreed both a resolution on growth and employment and also a new Title on Employment to be included in the EC Treaty. The content of both the Resolution and the Title are outlined in Chapter 9.

At first sight, it is difficult to envisage the Resolution and the Title making any significant short- to medium-term contribution to reducing the level of unemployment within the Union. Promoting a high level of employment is now to be written into the Treaty and the Resolution and Title do clarify the need for some form of coordination of policies within the Union. In reinforcing the autonomy of the member states, however, the possibility obviously remains for the member states to pursue different objectives and/or to use

Exhibit 15.2

The debunking of a caricature

Continental European workers are more flexible than is often supposed, says **Robert Taylor**

There is a view widely held – certainly in the UK and the US – that unemployment in continental Europe countries is largely a function of overly regulated labour markets.

Enthusiasts of the UK's supposedly more deregulated model claim its flexibility has been much more successful in creating jobs than the more structured and legalistic employment practices of its European competitors. Such practices are seen as a severe obstacle to employment growth and an important reason why these countries suffer from much higher unemployment than the UK.

But is this an accurate portrayal? Papers prepared for a conference in Ottawa last week suggest the labour markets of some continental European countries such as Holland, Sweden, Denmark and Finland enjoy a much larger degree of employment flexibility than is often supposed. The conference was staged by the Organisation for Economic Co-operation and Development and the Canadian government to discuss ways to change workplace strategies.

Surprisingly, Germany – often seen as one of Europe's least flexible labour markets – is in fact much more flexible than the popular image would suggest. An impressive study carried out by the Institute for Employment Research in Nuremberg* has shown just how wide a use of flexible employees there is in Germany.

It found so-called 'peripheral' staff (defined as those working on fixed-term contracts, staff on temporary contracts or sub-contract workers) accounted on average for 9 per cent of an enterprise's workforce – and that proportion appears to be increasing.

The study says that business policies and staff planning were found to take account of strategies to increase flexibility. It estimates 3.5m staff are working only a few hours a week.

The report also found a growing use of part-time employment across western Germany in as many as three-quarters of companies that employ over 200 workers. It has become 'a normal phenomenon rather than the atypical employment it used to be', says the report.

Companies were also found to be using a wide range of working-time patterns. As many as 53 per cent of German employees were working overtime, while just over a third stagger their working hours and 35 per cent work at weekends. It is far from the picture widely held in the UK and the US that German employees are fixated by a five-day, 35-hour working week.

The German study also found considerable flexibility in the way work is organised, with a wide use of new workplace strategies such as team-working, just-in-time production and delegation of decision-making to workers. These methods are evident in 57 per cent of companies employing between 50 and 499 workers and 81 per cent of larger companies. Even 21 per cent of small employers in the survey said they used such new methods.

Nor does the German evidence suggest companies are hindered – by either over-rigid law or cumbersome bureaucracy – from implementing redundancy plans, recruiting staff or reshaping existing work practices. Between 1982 and 1994 in western Germany, over 16m additional jobs were created with 6.3 per cent of them in the production sector. Some 15.2m jobs were lost. Annual employment turnover is running at about 11 per cent and rising in spite of the recession.

Part-time employment in western Germany accounts for 28 per cent of all people in jobs last year. The number of German workers on flexible hours rose to 83 per cent in 1995 from 77 per cent in 1993. Such figures suggest the German regulated labour market is a good deal more flexible in practice than its Anglo-American critics realise.

Further evidence of the flexibility of mainland Europe can be gleaned from the recently published annual employment report by the European Commission. This found employers across the European Union (except in Portugal) were recruiting more part-time than full-time workers. The increase in part-time employment was particularly noticeable not just in the UK but also in France, the Irish Republic and Finland.

The highest proportion of part-time workers is in the Netherlands where over 9 per cent of prime working-age men are now employed part-time. The report also found the increase in the use of temporary employment had been 'common to most member states'.

A study published last week by the UK's National Institute of Economic and Social Research also suggests that recruitment strategies aimed at increasing the proportion of non-standard or atypical workers in the labour force are increasing across Europe.

It found the share of part-time employment in the total employment growth rate rose by 0.4 per cent in the UK during the early 1990s compared with 1 per cent in France, 0.7 per cent in Germany and 0.6 per cent in Italy.

At the same time temporary employment has risen sharply in recent years in Germany and France where it now accounts for over 10 per cent of all jobs compared with the much lower figure of 6.3 per cent in the UK.

As Mr Padraig Flynn, the EU's social affairs commissioner, recently pointed out, the overriding objective of all European countries is to create 'a highly skilled, flexible workforce' for the next century and this involves 'equipping and deploying correctly the productive potential of the whole workforce'.

Crude point-scoring about which European country enjoys the most flexible approach to job recruitment should not divert attention from the similarity of employment trends. Each country may have varied public policy approaches to the labour market but they share much more in common than most are willing to admit.

Patterns of enterprise flexibility in Germany, obtainable in English translation from the Institute for Employment Research, Federal Employment Institute (Bundesanstalt für Arbeit) Regensburgerstr. 104, 90327 Nuremberg.

Source: Financial Times, 11 December 1996.

specific mechanisms that may not fit with the policies of the Union as a whole, although membership of EMU will affect the ability of member states to pursue their own and independent economic policies.

The Council will be able to make recommendations to individual member states in the light of the policies being pursued and their consistency with EU policy and that of the other member states, but ultimately there is no provision for sanctions to be taken. As has been amply illustrated throughout this and other chapters, there is plenty of scope for different interpretations of situations and their causes and the appropriate remedies.

There would seem to be some provision within the Title for financial support for the implementation of information gathering and exchange, comparative analysis and innovation through pilot projects, but the member states were not prepared to cede any authority to the Commission or the Council that might have enabled initiatives to be taken that resulted in any further harmonisation of member-state laws and regulations.

There is also doubt regarding the extent to which the requirement – that the objective of a high level of employment (unspecified) should be taken into consideration in the formulation and implementation of EU-wide policies and activities – will have an impact. In some respects, it seems akin to the process of mainstreaming (*see* Chapter 11), but the real crunch will no doubt come when this objective conflicts with others. An example of such potential is in the apparent dichotomy between the objective of a stable macroeconomy and the convergence criteria for achievement of a single currency and this objective of high levels of employment. It is impossible in the current climate to conceive that priority would be given to high employment if it posed a threat to the achievement of monetary and economic convergence.

There is a clear temptation to see both the Resolution and the Title as expressions of good intent that will ultimately achieve little. Promotion and acceptance were perceived by some as little more than an exercise in appeasing the interests of the labour movement and others (for example, the Scandinavian member states and the new Socialist government in France) who had been arguing the waste and social disruptiveness of unemployment. However, the inability to secure agreement on a diminution of the autonomy of the member states in the formulation and implementation of economic and employment policy implies that ultimately the agreements will produce little of substance.

It was suggested at the time of the IGC that the Title on Employment was accepted by Germany as the price to be paid in order to ensure that the Pact on Stability (*see* Chapter 9) was accepted – a trade-off between in particular the Germans and the French whose new left-wing government had campaigned long and hard on the importance of reducing unemployment.

There is no indication that priorities have changed and there is a clear likelihood that economic policy within the Union will continue to favour the pursuit of monetary union and competitiveness in the world economy through labour market flexibility and deregulation. Where necessary, these policies and priorities will be pursued in preference to others that might facilitate higher levels of employment such as public infrastructure investment.

Jobs Summit Nov 1997

At this summit meeting the EU leaders continued to give preference to the notion that priority should be given to policies to improve individual employability and training. The continuing emphasis was to be upon supply-side measures, deregulation of labour markets and tax reforms aimed at promoting business (especially the SME sector).

Each of the member states is to produce an annual action plan that will be collectively reviewed by the other member states.

Guidelines were agreed (Spain was granted an opt out) that commit the member states, by 2002, to providing a training opportunity to all under 25 year olds within 6 months of their becoming unemployed, 12 months for older unemployed. EU-wide coordinated approaches were rejected in favour of national level interventions, and major infrastructure expenditure as a means of job creation was also rejected.

The convergence criteria for monetary union remained a powerful conceptual influence.

Member state initiatives

While not the main focus of this chapter or indeed this book, it may be illuminating to briefly describe some of the initiatives that member states have taken since the topic of unemployment attained its place at the forefront of the EU agenda in 1993. It has already been noted that one of the debates within the Union is the appropriateness of Union-level action compared with member states retaining responsibility and autonomy, and this debate inevitably also involves the issues of subsidiarity and sovereignty (*see* later example from Saxony). There is no intention to include here exhaustive accounts of the measures taken in each of the member states; the following are intended to be no more than indicative.

There are different perspectives, diagnoses and traditions within the Union and one would expect to see these reflected in the variety of 'solutions' implemented across the Union by the member states. There are also different political agendas influencing the actions of the respective governments.

As already noted, the Amsterdam agreements did not limit this autonomy at the member-state level though the member states did confirm the need for Union-level objectives to be adopted and for much greater efforts to be made to coordinate at the level of the Union the initiatives and programmes taken at the member-state level. It is far too early to assess the impact of these agreements but given that this was not sudden or unexpected and given that the debate has been ongoing since the early 1990s we might expect to see some common ground or evidence of common directions being taken within the member states. (*See* Exhibit 15.3.)

The trends in and rates of unemployment within the member states are given in Table 4.5. As is evident from this, there are considerable variations in the levels and experience of unemployment. The examples below are not intended to provide a blueprint of good practice; they are simply illustrations of the kind of measures adopted and the directions taken.

Denmark

Early in 1994, the government launched a scheme which sought to preserve jobs as well as achieve other social objectives and to do so by encouraging agreements between managements and workers. These agreements enabled workers to take up options for sabbatical, educational and parental leave, thereby providing work opportunities for others. One of the most frequently quoted of these agreements is one relating to bus drivers in

Exhibit 15.3

A European strategy emerges [FT]

Robert Taylor highlights the convergence of employment strategies across the EU

Employment policy is going to be given a higher priority inside the European Union, at least if one of the outcomes of this week's Amsterdam intergovernmental conference is to be believed.

Whether such a commitment goes beyond broad-brushed rhetoric at future job summits where heads of government boast about the wonders of their own labour market models and close their ears to alternative opinions remains doubtful. The experience of the job summits held by the Group of Seven leading industrial nations in Detroit in 1994 and Lille last year does not suggest such gatherings produce any significant results.

An arid argument over who has the most efficient labour market could be avoided if all the EU states including the UK digested an impressive collection of labour market studies of each member state which is being published by the European Commission.

Not all are yet available. We must wait for those from France, Spain and Germany. However, enough have appeared to suggest the public debate about employment flexibility, stimulated in part by the unalloyed enthusiasm of the UK prime minister, Mr Tony Blair, for the UK approach, needs to recognise all is not what it seems. In fact, mainland European countries are now typified not only more by their rich diversity than conformity in the way they manage labour markets but also by the emergence of a commonly recognised strategy. It was always simplistic to contrast a lightly regulated neo-liberal UK employment model with a burdensome continental European system.

A number of examples can be found of employment systems which are a good deal more sensitive to market forces than the UK. Take the Netherlands, for example, a model much admired by Chancellor Helmut Kohl of Germany. The EU report argues: 'It has become more easy for employers to get rid of workers and to prolong temporary and flexible contracts. Regulations concerning working hours have become more flexible with shops being allowed to stay open longer. It has become less easy to receive social benefit and many benefits such as that for disability have been severely cut.' Sickness protection has been turned over to the private sector. The public employment system is no longer a state service.

Sweden has had active labour market measures such as training and job subsidies for a long time. Welfare to work is nothing new. Now the ruling Social Democrats are intent on reforming employment regulations, trying to make it easier for employers to carry through dismissals although in Sweden's recent recession compulsory redundancies were avoided. A jobless person in Sweden can no longer alternate between unemployment and a labour market scheme indefinitely, following the introduction in January of a three-year maximum limit.

In neighbouring Denmark employment strategy is aimed at increasing effective labour supply to employers rather than trying to reduce labour supply to reduce unemployment. This has meant tightening rules covering benefit eligibility and shortening the total benefit period as well as creating individually adapted training and education schemes.

The EU studies ought to correct the widely held view that there are two labour market models competing with one another

---

The new Danish emphasis is on increasing employee productivity through lifelong learning schemes. Increasingly, Denmark is moving away from a passive benefit approach to structural unemployment with a concentration on preparing the jobless for work through tougher limits on benefits and more encouragement for employability.

In Italy last September an agreement was signed by the government, employers and trade unions which emphasised the need for employment flexibility which was described as 'the main principle of labour market innovation'. The new approach is based on decentralising the bureaucracy, cutting employer taxes, encouraging temporary employment, and more training and education. In contrast, the report on corporatist Austria acknowledges 'employer calls for deregulation have so far not entered the employment policy debates and any greater flexibility which has occurred has been on the basis of plant level agreements'.

One of the most successful reductions in structural unemployment has taken place in Ireland but, as the EU report indicates, this was not primarily due to labour market reforms involving deregulation so much as co-ordinated wage restraint and tax relief although the creation of a new local employment service last year has provided access points to the unemployed through the provision of guidance, training, education and temporary employment programmes.

All of the EU studies published so far suggest substantial labour market reform has been introduced in most member states during the past few years in response to high unemployment. There are important differences between the approaches of member states reflecting national traditions and laws but a broad and common European strategy is also becoming more discernible.

This is focused on the improvement in the employability of the jobless through expanded training and education projects, a modernisation of the employment services with a more active and targeted approach to the needs of the jobless and a tightening of the social benefit rules covering the qualification rights of those without work.

Efforts are also being made to reduce recruitment regulations on employers hiring younger workers to provide a mix of incentives and subsidies in order to encourage employment, particularly by small and medium-sized enterprises.

The EU studies ought to correct the widely held view that there are two distinctively different labour market models – one mainland Europe, the other US/UK competing with one another. Far more convergence is taking place in employment strategies across the EU than many people have yet realised. This does not mean that mainland European countries have embraced the so-called neo-liberal, flexible deregulated US/UK approach. Most continue to worry about the need for social cohesion and exclusion and the role of public policy.

But an important shift has taken place among policy-makers about what kind of employment strategy should be pursued in countries, bringing a more market-sensitive approach to the problem. Whether it will help to provide satisfactory work for Europe's estimated 20m registered jobless is another question.

The reports are obtained from the EU Office For Official Publications in Luxembourg, priced Ecu29.50 each.

Source: *Financial Times*, 18 June 1997.

Copenhagen and their employer which allowed them to take a one-week sabbatical every nine weeks. It was estimated that this created/preserved jobs for 80 colleagues.

Later in the year the government initiated an extension of the state's partial early retirement scheme whereby people could choose to partially retire early and receive an allowance/pension in respect of the hours that they chose not to work. The scheme applied only to those between the ages of 60 and 66.

In 1996, new regulations for claiming unemployment benefit were introduced whereby the length of time for which benefit could be claimed was to be reduced and the unemployed person was to be required to accept all reasonable offers of work from the employment services. Allied to this were further provisions and requirements for the unemployed to engage in training and work experience schemes.

It has been estimated that some 54 000 people were engaged in active schemes of one kind or another in 1995.

Belgium

Early in 1994, the Belgian government agreed on a number of initiatives to boost employment for the three-year period through to 1997. In many respects the object was to improve employment by sharing work; the agreement therefore gave greater freedom to employers to impose/agree shorter working hours, implement early retirement on a half-time basis, extend employee rights to career breaks, limit overtime working and even implement a four-day week on condition that any such measures were to be balanced by additional recruitment. This initiative also allowed a reduction of 10 per cent on normal rates of pay in respect of 'starter jobs' for those under 30 with less than six months' work experience (EIRR, February 1994). Similar reductions in wages were also available to employers who were prepared to give at least traineeships of at least six months to young people who had been out of work for at least nine months (a PEP contract – a first work experience contract).

Another scheme enabled employers, employing a person under 26 years of age who had been out of work for at least six months, to avoid social contributions for up to three years. This latter scheme proved to be expensive and it is estimated that only some 11 per cent of the expenditure was effective in creating additional employment (European Commission, 1996c, p. 139).

In the spring of 1996, preparations were made via a tripartite agreement to halve the rate of unemployment by early in the next century. The essence of this agreement was wage restraint in return for job creation, but there was also agreement that non-wage labour costs would be reduced gradually and that part-time working would be facilitated and encouraged.

In the summer of 1996, the government was prompted by the relative failure of the above voluntary measures and agreements to introduce laws which gave them executive powers to set wages, raise taxes and cut social security benefits. These powers were taken in order to ensure that Belgium could meet the convergence criteria for monetary union and were not necessarily the policies that would produce solutions to the problems of unemployment.

Germany

The German government has continued by and large to take initiatives via the traditional route of achieving tripartite consensus so that early in 1994 there was a pact between the parties that sought to link wage restraint with reductions in working hours, enhanced job security and cuts in the social costs of employing certain types of worker.

Later in the same year, the government launched its Action Programme on Growth and Employment and, as part of this, measures were taken to encourage part-time working particularly among those in full-time work who wanted to work less. Estimates at the time indicated that in excess of 500 000 jobs could be created this way (*see* IDS European Report, July 1994 and also Hollinshead and Leat (1995, p. 133)).

Some of the difficulties of taking effective action have been illustrated in Germany by the resistance of the trade unions to proposals to liberalise shop opening hours which are quite restrictively regulated. Estimates in 1995 suggested that reform could create up to 50 000 new jobs. Clearly proposals of this kind to create jobs can be considered from two perspectives and the trade unions in their opposition to such moves are clearly acting as insiders and arguably against the interests of those unemployed – the outsiders.

Towards the end of 1995 and into 1996 there was considerable pressure upon government and the employers to respond positively to the proposal that was instigated by the engineering and metal workers' union (IG Metall) to agree an alliance for jobs – the alliance to be between the corporate actors. The essence of the proposal was an agreement on the part of the union to restrict wage demands in return for the creation of jobs. The original proposal was widened as more parties became interested in the notion and the government soon put forward a plan that sought a trade-off between pay restraint, reductions in company taxes and social security contributions and job creation.

These discussions prompted suggestions at EU and member-state level to extend the idea of a pact for employment to the level of the Union. In January 1996 the Secretary General of the ETUC called for such a pact to be agreed at EU level and this was supported by several other member states. There was a clear link between these calls and the proposals of the President of the Commission referred to earlier.

However, the search for a tripartite pact for jobs did not readily solve the problems and by the spring and early summer of 1996 the German government found itself under attack from trade unions worried about government plans to reduce pensions, reduce unemployment and other welfare payments, raise the retirement age, freeze child benefit, impose a two-year wage freeze and curb early retirement programmes. This last initiative was in part a response to the greatly enhanced take-up of such schemes, as the economy declined.

Later in 1996 and with unemployment still rising in Germany, an incident in Saxony illustrated the difficulties faced by EU institutions trying to coordinate employment policy across the Union and also the problems posed when there appear to be internal inconsistencies between one element of EU policy and another. In August 1996, there was a serious dispute between the local government in Saxony and the Commission over the issue of £100 million of job-creating subsidies to Volkswagen to build two factories and create 23 000 jobs. The Commission argued that the grants infringed competition policy; the local government defied the Commission and took the view that it was only at local level that such decisions should be taken. 'Brussels centralism' came under severe attack.

Compromise was apparently achieved in September 1996 on the basis that there would be no return of monies already paid to VW by the local government in Saxony, even though the Commission had argued the payments illegal. In return there were to be no further such payments. Initial indications were that the company received approximately half of the amount above.

Unemployment continued to rise into 1997 and was substantially higher in the new Länder than in the old West, with rates being close to 15 per cent and 10 per cent respectively.

France

In France, a number of well documented initiatives have been taken by successive governments. One of the earliest in the middle of 1994 was a scheme which effectively enabled state-subsidised short-time working over an extended period of 12 to 18 months, the object being to avoid redundancy. The government also proposed in 1994 to extend the scheme whereby employers could gain exemption from social costs in respect of labour hired from among the ranks of the long-term unemployed. In this case the definition of long term was more than three years. Arrangements were also made to allow employers a reduction on social charges in respect of young labour hired to replace older labour that either experiences a reduction in working time or retires early.

Further initiatives were taken by the new Chirac government soon after its election in mid-1995. Chirac had campaigned vigorously on the issue of unemployment and had been critical of previous governments' record. There was therefore considerable pressure upon them to act. Consequently, a number of measures were proposed within the first couple of months:

- *The CIE – the employment initiative contract*. This gave employers complete exemption from social costs on the pay of people recruited from the ranks of the long-term unemployed (in this case more than one year) up to the level of the SMIC (salaire minimum interprofessional de croissance) – the minimum wage. The exemption was for a maximum of two years. There was also to be a monthly incentive payment to the employer and together the proposals amounted to a 40 per cent reduction in labour costs in respect of an employee on the SMIC. It was estimated that some 350 000 people would be placed under the scheme in 1996.

- *The CAE – the access to employment contract*. This sought to provide more opportunities for those young people undergoing work-based training, the intention being to facilitate their integration into work (*EIRR* 258, July 1995).

The intention was to finance these programmes by cutting public expenditure in other areas including some welfare payments; towards the end of 1995 there was considerable social and industrial unrest at these and other measures directed at reducing public expenditure and government borrowing with a view, at least in part, to meeting the convergence criteria for monetary union. As the year wore on and the EMU pressures to cut public spending and government debt grew, the government concluded that it was not possible to spend its way out of unemployment and it was at this time that reducing the length of the working week increased in its appeal as a solution. The government sought to encourage employers and unions to voluntarily reach such agreements but this was backed up by the threat of legislation if they failed. In October 1995, the central employers' association and the five major trade union organisations agreed an early retirement package that was to comprise a trade-off between early retirement at up to 65 per cent of pay, pending entitlement to a state pension, with replacement of the early retirees by staff on permanent contracts and drawn from the ranks of the young unemployed.

In February 1996, the Prime Minister illustrated one of the difficulties confronting governments when they decide to give employers subsidies to promote job creation, and the employers take the money but don't actually create the jobs. (*The Guardian*, 3 February 1996).

Juppe was quoted as saying:

We will not further reduce employers social charges unless we feel that we are getting something for something, such as a massive pledge to employ young people.

As unemployment continued to rise through the summer of 1996, the government introduced measures to reduce public expenditure which included proposals for job cuts in the public sector.

The relative failure of the government to substantially reduce the level of unemployment played a major role in the election in 1997; the Socialist parties regained government promising to take measures to deal with the problem and, as already noted, the new French government was active in seeking to include in the revised EC Treaty a chapter on employment. In the summer of 1997 the government proposed a conference of the important actors to consider how to fulfil its election pledges to create 700 000 new jobs for the young unemployed and to reduce the working week to 35 hours without reductions in pay.

Italy

In February and March 1994, the government took the opportunity to make use of:

- the *Cassa Integrazione Guadagni* (CIG) – the Earnings Maintenance or Wage Compensation Fund – which pays laid off employees up to 80 per cent of their earnings and is designed to assist restructuring and keep people in employment; and
- *solidarity contracts* which in this context refer to agreements providing for work sharing and reductions in working time and pay (*see* Mosley and Krupp (1996)).

In February, it brought Fiat and its employees together in a deal which involved public funding of job losses and the introduction of reduced hours of work and work sharing as an alternative to even more job losses. The Fiat funding was for 6500 early retirements and 3500 solidarity contracts and additionally provided for state-subsidised retraining and job seeking.

In March, the government acted again in the state-controlled steel group, Ilva, and the agreement was to fund 10 500 early retirements with a further 1200 being saved through solidarity contracts.

The centre-left government, elected in the spring of 1996 and called 'the olive tree alliance', was confronted with many of the same problems as those in neighbouring member states – large public sector, massive fiscal deficits, high unemployment and high government debt. The determination to join and pressures of monetary union may not be so great in Italy; however, it seemed likely that the government would be forced to give priority to public sector finances, rather than to employment and job creation/preservation.

CONCLUSIONS

There are a number of dilemmas confronting the Union at the end of the twentieth century.

One of these concerns the degree to which economic policy can or should be determined, controlled and coordinated at the level of the Union. The achievement of monetary union, allied to the Stability Pact now agreed, should mean that member states, once members of EMU, will have less autonomy to pursue independent economic and fiscal policies. However, the 1997 agreements at Amsterdam also illustrate the difficulties of trying to persuade member states to give up their autonomy to determine such policies. Agreement was obtained on the need to cooperate, share information and experiences, and for the Commission and the new Employment Committee to coordinate, but no agreement was achieved that policies geared towards the reduction of unemployment should be determined centrally. Such a process is resisted by forces concerned about issues of sovereignty, national interest, federalism, capacity and the particular approach to be adopted.

This final point is probably one of the more critical: there are differences of view, value and tradition throughout the Union and at all levels of it. In many of the member states, there is a tradition of corporatism/tripartism and social or welfare capitalism – that is, capitalism mitigated by concerns for equity and social justice. At Union level this tradition can be seen to imbue the preferred approach of the Commission and the trade union movement, whereas the new orthodoxy of neo-Classicism and monetarism can be seen to inform the convergence criteria for monetary union and the preferred approach of the central banks, some of the member-state governments (led until 1997, and maybe beyond, by that of the UK) and the employers associations.

In recent times, the neo-Classical diagnosis and prognosis have appeared to be winning the hearts and minds of member states with the French and German governments apparently in the vanguard of change. This has been prompted by a determination to be at the forefront of those qualifying for membership of the single currency, the nature of the convergence criteria, and by the apparent success of the UK economy in securing a reduction in unemployment through the implementation of labour market and social and welfare policies emphasising the operation of market forces and the elimination of structural and institutional rigidity. This labour market 'flexibility' and reliance upon market forces was also supported by arguments relating to the need to keep labour costs in line with third-world competition since more employment is dependent upon growth and growth is dependent upon being competitive.

Associated with this debate and implied by the respective approaches are the discussions concerning the relevance to employment levels of macroeconomic versus microeconomic policy and interventions, the usefulness of active as opposed to passive labour market initiatives, and the relevance of supply-side as opposed to demand-side remedies.

There is evidence that the Union – as represented by the Council, the Commission and some member states – has been moving in the direction of microeconomic, supply-side and active initiatives and interventions. The Commission would appear to be the more reluctant in its espousal of this new orthodoxy and there is evidence of its desire not to lose sight of social costs and implications and the traditional tripartite approach which implies a search for consensus.

The consequences of these developments – which one suspects are at least as much motivated by a determination to meet the Maastricht convergence criteria as by the belief that they will contribute to the reduction of unemployment – are difficult to predict. However, unemployment in France and Germany was still historically high in late 1997 and, based on the UK experience of implementing and operating similar policies over a number of years, the most likely and predictable consequences would be:

- increasing employment and employee insecurity;

- a larger part-time labour force;
- women constituting a larger proportion of the total at work;
- declining wages;
- increasing inequality and poverty; and
- the empowerment of both capital and management at the expense of labour, the labour movement, representation and democracy.

The evidence of the UK does not necessarily vindicate the new approach; unemployment has risen with each business cycle.

There are of course alternative prescriptions, some of which are essentially Keynesian and expansionist, arguing that the way to create employment is through an expansion of demand and that there is very little evidence to suggest that supply-side measures actually do result in additional employment.

This expansion can be achieved through growth stimulated by investment which is in turn stimulated by low interest rates, not by the tight monetary policy associated with the neo-Classical and monetarist prescription. It is important, however, that the growth is labour intensive or employment rich. We have noted that the EIB has a major role to play in this policy and it is to be expanded as a result of the Amsterdam agreements but targeted at the SME sector and at major infrastructure projects (TENs).

Other means by which demand can be created is through the expansion or re-directing of public expenditure so that it is used to finance job creation rather than unemployment. There are many variations on the 'welfare to work' schemes referred to earlier in the text and there is scope for them to effectively create jobs, although, as French experience would appear to indicate, there is a danger that the money will be taken but that the extra jobs will not be created. There are also obvious affinities here with the move towards active labour market interventions mentioned earlier.

Lower interest rates are one of the benefits claimed for monetary union: international confidence and stability will be enhanced and interest rates will not then be used as a mechanism for influencing exchange rates since these will effectively be fixed.

A willingness to go down this road to employment will inevitably be influenced by individual views of the likely impact that such policies might have upon and for inflation, assessments of the natural or non-accelerating inflation rate of unemployment, and judgments regarding the possibility that a tighter labour market might enhance trade union power and their propensity – for example, by taking advantage of their insider position – to use it to drive up wages at the expense of competitiveness and the unemployed. It is partly to allay such fears that proponents of this and similar prescriptions tend to promote the notion of consensus and tripartite regulation of outcomes.

Inevitably the attraction of such a recipe will be a product of individual perceptions of the impact of unemployment on social cohesion and an expansion of crime. Some may feel that these social threats are qualitatively greater than the threat to the international competitiveness of the Union which is projected as the inevitable downside of such 'neo-Keynesian' demand-side, investment-driven expansionist policies.

However, it may be that the threat to competitiveness is not so great as perceived by the neo-Classical view. It can be argued that:

- the vast majority of the Union's trade is internal and this could be expanded;

- as the lower cost competition economies become successful, they will tend to become high-cost economies, thereby losing their competitive edge over Europe; and

- the desire of the USA and others to introduce labour standards as conditions upon free trade in order to prevent competition on the back of exploitation and child labour will, if imposed, significantly influence the relative competitiveness of developed and under-developed countries.

In any event to determine policy on the basis that the developed economies of Europe must reduce:

- both wage and non-wage labour costs, and thereby living standards, in order to compete with the so-called Tiger economies;

- the degree of protection afforded employees at work so that flexibility is enhanced;

- public expenditure, inflation and government borrowing (including unemployment and other welfare benefits) in order to provide the unemployed with an incentive to work and to meet the criteria for monetary union,

does seem to many to be the council of despair and a recipe for ever widening inequality, deepening poverty, greater social unrest and exclusion and (if the comparison with the USA is relevant) an increase in crime. Effective supply-side measures geared towards improving the quality of the labour force and thereby its employability and security may mitigate these effects but we still have an effective impasse on the issue of who is to pay for them and how. Certainly those who are unemployed and have poor skills cannot.

There is little reason to believe that reducing benefits acts as an effective mechanism for getting the long-term unemployed back into work, since it is this group that is in least demand as their skills decline and their empathy with a work environment and culture erodes. A more effective alternative may be to reduce the disincentive effect of low wages in many service-sector jobs by ensuring that those who voluntarily leave the ranks of the unemployed and take such low-productivity, low-wage work should in fact continue to receive a portion of their social security benefits. Care would have to be taken that the state does not then subsidise inefficient employers who then continue to exploit their employees.

References

Adnett, N. (1996) *European Labour Markets: Analysis and Policy*. Longman.

Casey, B. (1993) 'Employment promotion', in Gold, M. (ed) *The Social Dimension – Employment Policy in the European Community*. Macmillan.

Cecchini, P. (1988) *The European Challenge: 1992 – The Benefits of a Single Market*. Wildwood House.

EIRR (European Industrial Relations Review) 241, Feb 1994.

EIRR (European Industrial Relations Review) 258, July 1995.

European Commission (1988) *The Economics of 1992. European Economy No. 35*. European Commission.

European Commission (1993b) *White Paper on Growth, Competitiveness, Employment*. European Commission.

European Commission (1994a) *Employment in Europe 1994*. European Commission.

European Commission (1994c) *White Paper on Social Policy*. European Commission.

European Commission (1995b) *European Strategy for Employment*. European Commission.

European Commission (1996c) *Employment in Europe 1996*. European Commission.

European Commission (1997c) *Annual Report from the Commission. Equal Opportunities for Women and Men in the European Union – 1996*. European Commission.

European Report, 2134, May 1996.

Hollinshead, G. and Leat, M. (1995) *Human Resource Management: An International and Comparative Perspective on the Employment Relationship*. Pitman Publishing.

IDS *European Report* 387, March 1994.

Layard, R. and Nickell, S. (1987) 'The Labour Market', in Dornbusch, R. and Layard, R. (eds) *The Performance of the British Economy*. Clarendon, pp. 131–79.

Mosley, H. and Krupp, T. (1996) 'Short-time Work in Structural Adjustment: European Experience', *European Journal of Industrial Relations*, 2(2), 131–51.

OECD (1994) *The OECD Jobs Study: evidence and explanations*. OECD.

OECD, *Economic Outlook Series*. OECD.

OECD (1995) *Employment Outlook 1995*. OECD.

OECD (1996) *OECD Jobs Study: Taxation, Employment and Unemployment*. OECD.

Parkin, M. and King, D. (1992) *Economics*. Addison Wesley.

Topel, R. (1993) 'What we have learned from empirical studies of unemployment and turnover?', *American Economic Review*, 83(2), 110–15.

UNICE (1994) *Making Europe More Competitive – towards world class performance*. UNICE.

SOME PERSONAL REFLECTIONS
AND CONCLUSIONS

In this final section I would like to draw together some of the conclusions arrived in the earlier chapters and also allow myself some personal reflections on the issues that have emerged.

There seems to be little doubt about the issue or challenge that is currently perceived to be the greatest facing the Union – the challenge of unemployment. As we have seen in the body of this book, the debate about how to resolve this problem has become one that is very much concerned with other human resource issues such as VET, equality between the sexes, new forms of work organisation, labour mobility and immigration. It is also clear that the debates about solutions to this problem have opened up or at least brought into the open other debates about the nature of labour markets, the relevance of the traditions of social protection and regulation and the role that can and should be played at the level of the Union. Indeed, it is possible to contend that the enormity of this problem has cast into the ring the future of the Union – not so much whether it will continue, but the form that it will take and the role that it will perform. Perhaps particularly important is the question as to whether the Union will or can remain a union that genuinely adheres to the principles and practices of social democracy. Very much tied into these debates are also the futures of the various EU institutions, the decision-making processes and some of the guiding principles.

The focus of this book is very much upon human resource issues but it is impossible to completely divorce these matters from others, as evidenced by the debate on unemployment. Conversely, debates on matters such as the decision-making processes, the role of the EP or the extent and nature of the democratic deficit impinge inevitably upon the human resource issues – as evidenced by the debate about subsidiarity.

The recent definitions of the principle of the subsidiary have tended towards a narrowing of the scope for action to be taken at the level of the Union. There are grounds for arguing that initiatives and action at the level of the Union may be so prejudiced by a rigid adherence to this principle that certain particular interests may not obtain the attention and support that they need and deserve.

There are of course transnational issues that can only be dealt with at the level of the Union – for example, initiatives and action to combat the power of the multinational organisation to pick and choose between different regimes within the Union. However, if adherence to the principle of subsidiarity implies that it is only matters of this kind that will be addressed at Union level and that fewer and fewer initiatives will be pursued that impinge upon national regimes, the danger is that the socially and morally desirable processes of upward harmonisation of terms and conditions of employment, employee rights and working conditions, living standards and other mechanisms of social protection are put at risk. Unfortunately, subsidiarity is only one of the many threats to the rights and interests of employees that can be detected within the Union and can be seen to be influencing the positions adopted and the policies pursued.

As noted in Part One of this book there are a number of different ideological and regulatory traditions within the member states that form the Union. In the majority of the member states these ideological positions have facilitated systems of fairly extensive social protection. There are differences of degree and nature but they have all tended to accept the principle of intervention and the need for government to regulate the labour market, insist upon minimum employee rights and promote social justice.

The Commission has traditionally pursued policies and taken initiatives consistent with the Roman–German tradition of a core of fundamental rights and freedoms guaranteed by the Constitution. There is evidence that this is still the inclination of the Commission Directorates with responsibility for Social Affairs. This perspective is also shared by the majority of the political groups within the Parliament.

The debate on unemployment which has occupied the member states, Commission and other interests substantially since the early 1990s illustrates these preferences, with the Commission often arguing that while it may be desirable to reduce the regulation of the labour market and labour costs so as to encourage employment, this should not be achieved at the expense of social justice and the weakest and poorest members of the Union. It is also clear, however, that there are other interests within the Commission – for example, those with responsibility for Competition policy – that appear to be distancing themselves from the traditions of the Roman–German system of regulation and social protection. They seem more willing to countenance deregulation as a necessary response to the pressures of international competition, the need to reduce labour costs and the need to enhance flexibility in terms of response to the market and labour usage.

In this context, the UK architects of deregulation appear to have successfully presented it as a source of competitive advantage in the global marketplace, as a means of attracting foreign capital investment and thereby as a solution to the lack of job creation and employment in Europe. Indeed we may well have witnessed the emergence of a new credo, a new framework within which human resource and other social issues are to be addressed within the Union. Such a model may become more widespread as governments confronted with high unemployment, high employment and welfare costs, and highly regulated and inflexible labour markets are attracted to deregulation and cost cutting and who extend this new approach to their involvement at an intergovernmental level within the Union.

Grahl and Teague (1991) envisaged the development of two distinct trajectories that were compatible with greater flexibility – the *constructive* and *competitive* trajectories. The constructive trajectory depicts strategies which seek to combine greater flexibility with the traditions of social protection and cohesion and with an emphasis upon output-expanding activity. The competitive trajectory depicts strategies based on the deregulated, market-oriented, low wage and employment costs and anti-trade union model developed in the UK.

Grahl and Teague were of the opinion that the institutions and structures of welfare capitalism and social protection, combined with widespread social and political opposition, had limited and might continue to significantly limit the extent to which the competitive model might be given effect in many of the member states. However, as time has passed, not only have more national governments within the Union been tempted into following the UK lead, but there are reasons to believe that these views and judgements have also begun to permeate influential groupings within the Commission.

Social protectionist traditions are also under threat from a different direction; the convergence criteria for the achievement of qualification for monetary union have also begun to encourage several governments to re-appraise the feasibility of maintaining the welfare state. Their determination to comply with the convergence criteria has encouraged them to begin to pursue deflationary policies and has further encouraged the process of reducing the scale and scope of the welfare state and social protection. The demographic developments and predictions examined in Part One of this book add to the pressures for such reform.

Many have also argued that monetary union and the particular convergence criteria chosen will lock into the Union high levels of unemployment, low growth and a balance of power which favours capital at the expense of labour.

The new found adherence to and promotion of the need for a flexible and adaptive labour force poses another threat to the interests of labour – a threat not necessarily mitigated by the promise that the flexibility is necessary to engender competitiveness and that this greater competitiveness will in the longer run provide the employment that the people of the Union need. There seems to be an only too visible risk that the enhanced competitiveness will not provide the jobs that are promised and that the long-term consequence of the acceptance of this argument will be more exploitation of the labour resource and more inequality and social exclusion. Those without the skills in demand and with few if any rights to protection at work will be replaced by technology, and multinational capital will locate its resources on a global scale.

The sanguine approach of Grahl and Teague (1991) is no longer justified in these final years of the century. We may well be witnessing the terminal decline of the Roman–German regulatory model and social protectionism and its replacement by a model that encompasses among its major features:

- a rejection of the principles of social protection and the welfare state;
- acceptance of greater levels of inequality and social exclusion;
- deregulated labour markets and an emphasis upon labour flexibility and cost reduction;
- weakened trade unions and less employee protection;
- an emphasis upon individualism, individual contract and employee involvement and commitment to organisational goals;
- devolution and decentralisation of decision making and the dismantling of national/ sectoral industrial relations institutions;
- less employee participation, less collective bargaining and joint decision making and enhanced managerial prerogative.

Many readers may regard this assessment as unfair and as both too radical and too gloomy a viewpoint of the prospects for labour in the EU; they may point to the many positive initiatives that have been taken over the years to both support and protect the interests of labour. They may also cite the Amsterdam agreement – with its proposals to incorporate into the Treaty a Title on Employment and a new Social Chapter and to extend the role of the EP in the decision-making process – as evidence that the fears expressed here are unjustified and misplaced. However, the future of the social dimension is not looking particularly positive, confronted as it is by the deregulatory lobby.

It is in this context that I would argue the need for:

- the central institutions to pay less attention to the principle of subsidiarity;
- a widening of the scope of the subject matter to which the QMV procedures apply;
- a more powerful and initiatory role for the European Parliament;

- a strengthening of the roles of the Social Partners;
- legislative support for the rights of association and to engage in collective bargaining;
- similar support for the rights of employees as stakeholders in organisations;
- a more determined attempt to regulate the activities of multinational capital, difficult though this will be;
- fewer exceptions to be made for the SME sector in the measures and actions that are taken; and
- a more critical approach to be taken to the issue of labour flexibility, so that flexibility is enhanced by and through the acquisition of skills but not at the expense of the rights and living standards of many members of the labour force within the Union.

If this is not addressed and the trends identifiable in the last five years continue, we can expect increasing disenchantment with the Union among the population and an enhanced potential for social exclusion and social unrest.

Mike Leat

BIBLIOGRAPHY

ACAS (1988) *Labour Flexibility in Britain. Occasional Paper No. 41.* HMSO.

Addison, J. and Siebert, W. (1994) 'Vocational Training and the European Community', *Oxford Economic Papers*, 46, 696–724.

Addison, J. and Siebert, W. (eds) (1997) *Labour Markets in Europe: Issues of Harmonisation and Regulation.* Dryden Press.

Adler, N. J. (1997) *International Dimensions of Organisational Behaviour* (3rd edn). South Western.

Adnett, N. (1996) *European Labour Markets: Analysis and Policy.* Longman.

Atkinson, J. (1984) 'Manpower Strategies for the Flexible Organisation', *Personnel Management*, Aug, 28–31.

Barber, L. (1996) 'Court rules on EU jobs barriers', *Financial Times*, 3 July.

Barnes, I. and Barnes, P. (1995) *The Enlarged European Union.* Longman.

Barrell, R. and Pain, N. (1997) 'EU: an attractive investment. Being part of the EU is good for FDI and being out of EMU may be bad', *New Economy*, 4(1).

Barrett, B. and Howells, R. (1995) *Occupational Health and Safety Law* (2nd edn). Pitman Publishing.

Bartlett, C. A. and Ghoshal, S. (1989) *Managing Across Borders: The Transnational Solution.* Harvard Business School Press.

Batstone, E. and Gourley, S. (1986) *Unions, Unemployment and Innovation.* Blackwell.

Bean, R. (1994) *Comparative Industrial Relations* (2nd edn). Routledge.

Beatson, M. (1995) *Labour market flexibility. Employment Deptartment Research Series No. 48.* HMSO.

Becker, G. (1957) *The Economics of Discrimination.* The University of Chicago Press.

Becker, G. (1975) *Human Capital: a theoretical and empirical analysis.* NBER.

Beer, M., Spector, B., Lawrence, P. R., Quinn Mills, D. and Walton, R. E. (1984) *Managing Human Assets.* Free Press.

Benoit-Guilbot, O. and Gallie, D. (eds) (1994) *Long term Unemployment.* Pinter.

Bertrand, O. (1991) 'Comparing Skills and Qualifications in Europe', in Hantrais, L. *et al Education, Training and Labour Markets in Europe, Cross-national Research Papers No. 4.* University of Aston.

Blanpain, R. (1992) *Labour Laws and Industrial Relations of the EU.* Deventer, Netherlands. Monthly Review Press.

Braverman, H. (1974) *Labour and Monopoly Capital: The Degradaton of Work in the 20th Century.*

Brew, K. and Garavan, T. N. (1995) 'Eliminating Inequality: Women Only Training', EJIT (European Journal of Industrial Training) Part 1, 19(7), 13–19 and Part 2, 19(9), 28–32.

Brewster, C. (1995) 'HRM: The European Dimension', in Storey, J. (ed) *Human Resource Management : A Critical Text.* Routledge, pp. 309–31.

Brewster, C., Hegewisch, A. and Mayne, L. (1994) 'Flexible Working Practices: The controversy and the evidence', in Brewster, C. and Hegewisch, A. (1994) *Policy and Practice in European HRM.* Routledge, pp. 168–93.

Brewster, C., Hegewisch A., Mayne, L. and Tregaskis, O. (1994) 'Employee Communication and Participation', in Brewster, C. and Hegewisch, A. (1994) *Policy and Practice in European HRM.* Routledge, pp. 154–67.

Brewster, C. and Hegewisch, A. (1994) *Policy and Practice in European HRM. The Price Waterhouse Cranfield Surrey*, Routledge.

Bridgeford, J. and Sterling, S. (1994) *Employee Relations in Europe*. Blackwell.

Bright, C. (1995) *The EU: Understanding The Brussels Process*. Wiley.

Briscoe, D. R. (1995) *International Human Resource Management*. Prentice-Hall.

Burgess, P. (ed) (1993) *Training and Development* (European Management Guides). Institute of Personnel Management and Incomes Data Services.

Carley, M. (1993) 'Social Dialogue', in Gold, M. (ed) *The Social Dimension – Employment Policy in the European Community*. Macmillan.

Casey, B. (1993) 'Employment promotion', in Gold, M. (ed) *The Social Dimension – Employment Policy in the European Community*. Macmillan.

Cecchini, P. (1988) *The European Challenge: (1992) The Benefits of a Single Market*. Wildwood House.

Centre for Economic Policy Research (CEPR) (1995) *Unemployment – Choices for Europe*. CEPR.

Coates, K. and Holland, S. (1995) *Full Employment for Europe*. Spokesman.

Coopers & Lybrand (1995) *European Works Councils. Consultation and Communication in European Companies – A Survey*. Coopers & Lybrand.

Corry, D. (ed) (1996) *Economics and European Union Migration Policy*. IPPR.

Cotton, J. L. (1993) *Employee Involvement*. Sage.

Council of the European Union (1997) *Intergovernmental Conference Draft Treaty*. Office for Official Publications of the European Communities.

Coussey, M. and Jackson, H. (1991) *Making Equal Opportunities Work*. Pitman Publishing.

Cox, S. (1993) 'Equal Opportunities', in Gold, M. (ed) *The Social Dimension – Employment Policy in the European Community*. Macmillan.

Cressey, P. (1993) 'Employee Participation', in Gold, M. (ed) *The Social Dimension – Employment Policy in the European Community*. Macmillan.

Crouch, C. (1982) *The Politics of Industrial Relations* (2nd edn). Fontana.

Crouch, C. (1995) 'Exit or Voice: Two Paradigms for European Industrial Relations After the Keynesian Welfare State', *European Journal of Industrial Relations*, 1(1), 63–81.

Davidson, M. and Cooper, C. (1992) *Shattering the Glass Ceiling*. Athenaeum Press.

de la Dehesa, G. and Snower, D. (1995) *Unemployment Policy*. Cambridge University Press.

Dudley, J. W. (1993) *1993 and Beyond* (3rd edn). Kogan Page.

Due, J., Madsen, J. S. and Jensen, C. S. (1991) 'The Social Dimension: Convergence or Diversification of Industrial Relations in the Single European Market', *Industrial Relations Journal*, 22(2), Summer, 85–102.

Edwards, P. (1995) 'The Employment Relationship', in Edwards, P. (ed) *Industrial Relations: Theory and Practice in Britain*. Blackwell.

Elias, P. (1994) 'Job related Training, Trade union Membership, and Labour Mobility: a Longitudinal Study', *Oxford Economic Papers*, 46(4), 563–78.

Etzioni, A. (1975) *A Comparative Analysis of Complex Organisations*. Free Press.

European Commission (1988) 'The Economics of 1992', *European Economy* No. 35.

European Commission (1992) *PEPPER: Promotion of Employee Participation in Profits and Enterprise Results*. European Commission.

European Commission (1993a) *Employment in Europe 1994*. European Commission.

European Commission (1993b) *White Paper on Growth, Competitiveness, Employment*. European Commission.

European Commission (1993c) *Fourth Action Programme on Health and Safety at Work* (to cover the period 1996–2000) European Commission.

European Commission (1994a) *Employment in Europe 1994*. European Commission.

European Commission (1994b) *Europe for Safety and Health at Work*. European Commission.

European Commission (1994c) *White Paper on Social Policy: The Way Forward for the Union*.

European Commission.

European Commission (1995a) *Employment in Europe 1995*. European Commission.

European Commission (1995b) *European Strategy for Employment*. European Commission.

European Commission (1995c) *Third Social Action Programme*. European Commission.

European Commission (1995d) *The White Paper: Teaching and Learning: Towards the Knowledge Based Society*. European Commission.

European Commission (1996a) *Code of Practice on The Implementation of Equal Pay for Work of Equal Value for Women and Men*, COM (96) 336. European Commission.

European Commission (1996b) *The Demographic Situation in the European Union 1995*. European Commission.

European Commission (1996c) *Employment in Europe 1996*. European Commission.

European Commission (1996d) *A Review of Services for Young Children in the European Union (1990–1995)* European Commission Network on Childcare and other Measures to reconcile Employment and Family Responsibilities.

European Commission (1997a) *Agenda 2000*. European Commission.

European Commission (1997b) *Amsterdam European Council 16 and 17th June Presidency Conclusions*. SN 150/97. European Commission.

European Commission (1997c) *Annual Report from the Commission. Equal Opportunities for Women and Men in the European Union – 1996*. European Commission.

European Commission (1997d) *Green (Consultative) Paper, Partnership for a New Organisation of Work*, COM (97) 128. European Commission.

European Commission (1997e) *PEPPER II: Promotion of Participation by Employed Persons in Profits and Enterprise Results (including Equity Participation) in Member States*, COM (96) 697. European Commission.

European Communities Publication Office (1997) *Eur-Op News*, 2.

European Foundation for the Improvement of Living and Working Conditions (1996a) *Annual Report for 1995*. EFILWC.

European Foundation for the Improvement of Living and Working Conditions (1996b) *Equal Opportunities and Collective Bargaining in Europe. 1 Defining the Issues*. EFILWC.

European Foundation for the Improvement of Living and Working Conditions (1996c) *Policies on Health and Safety in Thirteen Countries of the European Union Vol II: The European Situation*. EFILWC.

European Foundation for the Improvement of Living and Working Conditions (1996d) *Preventing Racism at the Workplace – A Summary*. EFILWC.

European Industrial Relations Review (EIRR) 241, Feb 1994.

European Industrial Relations Review (EIRR) 254, Mar 1995, 'Race, Employment and the Law in Europe', 15–19.

European Industrial Relations Review (EIRR) 258, July 1995.

European Parliament Budget Committee (1996) *Report on Financing of Enlargement of EU 11/96*.

European Parliament (1997) *EP News*, July.

European Report, 2082, 8 Nov 1995.

European Report, 2126, 24 Apr 1996.

European Report, 2132, May 1996.

European Report, 2134, May 1996.

ETUI (European Trade Union Institute) (1995) *Les comités d'entreprises européens: inventaire des entreprises concernées*. ETUI.

Eurostat (1997) *Statistics in Focus, Population and Social Conditions*, 2. 1977 *European Works Council Bulletin*, Issue 3, May/June 1996, Industrial Relations Research Unit (IRRU) Warwick. IRRU.

Fenton O'Creevey, M. and Nicholson, N. (1994) *Middle Managers: their contribution to employee involvement*. Employment Department Research Series No. 28, HMSO.

Ferner, A. and Hyman, R. (eds) (1992) *Industrial Relations in The New Europe*. Blackwell.

Fernie, S. (1995) 'Participation, contingent pay, representation and workplace performance: evidence from Great Britain', *British Journal of Industrial Relations*, Sept.

Fernie, S. and Metcalf, D. (1995) 'Works Councils are the Future, but there is no need to be afraid', *The Guardian*, 22 May.

Field, F., Halligan, L. and Owen, S. (1994) *Europe isn't Working*. Institute of Community Studies.

Finegold, D. and Soskice, D. (1988) 'The Failure of Training in Britain: Analysis and Prescription', *Oxford Review of Economic Policy*, 4(3), 21–53.

Flanders, A. (1970) *Management and Unions*. Faber.

Ford, G. (1991) *Fascist Europe: The Rise of Racism and Xenophobia*. Pluto Press.

Ford, V. (1996) 'Equality Versus Diversity – Partnership is the secret of Progress', *People Management*, Feb, pp. 34–6.

Fox, A. (1996) *Industrial Sociology and Industrial Relations*. Royal Commission Research Paper No. 3. HMSO.

Gaffikin, F. and Morrisey, M. (1992) *The New Unemployed: Joblessness and Poverty in the Market Economy*. Zed Books.

Gallie, D., Marsh, C. and Vogler, C. (eds) (1994) *Social Change and the Experience of Unemployment*. Oxford University Press.

Garrahan, P. and Stewart, P. (1992) *The Nissan Enigma: Flexibility at Work in a local economy*. Mansell.

Geary, J. and Sisson, K. (1994) *Conceptualising Direct Participation in Organisational Change: The EPOC Project*. European Foundation for the Improvement of Living and Working Conditions.

Geary, J. F. (1995) 'Work Practices: The Structure of Work', in Edwards, P. (ed) *Industrial Relations: Theory and Practice in Britain*. Blackwell.

Ghauri Pervez, N. and Prasad, S. B. (1995) *International Management: A Reader*. Dryden Press.

Goetschy, J. and Rozenblatt, R. (1992) 'France: the Industrial Relations System at a Turning Point', in Ferner, A. and Hyman, R. (eds) *Industrial Relations in The New Europe*. Blackwell, pp. 404–44.

Gold, M. (1993) *The Social Dimension – Employment Policy in the European Community*. Macmillan.

Gold, M. and Hall, M. (1994) 'Statutory European Works Councils: The Final Countdown?', *Industrial Relations Journal*, 25(3), 177–86.

Grahl, J. and Teague, P. (1991) 'Industrial Relations Trajectories and European Human Resource Management', in Brewster, C. and Tyson, S. (eds) *International Comparisons in Human Resource Management*. Pitman Publishing, pp. 67–91.

Gregory, A. and O' Reilly, J. (1996) 'Checking Out and Cashing Up: The prospects and paradoxes of regulating part-time work in Europe', in Crompton, R., Gallie, D. and Purcell, K. (1996) *Changing Forms Of Employment : Organisations, Skills and Gender*. Routledge.

Griffiths, A. and Wall, S. (1996) *Applied Economics*. Longman.

Guest, D. (1987) 'Human Resource Management and Industrial Relations', *Journal of Management Studies*, 24(5), 503–21.

Guest, D. (1992) 'Employee Commitment and Control', in Hartley, J. F. and Stephenson, G. M. (eds) *Employment Relations*. Blackwell.

Hall, E. T. (1976) *Beyond Culture*. Doubleday.

Hall, E. T. and Hall, M. R. (1990) *Understanding Cultural Differences*. Intercultural Press.

Hall, M. (1992) 'Behind European Works Councils Directives: The European Commission's Legislative Strategy', *British Journal of Industrial Relations*, 30(4).

Hall, M. (1994) 'Industrial Relations and the Social Dimension', in Hyman, R. and Ferner, A. (eds) *New Frontiers in European Industrial Relations*. Blackwell.

Hall, M., Carley, M., Gold, M., Marginson, P. and Sisson, K. (1995) *European Works Councils – Planning for the Directive*. Eclipse Group and Industrial Relations Research Unit, Warwick.

Hantrais, L. (1995) *Social Policy In the European Union*. Macmillan.

Hegewisch, A. and Brewster, C. (1994) 'Equal Opportunities Policies in Europe', in Brewster, C. and Hegewisch, A. (eds) *Policy and Practice in European Human Resource Management*. Routledge.

Hegewisch, A. and Brewster, C. (1994) *European Developments in Human Resource Management*. Kogan Page.

Heller, F. (1992) (ed) *Decision Making and Leadership*. Cambridge University Press.

Hendry, C. (1994) 'The Single European Market and the HRM response', in Kirkbride, P. (ed) *Human Resource Management in Europe*. Routledge.

Hendry, C. (1995) *Human Resource Management: Strategic Approach to Employment*. Butterworth–Heinemann, Chap 19.

Herzberg, F. (1966) *Work and the Nature of Man*. World Publishing.

Hickson, D. J. and Pugh, D. S. (1995) *Management Worldwide*. Penguin.

Hill, S. (1991) 'How Do you Manage a Flexible Firm: the Total Quality Model', *Work, Employment and Society*, 5(3), 397–415.

HMSO (1996) *White Paper: A Partnership of Nations*. HMSO.

Hodgetts, R. M. and Luthans, F. (1994) *International Management* (2nd edn). McGraw-Hill.

Hodgetts, R. M. and Luthans, F. (1997) *International Management* (3rd edn). McGraw-Hill.

Hoecklin, L. (1995) *Managing Cultural Differences: Strategies for Competitive Advantage*. Economist Intelligence Unit and Addison Wesley.

Hofstede, G. (1980) *Culture's Consequences: International Differences in Work Related Values*. Sage.

Hofstede, G. (1991) *Cultures and Organisations: Software of the Mind*. McGraw-Hill.

Hofstede, G. (1994) 'The business of international business is culture'. *International Business Review*, 3(1), 1–14. Reprinted in Jackson, T. (1995) *Cross Cultural Management*. Butterworth–Heinemann.

Hofstede, G. and Bond, M. (1988) 'The Confucius Connection: From Cultural Roots to Economic Growth', *Organisational Dynamics*, Spring.

Holden, L. (1991) 'European Trends in Training and Development', *International Journal of Human Resource Management*, 2(2), 113–31.

Holden, L. and Livian, Y. (1993) 'Does Strategic Training Policy Exist? Some Evidence From Ten European Countries', in Hegewisch, A. and Brewster, C. (eds) *European Developments in Human Resource Management*. Kogan Page.

Hollinshead, G. and Leat, M. (1995) *Human Resource Management: An International and Comparative Perspective on the Employment Relationship*. Pitman Publishing.

Holt Larson, H. (1994) 'Key Issues in Training and Development', in Brewster, C. and Hegewisch, A. (eds) *Policy and Practice in European HRM*. Routledge.

Honekopp, E. (1996) 'Old and new labour migration to Germany from Eastern Europe', in Corry, D. (ed) *Economics and European Union Migration Policy*. IPPR.

House of Lords Select Committee on the European Communities (1990) *Vocational Training and Re-Training*. HMSO.

Humphries, J. and Rubery, J. (eds) (1995) *The Economics of Equal Opportunities*. Equal Opportunities Commission.

Hyman, J. and Mason, B. (1995) *Managing Employee Involvement and Participation*. Sage.

Hyman, R. (1995) 'Industrial Relations in Europe: Theory and Practice', *European Journal of Industrial Relations*, 1(1), 17–46.

Hyman, R. and Ferner, A. (eds) (1994) *New Frontiers in European Industrial Relations*. Blackwell.

I D E Research Group (1981) *Industrial Democracy in Europe*. Clarendon.

I D E Research Group (1993) *Industrial Democracy in Europe Revisited*. Oxford University Press.

IDS European Report 387, Mar 1994.

Ietto-Gillies, G. (1997) 'Working with the big guys: hostility to transnationals must be replaced by cooperation', *New Economy*, 4(1).

Institute of Personnel and Development (1994) *The Culture Factor. Corporate and International Perspectives*. IPD.

IPD European Update. July 1994.

IPD Report, 'Working to Learn', July 1997.

IPD Update. March 1996, p. 16.

Jackson, T. (1995) *Cross Cultural Management*. Butterworth–Heinemann.

James, P. (1993) 'Occupational Health and Safety', in Gold, M. (ed) *The Social Dimension – Employment Policy in the European Community*. Macmillan.

Jenson, J., Hagen, E. and Reddy, C. (1988) *Feminisation of the Labour Force: Paradoxes and Promises*. Polity Press.

Jewson, N. and Mason, D. (1986) 'The Theory and Practice of Equal Opportunities Policies: Liberal and Radical Approaches', *Sociological Review*, 34(2), 307–34.

Jones, A. K. V. (1990) 'Quality management the Nissan way', in Dale, B. and Plunkett, J. (eds) *Managing Quality*. Philip Allan, pp. 44–51.

Journal of European Industrial Training, 21(4), vi.

Joynt, P. and Warner, M. (1996) *Managing Across Cultures*. Thomson.

Keep, E. and Rainbird, H. (1995) 'Training', in Edwards, P. (ed) *Industrial Relations: Theory and Practice in Britain*. Blackwell.

Keller, B. (1994) *Towards a European System of Collective Bargaining? Perspectives before and after Maastricht. Leverhulme Public Lecture*. Industrial Relations Research Unit, University of Warwick.

Kelly, J. and Kelly, C. (1991) 'Them and Us: social psychology and the new industrial relations', *British Journal of Industrial Relations*, 29(1), 25–48.

Kennedy, C. (1992) 'ABB: model merger for the new Europe', *Long Range Planning*, 25(5), 10–17.

Kennedy, P. (1993) *Preparing for the 21st Century*. Fontana.

King, C. (1993) *Through the Glass Ceiling*. Athenaeum Press.

Kirkbride, P. (ed) (1994) *Human Resource Management in Europe*. Routledge.

Knudson, H. (1995) *Employee Participation in Europe*. Sage.

Lane, C. (ed) (1989) *Management and Labour in Europe*. Edward Elgar.

Lane, C. (1989) 'New Technology and Changes in Work Organisations', in Lane, C. (ed) *Management and Labour in Europe*. Edward Elgar, pp. 163–95.

Lane, C. (1990) 'Vocational Training and new production concepts in Germany: some lessons for Britain', *Industrial Relations Journal*, 21(1), 247–59.

Lasok, D. and Lasok, K. P. E. (1994) *Law and Institutions of the European Union* (6th edn). Butterworths.

Lawler, E. (1986) *Higher Involvement Management*. Jossey Bass.

Layard, R. and Nickell, S. (1987) 'The Labour Market', in Dornbusch, R. and Layard, R. (eds) *The Performance of the British Economy*. Clarendon, pp. 131–79.

Leeds, C., Kirkbride, P. and Durcan, J. (1994) 'The Cultural Context of Europe: A tentative mapping', in Kirkbride, P. (ed) *Human Resource Management in Europe*. Routledge.

Legge, K. (1995) *Human Resource Management: Rhetorics and Realities*. Macmillan.

Leibfried, S. and Pierson, P. (1995) *European Social Policy: Between Fragmentation and Integration*. The Brookings Institute.

Liff, S. (1995) 'Equal Opportunities: Continuing Discrimination in a Context of Formal Equality', in Edwards, P. (ed) *Industrial Relations Theory and Practice in Britain*. Blackwell.

Mabey, C. and Salaman, G. (1995) *Strategic Human Resource Management*. Blackwell, Chap 3.

Marchington, M., Wilkinson, A., Ackers, P. and Goodman, J. (1995) 'Involvement and Participation', in Storey, J. (ed) *Human Resource Management: A Critical Text*. Routledge.

Marchington, M. and Wilkinson, A. (1996) *Core Personnel and Development*. IPD.

Marchington, M., Wilkinson, A., Ackers, P. and Goodman, J. (1992) *New Developments in Employee Involvement*. Employment Department Research Series No. 2. HMSO.

Marginson, P. and Sisson, K. (1994) 'The Structure of Transnational Capital in Europe: the Emerging

Euro-company and its Implications for Industrial Relations', in Hyman, R. and Ferner, A. (eds) *New Frontiers in European Industrial Relations*, Blackwell.

Marginson, P. and Sisson, K. (1996) 'Multi-national Companies and the Future of Collective Bargaining: A Review of the Research Issues', *European Journal of Industrial Relations*, 2(2), 173–97.

Marsden, D. and Ryan, P. (1991) 'Initial Training, Labour Market Structure and Public Policy: Intermediate Skills in British and German Industry', in Ryan, P. (ed) *International Comparisons of Vocational Training for Intermediate Skills*. Falmer Press.

Maslow, A. (1943) 'A Theory of Human Motivation', *Psychological Review*, 50, 370–96.

Maurice, M., Silvestre, J.-J. and Sellier, F. (1980) 'Societal Differences in Organising Manufacturing Units: A Comparison of France, West Germany and Great Britain', *Organisational Studies*, 1, 59–86.

Mazey, S. (1988) 'European Community Action on Behalf of Women: The Limits of Legislation', *Journal of Common Market Studies*, 27(1), 63–84.

McEwan Scott, A. (ed) (1994) *Gender Segregation and Social Change – Men and Women in Changing Labour Markets*. Oxford University Press.

McClelland, D. C. (1987) *Human Motivation*. Cambridge University Press.

Meade, J. E. (1995) *Full Employment Regained*. Cambridge University Press.

Michels, R. (1966) *Political Parties*. Free Press.

Michie, J. and Grieve-Smith, J. (eds) (1994) *Unemployment in Europe*. Academic Press.

Millward, N., Stevens, M., Smart, D. and Hawes, W. R. (1992) *The 1990 Workplace Industrial Relations Survey, Workplace Industrial Relations in Transition*. Dartmouth.

Mole, J. (1990) *Mind your Manners: Managing Culture Clash in the Single European Market*. Industrial Society.

Mosley, H. and Krupp, T. (1996) 'Short Time Work in Structural Adjustment: European Experience', *European Journal of Industrial Relations*, 2(2), 131–51.

Mowday, R. T., Steers, R. M. and Porter, L. W. (1982) *Employee–Organisation Linkages: The Psychology of Commitment, Absenteeism and Turnover*. Academic Press.

Moye, A. M. (1993) 'Mondragon: Adapting co-operative structures to meet the demands of a changing environment', *Economic and Industrial Democracy*, May.

Nickell, S. and Bell, B. (1995) 'The collapse in demand for the unskilled and unemployment across the OECD', *Oxford Review of Economic Policy*, 11(1), 40–62.

Nicolaides, P. and Thomsen, S. (1991) 'The Impact of 1992 on Direct Investment in Europe', *European Business Journal*, 3(2), 8–16.

O'Brien, G. (1992) 'Changing meanings of work', in Hartley, J. and Stephenson, G. (eds) *Employment Relations*. Blackwell, pp. 44–66.

OECD (1995) *Employment Outlook 1995*. OECD.

OECD (1995) 'The incidence of profit sharing in OECD countries'. *Employment Outlook*. OECD.

OECD (1996) *OECD Jobs Study: evidence and explanations*. OECD.

OECD (1996) *OECD Jobs Study: taxation, employment and unemployment*. OECD.

OECD (1997) *Financial Market Trends*. June. OECD.

O'Leary, S. (1996) *European Union Citizenship. The Options for Reform*. IPPR.

Oliver, N. and Wilkinson, B. (1992) *The Japanisation of British Industry: New Developments in the 1990s*. Blackwell.

Paque, K.-H. (1997) 'Does Europe's Common Market Need a Social Dimension? Some Academic Thoughts on a Popular Theme', in Addison, J. T. and Siebert, W. S. (eds) *Labour Markets in Europe: Issues of Harmonisation and Regulation*. Dryden.

Parker, M. and Slaughter, J. (1988) *Choosing Sides: Unions and the Team Concept*. Boston Labour Notes.

Parkin, M. and King, D. (1992) *Economics*. Addison Wesley.

Peabody, D. (1985) *National Character*. Cambridge University Press.

Perlmutter, H. (1969) 'The Tortuous Evolution of the Multi-national Corporation', *Columbus Journal of World Business*, 4(1), 9–18. Reprinted in Ghauri Pervez, N. and Prasad, S. B. (1995) *International Management: A Reader*. Dryden Press.

Pickard, J. (1993) 'The Real Meaning of Empowerment', *Personnel Management*, 25 Nov, 28–33.

Pillinger, J. (1992) *Feminising the Market – Women's pay and Employment in the European Community*. Macmillan.

Pinder, J. (1995) *European Community. The Building of a Union*. OPUS.

Piore, M. J. and Sabel, C. (1984) *The Second Industrial Divide*. Basic Books.

Pollert, A. (1988) 'The Flexible Firm: Fixation or Fact', *Work, Employment and Society*, 2(3), 281–306.

Poole, M. (1986) 'Participation through representation: a review of constraints and conflicting pressures', in Stern, R. and McCarthy, S. (eds) *International Yearbook of Organisational Democracy. 3 The Organisational Practice of Democracy*. Wiley, pp. 251–76.

Poole, M. and Mansfield, R. (1992) 'Managers' Attitudes to Human Resource Management: Rhetoric and Reality', in Blyton, P. and Turnbull, P. (eds) *Reassessing Human Resource Management*. Sage.

Prais, S. J. (1991) 'Vocational qualifications in Britain and Europe: theory and practice', *National Institute Economic Review*, May.

Rainbird, H. (1993) 'Vocational Education and Training', in Gold, M. (ed) *The Social Dimension: Employment Policy in the European Community*. Macmillan.

Ramsay, H. (1992) 'Commitment and Involvement', in Towers, B. (ed) *The Handbook of Human Resource Management*. Blackwell.

Randlesome, C. (1993) *Business Cultures in Europe* (2nd edn). Butterworth–Heinemann.

Rees, B. and Brewster, C. (1995) 'Supporting Equality: Patriarchy at Work in Europe', *Personnel Review*, 24(1), 19–40.

Rees, T. (1995) *Women and the EC Training Programmes – Tinkering, Tailoring and Transforming*. SAUS Publications.

Regalia, I. (1996) 'How the Social Partners View Direct Participation: A Comparative Study of Fifteen European Countries', *European Journal of Industrial Relations*, 2(2), 211–34.

Regini, M. (1995) 'Firms and Institutions: The Demand for Skills and their Social Production in Europe', *European Journal of Industrial Relations*, 1(2), 191–202.

Rivest, C. (1996) 'Voluntary European Works Councils', *European Journal of Industrial Relations*, 2(2), 235–53.

Robinson, A. and Perotin, V. (1997) 'Is profit sharing the answer?', *New Economy*, 4(2).

Roethlisberger, F. J. and Dickson, W. J. (1939) *Management and the Worker*. Harvard University Press.

Rogers, J. and Streeck, W. (eds) (1995) *Works Councils: Consultation, Representation and Co-operation in Industrial Relations*. University of Chicago Press.

Ronen, S. (1986) *Comparative and Multi-national Management*. Wiley.

Ronen, S. and Shenkar, O. (1985) 'Clustering Countries on Attitudinal Dimensions: A Review and Synthesis, *Academy of Management Journal*, Sept, 435–54.

Rubery, J. and Fagan, C. (1993) 'Occupational Segregation of Women and Men in the European Community', European Commission Equal Opportunities Unit. *Social Europe Supplement*, 3/93. Office for Official Publications of the European Communities.

Rubery, J. and Fagan, C. (1994) 'Does Feminisation Mean a Flexible Labour Force?', in Hyman, R. and Ferner, A. (eds) *New Frontiers in European Industrial Relations*. Blackwell.

Salt, J. (1996) 'Economic developments within the EU: the role of population movements; in Corry, D. (ed) *Economics and European Migration Policy*. IPPR.

Sassoon, D. (1996) *Social Democracy at the Heart of Europe*. IPPR.

Schein, E. (1988) *Organisational Psychology*. Prentice-Hall.

Schneider, S. C. and Barsoux, J.-L. (1997) *Managing Across Cultures*. Prentice-Hall.

Schregle, J. (1976) 'Workers' participation in decisions within undertakings', *International Labour Review*, 113, 1–16.

Schulten, T. (1996) 'European Works Councils: Prospects of a New System of European Industrial Relations', *European Journal of Industrial Relations*, 2(3), 303–24.

Singh, R. (1992) 'Human Resource Management: a sceptical look', in Towers, B. (ed) *The Handbook of Human Resource Management*. Blackwell, pp. 127–43.

Sisson, K. (1994) *Personnel Management*. Blackwell.

Soskice, D. (1993) 'Social skills from mass higher education: re-thinking the company initial training paradigm', *Oxford Review Of Economic Policy*, 9(3), 101–13.

Sparrow, P. and Hiltrop, J. (1994) *European Human Resource Management In Transition*. Prentice-Hall.

Storey, J. (1992) *Developments in the management of human resources*. Blackwell.

Straubhaar, T. (1988) 'International Labour Migration Within a Common Market: Some Aspects of EC Experience', *Journal of Common Market Studies*. Sept.

Strauss, G. (1979) 'Workers participation: symposium introduction', *Industrial Relations* 18, 247–61.

Streeck, W. (1989) 'Skills and the Limits of Neo-Liberalism: The Enterprise of the Future as a Place of Learning', *Work, Employment and Society*, 3(1), 89–104.

Streeck, W. (1991) 'On the Institutional Conditions of Diversified Quality Production', in Matzner, E. and Streeck, W. (eds) *Beyond Keynesianism: The Socio-Economics of Production and Employment*. Edward Elgar, pp. 21–6.

Streeck, W. (1994) 'European Social Policy after Maastricht: The Social Dialogue and Subsidiarity', *Economic and Industrial Democracy*, 15(2), 151–77.

Symes, V. (1995) *Unemployment in Europe – Problems and Policies*. Routledge.

Tapinos, G. (1994) 'Regional economic integration and its effects on employment and migration', *Migration and Development – New Partnerships for Co-operation*. OECD.

Tarrow, S. (1996) 'The Europeanisation of Conflict: Reflections from a Social Movement Perspective', *West European Politics*, 18(2), 223–51.

Tayeb Monir, H. (1996) *The Management of a Multicultural Workforce*. Wiley.

Taylor, F. W. (1911) *Principles of Scientific Management*. Harper and Row.

Taylor, R. (1996) 'Health "affected by working time"', *Financial Times*, 12 Nov., p. 12.

Taylor, R. (1996) 'Impact upon employers an employees', *Financial Times*, 13 Nov., p. 10.

Teague, P. (1989) *The European Community: the Social Dimension*. Kogan Page.

Topel, R. (1993) 'What have we learned from empirical studies of unemployment and turnover?', *American Economic Review*, 83(2), 110–15.

Torrington, D. (1994) *International Human Resource Management*. Prentice-Hall.

Trompenaars, F. (1988) *The Organisation of Meaning and the Meaning of Organisation* modified printed version of Doctorate dissertation. University of Pennsylvania.

Trompenaars, F. (1993) *Riding the Waves of Culture – Understanding Cultural Diversity In Business*. Economist Books.

Tsoukalis, L. (1997) *The New European Economy Revisited* (3rd edn). Oxford University Press.

Turnbull, P. (1988) 'The Limits to Japanisation – just-in-time, labour relations and the UK Automotive industry', *New Technology, Work and Employment*, 3(1), 7–20.

Turner, L. (1996) 'The Europeanisation of Labour: Structure before Action', *European Journal of Industrial Relations*, 2(3), 325–44.

UNCTAD (United Nations Conference on Trade and Development) (1994) *World Investment Report 1994: Transnational Corporations, Employment and the Workplace*. United Nations.

Undy, R. and Kessler, I. (1995) *The changing nature of the employment relationship. Presentation to the IPD national conference*.

UNICE (1994) *Making Europe More Competitive – towards world class performance*. UNICE.

United Nations (1995) *World Investment Report for 1995*. United Nations.

van den Broeck, J. (1996) *The Economics of Labour Migration*. Edward Elgar.

Visser, J. (1993) 'Union Organisation: Why Countries Differ', *The International Journal of Comparative Labour Law and Industrial Relations*, Autumn, pp. 206–21.

Visser, J. and Ebbinghaus, B. (1992) 'Making the most of Diversity? European Integration and Transnational Organisation of Labour', in Greenwood, J., Grote, J. R. and Ronit, K. (eds) *Organised Interests and the European Community*, pp. 206–37.

Walby, S. (1990) *Theorising Patriarchy*. Blackwell.

Walker, K. F. (1974) 'Workers' participation in management: problems, practice and prospects', *Bulletin of the International Institute for Labour Studies*, 12, 3–35.

Wall, T. D. and Lischeron, J. A. (1977) *Worker Participation: A Critique of the Literature and some Fresh Evidence*. McGraw-Hill.

Wickens, P. (1987) *The Road to Nissan*. Macmillan.

Wilkinson, A., Marchington, M., Ackers, P. and Goodman, J. (1992) 'Total Quality Management and Employee Involvement', *Human Resource Management Journal*, 2(4), 1–20.

Wise, M. and Gibb, R. (1992) *A Single Market to a Social Europe*. Longman.

INDEX